FIVE RISING DEMOCRACIES

GEOPOLITICS IN THE 21ST CENTURY

For a quarter century since the fall of the Berlin Wall, the world has enjoyed an era of deepening global interdependence, characterized by the absence of the threat of great power war, spreading democracy, and declining levels of conflict and poverty. Now, much of that is at risk as the regional order in the Middle East unravels, the security architecture in Europe is again under threat, and great power tensions loom in Asia.

The Geopolitics in the 21st Century series, published under the auspices of the Order from Chaos project at Brookings, will analyze the major dynamics at play and offer ideas and strategies to guide critical countries and key leaders on how they should act to preserve and renovate the established international order to secure peace and prosperity for another generation.

FIVE RISING DEMOCRACIES

AND THE FATE OF THE INTERNATIONAL LIBERAL ORDER

TED PICCONE

Brookings Institution Press
Washington, D.C.

The Brookings Institution is a private nonprofit organization devoted to research, education, and publication on important issues of domestic and foreign policy. Its principal purpose is to bring the highest quality independent research and analysis to bear on current and emerging policy problems. Interpretations or conclusions in Brookings publications should be understood to be solely those of the authors.

Library of Congress Cataloging-in-Publication data

Names: Piccone, Theodore J., author.
Title: Five rising democracies : and the fate of the international liberal order / Ted Piccone.
Description: Washington, D.C. : Brookings Institution Press, [2016] | Includes bibliographical references and index. | Description based on print version record and CIP data provided by publisher; resource not viewed.
Identifiers: LCCN 2015049705 (print) | LCCN 2015040754 (ebook) | ISBN 9780815725787 (epub) | ISBN 9780815726951 (pdf) | ISBN 9780815727415 (hardcover : alk. paper) | ISBN 9780815725794 (pbk. : alk. paper)
Subjects: LCSH: New democracies—Case studies. | Democracy—Case studies. | Democratization—Case studies. | Democracy—India. | Democracy—Brazil. | Democracy—South Africa. | Democracy—Turkey. | Democracy—Indonesia.
Classification: LCC JC423 (print) | LCC JC423 .P454 2016 (ebook) | DDC 321.8—dc23
LC record available at http://lccn.loc.gov/2015049705

9 8 7 6 5 4 3 2 1

Typeset in Sabon

Composition by Westchester Publishing Services

To Susan and our three beautiful birds in the trees
and, forever, to my parents,
Dante and Margaret

Contents

Preface and Acknowledgments

The future beckons to us. Whither do we go and what shall be our endeavour? To bring freedom and opportunity to the common man, to the peasants and workers of India; to fight and end poverty and ignorance and disease; to build up a prosperous, democratic and progressive nation, and to create social, economic and political institutions which will ensure justice and fullness of life to every man and woman. . . . To the nations and peoples of the world we send greetings and pledge ourselves to cooperate with them in furthering peace, freedom and democracy.

JAWAHARLAL NEHRU, *on the occasion of India's*
independence, August 14–15, 1947

The world in which emerging powers and responsible stakeholders promoting common security and prosperity has yet to arrive, but it's within our grasp to see that happen.

VICE PRESIDENT JOSEPH BIDEN,
John F. Kennedy Library, October 2014

AT A TIME WHEN the worst excesses of human depravity appear in high fever and impervious to remedy, it is worth drawing back from the crises of the day to consider the longer arc of history. Trends the world over—the crushing of the Arab Spring, the machinations of revanchist Russia, the rise of nondemocratic China, the entrenched retrogression of democracy in places like Venezuela and Thailand, the proliferation of outrageous acts of terrorism against the innocent, and the thwarted striving of millions of migrants for a better life—suggest we are even further away from realizing the vision India's independence leader so eloquently articulated nearly seventy years ago. This dystopic perspective, however, is not the whole story. A deeper look at trends of freedom, opportunity, and development, particularly in some of the world's rising democracies, offers a more hopeful picture, not only for their own societies but for the larger cause of human rights and rule of law around the world.

Home to a quarter of the world's population, five emerging democratic powers—India, Brazil, South Africa, Turkey, and Indonesia—have a special and powerful role to play as examples of human progress in political, economic, and development terms. Moreover, their potential contributions as prosperous democracies actively committed to protecting international security, fundamental freedoms, and human development will likely, in my view, determine the fate of the international liberal order so painstakingly constructed over the past seven decades. Will they rise to the challenge of becoming responsible stakeholders prepared to shape the international agenda in favor of human rights and democratic development? Or will they choose the path of narrowly self-interested swing states oriented toward more parochial concerns and aligned with nondemocratic powers regardless of how those states treat their citizens? This book seeks to answer these questions, and many others, by taking a historical perspective grounded in liberal internationalism, current geopolitical realities of multipolarity, and an intensive empirical review of these five nations' behavior in domestic and foreign policy arenas.

I came to this subject as an intellectual labor of love to understand how and why democracies qua democracies occupy a distinctive place on the global stage and how they can and should shoulder a heavier burden in the age-old quest for international peace and development. I approach the subject from my hybrid experience as an observer and practitioner of international law and politics, one admittedly rooted in American values but sensitive to and cognizant of the multiple ways in which human rights and democracy have universal appeal and application. As an optimist, I believe the international liberal order can be improved despite the onslaught of challenges it faces. It is impossible, however, to imagine a better world without a solid foundation of democratic societies that respect human rights and practice tolerance and cooperation. Only on that basis may a coherent and functioning international liberal order rest.

This perspective helps explain my preoccupation with the trajectory of these five big democracies, which represent critical building blocks of a more democratic commons. To the skeptics, including those rightfully critical of the double standards that both established and emerging democratic states practice in their relations with others, I would argue that a descent to the lowest common denominator would only exacerbate the world's troubles; worse, such an attitude undermines the very idea of democracy and human rights—that individuals have a right and a responsibility to hold their governments' behavior at home and abroad to a higher standard.

The historical context for this study is also critical to understanding why these issues matter now. In the decades following the tumult and atrocities of World War II, the international community constructed a global human rights order founded on universal norms that place every individual's right to human dignity at the center. To give meaning to this concept, states adopted treaties that defined the scope and content of a wide variety of political, civil, economic, social, and group rights. Working through the United Nations and a growing number of regional organizations, they forged a variety of tools to monitor how states implement their obligations and to encourage protection of such rights in real time. Building this order was one of the great accomplishments of the second half of the twentieth century. Implementing these norms, however, remains one of the greatest challenges of the twenty-first century.

Alongside the emergence of a global human rights system, states began expressing a growing preference for the spread of liberal democracy as the most effective and legitimate form of governance capable of protecting basic human rights, fostering economic development, and advancing international peace and security. At first, this linkage between democracy, development, and peace was voiced mainly by more established democracies in the West that saw hope in building a world, in Woodrow Wilson's famous phrase, "safe for democracy." The Soviet Union's elevation of a competing model of authoritarian socialism further sharpened this argument. But as the Soviet empire collapsed and the number of democracies in the world tripled from 39 in 1974 to a high of 125 in 2014, the interest in fostering international cooperation to defend and protect democracies ballooned. Leading thinkers and practitioners from the development arena added their voices to the debate by focusing on the critical contribution of politics, "good governance," and the rule of law to

fighting poverty and building more prosperous societies. With the proliferation of initiatives and institutions built around promoting core concepts of transparency, accountability, and citizen participation, we can
confidently identify a distinct international human rights and democracy
order as a cornerstone of the wider international liberal order.

Shifting power balances in the world, however, are shaking the foundations of the international liberal order and revealing new fault lines at
the intersection of human rights and international security. In one camp,
states dominated by autocratic leaders and closed political systems remain
as wedded as ever to traditional concepts of sovereignty and noninterventionism regardless of the brutality of abuses on the ground. Their
definitions of national security are rooted in defending authoritarian systems and maintaining power without external interference. In the other
camp, the United States and other powerful democracies of the West remain bound to the idea that building a world of stable, prosperous democracies that compete but do not go to war with one another will best
ensure their security and prosperity. While they continue to underwrite
most international activities to protect and promote rights and democracy, this group is increasingly focused on managing their own domestic
challenges and resource constraints and the rise of nonstate actors with
competing agendas.

In the middle of these two groups reside the rising democracies, states
emerging from colonialism, apartheid, and/or military dictatorship (previously supported by the West) but now firmly rooted in constitutional
democracy, civilian control of the military, and market-oriented economic policies that have lifted millions of people out of poverty and
toward the middle class. Although their political and economic liberalization processes continue to face a number of significant hurdles, they
appear to be on an irreversible path of deeper democracy.

Five of these rising democracies—India, Brazil, South Africa, Turkey,
and Indonesia—stand at ground zero. As their stars rise (and occasion-
ally fall) on the international stage, they offer important examples of the
compatibility of political liberties, economic growth, and tolerance of
religious and ethnic differences. Yet their conceptions of national security and foreign policy as they relate to the international human rights
and democracy order are muddled, stuck between notions of neutrality
and strategic autonomy, on the one hand, and a principled concern for
international stability earned through democratic processes, transparency, and the rule of law, on the other. Given their continued rise on the

world stage, these five nations' individual and collective approaches to the turmoil of political and economic change under way in the world will determine in many respects the fate of an international liberal order founded on principles of democracy and human rights and could offer an important antidote to the contrasting visions of China and Russia.

This book tries to assess where these five countries are headed at the intersection of human rights and foreign policy. It first examines the demonstrable progress each has made since its transition to a more open society accelerated in the past two decades and what those examples offer to the rest of the world. The evidence demonstrates that these five democracies have delivered significant dividends across multiple indicators of economic, social, and political development. This empirical analysis leads to two critical findings: first, that their chosen paths toward democratic development helped fuel their own successes in providing better livelihoods for their citizens, and, second, that these achievements translated into more ambitious, activist, and credible claims for leadership at the regional and global levels.

Chapter 2 sets the context for the remainder of the book by discussing the current state of the global democracy and human rights order as a laboratory for understanding the contours and contradictions of emerging democratic powers and outlining the main areas of convergence and divergence between them and more established democracies. It will show how the creation of the UN Human Rights Council in 2006 and the burgeoning activity of international and regional human rights mechanisms and courts demonstrate a growing consensus around issues of monitoring and accountability for behavior that transgresses universal norms. Greater activism on a widening array of new issues (the effects of climate change, business and human rights, and LGBTI rights, to name a few) and introduction of new concepts like human security, responsibility to protect civilians (R2P), and international criminal courts are gaining adherents but are still fragile. Nonetheless, deep cleavages persist within the camp of democracies as well as between democracies and non-democracies on issues of principles and methods.

Chapters 3–7 then dive into a deeper analysis of each of the five countries' foreign policies, evaluating the relationship between their status as rising democracies and their national security strategies pertaining to human rights. The growing internationalization of their economic, energy, migration, and trade relations and the trade-offs in the face of human rights and humanitarian crises in other countries are assessed.

A special focus on their respective approaches to the Arab uprisings, as well as to events in their own regions and their behavior at the United Nations, grounds the analysis. Each country chapter also explores the most important domestic drivers of foreign policy decisionmaking, the points of influence, and the missing actors. Finally, chapter 8 presents policy recommendations for the international community of democracies as those nations seek to understand, accommodate, and influence "the rising five" and their growing voice on the world stage. This final chapter will suggest how democracies of different stripes can find common ground around a core set of priorities, from protecting freedom of the Internet and defending civil society to advancing economic and social rights and battling corruption.

THE BOOK RELIES EXTENSIVELY on field research conducted around the world and both quantitative and qualitative information gathering. I was inspired to tackle this project during a working visit to Indonesia, where I attended the World Movement for Democracy Assembly and carried out interviews for my previous book on how the UN's independent human rights experts conduct their work at the national level. The formal launch of the project took place in April 2011 when Foreign Policy at Brookings partnered with Marc Plattner and the National Endowment for Democracy (NED) to commission research papers by experts from Brazil, India, Indonesia, South Korea, South Africa, and Turkey and hosted a discussion of their findings at a one-and-a-half-day conference at Brookings.[1] There I presented a paper on how these states perform on democracy and human rights in international fora, which was published, along with other conference papers, in the *Journal of Democracy* in October 2011. I undertook a series of field visits to the five countries, where I met with dozens of government officials, parliamentarians, scholars, businesspeople, activists, and journalists to learn firsthand their views on the intersection of foreign policy and human rights. I also participated in relevant conferences and workshops in Brazil, Turkey, South Africa, India, Indonesia, Italy, Abu Dhabi, and New York, where the themes of the research were discussed with experts and practitioners from around the world. We also convened a roundtable session in Montreal on the margins of the CIVICUS World Assembly in September 2012 with activists from India, Indonesia, and South Africa to consider and further refine my initial findings.

In addition to my field research, I conducted high-level meetings in New York City and Washington, D.C. In New York, I met with officials from the Brazilian, Indian, Turkish, South African, and U.S. permanent missions to the United Nations. These were particularly timely meetings as three of these states then sat as nonpermanent members of the UN Security Council wrestling with key votes around the Arab Spring and on issues relating to the Responsibility to Protect (R2P) doctrine. A milestone was the convening of a workshop in November 2012 to explore potential areas of cooperation between emerging and established democracies. We brought together senior officials in the multilateral affairs, policy planning, and human rights policy offices of the foreign ministries and nongovernmental experts from academia and civil society in India, Brazil, South Africa, Indonesia, Turkey, the United States, and the European Union. The private, off-the-record dialogue provided key insights into varying approaches to the Arab uprisings, R2P, democracy promotion, and the human rights elements of foreign policy, which were summarized in a report available on the Brookings website.[2]

To further flesh out the main findings of the research, I produced a number of shorter pieces, including "Will Rising Democracies Adopt Pro-Human Rights Foreign Policies?," *South African Institute for International Affairs* (2014); "The Path to Progress? How Democratic Development Drives Five Rising Leaders" (with Ashley Miller), *Gorus* (Turkey, 2013); "Indonesian Foreign Policy: 'A Million Friends and Zero Enemies'" (with Bimo Yusman), *The Diplomat* (February 14, 2014); *Global Swing States and the Human Rights and Democracy Order* (German Marshall Fund, November 2012); and *Rising Democracies and the Arab Awakening: Implications for Global Democracy and Human Rights* (with Emily Alinikoff) (Brookings Institution, January 2012).

Throughout the research and writing process, I was blessed with a multitude of brilliant colleagues, dedicated and hardworking research assistants and interns, and a diverse band of devoted partisans of democracy and human rights around the world. I am especially indebted to the leadership team at Brookings, notably Strobe Talbott, Martin Indyk, and Bruce Jones, for their patience and support, particularly after a slight detour in the mountains of France; an added thanks to Strobe for his decision to give me a break from writing so that I could have the privilege of directing the Foreign Policy program in 2013–14. I owe a debt of gratitude also to Charlotte Baldwin for admirably backing me up in so many ways and to the professionalism and friendship of Elisa Glazer, Gail Chalef, and Julia Cates. I am honored to work with a group of Brookings scholars who gave me essential feedback and encouragement along the way, especially Kemal Kirişci, Fiona Hill, Harold Trinkunas, Joseph Liow, Lex Rieffel, Roberta Cohen, Bruce Jones, Tom Wright, and Guillermo Vuletin, among others; a particularly loud cheer goes to Michael O'Hanlon, a true master of scholarship, for producing thoughtful, constructive, and collegial comments at a critical phase of the drafting. I am indebted also to other experts who gave selflessly of their time and insights, including Camila Asano, Peggy Hicks, Mandeep Tiwana, Monica Moyo, Paul Graham, Hakan Taşçi, Louis Bickford, Ketut Erawan, Steve Grand, Daniel Kurtz-Phelan, Jerry Fowler, Nicole Fritz, and Vassilis Coutifaris in addition to many others who met with me to share their thoughts and insights on the topic.

My research team made all the difference in getting a project of this magnitude and complexity across the finish line. Emily Alinikoff kicked off the work with her can-do perseverance and research agility, especially on the Arab Spring topics. Ashley Miller picked up the baton from Emily and carried it brilliantly in so many ways, from organizing productive exchanges among experts in Washington and around the world to constructing databases and graphics, drafting written materials, and managing a cohort of interns who provided invaluable support and assistance. They include Consuelo Amat, Emma Borden, Nick Gibian, Kevin Grossinger, David Herman, Anuva Jain, Carmen Muñoz, Meredith Rahn-Oakes, Medha Raj, Michael Ramirez, Kevin Tutasig, Robert Ward, and Bimo Yusman.

Partners around the world offered input and provided opportunities to develop my ideas, and they were critical to the success of this project. I owe special thanks to Ahamad Dawwas and Greentree; Nicola Reindorp and Crisis Action; Marc Limon and the Universal Rights Group; Lucia Nader and Conectas Direitos Humanos; Steven Gruzd and the South African Institute for International Affairs; Daniel Kliman and the German Marshall Fund of the United States; Richard Fontaine and the Center for a New American Security; Richard Youngs and Diane de Gramont and the Carnegie Endowment for International Affairs; the National Democratic Institute; and Brookings India. Likewise, this project would not have been possible without the vision and support of our donors. I am especially grateful to the Embassy of the Netherlands in Washington, D.C., the Ford Foundation, and the Carnegie Corporation. The

Foreign Ministry of the Swiss Federation provided early support, as did the Foundation to Promote Open Society/Open Society Institute. Generous support was also provided by the Ministry of Foreign Affairs of the Republic of Finland and the Ministry of Foreign Affairs of the Kingdom of Norway. Brookings recognizes that the value it provides is in its absolute commitment to quality, independence, and impact. Activities supported by our donors reflect this commitment, and the analysis and recommendations are determined solely by Brookings scholars. Any faults of fact or judgments rest, as always, with me.

CHAPTER ONE

The Road to the Rise

How Democracy and Development
Powered the Five

TURN THE CLOCK BACK to 1984. The world was gripped by the nasty Cold War between the United States and the Soviet Union, and their allies and proxies. Wars in Central America raged. Dictators reigned in large swathes of the developing world. Nelson Mandela sat in jail for the twentieth year. Thousands were killed in India in the wake of the assassination of Prime Minister Indira Gandhi and the toxic gas leaks in Bhopal. General Suharto ruled Indonesia, the world's largest Muslim country, with an iron fist. Brazil's military junta was entering its twentieth year in power. And the threat of nuclear apocalypse cast its long shadow around the globe.

By 2014, just thirty years later, the world looks very different. The Soviet Union is gone; China and India have lifted hundreds of millions of people out of despair; Europe is unified, whole, and free; Africa boasts the world's fastest growing economies; the threat of nuclear war has receded; and all but one country in the Americas have emerged as viable democracies. Deaths caused by conflict have declined dramatically, from 53,286 in 1989 to 21,259 in 2013, and the number of interstate and internal conflicts have declined, as well.[1] Economic growth and trade have exploded in every region, and the Internet has become a ubiquitous and essential feature of commerce, culture, and politics. New problems have emerged or intensified—transnational terrorism, climate change, failing states, forced migration, cyber warfare, and humanitarian crises. By

Figure 1-1. High Majorities Believe Democracy Is a Good System for Governing Their Country

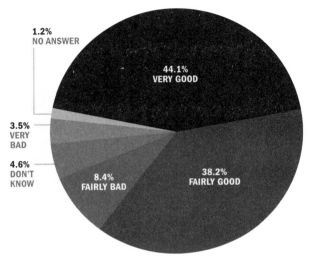

Note: 86,274 individuals from 57 countries were queried. Respondents heard descriptions of various types of political systems and asked whether each was a very good, fairly good, fairly bad, or very bad way of governing this country. Respondents were asked what they thought about "having a democratic political system."

Source: World Values Survey, Wave 6 (2010–14), question V130.

most measures, however, the world today is a much better place for the average human being, who is now living longer, with more years of education, some shelter and electricity, and in better health. Since 1990 extreme poverty rates have been cut in half, more boys and girls are in school, child mortality has declined significantly, and more people have access to safe drinking water.[2]

Among the most notable changes in the intervening three decades is the expansion of democracy and human rights in every corner of the globe. In 1989, 69 countries (41 percent of the world's countries) were electoral democracies, but as of 2014, there were 125 (63 percent of all countries). In 1989, 2.28 billion people lived in electoral democracies. Today the number is 4.18 billion, almost twice the number of just twenty-five years ago.[3] Public opinion polling conducted in every region of the world shows that most people strongly prefer to live in democratic systems that allow free elections and protect civil rights, and most people believe in the effectiveness of democracy as a system of governance (see figure 1-1).[4] States

Figure 1-2. High Majorities Consider Living in a Democracy to Be Important

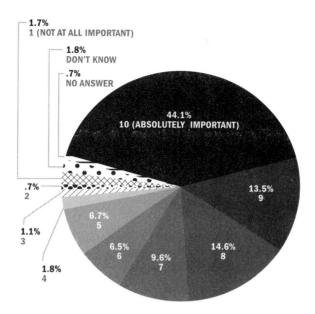

Note: 86,274 individuals in 57 countries were queried. Respondents were asked, "How important is it for you to live in a country that is governed democratically? On this scale where 1 means it is 'not at all important' and 10 means 'absolutely important,' what position would you choose?"

Source: World Values Survey, Wave 6 (2010–14), question V140.

large and small, east and west, north and south have adopted more open, pluralistic, and competitive systems of governance, giving more people a stake in how they are governed (see figure 1-2). Tendentious rhetoric aside, there is also growing convergence around the core elements of liberal democracy—periodic, free, and fair elections, with secret ballots and universal suffrage, run by independent electoral bodies; the rule of law guaranteed by independent judiciaries; respect for universal human rights, including political and civil rights; multiparty political systems and a robust and independent civil society; civilian control of the military; and freedom of the press.[5]

Dramatic episodes of democratic change over the past three decades have captured the world's imagination as "people power" rose up and defeated long-standing autocrats in the Philippines, Chile, Poland, and Korea. Spain successfully transitioned from Franco's iron fist to a strong parliamentary system with a weakened monarch. Mexico moved from one-party control under a democratic facade to peaceful transfers of power to opposition parties. The European Union expanded from twelve members in 1989 to twenty-eight today, all of which meet shared criteria for democratic governance, rule of law, and human rights. As the tide turned, and the democratic wave reached yet more shores, some even hoped that the end of history was near and that liberal representative government would rule the land.[6] Recent history, however, is replete with examples of the profound difficulties of converting popular aspirations for voice, transparency, and accountability into viable forms of democratic governance. Aside from the positive example of Tunisia, the Arab Spring has turned into the Arab nightmare with civil wars raging from Yemen and Iraq to Syria and Libya. They remind us that the story of democratization is the tale of the proverbial "two steps forward, one step back." Scores of stagnating illiberal democracies are stuck in neutral or sliding backward on their path toward more liberal systems, while more developed democracies contend with apathy, elite capture of politics, rising nationalism and populism, and growing polarization.

In this sea of change, five major countries—India, Brazil, South Africa, Turkey, and Indonesia (to which I refer throughout this book in short form as IBSATI)—stand out for three reasons:

1. They leaped from closed, authoritarian, illiberal governance to more open, representative, and accountable political and economic systems.

2. They made impressive progress in delivering better standards of living for their citizens, and their success as aspiring democratic powers could potentially impact other societies striving for change.

3. Their remarkably diverse populations, evident in multiple languages, ethnicities, and religions, distinguish them from more homogeneous and relatively cohesive societies such as Poland, South Korea, and Chile.

Their standing in the global community is changing as well: together, their citizens represent 25 percent of the world's population, whereas their economies account for only 8 percent of global GDP, suggesting high potential for more growth to come. IBSATI countries' average GDP growth rates over the past thirty years have been consistently above the global average, sometimes (from 2003 to 2008, and again in 2010 and 2011) as much as 50 percent higher. They also weathered the 2008 financial crisis effectively—their growth rates did not drop as low as the global average, and they bounced back quickly. IBSATI countries as a group perform better than authoritarian China in certain economic measurements, as well. For example, in recent years their average GDP per capita has consistently exceeded China's until 2014, when GDP per capita in China surpassed the IBSATI average owing to contractions in Turkey and South Africa (GDP per capita in Brazil, India, and Indonesia all continued to grow).[7] IBSATI countries have performed admirably in attaining Millennium Development Goals (MDGs); four of the five countries outstripped the global average in the percentage of the population with access to improved drinking water, and in lowering rates of child mortality.[8] There are other powerful examples of rising democracies, namely, Mexico and South Korea, both important stories of political, economic, and social progress in the past three decades. For a variety of reasons, including their particular geographic, security, and economic relationships with their immediate neighbors (the United States and North Korea, respectively), they were not included in the study.

This chapter documents how these five rising democracies emerged from legacies of military rule, colonial control, apartheid, authoritarianism, and statism to more dynamic, decentralized, and democratic societies. It examines the historical turning points when national identities and policies shifted toward a new path of greater openness, both domestically and internationally. From those key moments of transition, the chapter demonstrates the progress each country has made across a whole range of indicators, from political rights and civil liberties to GDP per capita, literacy, maternal mortality, public expenditures for health and education, and other indicia of human development. It also tells the story of how each country has entered the globalized marketplace through an increasing reliance on international trade, migration, remittances, energy, and foreign investment flows.

The data, drawn from a broad spectrum of sources, reveal two critical findings about these five countries: first, that their chosen paths toward more democratic models of development helped fuel their own successes in providing better livelihoods for their citizens, and, second, that these achievements translated into more ambitious and activist claims for leadership at the regional and global levels. As their credibility and soft power as democratically governed states delivering economic and social development for millions of their citizens have grown, their demands for a greater say in global governance have expanded, posing new challenges to the international order, particularly regarding the promotion of liberal norms of democracy and human rights. Their potential to provide positive examples to other countries, particularly vis-à-vis competing systems of hybrid authoritarianism, will also depend on how quickly and how well they can close major gaps in political, economic, and social goods. The job, in other words, is unfinished, and these five countries' weight in global affairs will rise and fall on their ability to meet international standards and their own publics' rising demands.

TURNING POINTS TOWARD LIBERALIZATION

Every national story of democratic transition is composed of a multitude of unique twists and turns. Each case also features a fork in the road between two paths—one of liberalization and representative governance, and the other of autocracy and isolation. This inflection point is identified in this study as T1. As the analysis below contends, the leaders, and more important the citizens, of these five rising democracies chose the more difficult but ultimately more durable and rewarding road of democratic development at critical moments of their national histories.

Brazil (T1 = 1985)

After its declaration of independence from Portugal in 1822, Brazil experimented with a range of governmental systems from monarchy and federal republicanism to parliamentary democracy and dictatorship. In 1964, conservative forces aligned with the military, with the support of the United States, overthrew the elected leftist president, João Goulart, ushering in a twenty-one-year period of military rule known for both repression of political opponents and fast economic growth based on state ownership of key sectors of the economy. For much of this time, political parties were banned, direct elections of mayors and governors were canceled, activists were tortured, and the military controlled all aspects of national security. As the military loosened its grip on power in the late 1970s and early 1980s, opposition parties began to consolidate their bases of support. In January 1985, they won enough votes in the electoral college to elect a civilian president, Tancredo Neves, and vice president, José Sarney. Neves tragically died before assuming office, leaving it to Sarney to cope with spiraling foreign debt, rampant inflation, and a fragile transition to democracy. During his term, a constituent assembly drafted a new constitution that secured individual rights and civil liberties, criminalized coups d'état, and established various forms of direct popular participation in governance.

Brazil's economic woes, however, continued. Fernando Collor de Mello, Brazil's first directly elected president in twenty-nine years, battled hyperinflation, which reached 30,000 percent in 1990, through a series of wage and price freezes, privatizations, free trade, and fiscal reforms. Just two years into his term, however, Collor faced an impeachment trial for an influence-peddling scheme and resigned, handing power to Vice President Itamar Franco. Despite an economy still reeling from hyperinflation and rising unemployment, Franco rejected calls for a military-led coup aimed at purging a corrupt congress and judiciary, and opted instead for an ambitious and ultimately successful scheme to control inflation, known as the Plano Real, managed by his finance minister, Fernando Henrique Cardoso. During this period and under Cardoso's subsequent two-term presidency, the Brazilian economy stabilized and began to grow, laying the path for takeoff under President Luiz Inácio Lula da Silva in 2002. A former shoeshine boy and labor activist once jailed for organizing strikes, Lula expanded social welfare programs, lifting millions out of acute poverty, and presided over dramatic economic growth, new infrastructure, and a successful bid to host the 2014 World Cup and 2016 Summer Olympics. His designated successor, Dilma Rousseff, who once fought with urban guerrillas against the military dictatorship and was reportedly tortured while in prison, handily won elections in 2010 and more narrowly in 2014. She now faces twin political and economic crises fueled in part by strong demands for accountability for massive corruption led by Brazil's network of independent prosecutors, auditors, and judges.

In less than three decades, Brazil has moved from military dictatorship to multiparty democracy and even elected a former female guerrilla to run the country. It faces a myriad of challenges, notably high levels of inequality, rising unemployment, entrenched political corruption, and criminal violence. Nonetheless, its politics are more inclusive, human rights abuses have declined and are more likely to be investigated and punished by an increasingly assertive judiciary, the military is under civilian control and has abandoned nuclear weapons, and its economy has lifted millions of Brazilians out of poverty.

India (T1 = 1991)

India's relatively rapid transition from the end of British colonial rule to independence as a federal republic with a new constitution and nationwide elections by 1952 marks it as an early and special case of post–World War II democratization.[9] Its pre-independence experimentation with political pluralism, particularly under the Congress Party, laid the groundwork for a wide diversity of Indian voices to have a say in political life.[10] It has performed particularly well in competently administering free and fair elections in enormously complex circumstances, which have led to multiple peaceful transfers of power. On the economic front, however, India pursued a state-driven "mixed economy" structure that emphasized protectionist policies, centrally planned industrialization, and heavy restrictions on everything from imports to business licenses. By the mid-1980s, India's economy had fallen behind South Korea, Spain, Singapore, Taiwan, and others that followed a more competitive economic model open to the global economy. Some pro-business policies were passed in the 1980s to encourage private businesses, including de-licensing of key sectors, but by 1990 the Indian economy was nearly bankrupt. By the summer of 1991, India's debt had reached $70 billion and the looming crisis prompted radical change.

In mid-1991 Prime Minister Narasimha Rao from the Congress Party and his finance minister, Manmohan Singh (later prime minister), initiated a vast economic reform program to stave off an acute liquidity/debt crisis. The hallmarks were the following:

—Opening many sectors to private investment (including power, steel, oil, air transportation, telecommunications, ports, mining, pharmaceuticals)

—Encouraging foreign direct investment, except in certain consumer goods sectors

—Abolishing industrial licenses for all industries to encourage competition and reduce red tape

—Liberalizing the services sector

—Devaluing the rupee

—Shifting from a fixed exchange rate to a market-based exchange rate

—Reducing certain tariffs as well as gradually liberalizing trade policy (which notably applied mainly to extraregional trade partners, not India's immediate neighbors)

—Liberalizing capital markets and encouraging private mutual funds

Since 1991, India's growth has been consistent and high. It has joined the ranks of the world's fastest-growing economies, giving rise to a massive, technically skilled Indian middle class. The financial slowdown of 2012 notwithstanding, India's economy, coupled with its more open and well-established competitive political structure, is poised to reap big gains in the coming years under newly elected prime minister Narendra Modi, whose coalition controls a majority in Parliament. On the political front, India remains a fairly solid middle performer but faces some fundamental challenges. Its failure to gain territorial control of its northeast and Maoist-controlled areas as a result of long-standing conflicts with indigenous communities, along with its ongoing contest with Pakistan for control of the Jammu and Kashmir region, has generated a host of human rights abuses that remain relatively immune to punishment thanks to the expansive Armed Forces Special Powers Act. It has a slew of constitutional and legal provisions that India's Supreme Court has interpreted in progressive ways,[11] but enforcement by national and state governments is weak and underresourced. A resurgence of Hindu nationalism has led to outbursts of anti-Muslim violence, and civil society and media face intense scrutiny and criticism by government officials.

Indonesia (T1 = 1998)

Before its financial crisis in 1997 and the *reformasi* period initiated in 1998, Indonesia was a good example of an authoritarian political system that also enjoyed strong economic growth. Most of the period under President Suharto (1967–98) was characterized by macroeconomic stability and a strong economy that benefited the majority of Indonesians. It was also marked, however, by severe limits on political parties, critical media and civil society, and an expansive role for the military in governance.

Because of high oil export prices in the 1970s and 1980s, Indonesia was able to invest heavily in a technologically advanced manufacturing sector, earning it the World Bank's moniker of "East Asian Miracle" in 1993. The Asian financial crisis of 1997, however, revealed the fragility of the Indonesian economy, which the Suharto government had distorted with domestic subsidies, export restrictions, massive corruption, and other statist policies. With the 1997–98 downturn of the Indonesian economy (GDP dropped an officially estimated 13 percent and inflation rose to nearly 60 percent in 1998), the economic conditions that had justified Suharto's rule no longer existed, and he began to face calls for resignation. Public outcry against "Corruption, Collusion, and Nepotism" (*Korupsi, Kolusi, dan Nepotisme*) grew louder and, after 1996, they were particularly directed at Suharto and his family. (In 2004, Transparency International retroactively deemed Suharto the most corrupt leader of all time.) Simultaneously, interethnic divisions that economic growth had softened resurfaced in the late 1990s. Some conflicts manifested along party lines and turned deadly in the lead-up to the May 1997 general election.

The Suharto regime's initial response to the economic downturn was to float the currency (rupiah), raise interest rates, and tighten fiscal policy, but these measures were not enough to rescue the economy. In October 1997 Indonesia and the International Monetary Fund (IMF) brokered an economic reform agreement for macroeconomic stability, which in-cluded cutting off subsidies to a car company owned by one of Suharto's sons, dissolving a clove monopoly owned by that son, and canceling two power plant projects in which another son had a stake. In May 1998, while Suharto was in Egypt, demonstrations and violence broke out and ultimately culminated in Suharto's resignation on May 21, 1998. Shortly thereafter, his successor, B. J. Habibie, released political prisoners, lifted the Suharto-era controls on political parties and the press, and ended the military's formal role in government administration. After a rocky pe-riod marked by shifting coalitions, the rise of Islam in politics, the impeachment of President Wahid, separatist conflicts, and tumult and ultimately independence for East Timor, Indonesia settled into a stable period of steady democratization and growth under President Yudhoy-ono (2004–14). During this time, Indonesia's economy took off, middle classes expanded dramatically, and political accountability improved, demonstrating the compatibility of democracy and development. Elec-tions in 2014 led to the ascension of the first president not from the old guard of Jakarta's elite, signifying a durability to the electorate's demands for change.

South Africa (T1 = 1994)

Uniquely in modern history, apartheid South Africa represented the gross injustice of a system of governance that rested its authority on mi-nority white control of a majority black population. Although the United Nations began denouncing South Africa's apartheid regime in the early

1960s and initiated a voluntary arms embargo in 1963, international efforts grew more aggressive as the regime dug in its heels in the face of rising resistance both inside and outside the country. Over time, the United Nations, other international organizations, and the United States implemented a series of economic sanctions on South Africa in an effort to pressure the National Party to enter negotiations with the antiapartheid opposition movement, the African National Congress (ANC).

South Africa finally submitted to sanctions criteria in 1990 by repealing the state of emergency that was in place at the time, removing the legal sanctions for racial segregation, releasing political prisoners—most famously, ANC leader Nelson Mandela who had been jailed for twenty-seven years—and legalizing and negotiating with opposition parties. In 1991 Parliament voted to repeal the legal framework that supported apartheid while negotiations continued on an interim constitution that would usher in a new era of majority-rule democracy. It was not until April 1994, however, that free and fair elections were held and the ANC, once the target of state violence, took power with 252 of 400 Parliament seats. Nelson Mandela was elected president and established a government of national unity. Subsequently, a progressive constitution and bill of rights were adopted and a Truth and Reconciliation Commission was formed to document past abuses and hold perpetrators accountable if they did not confess. A succession of free and fair elections were held, overseen by an independent electoral commission, and South Africa established itself as a relatively stable democracy while confronting a myriad of social, economic, and public security challenges. Under President Jacob Zuma, South Africa remains under the control of the ANC, a lethargic bureaucracy and a stilted model of reform increasingly beholden to China.

Turkey (T1 = 2002)

For much of the twentieth century, Turkey was governed under a strictly secularist constitution that outlawed any role for Islam in national politics. Mustafa Kemal Atatürk, the founder of Turkey's republic after the fall of the Ottoman Empire in 1923, shut down religious schools and courts and blocked any opposition to the political/military alliance he directed. Turkey did not hold democratic elections until 1950, when a newly formed opposition party came to power. For most of the post–World War II period, however, Turkey suffered through a series of failed civilian governments and military coups d'état, often provoked by the traditional Kemalist fear of Islamist influence and control. It also struggled through armed conflicts in neighboring northern Cyprus and against armed groups affiliated with Turkey's sizable Kurdish minority. In 1996 its first pro-Islamic government since 1923 came to office but was pushed out of power by the military the following year, followed by a banning of the pro-Islamic Welfare Party, the largest party in Parliament. Throughout this period, many Turks lived in fear of the so-called deep state—the notion of a shadow government that persecuted those who threatened the secular order. While 1997 marked the last time the military intervened to bring about a more secularist government in Turkey, the Constitutional Court continued to defend secularism until 2002. It banned the Islamist-based Refah Partisi in 1998 and its successor, the Fazilet Partisi, in 2001 on the grounds that they violated article 2 of the Turkish constitution, which states that Turkey is a secular republic. Meanwhile, successive governments adopted some reform measures to liberalize politics and the economy, including expansion of women's rights, abolition of the death penalty, and lifting of bans against Kurdish-language education and broadcasting.

It was not until November 2002, following the collapse of another coalition government, that the newly formed Islamist Justice and Development Party (AKP) won a majority of seats and, after some constitutional changes, Recep Tayyip Erdoğan came to power as prime minister. The 2002 election led to Turkey's first single-party government since 1987 and first two-party Parliament in forty-eight years. From 2002 to 2014 the Turkish government was stable as the AKP won three consecutive elections by steadily increasing margins of victory. With an eye on future European Union membership, the AKP government also passed laws relaxing restrictions on freedom of expression and dramatically cut down the role of the military in politics, albeit with much turmoil and controversy. A rigorous economic stabilization program, aided by strong political support from a more stable parliamentary majority and assistance from the IMF, reduced public debt and inflation and raised the fiscal surplus.[12] During this period (2002–13), the Turkish economy grew by an unprecedented 253 percent, lifting millions of Turks into the middle class. The economic and political successes of the Erdoğan government, however, have emboldened it to centralize authority, weaken checks and balances, politicize the judiciary, and take harsh measures against opponents in the media, civil society, and the military, tarnishing its potential as a democratic example for other Muslim societies.[13] Parliamentary elections held in June 2015 temporarily restored some balance in the political equation, and the Constitutional Court has recently ruled against the Erdoğan government and in favor of a journalist who was arrested in December 2014 government sweeps. But the AKP's strong showing in snap elections in November 2015 means the jury is still out on whether Turkey can consolidate its status as a leading Muslim-majority democracy.

SIGNS OF PROGRESS: DEMOCRATIC GOVERNANCE, FREEDOMS, AND RULE OF LAW

The progress these five countries have experienced since their respective transitions toward liberalization got under way can be measured across multiple indicators that capture the state of democratic governance, civil and political rights, and open and accountable systems. For the purposes of this analysis, I reviewed historical data from Freedom House's Freedom in the World ratings, the Polity IV Index Project, the World Bank Institute's Governance Indicators, Transparency International's Corruption Perceptions Index, and Bertelsmann Stiftung's Transformation Index, among others. I also cross-checked the data with the more recent Economist Intelligence Unit's Democracy Index, bearing in mind that while the general categories are analogous, time ranges and specific indicators vary across databases.[14]

As described earlier in the chapter, for each of the five IBSATI countries, a critical year of transition to liberalization has been identified. Throughout the study, this transition year is identified as T1. The transition years are different for each of the five countries, based on their unique histories of political and economic development. Important inflection points are sometimes stated in reference to T1. For example, T1-4 is four years before the transition year. The in-text quantitative comparisons, wherever possible, begin with the averages of the five-year period preceding a country's turning point of transition, inclusive of the transition year (T1-4 to T1), and end with the most current period for which data were available. (Figures do not reflect the average of the five-year period preceding the turning point but rather show individual data points by year.)

Not surprisingly, given the highly restrictive state of affairs before each country's period of liberalization, we see significant and early improvements in their adherence to international norms of democratic governance, political rights, and civil liberties. For example, Brazil and

South Africa moved from Freedom House's "partly free" category at T1-1, to "free" in T1, a spot they have held almost every year since then. Indonesia jumped even further, from "not free" in 1997 to "free" in 2005.[15] India stayed in place as a "free" state given its longer experience with democracy, and Turkey floated in the "partly free" category (although with a more recent downward trend).

Polity IV data confirm these shifts from autocracy to democracy during the relevant transition years (India, again, being the exception as its political transformation occurred much earlier). On the Polity IV indicators of the regulation, competition, and openness of executive recruitment, all five states have stable and transparent rules for selecting heads of state and government in a competitive manner. Similarly, all five have healthy levels of constraints on executive power through accountability mechanisms like a legislature, political parties, or the judiciary, although Turkey is backsliding.[16] In the area of political competition and opposition, which measures the degree of regulation of political participation and restrictions on political competition, all five score close to the top of the Polity IV charts, indicating that there are relatively stable and enduring secular political groups that regularly compete for political influence at the national level with voluntary transfers of power to competing groups and little coercion or disruption.[17] These data underscore the consolidation in all five countries of democratic practices that foster political stability, civil peace, and social cohesion, which in turn support a wealth of other benefits to society at large, including higher socioeconomic development and quality of life, as will be demonstrated later in the chapter.

Scores from Freedom House for political rights and civil liberties before and after each country's transition also improved substantially, although they have largely flattened or even declined slightly in recent years (see figure 1-3). The same can be said for ratings regarding press freedom, that is, substantial improvement in the early years followed by more recent stagnation and worrisome backsliding, although Indonesia's scores have improved since the fall of Suharto in 1998.[18] Similarly, according to a wide range of governance data analyzed and synthesized by the World Bank Institute since 1996, these five democracies improved on most "good governance" indicators after their initial break from more closed systems. Performance more recently, however, has stagnated or declined in some areas, especially in Turkey. On the World Bank's category of "voice and accountability," which captures perceptions of the extent to which a country's citizens are able to participate in selecting

Figure 1-3. Freedom House Political Rights and Civil Liberties Scores 1984–2014

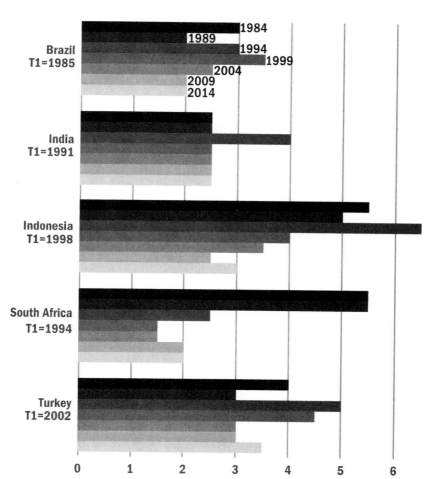

Note: On a scale from 1 to 7, 1 represents the most free and 7 represents the least free. The average score for the year of transition for the IBSATI countries (T1) was 3.4. The average score for the IBSATI countries in 2014 was 2.6.

Source: Freedom House, "Freedom in the World," 2015.

their government, as well as freedom of expression, freedom of association, and a free media, Brazil, Indonesia, and Turkey have advanced significantly during their initial periods of democratization, while India has remained flat and South Africa has fallen, although it still scores higher than any of the other four. In the area of women in politics, all five countries witnessed moderate to substantial increases between 1990 and 2013 in the percentage of parliamentary seats held by women, ranging from a high of 42.3 percent in South Africa (the fourth highest in the world) to 8.6 percent in Brazil.[19] (For reference, the global average for female participation in parliaments is about one in five.[20])

In another key area of democratization—security sector reform and civil–military relations—all five countries have benefited from a more stable international environment after the Cold War as civilian leaders sought to assert primacy over unwieldy and powerful military establishments. Military expenditures as a percentage of GDP, for example, declined in four of the five countries compared with the period before transition.[21] The size of militaries as a percentage of the population declined significantly, as well.[22] Civilian leaders made strides in reining in military prerogatives, took greater control of defense policy and bureaucracies, and generally shifted priorities from internal security to external missions such as peacekeeping, humanitarian assistance, and counterterrorism. The number of military personnel from IBSATI countries serving in international peacekeeping operations, for example, jumped significantly as all five countries sought both to redirect missions and demonstrate buy-in to the international order regime. Brazil and India, which also wanted to prove their bona fides for a seat on the UN Security Council, led the growth, increasing their troop contributions to UN peacekeeping missions from 27 (Brazil) and 35 (India) in 1990 to 1,697 (Brazil) and 8,139 (India) in 2014.[23] The peace dividend of their transformation years also allowed governments to reallocate resources toward other domestic priorities, such as social welfare and infrastructure development.

The Bertelsmann Transformation Index, which tracks the quality of both political and economic transformations based on such indicators as political participation, rule of law, and sustainable market economies, shows a steady improvement for four of the five countries since it began assessments in 2003.[24] All five except Indonesia were rated in 2013 as "advanced" in their transformation processes, while Indonesia jumped in the rankings of 129 countries from number 53 in 2006 to number 35 in 2014.[25] Their analysis supports the conclusion that liberalization of political and economic systems have gone hand in hand and reinforced one another. On perceptions of corruption, which Transparency International began surveying in 1995 to assess perceived levels of public sector corruption in 177 countries and territories, all five countries except South Africa improved their scores between 1995 and 2011.[26]

In terms of their transitions to market-based economies that respect property rights, regulatory and competition policies, and freedom of labor and capital, all five rising democracies demonstrate a pattern of liberalization, while retaining important roles for the public sector, especially in India and Brazil. The Bertelsmann Transformation Index, for example, which tracks, inter alia, private enterprise, property rights, and market organization and competition, found that all five countries except South Africa improved their scores between 2005 and 2013.[27] Similarly, the Wall Street Journal/Heritage Foundation Index of Economic Freedom, which uses a more conservative set of indicators, found better performance for all five countries between 1995 and 2014.[28] During this period, India, which underwent a concerted policy of economic liberalization, scored better on the tax burden on individuals and corporations and tariff and nontariff barriers to trade; Turkey also improved significantly in the tax burden category and on price stability and controls. On other indicators, performance varied across specific categories, but the net gain was positive.

A similar set of studies conducted since 1970 by the Fraser Institute, which rates countries on "economic freedom"—size of government and taxation, private property and the rule of law, soundness of money, trade regulation and tariffs, and regulation of business, labor, and capital markets—found greater liberalization of economic policies across the board in all five countries compared with periods before T1.[29] India, for example, jumped on a scale of zero to ten from a score of 4.9 in 1990, a year before its decision to liberalize its economy, to 6.5 in 2012. According to the authors, the study's findings of economic freedom correlate positively with such indicators as per capita income and economic growth, income disparity of the poorest 10 percent, political rights and civil liberties, corruption, literacy, and life expectancy.[30]

In sum, the weight of the evidence, whether it comes from more conservative approaches to economic freedom taken by Heritage and Fraser or the more center-left social democracy orientation of the Bertelsmann Index, strongly supports the conclusion that liberalization of political and economic structures in these five countries has created a virtuous circle of reform, especially in the early years of transition. The data also reveal, however, that these five countries largely sit in the middle of the relevant performance range, with little to no improvement in more recent years.[31] Public opinion polling in the IBSATI countries underscores this nonlinear path of transition and complicated demands for democracy.

According to the World Values Survey, a large majority of each country's population feels democracy is a "very good way" or "fairly good way" of governing their countries, and an equally large majority stresses how important it is to live in a democracy.[32] However, conceptions of what constitutes a democracy vary widely. Whereas most respondents feel that strong civil rights are an essential element of democracy, a substantial minority also feel that military intervention against an incompetent government (even a democratically elected one) is not inherently undemocratic.[33] The definition of democracy also differs from country to country, with income equality ranking as a high priority in Turkey while Indonesians place greater importance on gender equality and Brazilians on the free election of leaders.[34] Given such varied popular conceptions of democracy, the uncertain trend lines of IBSATI countries' democratic progress are perhaps unsurprising.[35]

SIGNS OF PROGRESS: ECONOMIC GROWTH AND HUMAN DEVELOPMENT

As the political dynamics of change swept through the five IBSATI countries from 1985 to 2002, their governments grew increasingly responsive to voters' demands for better living conditions and opportunities. Democratic governments adopted a series of measures to stimulate greater economic and job growth, invest in globalization and foreign trade, and expand social safety nets to lift more people out of poverty. In response, their economies took off, doubling and tripling in size, as figure 1-4 demonstrates.

Compared with the five-year average of GDP per capita in their respective periods before transition, the IBSATI countries grew a whopping 279 percent on average by 2013. Brazil led the pack with a sixfold increase in GDP per capita T1-4 compared with 2013, India's economy grew more than four times, Indonesia's more than 3.5 times, South Africa's doubled, and Turkey's grew 2.8-fold. When measured since 2002, the five countries continued to demonstrate high levels of economic growth per capita, led by Turkey, Brazil, and South Africa. In contrast to previous periods of boom and bust, growth was relatively steady and sustainable, as measured by the overall volatility of each country's growth, although the global recession of 2008 weakened stability somewhat, particularly in India, South Africa, and Turkey. Cash reserves increased and national debt as a percentage of GDP decreased in all but

Figure 1-4. GDP per Capita Has Markedly Improved Since Transition

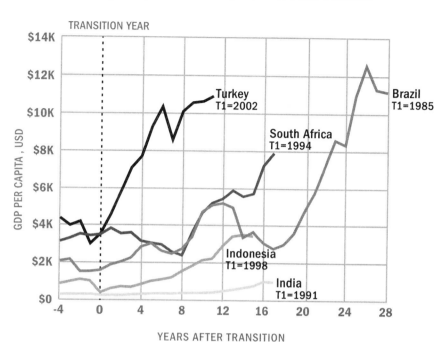

Note: Each country was assigned a different year of transition identified by the author as T1. The most recent data for each country are from 2014.

Source: World Bank.

India, evidence of more prudent macroeconomic management. As figure 1-5 shows, inflation notably decreased during their transition periods, or fluctuated within a relatively narrow band. This in turn lent stability and predictability to the economy, encouraged savings, and created conditions in which people could plan for their futures, all core elements of quality of life in developed democracies. Declining rates of population growth in all five countries contributed to these trends, as well.

On the downside, these spectacular growth rates were not accompanied by a significant decline in either unemployment or in inequality. Unemployment actually increased in Brazil, Indonesia, South Africa, and Turkey and stayed mostly flat in India. Inequality declined slightly in Brazil and Turkey after transitions were launched but increased in South Africa, India, and Indonesia. Coincident with these trends, and partly in

Figure 1-5. Average Inflation Decreases and Stabilizes after Transition

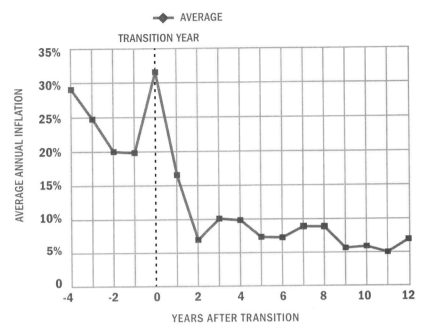

Note: Includes India, Indonesia, South Africa, and Turkey. Brazil not shown because hyperinflation in the 1980s and early 1990s skews average. The most recent data for each country are from 2014.

Source: World Bank.

response to popular demands for greater equity in development, each country took various steps to increase spending on social welfare, health care, food assistance, and conditional cash transfer programs. For example, under President Lula, Brazil substantially expanded the Bolsa Familia program, which makes cash transfers to eligible low-income households in return for conditions like keeping children in school.[36] Turkey instituted a national health care plan that dramatically increased public access to medical services from 69.7 percent of the population in 2002 to 99.5 percent in 2011.[37] More recently, India adopted legislation providing more food assistance to the country's still massive number of hungry families. The subsidized grain program is expected to benefit almost 70 percent of the population at a cost of approximately $4 billion a year.[38]

The result of these complementary transitions toward political and economic liberalization and increased social welfare expenditures was a meaningful increase in indicators of human development, as measured by the UN Development Program since 1980. The Human Development Index, which measures the average achievements in a country in three basic dimensions of human development (a long and healthy life, access to knowledge, and a decent standard of living), shows significant improvements in all five countries compared with pre-liberalization periods (see figure 1-6). On the high end, Brazil jumped from low to high levels of human development; on the low end, South Africa fractionally moved up within the medium-level category. Poverty rates, as measured by the percentage of the population living on $2 or less a day, dropped substantially in all five countries over the relevant time period before and after their turning points, with Brazil again leading the pack.

A closer look at some of the most important indicators in the health and education categories reveals a tangible difference in the quality of life for millions of people living in these five democracies compared with earlier periods. Life expectancy moved from an average of 63.6 years in the five-year period before each transition to 68.3 years as of 2012.[39] Both infant and maternal mortality rates decreased significantly. The great exception to this trend, South Africa, reflects the devastation wrought by the spread of HIV/AIDS and the ANC political leadership's tragic failure to address the crisis in a timely manner. Not surprisingly, public and private spending on health care continued to rise as politicians and the marketplace responded to the growing clamor for greater access to and better quality of care, as witnessed in major social protests seen in Brazil in 2013. A similar phenomenon took place in the realm of education—literacy rates grew across the board and more students reached higher levels of school, despite the rather anemic growth in public spending on education. Women enrolled at higher rates in secondary and tertiary education, especially in Turkey and India,[40] and the gender gap in youth literacy narrowed considerably. The MDGs provided a framework for tackling poverty globally, and the IBSATI countries generally tracked with or exceeded global norms in achieving them. From 1990 to 2015, great progress has been made in reducing extreme poverty and child mortality, increasing access to and equality of education, improving maternal health, and a host of other key development aims.[41] The IBSATI countries at least met if not exceeded the global average in improvements to child mortality and access to clean water (see figure 1-7

Figure 1-6. Human Development Improves after Transition

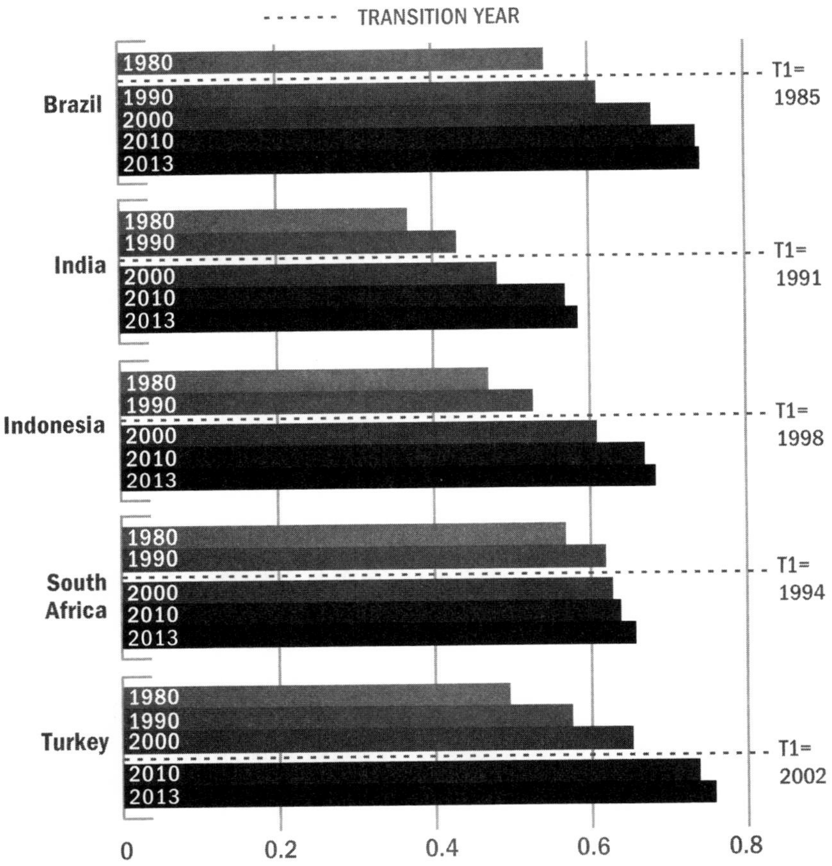

Note: The Human Development Index (HDI) is a summary measure of average achievement in key dimensions of human development, including life expectancy, health, education, and standard of living.

Source: United Nations Human Development Program, Human Development Index.

and figure 1-8). (Indonesia fell a bit short on access to clean water, and India also lagged slightly in addressing child mortality.) In most instances, they performed considerably better than non-democracies did in both these arenas.

New conceptual and quantitative work undertaken by Sakiko Fukuda-Parr and colleagues on measuring state progress toward fulfilling their

Figure 1-7. Children under Five Mortality Rate per 1,000 Live Births

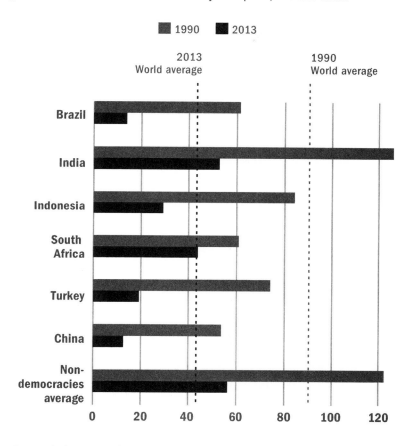

Note: United Nations Millennium Development Goal 4.A states, "Reduce by two-thirds, between 1990 and 2015, the under-five mortality rate." Non-democracies were selected from Freedom House "not free" countries, 1990 and 2013.

Source: United Nations Millennium Development Goals (mdgs.un.org/unsd/mdg/data.aspx).

international social and economic rights obligations confirm these trends. Their Social and Economic Rights Fulfillment (SERF) Index, which uses objective survey-based data published by national and international bodies, seeks to measure to what extent states are meeting their obligations to progressively respect and protect economic and social rights set forth in the Universal Declaration of Human Rights and the UN Covenant on Economic, Social, and Cultural Rights. The five indicators they employ cover the rights to food, education, health, housing, and decent work.

Figure 1-8. Proportion of Population Using an Improved Drinking Water Source

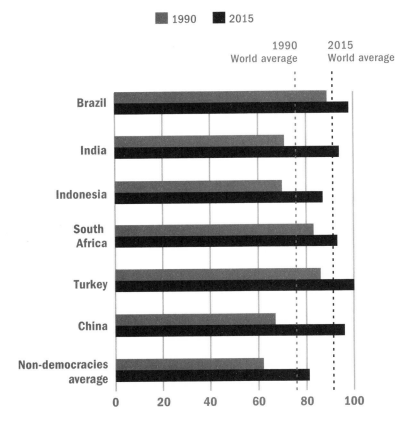

Note: United Nations Millennium Development Goal 7.C states, "Halve, by 2015, the proportion of people without sustainable access to safe drinking water and basic sanitation." Non-democracies selected from Freedom House, Freedom in the World "not free" countries, 1990 and 2014 (the most recent year for which scores are available).

Source: United Nations Millennium Development Goals (mdgs.un.org/unsd/mdg/data.aspx).

On average, all five rising democracies significantly improved their over-all scores between 2000 and 2010.[42]

EMBRACING GLOBALIZATION AND INTEGRATION

During earlier periods in each of the rising democracies' histories of varying degrees of autocracy and statism, political leaders pursued limited ambitions in the international sphere. The dominant theme of the Nonaligned Movement, for example, was all about staying out of big-power politics for fear of the collateral damage of associating oneself with one or the other superpower.[43] On economic terms, governments took a similar path as they sought to harness state control of the economy to advance ambitious plans for national development (along with self-aggrandizement and personal enrichment). Growth rates were strong at times but also volatile, a trend typical of autocratic regimes,[44] and costs in political and human rights terms were high.

As globalization accelerated in the 1990s, led by big economies like the United States, China, and Europe, the IBSATI countries jumped on the bus with policies designed to expand international trade, promote exports (of both primary and secondary goods and services), privatize state-owned enterprises, and welcome foreign direct investment. During this period and continuing today, these countries are diversifying their economic and trade relations, with big shifts from developed to developing economies as major trading partners. As noted in UNDP's Human Development Report for 2013:

> The world is getting more connected, not less. Recent years have seen a remarkable reorientation of global production, with much more destined for international trade, which, by 2011, accounted for nearly 60% of global output. Developing countries have played a big part: between 1980 and 2010, they increased their share of world merchandise trade from 25% to 47% and their share of world output from 33% to 45%. Developing regions have also been strengthening links with each other: between 1980 and 2011, South–South trade increased from less than 8% of world merchandise trade to more than 26%.[45]

IBSATI countries all contributed to these trends. For example, during the period before their respective transitions, exports of goods and services as a percentage of GDP represented on average 18.7 percent. By 2013, exports as a percentage of GDP rose to more than 23.6 percent on average,[46] indicating the growing dependence on global trade for economic growth. A similar though stronger pattern holds for imports. Trends have changed, however, as they relate to trading partners. Notably, over the past decade, the export destination mix of each IBSATI country has shifted away from advanced economies like the United States and Europe

Figure 1-9. Chinese FDI in IBSATI Countries Increases Dramatically in Recent Years (Year-End Stocks)

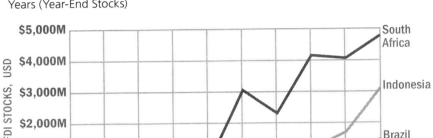

Note: Includes Brazil, India, Indonesia, South Africa, and Turkey.

Source: National Chinese Bureau of Statistics.

and toward other emerging economies. The majority of exports from Brazil and India, for example, go to emerging economies, particularly in Asia and the Middle East/North Africa.[47] The same is true of their import mix, in part attributable to rising energy imports,[48] but also due to the rise of Chinese production.

Before each country's turning point, China did not even register on the top five list of trading partners for any of the IBSATI countries. As of 2012, however, China became the number one source of imports for Brazil, India, Indonesia, and South Africa.[49] Similarly, as of 2012, exports to China from these same four countries were in the top three destinations.[50] Energy imports as a percentage of each country's energy use are also on the rise, except for Brazil, which has abundant domestic sources of hydropower, bioethanol, oil, and gas. Another notable shift is toward increased trade with countries in their respective regions, particularly for Indonesia and Turkey. Yet another sign of their growing reliance on external forces for economic growth can be seen in the big jump in foreign direct investment from 1994 to 2012, especially for India and Brazil. Foreign direct investment from China in particular rose dramatically between 2003 and 2012, especially to South Africa and Indonesia, as figure 1-9 shows.[51]

As the rising democracies transition from lower- to middle-income status and expand their economic spheres of interest around the globe, they are also shifting from being foreign aid recipients to foreign aid donors. Turkey stands out in this dimension, moving from $151.34 million in official development assistance (ODA) in 2001 to $3.3 billion in 2013, or 0.4 percent of gross national income, ranking it thirteenth on the list of most generous ODA donors in 2013.[52] Turkey was the world's third most generous donor of humanitarian assistance in 2013, above Germany, Japan, and France, and number one as a percentage of gross national income; Brazil reached number twenty-three, above Russia and China.[53] Brazil and India also have increased their ODA of late, though on a much more modest scale than Turkey. This should not come as a surprise given their place as leading recipients of ODA.[54] Indonesia also remains a major recipient of development aid. These trends suggest IBSATI countries, with the exception of Turkey, remain preoccupied with their national development demands and slow to step up to the international community's expectations that they will shift from being free riders to donors. The BRICS New Development Bank, which will provide concessional development financing to its members and other developing countries, is one indication this may now be moving in a more serious direction, but China, with its deep pockets, remains in the driver's seat.

These changes toward integration in the global economy have important implications for the IBSATI countries' respective rise as regional hegemons and carve out complementary economic and political spaces in their respective geographic zones to protect their national interests. They also bring home the remarkable shift in reliance on trade with China, which has become both Brazil's and South Africa's largest trading partner. These trends make it all the more likely that IBSATI countries, as they seek to gain a foothold in emerging economies (many of which are considered non-democracies or illiberal regimes),[55] will continue to avoid placing political conditions on their trade with countries that have bad democracy and human rights records.

The IBSATI countries' embrace of globalization can be seen in other important areas, touching millions of citizens in their daily lives. Access to the World Wide Web, for example, has exploded across the board, as have cell phone subscriptions. Large exile communities have settled in third countries for work and family reasons, sending billions of dollars home to their relatives and thereby lifting millions more out of poverty.[56] The numbers are particularly stunning for India, which received nearly $70 billion from Indians living abroad in 2012 alone, the highest amount in the world.[57] More and more students from IBSATI countries are traveling abroad for their studies, learning foreign languages, exploring new cultures firsthand, and developing networks of friendship and professional colleagues that are reshaping opinions about "the other." Bollywood films from India proliferate in the souks of the Arab world, while Brazilian music wafts through cafés from Oslo to Osaka, adding to the heady mix of a smaller, more integrated world and India and Brazil's own soft power.

The IBSATI countries' rise on the global stage has also generated greater interest in international tourism to their respective lands. From 2004 to 2012, receipts from international tourists grew steadily in all five countries as the ease and cost of air transport allowed more visitors from distant locales to visit areas once out of reach. Turkey's volume of visitors far outstripped the other four and has become an important factor in its high economic growth rates. It also operates as a constraint on its willingness to address the rising instability in its neighborhood for fear of inviting terrorist violence on its own soil, which would damage its increasingly tourism-dependent economy.[58] But the fundamental point remains: the planet is a more interconnected place now than when the IBSATI countries first embarked on their paths of liberalization, and they have been major players in this transformation, contributing to and benefiting from a more globalized world that is governed by shared rules of the road.

CONCLUSION

The evidence is overwhelming that the democratization and liberalization of political and economic systems in these five big rising democracies over the past three decades moved hand in hand with remarkable progress in the standards of living for millions of their citizens, proving that democratic forms of government and positive human development are compatible and, indeed, mutually reinforcing phenomena. The trajectory of many other democracies, from South Korea to Mexico to Poland and Chile, correspond strongly with this finding. The data from a wide variety of sources, both national and international, demonstrate that democracies deliver not only more open, responsive, and accountable governance and better respect for human rights, goods in and of themselves. They also produce positive development outcomes, more stable economies, and tangible improvements in citizens' lives, establishing the instrumental value of choosing a democratic path to development. This powerful combination of democratic legitimacy derived from governing with the consent of the people and development legitimacy as evidenced by tangible progress in peoples' lives gives them undoubted credibility as rising leaders on the world stage.

It should come as no surprise, therefore, that these states now claim a greater say in the decisionmaking process and leadership of the international institutions created since World War II. These and other rising democracies demand greater attention and power from the IMF and the World Bank to the World Health Organization and the World Trade Organization. In some areas, they are getting it—for example, G-20 membership, which all five IBSATI countries have—but mostly they are not. Some are particularly insistent on winning a permanent seat on the UN Security Council; advocates for such a change argue that their role as constructive leaders of the international liberal order hinges on giving them a greater say.[59] As they grow more impatient, they become more passive-aggressive vis-à-vis the international order, with a penchant for balancing the United States and Europe. Some are moving laterally to partner more deeply with nondemocratic countries like China and Russia, both bilaterally and through the BRICS group, and maintaining close ties to regimes like Zimbabwe, Venezuela, Cuba, and Iran. Their inclination to swing between the club of advanced democracies and the increasingly coherent group of authoritarian states raises doubts that they are ready to assume leadership roles in the international liberal order.[60] As one European diplomat remarked, they "can't be friends with everyone and still have global influence."

In response to these trends, traditional democratic powers should do more to find areas of convergence with the rising five democracies. They have, after all, what other leading claimants for greater influence in the world do not: political legitimacy afforded through modern popular sovereignty, derived by the consent of the people, as expressed in periodic and genuine free and fair elections, universal and equal suffrage, and secret ballots.[61] Recent declines in their respective records of respect for progressive norms of civil liberties, transparency, and accountability, however, are worrisome and may hurt the IBSATI group's claim for international leadership. It is difficult to discern whether, in the complex ebb and flow of politics, globalization, and nationalism, these five countries are more likely to remain in a gray zone or to advance in their liberalization agendas. In their transformations from closed to more open societies, these five rising democracies have chosen national development paths that skew centrist and moderate, with a hybrid mix of liberal and more state-centric political and economic policies. Compared with other democracies, they are neither shining stars nor declining laggards. This mixed outcome may be inherent to highly diverse and rapidly modernizing democratic societies that seek to reconcile competing demands through more democratic and hence slower, costlier, and more complex means. This hybrid trajectory is evident in their foreign policies, as well, as the remainder of this book explains. If progress continues to stagnate or reverses, their credibility as standard-bearers for the compatibility of democracy, peace, and development may fall.

These swing states have a dual responsibility: to deepen their commitments to the path of sustainable democratic development and to become more responsible leaders of the international liberal order. In turn, more advanced democracies should redouble their efforts to improve their own human rights records, listen and learn from their democratic brethren, and develop new ways and means of finding common ground to protect the democratic gains of the past thirty years.[62]

CHAPTER TWO

The International Human Rights and Democracy Order

Convergence and Divergence

AT THE HEART OF the contemporary international liberal order is the idea that the state's authority should be regulated to protect individual liberties and preserve the social contract to live in peace, prosperity, and security. On this foundation a structure for global governance is built that aims to manage conflicts, promote sustainable development, and protect human dignity. For such an order to work, it must have in place a set of norms, institutions, and instruments to protect and promote human rights and democratic systems of governance that, over time, have proven to be the best guarantors of those rights. For all of democracy's defects, humans have yet to invent a system of government that does a better job of securing human dignity in all its forms.

Fortunately, the key building blocks of such an international liberal order already exist, despite competing models of authoritarian governance that seek to obstruct and undermine encroachments on their traditional definitions of sovereignty.[1] Those building blocks were constructed largely (although not exclusively) by the world's democracies after World War II, but the fate of their handiwork will depend heavily on the capacity and conviction of other democracies—particularly the most influential rising democracies—to sustain and strengthen the international liberal order. To date, as explained later in the chapter, the evidence of their willingness to invest in the post–World War II order is contradictory—a predominant concern for parochial national interests has clipped their enthusiasm for what should have been a renaissance of the international liberal order after the fall of the Berlin Wall in 1989. But first we need to ask: what exactly is the international human rights and democracy order, and how has it evolved in the current context of mass communication, geopolitical competition, and new threats to the international order?

THE GLOBAL CONTEXT

Images of human suffering in places like Sudan and the Democratic Republic of the Congo, or of the triumph of popular protests in Ukraine and Tunisia, circle the wired globe in minutes. YouTube and Twitter document the flight of desperate migrants searching for greater freedom and security from the Mediterranean Sea to the Straits of Malacca. They are constant reminders that the greatest challenges facing the international order today are the struggles for human dignity rather than the grand ideological and territorial battles of the past. As core definitions of national security shift toward issues like economic security, transborder crime, migration, and climate change, the world is moving closer toward placing human security at the center of public policy. In essence, global politics in the twenty-first century has both a human face and a Facebook account.

The case of Malala Yousafzai, a Pakistani schoolgirl shot in the head by Taliban terrorists because of her campaign for girls' right to education, vividly demonstrates both the power of one person's courage to demand change and the platform offered by global communications to spread a profound message as simple as free, compulsory education for all children. Malala's speech to the UN General Assembly on July 12, 2013, which had garnered 1.45 million hits on YouTube by February 2015, came on the heels of a *New York Times* video documentary about her that was viewed more than one and a half million times in three years.[2] Similarly, one man's Internet campaign to shine a light on a warlord's crime of forcing children to become soldiers spread like wildfire in the span of days.[3] According to the Invisible Children campaign, the video about African warlord Joseph Kony was viewed 100 million times in just six days and generated almost $32 million in donations in one year.[4] The kidnapping of hundreds of schoolgirls by Boko Haram, anti-education militants in Nigeria, went viral in 2014, with millions of Facebook and Twitter messages spanning the globe to demand their release. In the first month of use, the hashtag #BringBackOurGirls was tweeted more than 3.3 million times, including by leaders like Michelle Obama.⁵ The legendary power of the pen to document injustice and inspire change has become the power of the video, a 24-7 reel of despair and hope. This explosion in global communications is driving the conversation toward convergence around liberal norms of democracy and human rights in every region of the world.

Broadly speaking, the attraction of the liberal democratic model and its track record of progress remain intact despite their imperfections and setbacks. Not coincidentally, nearly all the world's top performers on a variety of indicators of economic growth, income, and human development have adopted democratic systems of governance. The growing accountability of political leaders through free and fair elections is forcing them to place the voters' concerns for safe streets, decent jobs, good education, and basic health care as higher priorities for public spending. Sweeping ideologies of communism, fascism, and pan-Arab nationalism have been thoroughly discredited as incapable of addressing the increasingly complex challenges of satisfying public demands for human security and freedom broadly defined. As calls for political participation and social inclusion grow louder, both old and new democracies are expanding rights to decent health care, food, and education, gradually constructing social safety nets that guarantee at least a bare minimum of life's necessities. Even authoritarian states such as China and Russia feel some need to coat themselves with a patina of democratic legitimacy and have implemented elements of economic freedom unthinkable just two decades ago. China's defense of its own "democratic dictatorship" as a superior form of "capitalism with a human face"⁶ is looking increasingly hollow as corruption, contamination, and mass dislocation threaten its system from within, leading Beijing and Moscow to clamp down on bloggers, activists, artists, and lawyers. Whether judged by the comparative strength of the world's democracies or the inherent weaknesses of autocracies, democracy still stands as the most credible game in town, capable of responding to basic human demands for both political freedom and economic security.

As the real and perceived costs of outright war between states outstrip its benefits, states are freer to devote their resources to answering the voters' demands at home. While this trend may be sowing the seeds for future conflict over scarce resources of energy, food, and water, for now most states are more concerned about climbing the development ladder than with picking fights with neighbors. To meet their development goals, they depend increasingly on foreign trade and investment, weaving an ever-tighter web of integration and mutual dependence. Yet as they race to join the ranks of middle-income countries, concerns about the quality of governance and human rights in other states often take a backseat to other national interests, despite the fact that dysfunctional neighbors can threaten national security and impede their own development through spillover of conflict, refugee flows, terrorism, economic mismanagement, corruption, and criminal activity. Examples abound. Would Kenya be safer if Somalia were a functioning democratic state? Would al Qaeda have succeeded in attacking the United States, or Lashkar-e-Taiba carried off its massacre in Mumbai, if it had not found refuge in nondemocratic states like Afghanistan and Pakistan? Would North Korea be starving its people and rattling its nuclear weapons if it had followed the democratic path of its cousins to the south?

The relevance of internal governance to national and international security, which finds its philosophical origin in Immanuel Kant's democratic peace theory, are well embedded in the national security strategies of Western powers. Yet it remains worryingly underappreciated, at best, and ignored, at worst, among developing democracies. In the ideation and practice of foreign policy, national security interests narrowly defined have long predominated regardless of regime type. States choose, first and foremost, to defend their core national identities, resources, boundaries, and ideologies from the array of threats they face both regionally and globally. For centuries, imperial powers sought through force of arms to control resources, trade routes, and vast terrain far from their borders for their own selfish reasons cloaked in the name of the crown, religion, or "civilization." In the twentieth century, national security came to be defined by a fierce ideological battle between fascism and freedom, leaving behind millions of victims and delaying democratization in key states in Europe, Latin America, and Africa. In the modern era, competition for scarce resources, contested territory, military superiority, and nuclear supremacy dominate the national security discourse. Or so it seems.

Other trends suggest the emergence of a broader definition of national security, one that aims to enlarge the circle of democratically governed nations that exercise sovereignty in ways that protect rather than persecute their citizens and privilege negotiation and compromise over warfare. The concept behind this more expansive notion of national security, articulated (if not practiced enough) in the United States by every president since Woodrow Wilson, is that international peace and security are more likely in a world composed of liberal democratic states. As Michael Doyle, a leading proponent of the democratic peace theory, explains, liberal peace among democracies is achievable when all three factors—"republican representation, an ideological commitment to fundamental human rights, and transnational interdependence"—are in play.[7] First, as Doyle elaborates, warmongering is restrained in states where voters can turn out political elites and parliaments can check and balance the executive. In turn, transparent and contested democracies can more credibly signal to others that irrational aggression is unlikely and that cautious deliberation will prevail. Second, liberals also tend to trust and accommodate other liberal regimes—democracies still do not go to war against each other[8]—and distrust authoritarians as governing unjustly (thereby explaining why democracies are not immune from war with nonliberal regimes). Third, commercial and material incentives skew toward peaceful relations with states "governed by a rule of law that respects property and that enforces legitimate exchanges."[9]

A corollary to this thesis argues that democratic powers are more likely to accommodate the rise of other democracies but hedge or contest rising autocracies, an argument persuasively made by Daniel Kliman:

> Domestic institutions shape external perceptions of a nation's rise. On multiple levels, democratic government functions as a source of reassurance. Democracy clarifies intentions: decentralized decision-making and a free press guarantee that information about a state's ambitions cannot remain secret for long. In addition, checks and balances coupled with internal transparency create opportunities for outsiders to shape a rising power's trajectory. Other states can locate and freely engage with multiple domestic actors who all have a hand in the foreign policy of the ascendant state. Thus, democratic government mitigates the mistrust a new power's rise would otherwise generate.
>
> Autocracy has the opposite effect. By policing the media and confining foreign policy decisions to a select few, authoritarian government creates a veil of secrecy that obscures a rising power's intentions. Moreover, in a centralized and opaque political system, opportunities to shape strategic behavior are slim. Enforced secrecy prevents external powers from identifying and subsequently exploiting rifts within the government. And outsiders have few

domestic groups to engage because autocratic rule cannot tolerate independent centers of influence. Consequently, autocracy amplifies the concerns accompanying a powerful state's emergence.[10]

Applied to the real world, the democratic peace theory should lead policymakers to favor strategies that encourage strong democracies that by design feature greater transparency, horizontal and vertical accountability, and respect for human rights and the rule of law. Indeed, this principle of democratic enlargement remains a hallmark of U.S. policy, summed up by President Obama at the 2012 UN General Assembly:

> We believe that freedom and self-determination are not unique to one culture. These are not simply American values or Western values—they are universal values. And even as there will be huge challenges to come with a transition to democracy, I am convinced that ultimately government of the people, by the people, and for the people is more likely to bring about the stability, prosperity and individual opportunity that serve as a basis for peace in our world.[11]

The Third Wave of democratic transition under way since the late 1970s, with some support from more established democracies, validated this approach as one country after another, from Asia to Latin America to Eastern Europe, turned from closed to open systems of governance. Empirically speaking, there have been fewer conflicts with the spread of democracy: the world was more peaceful in 2014 than in all periods before the year 2000.[12] But judging from the pessimistic mood about the "freedom recession" of the last decade, and more recent talk of a return to the geopolitics of the Cold War, one would think that we have reverted to a Hobbesian world mired in the bare-knuckle trade-offs of a previous era of want and conflict. In fact, international consensus and cooperation around the aim of deepening democratic values and practices have come a long way from earlier eras of conflict and stagnation. Progress, however, is stuck for two main reasons. First, because authoritarian states are increasingly finding common ground to constrain and repress domestic and international movements for political change. And, second, because developing democracies are ambivalent and conflicted about their own role in strengthening the international liberal order.

To evaluate these propositions, I turn now to analyze key elements of the international democracy and human rights order and the intensity of support, or lack thereof, they receive from both developed and developing democracies. I also summarize the evolving views of the five rising democracies as they relate to emblematic concepts and events that shape the global order in this domain.

THE HUMAN RIGHTS AND DEMOCRACY ORDER OF THE TWENTY-FIRST CENTURY

In the decades following the atrocities of World War II, the international community, led by the United States, constructed a human rights order with a strong foundation of universal norms that place the individual's right to human dignity at the center. The Universal Declaration of Human Rights, adopted by all UN member states and translated into 407 languages and dialects, was the first international expression in modern history of the basic social compact between the governed and their rulers.[13] To give meaning to this concept, states adopted binding treaties that defined the scope and content of a wide variety of political, civil, economic, social, and group rights. Working through the United Nations and a growing number of regional organizations, they forged a variety of tools to monitor how states implement their obligations and to encourage protection of such rights in real time. Building this order was one of the great accomplishments of the second half of the twentieth century. Implementing these norms, however, remains one of the greatest challenges of this century.

Alongside the emergence of a global human rights architecture, states began articulating a growing concern for liberal democracy as the most effective form of government capable of protecting basic human rights, fostering economic development, and advancing international peace and security. At first this interpretation of Immanuel Kant's democratic peace theory was heard mainly from the United States, which saw hope in building a world, in Woodrow Wilson's famous phrase, "safe for democracy." Two world wars and a cold war between forces of liberal democracy and authoritarian communism eventually concluded in the 1990s with a resounding embrace of political freedom as millions tore down the iron curtain or broke free of colonial or military rule.

As the number of electoral democracies in the world tripled from 39 in 1974 to a high of 125 in 2014,[14] the interest in fostering international cooperation to defend and protect democracies ballooned. Given the twentieth century's record of volatile and often unsuccessful transitions to democracy, states were determined to create a more welcoming international environment weighted toward popular sovereignty expressed through free and fair elections as the litmus test of legitimacy.[15] Democratically elected civilian leaders, preoccupied with their own political survival in the face of militaries ready to pounce if they crossed certain red lines of national security, ideology, or economic management, agreed to marginalize governments that claimed power through extra-constitutional means like coups d'état.[16] A call for help to democratic neighbors could come in handy in an internal contest for political power, as seen in cases from Paraguay to Côte d'Ivoire and Burkina Faso. The end of the Cold War paved the way for greater civilian control of the military and a reorientation toward inclusive development and away from heavy-handed strategies of national security. This trend was reinforced by the growth in international peacekeeping and big increases in international development assistance. The added urgency of climbing out of economic crises, as in the case of Indonesia and Brazil, reinforced the international community's leverage to raise standards for greater transparency, accountability, and equity. Global and regional trade rules also became more important arbiters in mediating conflict and reinforcing globalization in the context of the rule of law.

HUMAN RIGHTS AT THE UNITED NATIONS

The United Nations, with its wide international membership and credibility, laid the groundwork for the modern global liberal order. As noted earlier, the Universal Declaration of Human Rights and subsequent human rights treaties and mechanisms were its foundation and still serve as the touchstone for an expansive definition of rights. In 1993, it created the senior post of High Commissioner for Human Rights and appointed a series of high-level figures to serve as "the conscience of the world." The office has a broad mandate to promote and protect human rights, prevent violations, provide technical and advisory services (at the request of the state concerned), conduct public education activities, and coordinate and manage a worldwide staff of more than 1,000 officers in regional and country field offices, in addition to approximately 700 human rights field officers serving in UN peace missions.

The liberal human rights and democracy order was reinforced at the United Nations' World Summit of 2005 when some 150 heads of state and government endorsed a plan of action that held up democracy, human rights, and the rule of law as among the cardinal principles of the global body.[17] In a document that touched all corners of the international agenda, the top leadership of every country acknowledged the interdependence of these issues with the two other pillars of the liberal order: international security and development. This consensus reflected the growing relevance and mainstreaming of democratic governance, transparency, human rights, and accountability in the broader international agenda. The road to such a proclamation, however, was long and rocky.

The UN Commission on Human Rights, established in 1946 to serve as the principal global forum for governments dealing with human rights, managed to negotiate a number of important treaties that later were adopted by the General Assembly and ratified by most states around the world.[18] It also established a series of working groups and independent experts commissioned to monitor compliance with international human rights norms and receive complaints on thematic and country-specific situations. It is important to recall that much of this early progress, including the key principle that internal affairs were not immune from international scrutiny, was spearheaded by India and other newly independent states from the Middle East, Asia, and Africa.[19] For much of its existence, however, the Commission was a victim of Cold War rivalries and manipulations by authoritarian states seeking to block international scrutiny of their human rights behavior. Western democracies were not immune to this tactic as they sought to deflect attention away from their own defects to the more urgent cases of repressive and failing states aligned with China and the Soviet Union.

As part of his comprehensive UN reform agenda, Kofi Annan, then secretary general, sought in 2004 to replace the Commission with something more credible. The result—the UN Human Rights Council, created in 2006—is an improvement over its predecessor, with greater buy-in from both developed and developing countries. The Council retained the Commission's authority to address country-specific situations, for example, and lowered the bar to convene special sessions to examine urgent cases. Key features of the Commission, such as the independence of its expert monitors and of the Office of the High Commissioner for Human Rights, as well as participation by civil society, were preserved or strengthened. Resources to deploy human rights monitors to the field were expanded, and a new Universal Periodic Review (UPR) mechanism to evaluate every country's human rights record was created. A process was established for encouraging competitive elections for seats on the Council, resulting, for the first time, in defeats for certain candidates with bad human rights records (for example, Iran, Venezuela, Sri Lanka, Azerbaijan, Belarus, and Syria), although others with similar records continued to be elected (for example, Cuba, China, and Saudi Arabia). A minority of states continue to oppose the principle of country scrutiny while simultaneously supporting certain long-standing exceptions like Israel, which is subject to an open-ended mandate on the occupied Palestinian territories and often biased treatment.

After some deserved disappointment with its actions, and inaction, in its first two years (a time when the United States effectively withdrew from the scene), the Council has turned an important corner—away from pointless debates about whether it has the authority to criticize countries (it clearly does) and toward very specific actions in a range of cases—from the historical change sweeping the Arab world to entrenched conflicts in North Korea, Myanmar, Eritrea, and Côte d'Ivoire. These include the rapid suspension of Libya as a member of the Council when violence erupted there in February 2011; the dispatch of special fact-finding teams to investigate human rights abuses in Libya, Syria, and Côte d'Ivoire; the appointment of fifteen commissions of inquiry, including pathbreaking work on crimes against humanity committed in North Korea; the creation of new special rapporteurs to address denial of rights in Iran, Belarus, and Eritrea; the halt of a damaging campaign to elevate "defamation of religion" to a human rights principle; and the opening of unprecedented debates and resolutions on the human rights of lesbian, gay, transgender, and bisexual people. The UPR process received 100 percent participation in its first cycle, an unheard of rate of engagement in any international proceeding, and led to new human rights treaty ratifications, more invitations to the Council's independent experts for country visits, greater interministerial coordination on human rights at the national level, and wider civil society participation in Geneva and in capitals.

These more assertive steps did not happen by accident. The Council, after all, is composed of governments, many of which have every interest in deflecting attention away from any international monitoring of domestic affairs. But an increasing number of them, particularly emerging democracies from Latin America, Africa, and Asia, are joining coalitions composed of traditional protagonists like the United States and Europe to support more, rather than less, international scrutiny of rights violations. The onset of the Arab Spring appears to have stimulated most states to move away from traditional noninterventionist posturing toward serious action to deal with real problems in real time, although laggards certainly still object. Other forces were involved—an increasingly networked and organized international human rights movement, greater public exposure of human rights crises, greater willingness on the part of transitioning countries to accept at least some scrutiny and technical assistance, and more democratic governments concerned with public opinion in their countries—and may pave the way for a new era in which governments feel more compelled than ever to take steps to deal with at least the most urgent situations.

Despite the relative progress of the human rights system over the past ten years, the international community faces a tangle of legal, bureaucratic, and poorly resourced mechanisms to address both urgent and chronic cases. The human rights treaty bodies, for example, are slow and cumbersome, and too many states are years behind fulfilling their reporting requirements and ignore the treaty bodies' decisions. Political resolutions from the UN Security Council or General Assembly that condemn violations may be massaged for months and ultimately watered down with little effect or blocked entirely, as seen in the case of Syria. Resources for human rights activities are grossly lacking. Funding for the United Nations' work on one of the three main pillars of the organization represents a mere 3 percent of the UN regular budget. The Responsibility to Protect doctrine (R2P), applied through NATO's armed intervention in Libya in a campaign for regime change, prompted blowback from key states that subsequently vetoed UN action to stop the Assad regime's brutal attacks in Syria. The International Criminal Court may issue indictments but has no power to arrest. From the impunity of a sitting president like Omar al-Bashir of Sudan for genocide in Darfur to the killing sprees led by an unspeakably brutal network of fanatics known as the Islamic State, there is no shortage of emergencies that test and even threaten the underpinnings of the human rights and democracy order. Enforcement of norms, unfortunately, will likely remain weak as states are not prepared to cede more sovereignty over their internal affairs, particularly to a Security Council perceived as fundamentally unequal and outmoded in its granting of veto powers to the five great powers that emerged after World War II.

THE COMMUNITY OF DEMOCRACIES

The main global forum for encouraging greater international cooperation among democracies began to take shape when Poland and the United

States hosted the first meeting of the Community of Democracies in 2000, the height of the post–Cold War democratic wave. The Community's mandate is to foster cooperation to strengthen democratic institutions, support adherence to common democratic values and standards, oppose threats to democracy, and coordinate support for new and emerging democratic societies.[20] The Community's early contributions to international politics resided more in the definition and expansion of core values,[21] and in the orientation of transitioning states to them than to concrete collective action, which remained for the United Nations or regional bodies to carry out, if at all.[22]

This emphasis on common values was expressed, in part, through a controversial process of determining who met the Community's standards of representative democracy and human rights and therefore qualified to participate in its ministerial meetings. On the recommendation of an international advisory committee, a self-appointed convening group of governments decided which states to invite as participants to biennial ministerial meetings; states in a transitional process toward democracy could be invited as observers.[23] At first, skeptics in the U.S. government and elsewhere were concerned that such a divisive process would be perceived by important states like China as an attempt to draw new Manichean lines in international affairs. France's then foreign minister, Hubert Védrine, saw the effort as a ham-handed attempt by Washington to lead a unipolar world in its image and went so far as boycotting the inaugural meeting.[24] Nonetheless, France stood alone as 107 states endorsed the founding Warsaw Declaration, which Poland's foreign minister, Bronisław Geremek, declared a fitting farewell to the Soviet Union's Warsaw Pact among its communist allies.

Lingering discomfort with this selectivity, particularly by states more inclined toward nonalignment and inclusion (like India and South Africa, both founding members of the initiative), prompted a rethink of the group's invitation process in 2010. A new governing council was formed to draw in states committed to a more operational Community of Democracies and invitations to ministerial meetings became more inclusive, at least on the margins (Russia and Venezuela, however, have remained unwelcome). The governing council is composed of twenty-seven states at varying levels of democratic consolidation, including important states like Japan, Korea, Mexico, and Nigeria, along with an executive committee and a troika system led most recently by Lithuania, Mongolia, and El Salvador (see table 2-1). (Notably, Brazil and Indonesia have kept

Table 2-1. The Community of Democracies Governing Council

CANADA	INDIA	PHILIPPINES
CAPE VERDE	ITALY	POLAND
CHILE	JAPAN	PORTUGAL
COSTA RICA	LITHUANIA	REPUBLIC OF KOREA
EL SALVADOR	MALI	ROMANIA
ESTONIA	MEXICO	SOUTH AFRICA
FINLAND	MONGOLIA	SWEDEN
GUATEMALA	MOROCCO	UNITED STATES
HUNGARY	NIGERIA	URUGUAY

Note: Of the dozens of countries that participate in the activities of the Community of Democracies, 27 form the Community's Governing Council, and act as the leaders of the Community.

Source: "Governments," Community of Democracies (2015).

their distance from the initiative.) This body, rather than the wider ministerial, is now the official governing authority, thereby diluting the influence of wavering or obstructionist states. It suspended Mali's membership on the council after the March 2012 military coup,[25] indicating that, at least when democratically elected governments are upended, standards will be enforced, even for founding members.[26] In early 2009, a Permanent Secretariat hosted by Poland was established with an international staff led by a diplomat seconded by the Swedish government. To help it get on its feet, Hillary Clinton, then secretary of state, pledged $1 million toward the secretariat and Mongolia's chairmanship.[27] In recognition of the diverse constituencies engaged in democracy building, the initiative includes parallel tracks of cooperation among parliamentarians, civil society, youth, and business leaders. In 2014, the Obama administration pledged an additional $3 million over three years to the Community of Democracies operations and to support its CD-UNITED initiative to strengthen civil society and democracy worldwide.[28] The United States will also host the group's next ministerial in 2017.

In addition to a rhetorical commitment to strengthening core democratic values and practices, the Community of Democracies has become modestly more operational and global in its reach. It provided critical early backing for a voluntary UN Democracy Fund (UNDEF) to support democracy-building initiatives implemented by civil society groups around the world. Since its establishment in 2005, UNDEF has received donations and pledges totaling more than $160 million from a wide range of countries, including India ($31.8 million), the United States ($56 million), Qatar ($10 million), and Japan ($10.1 million), as detailed in table 2-2.[29] The majority of UNDEF's funds go to projects run by local NGOs in Africa, Asia, eastern Europe, and Latin America, which range from supporting the development of democratic electoral processes in Azerbaijan to engaging and empowering student leaders in Jordan and providing human rights training to indigenous peoples in Mexico, Guatemala, Panama, and Peru.[30] The secretary general's advisory board, UNDEF's main governing mechanism, is composed of eighteen members, including the seven biggest donors between 2009 and 2011 (the United States, India, Sweden, Germany, Spain, Australia, and France); six states from different regions with "a proven commitment to democracy"; three members serving in an individual capacity; and two representatives of civil society organizations.[31] For a global body leery of engaging in member states' internal affairs, the willingness of such diverse states to put money behind a UN set of initiatives that encourage grassroots campaigns to hold governments accountable stands as an unheralded achievement. Complementary efforts by International IDEA, an intergovernmental initiative of Sweden composed of 28 established and newer democracies and dedicated to sharing comparative knowledge and experiences in support of democracy around the world, are another demonstration of the growing demand for and supply of democracy assistance.

Fitful attempts to establish a formal Democracy Caucus at the United Nations,[32] however, have proved more difficult, as governments like India and South Africa squirmed at the thought of having to choose between their traditional regional or South-South blocs and a new U.S.-led club of democracies in the halls of the General Assembly. Others worried that a high-profile bloc of democracies would unnecessarily antago-

Table 2-2. UN Democracy Fund Contributions (2005–15)

COUNTRY	CUMULATIVE AMOUNT	COUNTRY	CUMULATIVE AMOUNT
U.S.	$56,076,000	Senegal	$100,000
India	$31,762,543	Hungary	$75,000
Sweden	$16,931,757	Croatia	$71,000
Germany	$15,115,188	Peru	$72,681
Japan	$10,180,000	Israel	$57,500
Qatar	$10,000,000	Lithuania	$49,332
Australia	$9,212,424	Georgia	$24,943
Spain	$5,043,311	Panama	$27,000
France	$4,793,716	Argentina	$20,000
Italy	$2,947,800	Latvia	$15,000
Korea	$1,000,000	Estonia	$10,395
Ireland	$658,724	Bulgaria	$10,000
Poland	$612,276	Libya	$15,000
U.K.	$609,350	Mongolia	$10,000
Romania	$472,860	Cyprus	$5,000
Chile	$360,000	Ecuador	$5,000
Denmark	$265,018	Iraq	$5,000
Turkey	$235,000	Madagascar	$5,000
Czech Rep.	$195,780	Morocco	$5,000
Portugal	$150,000	Sri Lanka	$5,000
Slovenia	$127,924	Inst. on Governance	$2,230

= TOTAL $167,339,753

Note: Figures as of October 8, 2015.

Source: UNDEF, "Contribution Table."

nize powerful states like China and Russia. Cooperation among some states under the banner of the Community of Democracies, nonetheless, has occurred on issues such as elections to the Human Rights Council and some human rights resolutions in New York and Geneva.

The Community of Democracies has also organized international missions and technical assistance to developing democracies like Timor-Leste and Georgia and more recently to Tunisia and Moldova, and it has stepped up its activities in areas such as women's rights, protection of civil society, and education for democracy.[33] Its Working Group on Protecting Civil Society played an instrumental role in pressuring states to drop or amend rules that would restrict civil society and in winning the UN Human Rights Council's support for creation of a new special rapporteur on freedom of assembly.[34] In cooperation with the Club de Madrid, it launched the LEND network (Leaders Engaged in New Democracies), which provides a platform to facilitate timely assistance via voice/video/text communications connecting former presidents, prime ministers, and other leaders from around the globe to counterparts in transitioning democracies like Tunisia, Moldova, and Ukraine. A range of new initiatives were launched, as well, including the Asia Democracy Network, uniting democracy activists and policymakers throughout the Asia-Pacific region, and a new digital platform to support global education on democracy. The Community's original vision, however, remains unfulfilled, and, without the more active support of established democracies in Europe and key rising democracies like Brazil and India, it will likely continue to punch below its weight.

MAINSTREAMING DEMOCRACY AND RIGHTS IN THE DEVELOPMENT AND SECURITY AGENDAS

Since the demise of the UN's Commission on Human Rights, which balkanized human rights into the corridors of Geneva, the UN system has moved more deliberately toward integrating and mainstreaming a democracy and rights agenda into its two other core pillars of development and security. The international debate to move beyond the relatively effective UN Millennium Development Goals (MDGs) toward common benchmarks of sustainable development applicable to all governments reveals a widening if fragile consensus not only around fundamental objectives like expanding access to safe drinking water and quality education, rights previously articulated in UN treaties. It also reaffirms democratic concepts like accountability, rule of law, and transparency as essential ingredients for successful development outcomes.[35] In September 2015 governments formally adopted the Sustainable Development Goals, including a goal dedicated to access to justice and building accountable institutions. The UN Development Program (UNDP) led a comprehensive consultation process to encourage integration of governance and the rule of law into the new development framework.[36] UNDP was no stranger to these topics: it began mainstreaming rights and democracy elements in its development aid projects as far back as 2003 and puts a heavy focus on participation rights in development, including process rights, gender equality, and nondiscrimination. As of 2011, projects under the category of "democratic governance" consumed over a fourth of the agency's $4.6 billion budget.[37] A reallocation after 2011 led to an even greater emphasis on a broader category of similar activities to strengthen responsive institutions; combined, these themes constituted 49 percent of the 2014 UNDP budget.[38]

An ongoing concerted effort to mainstream human rights in the UN's security and political agenda gathered steam after the UN's failure to respond effectively to the brutal termination of the conflict in Sri Lanka. It eventually culminated in late 2013 when Secretary General Ban Ki-moon launched the Rights Up Front initiative. It aimed to improve the United Nations' capability of preventing and responding to large-scale human rights violations by making it a core systemwide responsibility.[39] Beyond targeted efforts like Rights Up Front, a number of UN agencies also concern themselves with human rights on a regular basis. The Electoral Assistance Division provides technical assistance on holding free and fair elections to dozens of countries. UNHCR, the UN refugee agency, is tasked with protecting refugees worldwide and helping those who are stateless find safe refuge.[40] UNESCO's mandate to protect freedom of expression, mobilize for education, protect cultural heritage, and pursue scientific cooperation spans a wide swath of the United Nations' human rights obligations.[41] A variety of special representatives, envoys, and advisers to the secretary general cover targeted human rights areas, including children and armed conflict, disability and accessibility, food security and nutrition, global education, migration, the prevention of genocide, and sexual violence in conflict, among others.[42] The Office of the High Commissioner for Human Rights has also stepped up its presence in New York and significantly expanded its role in briefing the UN Security Council on urgent human rights matters. Navi Pillay, former high commissioner for human rights, broke new ground by briefing the Security Council at least twenty times during her terms, more than double all her predecessors combined.[43] Protection of civilians is now a regular feature of UNSC mandates for peacekeeping, and, after a searing report on human rights abuses committed by the regime in North Korea, the Security Council decided to make the situation a standing item on its agenda. These are some signs of a growing recognition that the Security Council's mandate to address matters of international peace and security require it to consider the internal governance and rights behavior of its member states.

REGIONAL PILLARS OF THE INTERNATIONAL LIBERAL ORDER

At the regional level, the leading example of the postwar trend toward a human rights and democracy order is Europe's drive to build a union around a common commitment to democratic norms, human rights, and the rule of law. As the Berlin Wall collapsed, the attraction of a Europe "whole and free" pulled at least eight former communist states into the democratic fold. The violent upheavals in the Balkans have subsided in part because of the carrot of entry into the European Union and its common rule of law standards, which Croatia recently fulfilled as its twenty-eighth newest member. The European Union, along with the Council of Europe and its European Court on Human Rights and, to a lesser degree, the Organization for Security and Cooperation in Europe, rapidly increased their attention to the nuts and bolts of deeper democratization, greater transparency and accountability, legal protection of rights, and support of civil society.

In a similar though much less integrationist mode, Latin American countries emerging from military rule, with encouragement from the United States and Canada, found solace in the idea of a hemisphere of democratic states that would protect one another from a return to the political instability and repression of the recent past. Through the Organization of American States, and its companion inter-American human rights system, governments adopted mechanisms to intervene in cases of democratic interruptions and human rights violations.[44] These "democracy clauses" were put to good effect in a number of concrete cases when constitutional order was upended or impaired through military coups, executive grabs of power, street protests, and forced resignations. The Inter-American Commission and Court of Human Rights have issued pathbreaking decisions in areas like preventive measures to protect indigenous rights, and classifying disappearances as ongoing crimes for which no statute of limitations may apply.[45] These decisions rankled states like Brazil and Ecuador, which in 2012 led a "reform" effort that sought to weaken the system's effects, a contentious two-year process that ultimately led to a draw.[46] Brazil later distanced itself from Ecuador's maneuvers and even put forth a candidate for the Inter-American

Commission—Paulo de Tarso Vannuchi—who was ultimately elected, but its commitment to the system remains questionable.

Other regional human rights norms and institutions gradually strengthened during this period, as well. The Commonwealth states, affiliated historically with the United Kingdom, adopted their own declarations and diplomatic initiatives to support democratic transitions and condemned and isolated backsliding states like Pakistan, Nigeria, and Zimbabwe.[47] Following the Commonwealth Ministerial Action Group's (CMAG) decision that it had not made sufficient progress toward returning to democracy, Fiji was suspended in September 2009 (and was reinstated after holding new elections in September 2014), and the Maldives was suspended from the CMAG in 2012 and remains under close observation.[48] The African Union also reached consensus on embracing democracy and human rights principles with measures to protect democratically elected incumbents from unconstitutional disruptions, incentivize political and economic reforms through the New Partnership for Africa's Development (NEPAD), and establish an Africa-wide human rights system featuring a commission and a court. From Egypt to Madagascar, Central African Republic and Mauritania, the African Union continues to surprise observers with its proclaimed defense of constitutional democracy as the benchmark for full membership. Notably, the African Union immediately suspended Egypt after the military deposed President Mohamed Morsi in July 2013 and sent a ministerial delegation to Cairo to urge a return to electoral democracy. At the subregional level, the Economic Community of West African States (ECOWAS) has played a proactive role in responding to democratic backsliding, most recently in Burkina Faso in 2015.

Lagging far behind in the development of regional norms and institutions in the human rights and democracy space are the Arab world, some subregions of Asia, and the Organization of Islamic Cooperation (OIC—formerly the Organization of the Islamic Conference). Of these, only the South Asian Association for Regional Cooperation (SAARC) and the Association of Southeast Asian Nations (ASEAN) have developed a modicum of concern for the principles of democracy and human rights as defining criteria of their common identity. In 2011, for example, the eight-member SAARC, under the leadership of Bangladesh, adopted the Charter of Democracy, which "renounces unequivocally any unconstitutional change of an elected government in a Member State."[49] No mechanism exists, however, to institutionalize a collective response to threats to the democratic order, as recently occurred in the Maldives, and a common view in the region remains that SAARC is no more than a paper tiger. Similarly, while ASEAN has made surprising progress toward articulating commitments to democracy and human rights principles (more than half of its members are non-democracies), its Human Rights Commission has been criticized heavily for its lack of independence. Human rights experts were particularly dismayed by the adoption of an ASEAN Human Rights Declaration in 2012 that reintroduced elements of cultural relativism and other limits to universal human rights norms.[50] The Arab awakening, however, has provoked some interesting precedents in the Muslim world, including the suspension of Syria from both the Arab League and the OIC on human rights grounds. Overall, while progress is uneven, all regions feel at least some compulsion to address democracy and human rights as a sine qua non of international legitimacy.

NEWER CONCEPTS: THE INTERNATIONAL CRIMINAL COURT AND RESPONSIBILITY TO PROTECT

As global consciousness of the horrific human consequences of conflict grew, efforts to limit state sovereignty when governments grossly violated their responsibility to protect their citizens increased, as well. In 1998, states agreed to create a permanent international criminal tribunal, the International Criminal Court (ICC), which was established in 2002 when the Rome Statute came into effect. Unlike its ad hoc predecessors—the International Criminal Tribunal for the former Yugoslavia, the International Criminal Tribunal for Rwanda, and the Special Court for Sierra Leone—the ICC holds global jurisdiction over cases of genocide, crimes against humanity, and war crimes in signatory states, if the state is unwilling or unable to investigate and prosecute according to standards of due process.[51] It is known as the court of last resort for the gravest human rights abuses. This basis in complementarity provides an alternative to national judicial systems that may not be able to try powerful domestic leaders. For non-signatory states, the UN Security Council has the power to refer cases to the ICC, a political and diplomatic tool thus far only employed twice—in the situations in Darfur and Libya. In all other circumstances, the court is limited by a lack of universal jurisdiction—it can only prosecute crimes committed on the territory of a signatory or by a citizen of a signatory. For this reason, states in the midst of conflict have little incentive to sign on since they open their officials to prosecution. Most of the criticism against the ICC originates from Africa, which claims it has been unfairly the target of all ICC investigations since its inception twelve years ago (often at the request of African states) while countries in the global North run the court.[52]

As of November 17, 2015, 123 countries had ratified or acceded to the Rome Statute, up from 60 when it entered into force, and a total of 139 countries are signatories.[53] Conspicuously, the United States has never ratified the Rome Statute and is joined by Russia, China, and Saudi Arabia, among others. India refuses to sign or ratify the statute, arguing the scope of the statute is overly broad and the court subject to political influence.[54] India also wants to avoid any move that would place its on-going conflicts in such areas as Kashmir under the ICC's jurisdiction. Indonesia, also not a signatory, says it supports the statute in principle and even asserted the intention to ratify by 2008 in its 2004 National Plan of Action on Human Rights, a plan reaffirmed by Foreign Minister Hassan Wirajuda in 2007. Since then, Indonesia has backpedaled, with Defense Minister Purnomo Yusgiantoro stating in May 2013 that "there are many countries, including major democratic countries [such as the United States] that have yet to ratify the Rome Statute," and "we need more time to carefully and thoroughly review the pros and cons of rati-fication."[55] In conjunction with its efforts to enter the EU, Turkey has been under pressure to accede to the statute. Echoing the Indonesian government's position, the Erdoğan government committed to ratifica-tion in 2004 but backpedaled in 2008, insisting the court have jurisdic-tion over the crime of terrorism, as well (stemming from its long-standing struggle with the Kurdistan Workers Party, known as PKK).[56]

Of the IBSATI countries, only Brazil and South Africa are parties to the statute, but neither has thrown their full support behind it. Brazil was silent on the UNSC referral of Syria to the ICC in January 2013, a mo-tion currently blocked by China and Russia. South Africa has opposed the ICC's prosecution of Sudanese president Omar al-Bashir, in keeping with the African Union's 2009 vote to not cooperate with the ICC in-dictments against Bashir, despite calls for his arrest on charges of geno-cide and war crimes committed in the Darfur region of Sudan.[57] After the ICC's indictment of Kenyan president Uhuru Kenyatta and Deputy President William Ruto for election-related violence, opposition among African states intensified, citing concerns about "constitutional order, stability and integrity" when sitting heads of state were called to the court.[58] In October 2013, South Africa supported a failed Kenya-led bid to withdraw from the court but tensions remained high as it sought a deferral until after they completed their terms in office (the charges against Kenyatta have since been dropped). South Africa went a step further in June 2015 when it failed to arrest al-Bashir during his visit to the country for an African Union meeting, despite treaty and constitutional obligations and court judgments to the contrary.[59]

On the matter of North Korea and the ICC, IBSATI states were similarly wobbly. In November 2014, the UN General Assembly's Third Committee (responsible for humanitarian affairs and human rights issues) voted in favor of a draft resolution referring North Korea to the ICC for crimes against humanity as well as "targeted sanctions" for rampant human rights abuses. The 111–19 vote, with 55 abstentions, is merely a recommendation as the General Assembly does not have the power to refer the regime or its leader Kim Jong-un to the ICC. (The UN Security Council does have the authority to refer cases to the ICC, although Russia and China would likely veto this move.) Of the IBSATI countries, only Brazil and Turkey voted in favor of this resolution; India, Indonesia, and South Africa abstained, asserting that they "preferred constructive dialogue that respected the principles of sovereignty and territorial integrity."[60] On a separate amendment sponsored by Cuba to strip the ICC referral language from the text, India, Indonesia, and South Africa voted for the amendment, whereas Brazil abstained; only Turkey voted against it.[61] These positions drive home the deep resistance still felt against granting the ICC authority to investigate top officials for the worst crimes.

The principle of R2P is perhaps one of the most controversial emerging political norms driving a wedge between emerging powers and their more established counterparts. A preventative diplomacy tool designed to protect civilians from genocide, ethnic cleansing, war crimes, and other crimes against humanity, R2P is based on three mutually reinforcing pillars:

1. The state has the primary responsibility to protect its citizenry from these crimes.

2. The international community has a commitment to encourage and assist states to fulfill that responsibility.

3. The international community has a responsibility to take collective action under the UN Charter when a state fails in this responsibility.[62]

As Madeleine Albright and Rich Williamson have noted, R2P's overarching goal is to reinforce sovereignty by encouraging and, when needed, helping states protect their own citizens first through diplomatic, economic, and other measures, with collective military action being a rarity.[63]

Despite the fact that use of force is by no means the first step in the operationalization of R2P, in recent years R2P has become synonymous with Western-led regime change and humanitarian intervention, at least in the eyes of some rising democracies. With few exceptions, such democracies—especially India and Brazil—are exceedingly uncomfortable with the concept. While on the UN Security Council, India, Brazil, and South Africa all voted in favor of imposing sanctions on Libya and referring the case to the ICC in February 2011. But when R2P was invoked as the basis for the use of force and establishment of a no-fly zone, India and Brazil abstained just one month later. Since then, all three states have turned against intervention in the name of R2P, as evidenced most dramatically in the case of Syria.

Libya signified one of the first conscious applications of the R2P concept, and it sparked significant debate regarding its conceptual development and practical application. Many states, especially the IBSATI states, feared that R2P as written offered the world's powers a blank check to pursue national interests and instigate regime change under the guise of preventing atrocities.[64] In response to complaints that the UN Security Council was not sufficiently consulted and informed following NATO's implementation of Resolution 1973 authorizing the use of force in Libya, Brazil put forth a proposal titled "Responsibility While Protecting" (RWP). A reflection of the IBSATI countries' (and others, such as Russia and China) shared discomfort with Western-led use of force, RWP offered a comprehensive framework for increased reporting and accountability of military interventions. It also reinforced the need to exhaust all other policy options and conduct a thorough analysis of possible consequences before such interventions. In some respects it stalled conversation and polarized opinion by making R2P out to be something it is not—a pretext to pursue national interests instead of preventing atrocities—and took away the flexibility needed to respond quickly to imminent atrocities. But in others it reinforced global consensus for the new norm by reaffirming the core principle behind limited sovereignty in emergency situations. It also set parameters that allowed countries to reengage on the issue, brought new states into the R2P conversation, and rallied the three India-Brazil-South Africa (IBSA) countries.

RWP has largely fallen off the radar since its introduction in November 2011, but the effects of the larger conversation regarding R2P are far-reaching. From an earlier period of general international consensus in favor of atrocity prevention, divergence rather than convergence prevails on how to operationalize the concept, and the IBSATI countries continue to resist more robust interpretations of the doctrine. The implications are clear in the international community's woeful inaction in Syria.

In sum, as the above survey illustrates, developments since the democratic wave unleashed in the 1980s and 1990s have reinforced the underpinnings of an international democracy and human rights order of unprecedented scale and breadth. The enduring appeal of "democracy" and the legitimacy its authentic expression carries in mainstream global public opinion have encouraged governments to strive, even if only rhetorically and in self-interested ways, for more democratic structures of both national and global governance. As noted further in the next section, the IBSATI crowd leans in this direction, although with serious inconsistencies and caveats. China and Russia, along with allied states like Cuba, Syria, North Korea, and Pakistan, remain as the great outliers in this convergence toward consensus, and they are able to recruit swing states like India and Brazil from time to time, in damaging ways (for example, Ukraine). As the world fragments into shifting multipolar coalitions of convenience, the international liberal order could face a major setback if these swing states decide not to align their foreign policies with their internal characters as thriving, if imperfect, democracies.

HOW DO RISING DEMOCRACIES SHAPE THE HUMAN RIGHTS AND DEMOCRACY ORDER?

The international liberal order outlined above did not appear from thin air. It was the result of decades of incremental negotiation, compromise, and ultimately adoption by states of norms, instruments, and institutions to promote and protect human rights and democratic governance. While the gap between rhetoric and reality in this domain is wide, policymakers in the United States and other developed democracies have invested heavily in the task of supporting democracy and human rights abroad. Billions of dollars in foreign assistance from the United States, Canada, and the European Union are provided each year to help states build transparent and accountable institutions, reform judiciaries, defend human rights, and sustain civil society and free media.[65] This includes traditional programs of direct assistance to parliaments, judiciaries, and human rights defenders and newer U.S. programs like the Millennium Challenge Account, which offers major development assistance—more than $10 billion in poverty reduction compacts and $539 million in improvement threshold projects in just over ten years—to states that reach certain thresholds of democratic governance and anticorruption.[66] As evidence demonstrating the link between democratic governance and the effectiveness of development assistance grows,[67] international agencies like UNDP and World Bank are devoting more and more resources toward building state capacity on transparency and accountability, proxy terms for democracy assistance. In concrete terms, UNDP spends $1.5 billion yearly in support of democratic processes, making it one of the largest providers of such assistance worldwide.[68] In fiscal year 2014, U.S. spending on advancing democracy totaled $1.9 billion, with requests to Congress of $2.8 billion for fiscal year 2016.[69] The European Union utilizes a number of mechanisms to support democracy and human rights, including the European Instrument for Democracy and Human Rights (EIDHR), which has a budget of 292 million euro dedicated to supporting democracy and election observation from 2014 to 2017.[70] The EU also recently created the European Endowment for Democracy, which has begun taking a hard look at democracy support policies and opportunities for strengthened transatlantic cooperation.[71] Meanwhile, member countries—including former communist countries—continue to commit varying levels of bilateral funding to this objective.[72] In essence, the established democracies have more than carried their weight of the democracy enlargement project for decades.

As newer democracies have emerged around the world, have they become more willing to support democracy in other countries? In a comprehensive survey of the foreign policies of forty established and newer democracies between 1992 and 2002, a research team I co-led with Robert Herman found a direct correlation between the level of a country's internal democratic development and its support for democracy abroad. Using Freedom House rankings of political rights and civil liberties, and a series of case studies in which governments chose to (or not) support democratic transitions in other countries, nearly all states rated "free" earned scores as "good" or "very good" promoters of democracy abroad. Similarly, states rated "not free" or "partly free" had only a "fair" or "poor" record of defending democratic principles in their foreign relations.[73] This finding underscores both the practical implementation of the democratic peace theory in more developed democracies and the weakness of its adoption in weak and illiberal democracies. A 2014 assessment conducted by Freedom House reinforces these findings: newer democracies in Latin America, Africa, and Asia are less likely than the United States, European Union, and individual European countries to condemn democratic backsliding in third countries. In general, the countries examined in the report support elections abroad but do not take their policies a step further to promote democracy and human rights in their trade policies or responses to coups; they likewise fail to stand up to authoritarian states like China and Russia.[74]

As these newer democracies take hold, one would assume that democracy and human rights promotion would become a more widely adopted feature of their foreign policies. Indeed, a recent study evaluating the foreign policies of Central and Eastern European states (CEE) concluded that Poland, the Czech Republic, and Slovakia "are among the most active emerging democracy promoters. Even with limited capacity, these new democracies have leveraged their recent democratization experiences and local knowledge to contribute to the democratization of their neighborhood," marking them as complementary actors in the traditional democracy assistance strategies of the West.[75] The Baltic states, fearing the return of an antidemocratic Russia, have become positive contributors to democracy projects in countries like Belarus, Moldova, and Georgia. CEE governments also have been vocal supporters at the European Union of harder-line approaches toward authoritarian regimes in Cuba, Russia, and Myanmar. Nonetheless, their style of support tends to be one of constructive engagement, rather than naming and shaming, with a preference to work through multilateral instead of bilateral channels.

The farther one goes from Europe, itself a model of integration based on rule of law and democratic norms, and the transatlantic alliance, the more likely one is to find less intense support for policies that favor democracy and human rights. A number of indicators—from the votes taken at UN fora on human rights resolutions to the integration of democracy as an element of foreign aid—suggest that a concern for democracy and human rights in third countries still ranks low as a priority for such rising democracies as Brazil, India, South Africa, Turkey, and Indonesia. A study comparing the voting patterns of these five countries (plus the Republic of Korea) in three UN bodies—the Human Rights Council, the General Assembly, and the Security Council—concluded that they are inconsistent advocates for democracy and human rights on the international stage,[76] although recent trends are slightly more favorable.[77] Similar to more developed democracies, these states place primacy on other interests—security, economic, or ideological—and undervalue the instrumental role democratic governance and rule of law can play in reaching common goals of political stability, economic growth, regional and international peace, and sustainable development.

Reactions of these countries to the events surrounding the Arab Spring, including entrenched repression in Iran, reveal a tendency toward rhetorical support for representative democracy and the rule of law; even coercive interventions to prevent human rights abuses in Libya and to protect the results of free and fair elections in Côte d'Ivoire have garnered some approval. This wave of apparent concern for the democratic aspirations of citizens in Tunisia, Egypt, Yemen, and Libya came not only from democracies but from neighboring monarchies, as well, reflecting a mix of sectarian, nationalist, and economic interests motivating external support for changing how states govern themselves internally.

The high-water mark came in 2011 when the UN Security Council voted unanimously to condemn and sanction the Qaddafi regime in Libya under the banner of the responsibility to protect doctrine adopted at the World Summit in 2005.[78] When leading powers in Europe and the United States united around a resolution authorizing the use of force to prevent violence against unarmed civilians, wavering countries like India, Brazil, and China stood aside, opening the door to NATO airstrikes as the pointy end of what became a regime change policy. While successful in dislodging Qaddafi from power, the strong-arm tactics enraged states that have long upheld nonintervention and protection of sovereignty as the cardinal rule of international politics. As a result, states like South Africa, India, and Brazil have pulled back from more robust action in Syria, while Russia and China stand firmly against, despite the rising death toll there. A sampling of UN votes on human rights and the responsibility to protect, illustrated in table 2-3, indicates the erratic approach these countries have taken when it comes to integrating these issues in their foreign policies.

These dramatic developments on the world stage are a window on the emerging fault lines of international debates on human rights and national security. In one camp, states dominated by autocratic leaders remain more wedded than ever to traditional concepts of noninterventionism

Table 2-3. Key UN General Assembly Third Committee Votes

	SYRIA	IRAN	NORTH KOREA	MYANMAR
	Condemnation of Human Rights Record (122-13-44)	Condemnation of Human Rights Record (86-32-59)	Recommenda-tion to Refer DPRK to ICC (111-19-55)	Situation of Human Rights in Myanmar (98-25-63)
	November 2011	November 2011	November 2014	November 2011
Brazil	Yes	Abstain	Yes	Abstain
India	Abstain	No	Abstain	No
Indonesia	Yes	Abstain	Abstain	Abstain
South Africa	Abstain	Abstain	Abstain	Abstain
Turkey	Yes	Absent	Yes	Yes

Source: United Nations.

regardless of the brutality of abuses on the ground. Their definitions of national security are rooted in a defense of their own closed political systems and prolongation in power without external interference. In the other camp, powerful democracies of the West, often with political support for taking action against gross human rights abuses, remain committed to the aim of building a world of stable, prosperous democracies that compete but do not go to war with each other.

In the middle reside the rising democracies, states emerging from colonialism, apartheid, or military dictatorship (previously supported by the West) but now firmly rooted in constitutional democracy, civilian control of the military, and market-oriented economic policies. As their stars rise on the international stage, they offer positive examples of the compatibility of political liberties, economic growth, and tolerance of religious and ethnic differences. Yet their willingness to join forces with other democracies on the side of spreading and deepening democratic governance and respect for human rights is uncertain. The future direction of their conception of national security will determine in many ways the fate of the global democracy and human rights order.

Based on recent trends, the jury is out on whether they will become more vocal and confident partners in common endeavors to defend democracy and human rights. The following snapshot of the behavior of five of these countries—India, Brazil, South Africa, Turkey, and Indonesia—reveals a basic consensus on the values of democracy and human rights to both national and global orders, alongside a range of active, passive, and antagonistic behaviors on how best to advance them. A deeper treatment of each country is covered in chapters 3–7.

Brazil

Since its transition to democracy, Brazil's attitude toward the current human rights and democracy order has fluctuated between a willingness to build up international mechanisms to support political reform and serious skepticism toward initiatives led by traditional Western powers.

In general, Brazil's evolution from a relatively quiet, inward-looking, and defensive foreign policy to a more assertive regional and increasingly global strategy has coincided with its considerable domestic progress on democracy and human rights and economic growth. When it comes to using such influence to strengthen the existing global order, however, Brazil has played an ambiguous and somewhat unpredictable role. On the occasional episode when support for democracy or human rights abroad coincides with higher priority goals like consolidating regional leadership, protecting business interests, or winning a seat on the UN Security Council, Brazil tends to favor multilateral strategies that lean toward pro-reform outcomes. Its close cooperation with Washington on a global good governance initiative known as the Open Government Partnership is noteworthy less for its content, which appeals to the popular clamor against corruption, but for the willingness of Brazil to stand side by side with the United States to launch it. More often, as in the cases of Iran, Cuba, and Honduras, Brazil under President Lula and his handpicked successor, President Dilma Rousseff, has taken a more skeptical approach marked by a traditional defense of national sovereignty, suspicion of U.S.-led initiatives, and growing demands for global governance reform. Brazil's policy response to the Arab Spring has demonstrated this latter tendency more than the former.

In the context of the Arab Spring, Brazil has taken a largely hands-off, noninterventionist approach. Any action Brazil has taken or endorsed has been multilateral in nature, with a strong preference for

South-South cooperation and against harder-line interventions. It initially supported UN actions in Libya, then abstained on the use of force, a position that has hardened despite rising levels of violence in Syria. In between these two episodes, however, it did join the unanimous consent by the Security Council for UN forces in Côte d'Ivoire to use "all necessary means" to protect civilians caught up in postelection violence.[79] In the same vein, Brazil introduced a much-discussed proposal at the United Nations under the theme of "responsibility while protecting" that, on the one hand, reinforced its support for the R2P concept but, on the other, sought to constrain any use of force and prioritize the exhaustion of diplomatic measures.[80] In addition to its desire to check U.S. leadership, such measures reflect Brazil's preference for South-South solidarity, nonintervention, and deference to regional bodies to resolve conflicts, a stance that neatly serves its own purposes as a leader of UNASUR.

India

India, the world's most populous democracy, was a leader in the Non-Aligned Movement during the Cold War and the anti-imperialist and noninterventionist roots of its foreign policy run deep. Yet as it emerges as a global economic power, and a rival to China, its status as a secular, pluralist, and democratically governed state is slowly beginning to influence its behavior toward the international human rights and democracy order.

At the United Nations, India has mostly opposed or abstained from criticizing the human rights records of other states as an inappropriate intervention in internal affairs. Its robust support of the UN Democracy Fund and its modest role on the steering committee of the Community of Democracies reflect not only its decision to demonstrate healthy bilateral relations with Washington. They also evidence India's preferred approach of cooperative engagement through the United Nations and its passive promotion of democracy and human rights values. A key factor in its decision to participate in these two particular initiatives was its desire to forge closer ties with the United States, which worked hard under the George W. Bush administration to secure New Delhi's support. Like Brazil, India seeks to win a permanent seat on the UN Security Council. India is willing to associate itself with multilateral initiatives that support democratization in countries already on the democratic path and those that actively request assistance from India or the larger international community.[81] It also has been quick to use democracy-related forums on the international stage to distinguish itself from autocratic and corrupt regimes in neighboring Pakistan and the authoritarian capitalist model presented by China.

India's drive to best Pakistan for regional supremacy is the key factor that explains its active role in supporting the government in Kabul against the Taliban in Afghanistan.[82] Consonant with India's cautious support for democracy, and its desire for closer relations with Washington, it joined the international community's efforts to build Afghanistan's democratic institutions by supporting construction of the Afghan parliament building, parliamentary training, and material support for elections in addition to more than $1 billion in other forms of assistance. India also worked closely with the United States and the European Union to pressure the monarchy in Nepal to accept far-reaching constitutional changes and an eventual fall from power in favor of representative democracy.[83] Its behavior vis-à-vis political turmoil in the Maldives, on the other hand, has veered from direct intervention in 1988 to a more laissez-faire approach after the democratically elected president was deposed by conservative forces aligned with sympathetic police and military forces.

India is starting to find its comfort zone in speaking on the global stage in favor of democracy as a preferred foundation for international peace and cooperation while insisting that its assistance be sought and not imposed on others. In responding to the wave of demands for democracy and human rights across the Arab world, however, India has largely hunkered down in the noninterventionist camp, adamant that it supports democracy in principle but that it should not interfere in the affairs of other states.[84] India's largely passive response to the Arab Spring reflects its general approach to global democracy and human rights as well as its complicated economic and expatriate ties to the Middle East.

In Egypt and Libya, the Indian government categorized the uprisings as an "internal affair" and prioritized the safety of its citizens living there.[85] As international forces mobilized to protect civilians in Libya, India's noninterventionist posture tangibly manifested itself at the UN Security Council, where it sat as a nonpermanent member at the time. When the Council passed Resolution 1970, extending sanctions on certain Libyan officials and referring the situation to the ICC, India joined unanimous endorsement. A month later, however, India abstained when the Council authorized force to protect civilians and implemented a no-fly zone. In explanation of its abstention, India insisted that political measures ought to be the primary course of action for ending the violence.[86] India further bolstered its South-South solidarity credentials by endorsing the African Union road map for Libya, saying that decisions related to Africa "should be left to the Africans."[87]

India's natural noninterventionist tendency, coupled with its view that the NATO mission in Libya had exceeded the confines of its mandate, made it even less inclined to act in the context of violent crackdowns in Syria. Bilaterally, India continued its relationship with the Syrian regime, displaying its preference for mediation and political dialogue. A desire not to disturb relations with Iran, an ally of Syria and important oil supplier, also may have influenced India's initial reticence on the Assad regime's violent crackdown, although in March 2014 India obliged a U.S. request to cut its Iranian oil imports by two-thirds to help fulfill the terms of the interim nuclear agreement.[88] Similar circumstances and priorities influenced India's reaction to uprisings in Bahrain, where India has the additional complication of ensuring the safety of its more than 350,000 nationals—the largest of Bahrain's expatriate communities— residing in the island nation. As a nod to its historic bonds with Russia, it abstained on UN action critical of Moscow's blunt intervention in Crimea.

Overall, India's response to the Arab Spring is typical of its ongoing balancing act between supporting democratic values in principle, on the one hand, and noninterventionist pragmatism, on the other. However, it is important to highlight India's actions that have deviated from the noninterventionist approach, such as its endorsement of sanctions against Libya and referral to the ICC; its abstention (not opposition) on the Libya no-fly zone and intervention; and its vote in favor of the use of UN forces to protect civilians in Côte d'Ivoire. These efforts reveal that as India ascends to a leadership role, it is delicately attempting to maintain good relations with the West by supporting democracy while preserving its bona fides in the Nonaligned Movement.

South Africa

South Africa's remarkably peaceful transition from apartheid to constitutional democracy (under the inspiring leadership of Nelson Mandela and encouraged by an active and attentive international community) raised high expectations that it would favor international solidarity in support of other peaceful democratic movements both inside and outside

Africa. A beacon of democratic transition in southern Africa, it is expected to lead as others in its neighborhood struggle to consolidate their
democracies. But despite boasting a foreign policy predicated on a human
rights and democracy imperative, South Africa's cognizance of its own
colonial past and desire to distance itself from its apartheid-era reputation of regional hegemon leads it to favor pan-African and South-South
solidarity. Faced with entrenched economic and social challenges at
home, South Africa prioritizes relations that help it address domestic
priorities like rural development, creation of decent jobs, and crime
prevention. South Africa also displays a strong preference for playing a
mediator role, particularly with regard to regional conflict resolution,
prompting it to favor negotiated settlements and incremental changes lo-
cally over acting as a leader on democracy and human rights issues on a
wider stage. The result is an uneven and muted leadership record.

With regard to its own neighborhood, South Africa has leaned heavily on the tool of quiet diplomacy over public condemnations highlighted
in its approaches to the political and human rights crisis in Zimbabwe
and disputed elections in Côte d'Ivoire. Its preferred role as mediator in
several conflicts on the continent—Angola, Burundi, Kenya, Mozambique, Sierra Leone, Sudan, and others—has also led it to avoid taking
sides in internal political disputes. Favoring negotiated settlements of apparent incremental change but few results has led in these cases to muted
concern for democratic principles. Despite "flawed" 2013 presidential
elections, South Africa and the Southern African Development Community (SADC) asked all parties in Zimbabwe to accept the outcome of the
elections to stabilize the country, encouraged the United States and the
European Union to lift sanctions and set the country on a path toward
economic recovery.[89] In contrast, South Africa promptly termed the
overthrow of Egyptian president Mohamed Morsi "an unconstitutional
removal of the democratically elected president and the suspension of
Egypt's constitution," noting that it breached the norms and standards
adopted by the African Union.[90] Unusually direct in its criticism, South
Africa went on to offer to share its national reconciliation experiences
and practices with Egypt as it builds peace and stability in the aftermath
of the coup.

When it comes to endorsing international initiatives aimed at stabiliz-
ing internal or cross-border conflict, South Africa has regularly voted in
favor of UN or regional interventions and deployed military and police
personnel in support of such peacekeeping missions. When it served on

the UN Security Council in 2007–08, for example, it endorsed all seven resolutions related to creating or strengthening mandates on Sudan. Likewise, it supported all thirteen Security Council resolutions relating to the Democratic Republic of the Congo, including extending the arms embargo. Unlike India, South Africa voted for the Security Council's second resolution on Libya that authorized the use of force to protect civilians and the implementation of a no-fly zone. Its explanation of vote illustrated South Africa's concern for both protecting democracy and human rights and ensuring the sovereign integrity of a nation.

But South Africa's endorsement of strong international action quickly turned to criticism of NATO's turn toward regime change as it advocated for African-led mediation and attacked an international power structure that interferes with the principle of regional primacy. Its concern with NATO's overreach in Libya directly influenced its unwillingness to endorse Security Council action on Syria. South Africa abstained on an October 2011 Security Council vote that would have condemned Syrian authorities for their violent crackdown, vetoed by Russia and China, and maintained its neutral position in November 2011 at the UNGA's Third Committee when it abstained on a resolution condemning Syria's human rights abuses. It did engage Syria through an IBSA delegation that called on Assad in August 2011, but this first instance of trilateral IBSA diplomacy is an anomaly in South Africa's approach to the tragic case of Syria.

When South Africa's dueling values of strong rhetorical support for human rights and democracy and advocacy for pan-African and South-South solidarity come into conflict, the latter comes out on top nearly every time. Its overwhelming desire to leverage its own national experience to mediate conflicts and to respect the sovereignty of others overshadows all other policy priorities. The result is inaction, inconsistent leadership, and a democracy and human rights promotion record that leaves much to be desired.

Indonesia

Indonesia's transition from an authoritarian system to a relatively open, pluralist democracy in just ten years has been accompanied by a similarly notable reorientation in its foreign policy from a rejection of international norms of democracy and human rights as incompatible with "Asian values" to a leader in promoting such principles. This transformation, accompanied by consistently high levels of economic growth, a growing middle class, booming foreign direct investment, and internal and external peace (relatively speaking), is precisely its greatest asset when it comes to projecting its interests and values in the Asian region. Although it primarily focuses its attention on its neighborhood, Indonesia's democratic progress, coupled with its Muslim identity, have important implications for broadening the legitimacy of the global democracy and human rights order.

After decades of exercising a brand of self-protective isolationism and hostility toward external intervention in internal affairs, Indonesia has embarked on a regional strategy of preaching the merits of democracy to its neighbors. As President Susilo Bambang Yudhoyono explained in an address to the World Movement for Democracy in April 2010, democracy is entirely compatible with economic progress, Islam, modernity, and domestic peace.[91] Indonesian officials have not been shy about admitting the difficulties of their own transition but go on to underscore that the results were worth the messiness of democratic politics, a point that goes to the heart of Asian governments' obsession with stability. Beyond holding itself out as a successful example of democratic transition, Indonesia has taken some concrete steps to build up regional institutions and mechanisms to gently prod other governments in the region in a democratic direction, particularly Myanmar.[92]

Outside its neighborhood, Indonesia has been markedly less willing to take the rhetorical initiative on democracy and human rights. In the context of the Arab Spring, it has been ready to share lessons learned from its own transition only when prompted. Indonesia, which did not sit on the UN Security Council at the time, was cautious when it came to UN action on Libya. On Syria, Jakarta did not express criticism until violence escalated to a breaking point. Against its long tradition of abstaining or opposing name and shame resolutions at the United Nations, Indonesia supported both the Human Rights Council's special session on Syria in August 2011 and its subsequent establishment of a special rapporteur on Syria in December 2011. It also voted in September 2012 to extend the mandate of the HRC's Commission of Inquiry on Syria. Indonesia's silence on Bahrain, on the other hand, can be largely understood as an attempt to avoid problems with Gulf monarchies, which house millions of Indonesian migrant workers. Not unlike other democracies with their own sets of pressing security and economic interests, Indonesia navigates its relations in the Gulf, and the Middle East more broadly, with utmost concern for the well-being of its own citizens and the economic implications of overseas labor. Expressing solidarity with Egyptian Muslims in the wake of Morsi's ouster, Indonesia has strongly called on the international community to support reconciliation, and in August 2013 President Yudhoyono urged the UN "to take necessary actions to prevent humanitarian tragedy."[93]

Underlying Indonesia's support of the international human rights and democracy regime is pride in its democratic identity. President Yudhoyono explicitly acknowledged in a 2011 interview that "Indonesia can be a model where Islam and democracy exist hand in hand, with no contradiction between the two."[94] Its preferred approach so far is to build up regional norms and mechanisms, share its own experience when asked, and avoid lecturing.

Turkey

Turkey stands apart from the other swing states reviewed here because its transition to democracy is still uncertain, making it both an object and subject of international assistance. The attraction of accession to the European Union no doubt once played a major role in bringing Turkey's own domestic standards and practice of democracy closer to liberal international norms. But more recently, Turkey under Erdoğan has undergone a steady decline in respect for democratic and human rights norms, diminishing its once rising star as a liberalizing state capable of leading others. Even so, the story of Turkey's foreign policy on democracy and human rights suggests a positive impact of EU enlargement. It was precisely Turkey's gradual evolution from a secular, military-dominated state with weak checks and balances to a competitive, multiparty, and multiethnic system in which Muslim democrats now win elections that gave hope to observers that it could emerge as a leader of the democracy and human rights order. While the positive results of the June 2015 elections and recent Constitutional Court decisions overturning Erdoğan's attempts to shut down critics suggest a possible course correction is under way, Turkey will remain stunted in its projection of democratic soft power as long as Erdoğan entertains his autocratic tendencies.

Even before it embarked on a series of political reforms in 2002, Turkey was a relatively constructive albeit quiet player in supporting democratic transitions, mainly because of its alignment with the United States, NATO, and the European Union. Its primary motives in foreign policy, however, remain the protection of Turkey's economic, energy, and other strategic interests in Central Asia, Russia, the Middle East, and North Africa and the expansion of economic and trade ties to emerging markets in the global South. In seeking to maintain maximum flexibility as its economic interests and leverage expand, pragmatists in Ankara walk a careful line between rhetorical support for democratic pluralism and case-by-case neutrality when it comes to international action to protect democracy and human rights. This policy was dubbed in its early years as "zero problems with neighbors."

Even before the Arab uprisings, Turkey expressed rhetorical support for democratic transition and good governance in the Arab region and at the OIC, often as a way to burnish its own credentials. As early as January 2003, for example, Prime Minister Erdoğan made the case for the compatibility of Islam and democracy in the Middle East. "It is obvious that the Turkish example demonstrates the invalidity of the exceptionalism paradigm," he told an audience at Harvard University and later in Jeddah, Saudi Arabia. He went on to outline the case for a consistent, gradualist approach toward "deep democracy" based on widespread social consensus, establishment of stable institutions, gender equality, education, civil society, and transparency. He also emphasized the importance of peaceful external conditions, linking Israeli-Palestinian peace and the territorial integrity of Iraq to the prospects for successful democratization.[95] Ten years later, however, widespread protests against Erdoğan's government, prompted by opposition to the state's destruction of a public park in Istanbul, revealed his tendency to dismiss critics at home and abroad with the back of his hand. The Gezi Park episode, no doubt, and others since then have weakened his government's credibility to hold Turkey up as a model for others.

Nonetheless, as the wave of demands for democracy rise and fall across the Arab world, Erdoğan has grown increasingly aggressive in his demands for political reform in the region. In Egypt, Libya, and Syria, Turkey has been critical of regimes' hard-line tactics to suppress dissent and, with varying vigor, supportive of those demanding their rights. Amid protests in Egypt, Prime Minister Erdoğan was among the first world leaders to call on President Hosni Mubarak to step down, despite Turkey's stakes in expanding trade and investment. Mubarak's exit represented an auspicious opportunity for Turkey to assert its regional leadership as the ousted Egyptian strongman had represented prime competition for influence in the region. It did so in part by building capital

with the new democratically elected government of Mohamed Morsi—
in September 2012, Erdoğan offered to loan economically strapped Egypt
up to $1 billion. Just twenty-four hours after the army overthrew Morsi
on July 3, 2013, Turkish foreign minister Ahmet Davutoğlu called the
action "unacceptable" and a "military coup." Erdoğan followed suit, even
scolding the West for not calling the unconstitutional transfer of power
a coup.[96]

When it comes to Libya and Syria, Turkey has similarly supported
opposition forces, but its own security and economic interests strongly
influenced the timing and nature of the support. Turkey's initial silence
and refusal to criticize the Qaddafi regime coincided with intensive efforts to rescue its expatriates and mediate the conflict. Accordingly, Turkey at first opposed the UN Security Council's resolution to establish a
no-fly zone and the subsequent NATO intervention.[97] Eventually, however, Turkey decided to support NATO's efforts to dislodge Qaddafi, in
effect the reversal of where the IBSA states landed.

The uprisings in neighboring Syria represent the Arab Spring's most
complicated quagmire for Turkey. Turkey under Erdoğan had invested
precious time and resources in its relationship with the Assad regime,
and the normalization of diplomatic and trade relations with Syria had
been the crown jewel of Erdoğan's "zero problems with neighbors" policy.
The volume of trade between the two countries rose from $752 million
in 2004 to $2.3 billion in 2010. Aside from these economic risks, chaos in
neighboring Syria has very tangible implications for Turkish security as
hundreds of thousands of Syrians have sought refuge across the 822-kilo-
meter border the two countries share.

Initially and with these interests in mind, Turkey tried to use its influence to convince the Assad regime to pursue democratic reforms. But
after the July 2011 massacres in Hama, Ankara eventually grew tired of
Assad's failure to deliver on promised reforms. As the situation in Syria
further deteriorated and the Arab League agreed to isolate and sanction
the Assad regime, Erdoğan translated his critical rhetoric into action,
announcing economic sanctions and the suspension of the high-level
bilateral strategic cooperation mechanism "until a democratic administration comes to power."[98] In addition to hosting refugees, Turkey is also
proactively facilitating aid, including money and equipment, to opposition forces in Syria. Turkey was also the fourth largest humanitarian
donor in 2013, contributing more than $1.6 billion—much of which was
likely spent on housing Syrian refugees within Turkey.[99]

Like advanced democracies, Turkey will not stand up for an international rights–based response at every opportunity. More recently, its checkered behavior at home has soured its standing as a model for other democracies. It has, however, conveyed a willingness to defend these values, share its experience, and even impose sanctions to dislodge autocratic regimes.

CONCLUSION

The long-standing tug-of-war between directly competing principles of international order—between noninterference in domestic affairs, on the one hand, and the responsibility to respond collectively to gross violations of human rights and interruptions to democratic rule, on the other—puts special demands on democracies. As states devoted to core principles of human rights, accountability, and transparency, democracies bring an inherent legitimacy and value to the global debate around universal norms and their practical application to national and local levels of governance. It is precisely this identity that generates a moral and political duty to respond when democracies are threatened and popular aspirations for their rights are thwarted.

A parochial view of democracies' role in this debate would privilege national interests over and above a more collective response to humanitarian crises abroad. This is the amoral and ahistorical perspective that ignores both the vast suffering caused by dictators and autocrats bent on controlling their populations under the guise of sovereignty and the remarkable human progress that has occurred under democratic regimes. It also pretends that globalization in all its forms can be somehow constrained or reversed and ignores the long history of positive actions to support and consolidate earlier waves of democracy around the world.

A more enlightened foreign policy posits that support for a robust human rights and democracy order is both the smart and the right way to protect and strengthen a country's own system of democratic governance *and* its national security. This moment in history, with its prevalence of diverse democracies capable of delivering economic, national, and human security to their citizens, is particularly ripe for elucidating the pros and cons of this more expansive notion of national interest.

CHAPTER THREE

India

A Reluctant Leader

I do not wish to enter into any comparisons with other countries, and certainly we have done nothing in India to merit leadership of anybody. It is for us to lead ourselves; then only can we lead others properly.

JAWAHARLAL NEHRU, *India's first prime minister,*
March 8, 1948, to India's Constituent Assembly

TO OUTSIDERS, INDIA'S UNIQUE position as the world's largest democracy, along with the adoption of Mahatma Gandhi as a powerful global symbol of nonviolence and independence, has engendered expectations of leadership on democracy and human rights that continue to be disappointed. Inflated hopes for India as a proactive player on the world stage, however, can mislead observers to the real power of its role—as an example of social and economic progress achieved within the framework of liberal democracy.

A sprawling subcontinent of 1.2 billion people, 122 languages, hundreds of recognized castes and tribes,[1] and six significantly represented religious groups, India itself is a microcosm of a pluralistic global society still coming to grips with how to coexist in peace. Its birth at the forefront of the struggle against colonialism after World War II distinguishes it as a leading symbol of self-governance and equality of all peoples. India as a single nation, with all its complexities, probably would not exist without a democratic and federalist form of government; the division of powers between its capital New Delhi and its twenty-nine states and seven union territories has proven to be essential to its coherence and identity. Universal suffrage for all India's citizens, even the poorest sectors in remote rural areas, has helped disaggregate power and give everyone an opportunity to participate in public life. India's political system, over time, has responded to the most basic demands of its majority poor with a growing social safety net, including expanded efforts to implement the rights to food and education. Given its sheer size and complexity, the fate of India's grand experiment with democracy matters more to the international order than any of the other cases in this book, and perhaps more than any country in the world. As articulated in a 2012 report by a group of India's leading strategic thinkers, "The fundamental source of India's power in the world is going to be the power of its example. If India can maintain high growth rates, leverage that growth to enhance the capabilities of all its citizens, and maintain robust democratic traditions and institutions, there are few limits to India's global role and influence. The foundations of India's success will, therefore, depend on its developmental model."[2]

India's vaunted position as the world's largest democracy means even more in the context of its remarkable rise as an economic giant since the onset of liberalizing reforms more than two decades ago. As documented in chapter 1, democratic India has made dramatic progress in reducing poverty and delivering social and economic rights to its poorest citizens. It must, however, continue to move in this direction by addressing the dire demands for jobs, education, and health care for the millions still struggling to survive. If it does so, it has great potential as both a leading example of democratic development and a promoter of Gandhian values of tolerance, participation, and nonviolence. "Democracy is part of our national ethos," according to Jaswant Singh, former foreign minister and a leader of the ruling Bharatiya Janata Party (BJP). "It is inconceivable that we could operate as a nation otherwise. Foreign policy is merely an extension of our internal democratic identity."[3] It remains reluctant, however, to wed itself to the international human rights and democracy order, let alone to lead it, as it continues to struggle to bring millions of its citizens out of poverty, wrestle with severe discrimination and violence against women and traditional lower castes, and resolve long-standing domestic insurgencies. It also must cope with a complex and disorderly regional security environment that demands most of its attention, particularly China and Pakistan, and could derail its ascendance.

These factors explain the continued dominance of India's doctrine of noninterference in internal affairs, a sentiment that runs deep in the wake of eighty-nine years as a colonial subject of Britain and that has major implications for its posture toward external human rights norms and crises. Its well-known stance of nonalignment during the Cold War may have yielded important dividends in shielding India from involvement in expensive and divisive battles of that era. But its current trajectory as a globalizing, nuclear-armed power and its aspirations for a seat on the UN Security Council and other forms of global leadership are generating demands among opinion leaders for a different paradigm for engagement abroad. Its domestic politics, meanwhile, are increasing pressures for taking uncomfortable stands on human rights issues regarding Sri Lanka, Iran, and China (Tibet) at the same time its spiraling thirst for energy imports and dependence on remittances from the Indian diaspora constrain a more values-oriented approach to its foreign policy. It should come as no surprise, then, that India's leaders tend toward pragmatic realism and strategic autonomy in foreign policy as they tackle intense challenges at home.

INDIA'S DANCE WITH UNIVERSAL NORMS

Modern India was born at a revolutionary moment in world affairs. The midcentury war that spanned the globe coincided with, and contributed to, India's determined battle for independence, forcing Britain ultimately to yield its control of the subcontinent to two visionary statesmen who effectively employed the language of democracy and human rights in their own struggle for liberation and an end to imperialism. It was Mahatma Gandhi and Jawaharlal Nehru who called on the United Nations in its earliest days, for example, to protect the fundamental rights of Indian nationals in South Africa, an important early case of appealing to international norms to limit state sovereignty over internal affairs.[4]

South Africa's legislation in 1946 to limit voting and residence rights of Indians living within its borders, echoes of previous conflicts that Gandhi personally fought earlier in his career as a lawyer in South Africa,[5] sparked a lively campaign to condemn the action, led in New York by Nehru's powerfully persuasive sister, Vijaya Lakshmi Pandit. While the UN Charter's carefully negotiated provisions protecting domestic jurisdiction gave South Africa a leg up in the argument, India's appeal to the moral conscience of the world won the day.[6] Protection of Indian nationals abroad was, of course, paramount. Nehru claimed, however, that it was not "merely an Indian issue" but rather "a world cause" that concerned Asians, Africans, and all those struggling for "equality of opportunity for all races and against the Nazi doctrine of racialism."[7] The wave of disgust with the horrors of World War II, powerfully indicted in the Nuremberg trials, also generated an international political climate that favored India's case for UN action, a cause that coincided nicely with its own claims for an independent foreign policy and leadership in Asia and Africa. Meanwhile, its own communal violence in the 1947 partition crisis that led to the creation of Pakistan ironically, and tragically, escaped the same level of international scrutiny.

The UN debate over South Africa's policies of segregation highlighted the need to grapple with the place of human rights in the new organization's mandate. Here, too, India under Nehru played an important role in the negotiations that led to the Universal Declaration of Human Rights. Again, it did so because it directly facilitated its own interests at the time—in this case, writing a new constitution that would make peace among its disparate factions based on the concept of individual rights, checks and balances, and federalism.

As Nehru negotiated a division of powers with the princes of India during the Constituent Assembly of 1947–50, he drew a direct line between the international norms being drafted at the UN's Human Rights Commission and India's own fundamental charter: "I suppose certain fundamental rights are part of the Union structure. Presumably, they will apply to the whole of India. A certain guarantee of individual rights will be provided for in it. Today the [UN] Human Rights Commission is meeting in New York. Our representatives are there. The conception today is there are common individual rights which should be guaranteed the world over. Naturally I presume we shall accept any world charter to that effect."[8] Just as Nehru conceived of a new federalist India with rights and freedoms guaranteed by the center, sovereign nation-states would subject themselves to a charter of fundamental rights—the Universal Declaration of Human Rights—applicable to the world.[9] The larger cause of world peace and harmony among races became, in Nehru's view, inextricably enveloped in India's own destiny as a democratic republic at peace with its own diverse and often battling constituent parts.

The historical context of India's transition from a colonial subject to a democratic republic is important to keep in mind when analyzing

India's current approach to questions of democracy and human rights promotion. Gandhian and Nehruvian impulses run deep in Indian foreign policy and offer powerful messages that could anchor a more robust role for India as a leader in this field. Along the way, however, the struggle for Indian nationalism and development and the heavy emphasis on anticolonialism and noninterference in its foreign policy trumped any serious concern for democracy and human rights as a priority in the international order. Caught in the Cold War battle between the forces of open, competitive systems and closed, state-dominated ones—or in human rights terms, between individual political and civil rights and state-guaranteed economic and social rights—India chose a mix of the two: institutionalization of pluralist democracy and liberal political norms coupled with a heavy-handed approach to state-led development and protection of the economy. In foreign policy, it came down clearly on the side of avoiding entanglement, leading an international coalition devoted to neutrality between East and West, and championing the cause of the global South. When it came to human rights violations abroad, it mostly looked the other way.

DEMOCRACY AND HUMAN RIGHTS IN THE NEIGHBORHOOD

An abiding concern for nation building at home and noninterference abroad does not mean, however, that India was absent when democracy and human rights crises emerged in its own neighborhood. Several episodes during and after the Cold War evince India's willingness to take action when violence threatened its own domestic stability or coincided with its desire for leadership in a more stable South Asia, particularly against rivals Pakistan and China.

For example, when Pakistan's first democratic elections in December 1970 legitimized the claim of East Pakistan for an independent Bengali state, and the Pakistani army lashed out against leaders of the Bengali campaign, Prime Minister Indira Gandhi appealed to the international community on their behalf, to no avail. India was also gravely concerned about the enormous flow of refugees into poor, unstable areas. It then stepped in with direct armed strikes against the Pakistani military, which it accused of committing genocide against Hindus in then East Pakistan. It did so unilaterally, with no endorsement of the UN Security Council and much criticism from the United States and others. A party to the

Genocide Convention, India also conducted investigations of Pakistani army officers, held 195 individuals suspected of war crimes, and promised to help bring them to justice. By 1974, however, India turned down Pakistan's request to give the International Court of Justice jurisdiction of the matter and released all POWs as part of the 1972 Simla Agreement that led to Pakistan's diplomatic recognition of Bangladesh. The accused were returned to Pakistan, where they faced no charges of genocide or other crimes.[10] As in so many cases of conflict resolution, justice was delayed in pursuit of regional peace. More recently, Bangladesh's own internal process for investigating and prosecuting war crimes from that era has generated numerous convictions, harsh penalties, and popular support, but virtually no comment from New Delhi.[11]

In the Maldives, a small Muslim island nation in the Indian Ocean, a band of Maldivians with support from Tamil mercenaries took control of the capital in 1988 as President Maumoon Abdul Gayoom fled from house to house and appealed for international help. Prime Minister Rajiv Gandhi immediately dispatched 1,600 troops to restore order and returned the democratically elected president to power. It also helped capture the coup leaders as they fled to Sri Lanka and facilitated their return for trial and imprisonment in Male, the capital. India's move appeared as both a serious attempt to defend a fragile democratic neighbor and a means of reaffirming India's strategic presence in the Indian Ocean.[12] Gayoom went on to rule for another twenty years with little opposition. When a real multiparty contest was allowed to emerge in 2008, Gayoom lost to Mohamed Nasheed, who joined forces with other opposition parties to form a winning coalition. Nasheed's own turbulent term was cut short in 2012 when he resigned in the face of street protests and alleged military pressure. India's attitude this time was much more muted, and it refused to call for early elections.

India's reticence to take a stand this time may have had to do with its commercial interests—specifically, its desire to preserve a $500 million contract for Indian construction firm GMR to rebuild the main airport in Male. After the cancellation of that contract in November 2012[13] India shifted gears to more assertive engagement in February 2013 as the Indian High Commission in Male provided shelter to Nasheed, who was fleeing an arrest warrant issued after he failed to show up for a court hearing over allegations he mistreated a judge. The interim government of Waheed Hassan also challenged Nasheed's ability to run in parliamentary elections later that year, which prompted India to demand conditions for a fair election, its primary justification for providing Nasheed refuge.[14] The two countries appeared to have mended relations to some extent in January 2014 when President Yameen (elected in rather complicated November 2013 elections) visited Delhi, where both sides committed to resolving the GMR issue and improving relations.[15] However, when Maldivian authorities charged former president Nasheed with questionable terrorism-related charges in February 2015, India's new prime minister, Narendra Modi, canceled a scheduled trip to the country.[16]

The same year as its first intervention in the Maldives, India joined a coalition of states from the West in condemning the Burmese military's violent repression of the 8888 Uprising and endorsing international sanctions against the regime. Its long-standing sympathy for Aung San Suu Kyi, the opposition leader who took up exile in India for several years during the military's crackdown on activists, also played a role. It backed opposition media, offered asylum to student leaders, and helped them regroup and campaign from Indian soil.[17] As part of its policy of "complete disengagement" from the ruling junta in Burma,[18] India joined with Western governments to cosponsor a 1992 UN resolution condemning the military's human rights violations.[19] Gradually, however, India's leaders decided that isolating the military junta was hurting their own interests in preventing cross-border attacks in the northeast from insurgents based in Myanmar; China's move to fill the vacuum created by UN sanctions also raised concerns that Beijing could establish naval bases in the Bay of Bengal that could threaten India. New Delhi rather quickly shifted gears, choosing to influence the junta through engagement rather than isolation. As it found common ground with the generals in securing the border and investing in new infrastructure, India "continued to raise democracy with them at every high-level meeting," according to a former senior diplomat. "We told them it would be difficult to get out of isolation without internal changes," including a more inclusive constitution.[20]

India did not abandon the goal of moving Myanmar toward pluralist democracy but changed its tactics to accommodate India's security interests in controlling the border and containing China's expansion in the region. Even after the crackdown on the Saffron Revolution in 2007, India resisted international pressure to adopt tougher sanctions against Rangoon.[21] "Myanmar had to evolve on its own, at its own pace," explained a top former official.[22] It also argued that engagement translated into the kind of influence that facilitated other international priorities. It was in a better position, for example, to persuade the regime to allow the delivery of international food aid after cyclone Nargis devastated sections of the country in 2008.[23] India's strategy of engagement eschewed high-level political or military-to-military cooperation while sending a message to the junta that a broad-based, inclusive approach to governance would pave the way for better ties. Coupled with the continued pressure of international sanctions and scrutiny (India voted in favor of a UN General Assembly resolution regarding Myanmar's human rights situation in 2011[24]) and Myanmar's leaders' desire to become members in good standing in ASEAN, the engagement policy ultimately encouraged competitive elections and a return to limited civilian rule in 2011.[25] No doubt, the military regime's own desire for survival through a controlled transition from the top was decisive in its ongoing path of reform.

Myanmar still faces an enormous task of rebuilding basic governance capacity after decades of stifling, autocratic rule. In response, India has doubled its program to train civil servants from Myanmar to 500, including parliamentary staff. It has extended a $500 million concessionary line of credit to support capacity-building and infrastructure projects like railways and housing. India is also helping with new construction under way at a hospital named in honor of Gandhi, a new faculty of tourism, a new national police academy, and other projects on health, education, banking, and farming.[26] Modi continued this outreach during his first official visit to Myanmar in November 2014, meeting with President Thein Sein to review joint infrastructure projects. Modi also met with opposition leader Aung San Suu Kyi, who faces a constitutional ban on running for president, lauding her as a "symbol of democracy."[27] It is too early to say whether Myanmar's transition will succeed, but India's pragmatic decision to engage the dictators while supporting the democrats may continue to yield strategic and tactical benefits for years to come. It also undergirds the realists' call for engaging rather than isolating unsavory regimes as a preferred means of encouraging democratic reforms.

A similar dynamic prevails in neighboring Nepal where the Maoists' claim to power, a campaign that stretches to parts of northeastern India, raised fears of greater Chinese influence and a direct challenge to India's democracy. As the monarchy seesawed from a managed transition plan to a violent grasp for dominance, India's worst fears—a one-party state on its border run by allies of Beijing and in cahoots with its own insurgencies—became real. Unable to defeat them militarily, Nepal's political establishment, with assistance from India, in 2006 was able to reach an accommodation with the Maoists through an inclusive constitution that Indian experts helped to draft. The policy so far has worked in two respects: first, for India's economic and security interests—Maoists in India are no longer taking sanctuary in Nepal and India wants to beat China in the race to develop Nepal's hydropower sector for its own purposes—and second in terms of promoting long-standing Indian values.[28] The fact that about 6 million Indians live in Nepal is another strategic consideration. Prime Minister Modi elevated the relationship further in August 2014 when he became the first Indian prime minister to visit Nepal in seventeen years and announced a $1 billion credit for infrastructure development and energy projects.

Based on these and similar experiences in the region, the foreign policy establishment in New Delhi is coming around to the view that having "democratic neighbors is better for our security" than having dictators, as one leading authority put it.[29] "Liberal democracy is the natural order of political organization in today's world," argued Prime Minister Manmohan Singh in 2005, and "all alternate systems . . . are an aberration."[30]

This sentiment is particularly striking in the case of India's current views toward neighboring Pakistan. Genuine democracy there, according to a number of Indian diplomats and observers, would lead to less terrorism directed against India because the Pakistani military's close ties to Islamist radicals would come under greater civilian control. Concern that more competitive politics could lead to more conservative Islamist control of government has been muted—the average Pakistani voter is moderate, they point out, and with more Muslims living in India than Pakistan, people-to-people contacts are warm despite chilly official relations. The democratic security calculus may explain Prime Minister Singh's gradual return to a policy of bilateral rapprochement with Islamabad after the wrenching terrorist attacks in Mumbai were launched, with tacit military support, from Pakistani soil in 2008. The economic benefits of more open trade, which would yield immediate benefits to India, are also a factor.

On the other hand, views against democracy promotion within India's foreign policy circles remain loud. Even those experts who recognize the long-term value of having more states governed democratically and under the rule of law hold strong opinions against the heavy-handed tactics of more established democracies in the West. Warm words about a shared vision of a world of peaceful democracies are uttered, for example, in communiques between American and Indian officials. But in practice, regime change hangover from Iraq and, more recently, Libya, have poisoned the democracy promotion and R2P debate and fanned the flames of India's predilection toward inaction. The uncertainty of outcomes of political transitions also weighs heavily in New Delhi toward cautious realism and neutrality on regime type. The chaos of the Arab uprisings is particularly unsettling. As one Indian commentator remarked, "The United States has dismantled three secular, stable dictatorships (Tunisia, Egypt, Libya) and replaced them with Islamist instability and chaos, spreading as far as Mali, and gave renewed energy to Salafism and the Muslim Brotherhood," including in India.[31] Even democratic Turkey, the analyst claimed, is dreaming of a neo-Ottoman "commonwealth" that could harm India's interests in West Asia. The skeptics also argue that democratically elected leaders are more vulnerable to the push and pull of domestic politics, making bilateral and multilateral negotiations more difficult.[32]

Afghanistan poses a similar dilemma for India when it comes to the difficult nexus between terrorism, state building, and the military. As the U.S.-led war winds down, India is hoping for continued consolidation of Afghanistan's fragile democracy but fears the worse outcome of a spiral into chaos or a return of a Taliban allied with the Pakistani military against India. While it has avoided direct involvement in the conflict—it was not a member, for example, of the coalition forces that defeated the Taliban in Operation Enduring Freedom—it has become the largest regional provider of humanitarian and reconstruction aid, investing nearly $2 billion in the country over the past decade.[33] In 2011, the two countries signed a strategic partnership agreement, Afghanistan's first bilateral partnership since the 1979 Soviet invasion, to deepen bilateral cooperation on a wide range of security, political, trade, economic, educational, and cultural topics.[34] At the high political level, Afghanistan agreed to support India's claim for a permanent seat on the UN Security Council.

New Delhi's projects in Afghanistan include the provision of food aid, public health consultation through Indian medical missions, and vehicles for urban transportation projects. The Indian government has also overseen the reconstruction of the Indira Gandhi Institute of Child Health in Kabul and the Afghan parliament building, restoration of telecommunications infrastructure in eleven Afghan provinces, and construction of the Salma Dam power project. In addition, India has provided 500 long-term university scholarships for undergraduate and postgraduate education and constructed a vocational training center for women led by SEWA, a well-regarded Indian NGO. India's government has gotten its private sector engaged as well with billions in public-private investment in Afghanistan, including steel, copper, and iron ore mining.[35]

India's aid package to Afghanistan also includes direct support to projects related to good governance and democratization in such areas as capacity-building programs on diplomacy, standardization, public administration, and local governance. To this end, twenty Indian civil servants work exclusively with the Afghan government as coaches and mentors with programs supported by the UNDP. Afghanistan's Independent Election Commission and India's Election Commission—arguably one of the most transparent in the developing world—have regular exchanges, mutual visits for study and observation, and training activities. Officials of the Afghan National Assembly are trained in India's Bureau of Parliamentary Study and Training. The Indian government is also vocally supportive of democratization efforts in the country. After the assassination of the chairman of the Afghan High Peace Council in 2011, External Affairs Minister S. M. Krishna reiterated steadfast support of the people and government of India for Afghanistan's "quest for peace and efforts to strengthen the roots of democracy."[36]

India's strategic interests in building closer ties with Afghanistan while marginalizing Pakistani influence were in particularly sharp relief as the United States and other international forces prepared to withdraw troops in 2014. Toward that end, the Indian army's Border Roads Organization in 2009 constructed a major highway to a remote Afghan province as a way to bypass Pakistan and reduce Afghanistan's economic dependence on its eastern neighbor. In May 2013, India agreed to step up its direct support to Afghan security forces and promised to continue its strategic partnership despite terror attacks in September 2013 against Indians working in Afghanistan. India's steadfast support for Afghanistan's reconstruction has not gone unnoticed by Afghans themselves: a 2010 Gallup poll found that, as a result of aid efforts, Afghans prefer India's leadership to that of China or the United States. Further, they view India more positively as compared with any other surveyed Asia-Pacific country.[37]

INDIA'S SOFT POWER ON THE WIDER
REGIONAL AND GLOBAL STAGES

India's growing investment in its role as a provider of development assistance, particularly in its neighborhood, along with a long-standing concern for its image as a moral voice for the underprivileged South are two critical features of its exercise of soft power. Another tool is its use of multilateral institutions and fora to project leadership and protect its interests in upholding nonintervention principles and multipolarity. In the democracy and human rights realm, these strands often yield ambiguity and confusion.

India has long been reluctant to criticize specific countries for their human rights records.[38] On the other hand, it regularly supports thematic human rights resolutions of its liking at the UN General Assembly and the Human Rights Council in Geneva. India's uneven but ultimately constructive engagement on the UN debates to create the Human Rights Council in 2006 and to accept and apply the responsibility to protect doctrine in places like Libya and Côte d'Ivoire are just two signs of its decision to shape rather than undermine the rules of the liberal international order. It is a founding sponsor of the Community of Democracies, a global initiative whose main purpose is to create a welcoming and supportive environment for new democracies, but has been largely passive, insisting it refrain from evangelizing, and actively opposes attempts to single out specific states for criticism (except Pakistan). It is a top donor to the UN Democracy Fund, which supports the building blocks of civil society participation in governance. IBSA gives India a multilateral avenue to assert its status as a rising democratic power, distinct from two of its nondemocratic brethren in the BRICS. IBSA also provides the added convenience of posing no threat to its leadership in its own region given Brazil and South Africa's purported lack of interest or influence in South Asia.

The South Asian Association for Regional Cooperation (SAARC) offers yet another forum to talk up shared values of democracy and human rights. Its eight constituent members—Afghanistan, Bangladesh, Bhutan, India, Maldives, Nepal, Pakistan, and Sri Lanka—all profess allegiance to universal norms of democracy and human rights, admittedly with very mixed results to date. India, however, avoids playing any leadership role there, ostensibly out of concern it not appear as the regional hegemon, although the Modi government seems to be shedding that reluctance. A SAARC Charter of Democracy adopted in 2011,[39] which includes for the first time a mutual assistance clause in the case of unconstitutional disruptions, came about through Bangladesh's leadership, not India's. Proposals to create a SAARC human rights mechanism, a goal of human rights advocates in the region, remain largely on the drawing board; a new SAARC Center for Good Governance, proposed by India's home minister in September 2014 as a way to improve regional cooperation against terrorism, is a more palatable move for India's neighbors. In practice, SAARC's requirement for consensus, and blocking action between Pakistan and India, make it a thin reed on which to build regional diplomacy.

More recently, however, India's strategic thinkers have begun focusing on the need to consolidate their relations with South Asian neighbors if India is to achieve its broader global aspirations. As a report published in 2012, titled *Nonalignment 2.0: A Foreign and Strategic Policy for India in the Twenty-First Century*, argues, "India cannot hope to arrive as a great power if it is unable to manage [its] relationships within South Asia . . . India's ability to command respect is considerably diminished by the resistance it meets in the region."[40] Prime Minister Modi's government seems to be adopting this attitude as it moves quickly to elbow China aside and shores up relations with such countries as Nepal, Bhutan, Sri Lanka, and Bangladesh. Under Modi, India has begun pushing for further regional cooperation in the economic sphere, especially through multilateral organizations like SAARC.[41] Calls for free trade systems and economic cooperation among its South Asian neighbors have been met with enthusiasm from the community. Building on this policy, India could do much more to coach its neighbors toward pluralist, federalist, and secular systems, its strongest calling card in a region beset with majoritarian ethnic and religious cleavages that undermine democratic stability on its borders.[42] "No regional integration is possible," argued the *Nonalignment 2.0* authors in 2012, "unless there is ideological convergence on basic political values in the region . . . we have to collectively signal that all states in the region are committed to the pacification of violence, human rights, democracy and free trade."[43]

Beyond its immediate neighborhood, India has at times played an important role in supporting and enforcing the Commonwealth's principles and mechanisms to protect democracy among its members. The most relevant case is Fiji, a small Pacific island with a sizable Indo ethnic population that in 2000 experienced an unconstitutional seizure of power forcing from office the democratically elected president, Mahendra Chaudhry, who was of Indian descent. To defend ethnic Indo-Fijians from reprisals, New Delhi considered military intervention but ultimately chose to work with Australia to pressure Fiji's new rulers through suspension of relations with the Commonwealth and ASEAN.[44] It took more than a decade for Fiji to hold free and fair elections in 2014, which Prime Minister Modi recognized with the first Indian leader visit in thirty-three years and the announcement of a new bilateral security cooperation, scholarships, and a $75 million line of credit.[45]

These examples illustrate India's genuine but weak and ambivalent interest in encouraging democratic change outside its borders. They also evince some of the abiding principles and policies of India's style of democracy promotion: lead by example, not by preaching to others; listen to local demands and wait to be asked for assistance; avoid appearing as the regional bully and never impose; focus on technical assistance and institution building, like in areas of elections and civil service training that play to India's strengths; and avoid more overtly political forms of involvement. India's diplomacy on human rights issues demonstrates a similarly modest, low-profile approach. When negotiating positions at the United Nations or other multilateral institutions, basic principles like dialogue and consultation and avoiding confrontation, selectivity, or double standards prevail. Within these parameters, however, Indian diplomats have a lot of freedom to maneuver in the field. This means that, with the exception of particularly sensitive bilateral cases like Pakistan or Iran that are managed closely from New Delhi, Indian officials can (and often do) play a constructive if quiet role in the corridors of Geneva and New York.

At a deeper level, India's experience at the crossroads of major civilizations has taught it the value of strategic patience. Political change, argue many Indian elites, will come eventually to closed societies in the Middle East, but these are ancient cultures that will evolve gradually, not according to a U.S. electoral timetable. "Countries need time to change with dignity," explained one senior diplomat.[46] They also point out that the rise of conservative strands of Islam makes transition to democracy even more difficult and unpredictable. Transitions, therefore, should not be rushed—regime change would have happened eventually in places like Iraq and Libya, and at a much lower cost than the billions spent by the United States. As it relates to more robust interventionist concepts like R2P, Indian foreign policy is predictably cautious: "We need to make it clear to the international community that the circumstances under which armed intervention is warranted on behalf of these values needs to be very carefully weighed, and that universal norms and values cannot provide a fig-leaf for the pursuit of great power interests."[47]

FOREIGN POLICY AND DOMESTIC POLITICS

"Credible India?" asks the cover of *Forbes India* magazine in its special independence day edition of August 2012, a clever play on the government's promotional slogan of "Incredible India!" plastered on buses and tourist magazines around the world. Its author, Sundeep Waslekar, argues that India's leaders should forget the obsession with becoming a superpower and focus first on becoming a great nation.[48] This is a remarkably common sentiment heard both in and outside government.

After more than six decades of independence, India remains intensely preoccupied with its own economic and social development, and this fact drives its strategic outlook on international affairs. "The single most important objective of our foreign policy has to be to create a global environment conducive to the well-being of our great country," Prime Minister Singh told a gathering of top Indian diplomats in November 2013.[49] Its primary national security goals are to seek stable relations with neighbors (democratic or otherwise), secure resources for its rising energy demands, promote India's increasingly globalized private sector, and protect Indian nationals working abroad and sending $71 billion in remittances home each year—the highest quantity of remittances distributed to any country in 2013.[50] It also wants to burnish its soft power credentials and reputation for nonviolence and democratic governance and achieve a higher position of leadership in a multipolar world. It does not share an ideational preoccupation with the spread of liberal values in the world but welcomes more democratic outcomes in its own neighborhood and beyond and is willing to engage in such endeavors if in accord with its higher-priority development goals.

Indeed, its reluctance to get involved in criticizing other states for failing to meet international human rights norms stems largely from its hypersensitivity to external criticism of its own performance. This sentiment came to a head during the violent clashes in Kashmir in the late 1980s when Indian troops came under fire by groups like Amnesty International and Human Rights Watch for committing human rights abuses. "We have been victims of politically motivated charges" by others, complained one retired diplomat, who nonetheless went on to cite the steps the government took to enact new human rights policies and training to deter future violations and to persuade NGOs to undertake more balanced critiques.[51]

This defensive crouch continues today. "We don't want others to tell us what to do," one senior official said in explaining the government's wish for strategic autonomy, and "we extend that principle overseas."[52] A fear, reasonable or not, that the international community might actually intervene in India's approach toward Kashmir and terrorism casts a long shadow over its willingness to play a more activist role as a promoter of human rights. Indian diplomats also point to the country's robust culture of internal debate, independent media, active civil society, and competitive parliamentary politics as important factors in shaping their stiff-armed stance toward external criticism. "We have enough people telling us what to do," quipped one senior official, and "we don't want the United Nations or others to get involved."[53]

Despite the heavy resistance to UN interference in its affairs, the Indian government gradually is becoming more open to international mechanisms like the Human Rights Council's Universal Periodic Review (UPR) and its Special Procedures (independent experts). India sent an interministerial delegation led by its attorney general to Geneva in May 2012 to present its country's human rights report after a yearlong process of public comment and debate. It then accepted 83 of the 169 recommendations generated by governments with input from civil society.[54] In September 2011, India added its name to the list of countries extending a standing invitation to the Council's independent human rights experts. Since 2000, it has received or accepted visits from twelve rapporteurs or working groups, including a visit in 2013 by the UN Special Rapporteur on Violence against Women in the wake of the public uproar over rapes of women.[55] These steps suggest a greater willingness to accept international scrutiny of its rights record.

Civil society groups are using the UPR process to organize a coordinated effort to hold the Indian government's feet to the fire on its national and international human rights commitments. For example, the Working Group on Human Rights in India and the UN, a coalition of NGOs and independent human rights experts, partnered with the National Human Rights Commission to hold consultations throughout the country in preparation for the UPR's second cycle, which helped educate the public on international human rights principles and ensure the Council received a balanced critique of the human rights situation.[56] By all accounts, the "cooperative engagement" model of the UPR system seems to be having multiple positive effects in India—as a universal tool applicable to all states, it is seen as credible by the both the government and civil society, and its regular cycle of reviews encourages ongoing monitoring of and pressure for further reforms. "We know we can't live in an isolated box—we can look at best practices from around the world and use them," explained one diplomat.[57]

More recently, under the Modi government, various groups have alleged that the Indian government is clamping down on the civil society sphere. For example, in April 2015 the government suspended Greenpeace's foreign funding—a continuation of a recent trend that has seen the suspension of the foreign funding of sixty-eight other NGOs.

Activists have also charged that the government is cutting into their freedom of expression.[58] In a joint letter to Prime Minister Modi signed by 144 NGOs in May 2015, the government was accused of freezing funds, using intelligence reports to denigrate NGOs, demanding case-by-case clearance of fund disbursements, and placing groups on "watch lists." "As a result several NGO projects have shut down, donors are unable to support work, and there is an overall atmosphere of State coercion and intimidation in India's civil society space."[59] Amnesty International has likewise charged that the Modi government has done nothing to curb a rise in communal violence and has placed more importance on economic development than human rights issues.[60] A string of violent attacks against secular liberals have sparked renewed concern that Modi's inaction is facilitating the rise of far-right Hindutva groups.[61] Increasing tension over human rights issues at home threatens to further hinder India's willingness to be active globally lest it invite criticism of its own record. Nevertheless, India faces domestic and international pressure to deal seriously with such shortcomings, and civil society likely will continue to hold the Modi government accountable for its response despite the growing pressures against it.

Two of India's greatest challenges—violence against women and widespread corruption—are mobilizing citizens like never before and increasing pressure on government to heed international norms. The notorious case of the brutal rape and murder of a young professional Indian woman in 2013 brought millions of Indians to the streets to protest the long-standing denial and impunity of this endemic violence. Similarly, the anticorruption campaign led by the social activist Anna Hazare in

2011 and 2012 galvanized widespread activism in favor of stronger legislation and enforcement of laws against political corruption. An earlier effort to relax India's strict secrecy rules led to 2005's Right to Information Act, which, for the first time, grants citizens the right to request basic information from its government authorities. Although the ability to access government documentation and information is a huge step forward for freedom of expression in India, Amnesty International has criticized a few instances in which rights activists who have petitioned for government records were harassed and attacked by local authorities.[62]

As these developments illustrate, the reawakening under way in Indian society toward human rights and its interplay with an international human rights system that is growing in size and prominence are punching new holes in India's preoccupation with protecting sovereignty. In broad terms, India's growing interest in its soft power projection, which implicates a serious reputational concern for its human rights record (especially in contrast to rivals China and Pakistan), is pushing it to engage in the international human rights system in more constructive ways than in the past. As one senior official explained, "Reputation management means getting the human rights story on our side out there, to balance the bad news that the media delivers."[63] This concern, in turn, is providing leverage to a wider circle of stakeholders for inserting a human rights discourse in the way the government handles a range of sensitive topics, from food security and education to access to information and women's rights. Over time, this virtuous circle encompassing both domestic and international norms and practice will pressure India to concern itself not only with its domestic challenges but with the health of the international human rights system, as well. However, this virtuous circle remains at risk as long as the Modi government continues its recent backsliding in the human rights realm.

The convergence between the practical realities of India's natural preoccupation with its domestic affairs and its potential as a more consistent human rights actor internationally is demonstrated most recently in its relations with Sri Lanka. India, home to an estimated 60.8 million ethnic Tamils,[64] mainly concentrated in the state of Tamil Nadu, has long been seized with the turmoil in its island neighbor, home to 3.1 million Tamils.[65] It intervened directly in the long-running Sri Lankan civil war by supplying humanitarian aid in the 1970s. In 1987, it brokered an accord with both parties to the conflict and at their request sent peacekeepers to help stabilize and wind down the conflict. Instead, the Liberation Tigers of Tamil Eelam (LTTE) entangled Indian troops in the war, costing more than 1,000 Indian lives, including that of Prime Minister Rajiv Gandhi, murdered by a LTTE suicide bomber in May 1991.[66] Chastened by the episode, India retreated further into its noninterventionist pose.

Years later, that conflict finally ended in 2009 through a brutal military campaign against LTTE fighters that trapped thousands of civilians on the battlefield. India was confronted again with the dilemma of responding to a massive violation of human rights on its borders and largely punted. Its limp response played out at the UN with its vote in favor of a notorious Human Rights Council resolution that largely applauded Sri Lanka's campaign against terrorism.[67] The watered-down resolution did, however, commit Colombo to take certain steps to investigate the charges of violations against civilians. Privately and publicly, New Delhi used the resolution and bilateral communiques to press Sri Lanka to uphold these commitments but got nothing in return. When the United States pushed for a new UN resolution in 2012 criticizing Sri Lanka for failing to undertake a credible and independent investigation into the allegations, Sri Lanka launched a full-court press to block the action. In response, the Tamil community, both in India and abroad, undertook a vigorous campaign demanding India vote for the resolution, including a threat in 2013 by Dravida Munnetra Kazhagam, a Tamil-dominated party, to withdraw from the governing coalition.[68] Heavy media coverage of the violence in Sri Lanka, including footage of crimes against children, contributed to the fray.[69] Contrary to its usual stance of opposition or neutrality on resolutions criticizing specific countries, India voted for it in a contested vote of 24-15-8.[70] A confluence of factors—domestic politics, international lobbying, and India's frustration with Sri Lanka's dismissal of its concerns—tipped the scales in favor of Indian activism on a high-profile country-specific human rights issue. In at least this case, domestic politics tipped the balance toward a foreign policy aligned in favor of human rights.

Does the minor though much-discussed Sri Lanka episode foreshadow a turn toward a more concerted effort by India to break free of its traditional reliance on nonintervention and become a more reliable defender of liberal values? Unlikely in the short term, according to many observers, and India's return to the abstention column in the 2014 vote on Sri Lanka proves the point. But underlying trends in a globalizing and maturing India point toward a more proactive and self-confident society prepared to hold its government's foreign policy accountable to its core values of democracy and human rights. The government signaled its commitment to these values (at least in the case of Sri Lanka) in November 2013 when Prime Minister Manmohan Singh refused to attend the biannual Commonwealth Heads of Government Meeting in Colombo, citing human rights concerns in the host country under then president Rajapaksa.[71]

Several factors shaping India's foreign policy ecosystem point toward increasing interest and pressure for changes in its approach on these questions. Greater involvement by the Parliament, political parties, state governments, media, business, civil society, and think tanks on issues traditionally and jealously guarded by high officials in New Delhi is democratizing the foreign policy debate. Public attention to topics like human rights and corruption at home and abroad is growing. Fragmentation is under way, as local interests and lobbies demand changes in trade, energy, climate, and agriculture policies that tend toward protectionism and insularity. Other forces—an expanding and increasingly wired middle class, growing demand for overseas education and travel (particularly to the democratic West), rising industries dependent on exports of goods and services like pharmaceuticals and information technology, a muscular business lobby, and greater inclusion of traditionally marginalized classes in governance and politics—are cutting in a different direction, toward greater awareness of international norms, the rule of law, and the values of reform, transparency, and accountability. As one corporate leader explained, India's businesses want to invest overseas but "can't live in a situation where our investment depends on the whim of a single ruler."[72]

But as Sundeep Waslekar argues, India faces a crucial decision: will it assert itself sufficiently on the world stage to be a great power built by a great ruler (an aspiration Waslekar finds impractical and undesirable), or should it be content to become a great nation, built by citizens who have as much of a chance as their rulers of achieving greatness?[73] Beset with a daunting list of challenges—domestic insurgencies, widespread corruption, creaking infrastructure, failing schools, high inequality and poverty rates, deep discrimination against women, castes, and other underprivileged groups—can India graduate from its low-middle-income status to become a truly prosperous democracy?

Even if India became more interested in asserting greater leadership on democracy and human rights, would it have any effect? One of the most surprising constraints on India's ability to carve out any leadership role on the world stage is its anemic diplomatic capacities. The Ministry of External Affairs employs approximately 600 career diplomats to staff 120 missions, a fraction of the 229 missions staffed by a much smaller country, like Germany,[74] and dwarfed by powerful countries like Russia, China, and the United States.[75] Of the 1,000–1,200 new civil servants brought into government each year, only 25 or so enter the foreign service. Since the liberalization reforms of 1991, today's well-educated Indians have many more opportunities to work abroad and are no longer interested in taking a demanding job at a badly resourced diplomatic post to get ahead in the global economy. "We are running thin, and resistant to change," lamented one career diplomat.[76] A plan approved by Parliament to double the number of professional staff by 2015 and efforts to recruit civil servants from other ministries as lateral hires offer some promise but still fall far below what a rising power should have to defend and promote its interests and values abroad. Staffing at India's national security council is similarly stretched, with only forty-five professionals to cover a massive agenda. Prime Minister Singh's admonition to the diplomatic corps in November 2013 to do more with constant or declining resources suggests foreign policy will continue to take a backseat to India's other concerns.[77] While Prime Minister Modi's government is aware of the capacity problem, it will remain constrained in fulfilling its ambitious goals in the short term. It must also address the absence of any serious policy planning and research capacity in the foreign ministry.[78]

When Indian national security officials do have time to turn to a human rights agenda, they are likely to focus on issues of greatest concern to domestic audiences: child labor, child marriage, poverty, food security, right to education, and right to health are just some of the priorities cited. Although the central government has approached human trafficking in an uncoordinated and piecemeal manner, migrant rights and anti-trafficking issues have recently come to the fore, as well. The Ministry of Home Affairs (MHA) continues to establish Anti–Human Trafficking Units and in April 2013, national laws were strengthened to cover more crimes and punish traffickers more stringently.[79] India's National Human Rights Commission, an accredited National Human Rights Institution (NHRI) in UN parlance,[80] tries to foster awareness and hold the government accountable, and organizes trainings for government officials and police forces. In 2012–13, it conducted 114 such trainings.[81] But this broadly uncoordinated approach is highlighted in the structure of the Ministry of External Affairs, where there is no dedicated focal point for human rights or democracy—it is not within the primary wheelhouse of any minister, secretary, additional secretary, division, or office.[82]

The clear victory by Prime Minister Narendra Modi's Hindu nationalist BJP in May 2014 national elections ushered in a new more proactive phase in India's outreach to the world, driven principally by its drive for economic growth and investment and its aspirations for a greater voice in shaping the global order to its advantage. To the surprise of many observers, Modi also set a fast pace on an ambitious foreign policy agenda, including a subtle but marked shift toward support for democratic stability in its region and beyond. A "more energetic diplomacy that seeks a larger and deeper footprint in the world," according to Foreign Secretary Jaishankar, "is an expression of greater self-confidence. Its foreign policy dimension is to aspire to be a leading power, rather than just a balancing power . . . there is also a willingness to shoulder greater global responsibilities."[83]

A review of Modi's external affairs agenda during his first year in office tells us many things: his vision for making India work again, seizing the initiative in South Asia and the broader Asian theater, and proclaiming India as an inevitable success story worth betting on. There is, of course, great pragmatism in such an approach as India faces the daunting task of finding viable employment for its 800 million citizens under the age of thirty-five, which by some estimates would require generating at least 12 million jobs a year for the next twenty years.[84] But one also takes away from Modi's first year in office a deeply felt spiritual and philosophical worldview that promotes India's civilizational and cultural characteristics as unique contributions to the world. Modi speaks of India's vibrant democracy, its "unity in diversity" ethos, not only as the indispensable ingredient for governing its remarkably complex society but as the necessary path toward greater peace and coexistence in the world, a world that would allow his country to reach sustainable levels of development and prosperity. The decisiveness of his party's victory— the first time an opposition coalition has won a clear majority of seats over the traditionally dominant Congress Party, which has ruled India for forty-nine of the past sixty-seven years—has rekindled confidence in India's democracy and inspired hope in its burgeoning middle classes that they too will be able to enjoy the material benefits of India's prosperity someday.[85]

True to the Indian tradition of sharing but not boasting of its experience as the world's largest democracy, Modi has traveled around the region and the world praising countries like Mongolia, Mauritius, and Korea for their transitions from conflict toward democratic stability. He was the first sitting Indian premier in thirty-three years to visit Fiji, shortly after elections that restored democracy to the island and led to its readmittance to the Commonwealth of Nations. There he promised to expand defense and security cooperation, increase scholarships, and finance a cogenerated power plant and upgrades to the sugar industry. Upon becoming the first prime minister to visit neighboring Nepal in seventeen years, he announced a $1 billion credit for infrastructure development and energy projects and later rushed disaster relief to earthquake victims. On India's national independence day, Modi praised Nepalese youth for dropping their weapons in favor of plows and schoolbooks as they await a new constitution that Indian experts have helped draft. In Myanmar, Modi made a point of visiting democracy icon and opposition leader Aung San Suu Kyi, who impressed upon him the link between democracy and stability, citing India as an example of a country with a diverse, pluralistic population that can both develop and govern itself democratically.

The encouraging embrace of democratizers in the region is counterbalanced by the chilly unease that continues to overshadow relations with Pakistan and China. Similarly, Modi turned a cold shoulder toward the Maldives after its increasingly authoritarian government chose to prosecute a former president on questionable charges, leading Modi to cancel a scheduled trip to the country in February 2015. After the previous government in New Delhi declined to attend the Commonwealth Summit in Sri Lanka while it was governed by the autocratic president Rajapaksa, Modi traveled to Colombo after Rajapaksa's surprising electoral defeat. There he told the Parliament about India's success with "cooperative federalism" as a more positive antidote to the island's long-standing separatist conflict while stressing that the unity and integrity of Sri Lanka are "paramount."[86]

CONCLUSION

These examples suggest a subtle shift toward greater activism in India's generally passive if genuine support for democratic stability in its foreign policy. Its traditional style of democracy promotion emphasizes leading by example, not preaching to others; listening to local demands and waiting to be asked for assistance; avoiding the appearance of bullying its smaller neighbors; and focusing on technical assistance and institution building while eschewing more overtly political forms of involvement. Modi's "neighborhood first" policy, including its interest in greater integration, trade, and transport links, makes it more likely that it will use its expanding influence to support stronger institutions of democratic governance and rule of law and more overtly favor countries on the democratic path.

Modi brings to these subjects his own unique voice and experience. As a child of poverty who once served tea in a railway coach, Modi knows firsthand that democratic systems offer greater opportunities for mobility and prosperity. India also offers a particularly strong contrast to neighboring China, which, for all its economic and social progress, remains grossly deficient in terms of political rights and democratic values.

What sets Modi apart from his predecessors is his mission to help spread the experience of a more inclusive and democratic India not only to his fellow Indians but to the wider world. As a devout Hindu, Modi is not shy about preaching the virtues of what he considers not a religion but a way of life that encompasses all societies, a philosophy that teaches that "all should be happy, all should be healthy, all should live life to the fullest."[87] As India succeeds at home, "we increase our ability to help our friends," he told the Mongolian Parliament in May 2015. "This is the urge of the land of Buddha and Gandhi. This is the instinct born from our ancient belief in the world as one family."[88] He proceeded to connect the Lord Buddha's message of kindness and compassion for all to the foundational principles of democracy and human rights, as an ancient common heritage that will unite Asia, regardless of different forms of government, around peace and cooperation. In linking India's ancient Buddhist traditions with its soft power diplomacy, Modi may be able to set the right tone for India's peaceful nonthreatening rise in Asia while checking any Chinese soft power advantage.[89] He also broke new ground in winning widespread international support for a first ever and much touted International Day of Yoga, celebrated June 21 (summer solstice) as "an invaluable gift of India's ancient tradition."[90] These initiatives, which promote a more spiritual or cultural form of Indian nationalism, risk alienating India's large Muslim population, which remains on high alert after previous anti-Muslim violence in Modi's home state of Gujarat and a rise in Hindutva communal violence.[91]

The result for now is a highly fluid and unpredictable India that seeks strategic autonomy for maximum flexibility, promiscuous multilateral engagement, and minimal binding commitments that could drain treasure or prestige from its national hard and soft power banks.[92] Whether Modi's government will fulfill its promises of becoming a more responsible regional and global leader less afraid to assert its interests in a more democratic environment remains to be seen. As India opens to the world, however, the contest over its role will accelerate and new and louder voices will have a chance to demand policies that call to mind the Gandhian and Nehruvian values of tolerance, pluralism, and independence for all citizens—of India and the world.

CHAPTER FOUR

Brazil

In Pursuit of Strategic Autonomy

Oh country vast by nature, fair and strong, brave and colossus, thy future mirrors this thy greatness.
Brazil's national anthem, 1922

Of all the misguided quests that Brazil had undertaken over the years, few rivaled our efforts to attain our dream of world prominence. . . . But a history of awful follow-through meant that, in retrospect, such declarations always ended up looking rather brash.
PRESIDENT FERNANDO HENRIQUE CARDOSO *(1985–95),*
from his memoirs

BRAZIL HAS LONG SOUGHT a role in world affairs that would mirror its impressive physical attributes: its continental breadth, its status as the world's fifth largest country by size and population, and its rising place as the world's sixth largest economy. Yet its own experience of erratic growth, high inequality, and unstable politics has tempered its influence on the world stage and reinforced traditional views of national development as the top priority in both its domestic and international agendas. Since its transition to democracy in 1985, Brazil's dual strategy of pursuing its national economic interests and a higher profile in regional and global affairs has served it well. As cataloged in chapter 1, Brazil has surged forward over the past three decades with one of the world's largest increases in gross national product, major improvements in human development, and a relatively stable democratic political order.[1] Its seat at the table of the G-20 and BRICS and its viable bid for a permanent seat on the UN Security Council, its drive to establish regional institutions that stand apart from the United States, and its successful claim to host both the World Cup in 2014 and the Summer Olympics in 2016 are some of the fruits of its ambitious reach for a long-anticipated leadership role in the world.[2]

While Brazil may legitimately claim the mantle of an emerging democratic power, at peace with its neighbors and of growing weight economically, its preference for noninterference in internal affairs, abjuration of use of military force, and drive to establish itself as a leader of the global South often put it at odds with the traditional powers' concept of the international liberal order. This attitude is markedly on display in the realm of support for democracy and human rights, where Brazil has held firm, with some notable exceptions, to traditional principles of sovereignty and against coercive tactics to effect change in other countries. As former foreign minister Celso Amorim phrased it, "We don't give certificates of good behavior."[3] In a comparative study released by Freedom House in 2014, Brazil scored in the low end of the scale as a minimal supporter of democracy and human rights in the world.[4]

Given the personal and political trajectories of its three most recent democratically elected presidents—Dilma Rousseff, Lula da Silva, and Fernando Henrique Cardoso, all victims in one form or another of the military dictatorship of 1964–85—its lackluster performance in this arena comes as a surprise to many observers. Despite the Brazilian constitution's call to give priority to human rights in its international relations, Brazil has favored other historical strands in its foreign policy, such as self-determination, nonintervention, and peaceful conflict resolution.[5] Above all, it has sought strategic autonomy, that is, the flexibility to secure and defend its national interests without the constraints of alliances or conditions imposed by external actors. Over time, however, a growing awareness in Brazilian elite and middle-class circles of the country's constitutional and moral obligation to advance human rights both abroad and at home may pave the way for more progressive policies that better reconcile its interests with its values.

In the decades before it consolidated its position as Latin America's largest democracy, Brazil's principal preoccupation was to secure its borders and develop its continental "empire" without much reference to the rest of the world. Once Foreign Minister Rio Branco, the father of

Brazilian diplomacy, negotiated the legal national borders at the end of the 1910s, Brazil turned wholeheartedly to national development as the North Star of its foreign policy, an approach former foreign minister Celso Lafer labeled "goal-oriented nationalism," or nationalism as a means to development.[6] As it grew in strength, Brazil also sought *grandeza*, to be recognized as a great country with the capacity to be regionally and internationally influential.[7]

To achieve *grandeza*, its leaders chose the path of political autonomy, which has taken different forms over the years, as Brazilian political scientists Tulio Vegevani and Gabriel Cepaluni explain. These ranged from autonomy through distance from international regimes, which prevailed from the 1930s through the Cold War, to autonomy through participation in the international system, which predominated in the 1980s and 1990s.[8] Late in the Cardoso administration and institutionalized by both the Lula and Rousseff governments, Brazilian foreign policy has shifted toward autonomy through diversification by developing new alliances with partners from the global South as a way to reduce asymmetries in its relations with more powerful countries. An early statement of these lines of diplomacy came from President Jânio Quadros, who wrote in 1961:

> We gave up the subsidiary and innocuous diplomacy of a nation aligned with worthy though alien interests, and, to protect our rights, placed ourselves in the forefront, convinced as we were of our ability to contribute with our own means to the understanding of peoples . . . My country has few international obligations . . . Not being members of any bloc . . . we preserve our absolute freedom to make our own decisions in specific cases and in the light of peaceful suggestions at one with our nature and history.[9]

An important detour from the path of nonalignment came during the height of the Cold War when the military, encouraged by the United States, deposed the democratically elected government of João Goulart in 1964. The coup ushered in two decades of military rule in which opponents of the regime, including Fernando Henrique Cardoso, fled into exile, or, like Dilma Rousseff, stayed to take up arms against the government (see figure 4-1). Brazilian foreign policy then took sides with the United States against the Soviet Union and joined Operation Condor, a secret multinational campaign by military governments to eradicate

Figure 4-1. Dilma Rousseff before a Military Tribunal in 1970

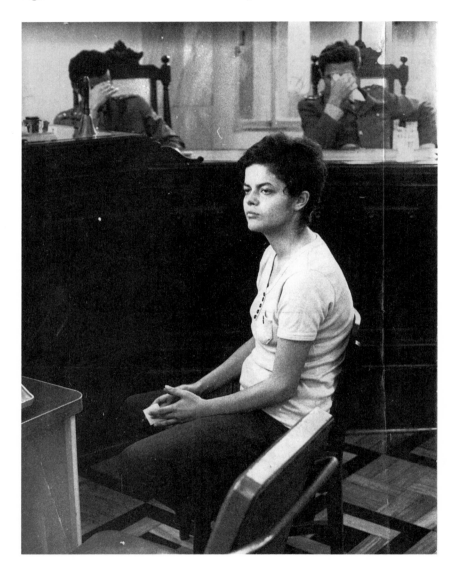

Source: Adir Mera/Public Archive of the State of São Paulo.

communist influence in the southern cone of South America. Declassified documents have also elucidated Brazil's role under President Médici
in rigging Uruguay's 1971 elections and in supporting Chile's military
coup d'état in 1973.[10]

By the mid-1970s, however, Brazil shifted away from the United
States, which under Jimmy Carter began to elevate human rights as a
feature of U.S. foreign policy, and toward a more independent policy of
"responsible pragmatism."[11] "What we seek is that all countries respect
us as we respect them," according to then foreign minister Azeredo da
Silveira. "Our foreign policy is a search to harmonize national interests.
First, with countries that are our neighbors, then with countries on the
American continent, on our maritime border, African countries and the
countries of the world."[12] Brazil looked to diversify its foreign trade
options and energy suppliers, attract capital, and open new markets.[13]
Brazil also began to move closer to Latin America, Europe, and Japan,
and shifted away from Israel toward Arab countries. In 1974, Brazil
recognized the People's Republic of China and soon after the former Portuguese colonies of Angola, Mozambique, and Guinea-Bissau.[14] Further,
the regime arrived at an agreement with West Germany to build nuclear
reactors in 1975 and renounced the military alliance with the United
States in 1977.[15] A review of Brazil-Cuba relations resulted in the 1986
reinstatement of relations with Cuba—ending a twenty-two-year policy
of nonrecognition.[16] Brazil pursued a nuclear technology development
program from the 1960s to the early 1990s but renounced all interest in
nuclear weapons after its transition to civilian rule. It was one of the earliest supporters of the Treaty of Tlatelolco (1968), which established a
nuclear-weapons-free zone in Latin America, and officially acceded to
the Nuclear Non-Proliferation Treaty (NPT) in 1998.[17]

As Brazil emerged from twenty-one years of military dictatorship in
1985, it began gradually to incorporate a concern for democracy and
human rights in its foreign policy as a way to lock in the gains it and
many of its neighbors had made. In 1985, Brazil joined the American
Convention on Human Rights (Pact of San Jose), the United Nations
human rights treaties, and the UN Convention against Torture.[18] Brazil
supported the inclusion of a reference to democracy in the new preamble
to the Organization of American States (OAS) Charter, which consolidated the organization's mission to support civilian rule in the hemisphere.[19] Brazil's redemocratization process also was instrumental in
enhancing trust between Brazil and its historical rival Argentina, now as

a restored democracy.[20] Under President Cardoso, this trend accelerated as Brazil supported or led efforts to further the cause of democratic transitions in its region through multilateral institutions like the OAS, the Southern Cone Common Market (Mercosul), and the Rio Group. This initially came in the form of democracy clauses, a type of insurance policy that conditioned membership in each organization on a state's adoption of constitutional representative democracy; an interruption of such status triggers a vote of suspension and diplomatic intervention to restore democracy.[21]

After these initial steps to solidify the region as a zone of democracy and peace, Brazil's record of mainstreaming democracy and human rights in its foreign policy began to waver.[22] Its global ambitions and quest for economic growth increasingly outweighed a concern for human rights in cases like Iran, China, Angola, and Russia. The result is a "human rights lite" policy in which special domestic concerns around racism, food security, and LGBT rights are promoted internationally while harder issues that could jeopardize its strategic autonomy like Responsibility to Protect (R2P) and Syria are avoided or opposed. Its expanding role as a development aid donor is largely devoid of any concern for democratic governance or human rights. It has studiously avoided any serious effort to criticize countries it sees as key economic or ideological partners, for example, China, Venezuela, or Cuba, and increasingly has found common ground with its diverse partners in the BRICS group, including Russia and China. These issues, however, are often subjects of lively debate in Brazilian politics and media. An active civil society is increasingly stretching its agenda beyond domestic concerns and pressuring the government to rethink its traditional noninterference approach to human rights issues abroad. And the government's willingness to tackle the painful legacy of its own past through the establishment of a national truth commission is a sign that Brazil's greatness, as a leading example of a democratic country willing to use its soft power to advance liberal values, may yet be achieved.

To do so, it must face a host of internal challenges that regularly pull it back from achieving its dream of *grandeza*. The dramatic revelations in 2014–15 of a massive kickback and bribery scheme potentially involving $800 million from state-controlled energy conglomerate Petrobras redirected to the pockets of politicians, parties, middlemen, and political cronies are both a painful reminder of the deep corruption in the Brazilian system and the encouraging efforts to address it. Other cases of waste and fraud surrounding the construction of stadiums for mega-sporting events, the displacement of slum dwellers to make way for new infrastructure, failing health and education systems, and persistent zones of criminality and violence alongside police brutality and impunity all point toward a growing crisis of confidence in Brazil's ascendancy as a rising democratic power. These problems are exacerbated by a serious economic crisis brought on by the end of the Asian-led commodities boom, rising inflation, unmet pension needs, and a political system that requires constant vote trading and favor peddling to manage fractious coalitions in congress. On the upside, Brazil's political trajectory as a stabilizing democratic power with an assertive and independent judiciary, robust media and civil society, and civilian control of the military bodes well for managing through the current crisis. As its domestic troubles grow, however, Brazil's more ambitious foreign policy agenda will necessarily be curtailed, as well.

BRAZIL IN ITS NEIGHBORHOOD

> Brazil can't be the gendarme of Latin America, but it can play a pedagogical role with reference to democracy.
> FERNANDO HENRIQUE CARDOSO, *interview with El País International*, June 15, 2010

After the economic and political turbulence of the early years of Brazil's modern democracy, Brazil settled down under the leadership of Fernando Henrique Cardoso, the finance minister largely responsible for the successful currency devaluation plan that tackled hyperinflation. As president, Cardoso doubled down on Mercosul as Brazil's "destiny." But for many years, Brazil's desire to shape Mercosul as a platform for its insertion into the global economy was not matched by a willingness to bear the economic costs of it becoming a true customs union.

Cardoso's administration embraced the goal of strengthening a South American pole of influence in the context of an international environment in which the United States and the mainstream values and institutions of the post–World War II order predominated. This steered Cardoso and his foreign minister, Luiz Felipe Lampreia, toward preserving Brazil's autonomy by conforming to and shaping an international regime that would ultimately both constrain the superpower and deliver concrete benefits to a transforming Brazil. "The Brazil that enters the twenty-first century is a country whose primary objectives for internal transformation and development are in harmony with values universally disseminated on the international level," Cardoso explained in 2000.[23] In the words of Lampreia, "critical convergence" would guide Brazil's foreign policy, "because transformations in Brazil have brought us, of our own choosing, into the central current of world history in an era when political democracy and economic liberty are the fundamental reference points."[24]

From this line of thinking flowed a series of actions in which Brazil under Cardoso played a leading role to support democracy and resolve regional conflicts, as in the case of the Peru-Ecuador conflict in 1995–96. Cardoso was the principal advocate for using Brazil's growing leverage to advance political reforms in the region, for example, through adoption of democratic criteria for Mercosul membership.[25] Cardoso's presidency also actively supported a series of reforms to the OAS and Rio Group charters to reinforce collective rejection and response to "sudden and irregular interruptions to the constitutional order."[26] These measures were embraced as an effective diplomatic tool to help break the historical cycle of coups d'état that led to decades of military rule and weak civilian governments not only in Brazil but throughout Central and South America. It took a similar pro-democracy approach in other fora like the Ibero-American Summits and in the formative years of what is now known as the Union of South American Nations (UNASUL).[27] Cardoso was outspoken in favor of democracy as a common identity for the region, declaring in a speech in South Africa in 1996, at the height of democratic turbulence in the region, "Peace, democracy, and political dialogue are also distinctive traits of South America, elements of our historical evolution. Democracy is the best guarantee for effective change. Democracy ensures predictability, coherence in the transformation process, and continuity with accountability. We are committed to supporting democracy in the region."[28]

As the region underwent a series of tumultuous transitions to civilian democratic rule in the 1990s, these democracy standards were repeatedly put to the test. Throughout Cardoso's presidency, Brazil responded swiftly to overt interruptions of democracy in Paraguay, Guatemala, Venezuela, and Ecuador both bilaterally and by supporting the OAS, Rio Group, and Mercosul diplomatic initiatives to restore constitutional rule during periods of political crises.[29] In these cases, Brazil's insistence that constitutional rule in the region be preserved was primarily designed to protect its own democratic trajectory, and secondarily to reinforce international norms and multilateral diplomacy as a hedge against external interference from the United States, which had a history of supporting military coups in the region. In the case of Haiti's coup in September 1991, for example, Brazil supported collective action at the OAS and the UN to restore President Aristide to power but drew the line against the use of force proposed by the United States. Ten years later, during the short-lived coup against democratically elected Hugo Chávez in 2002, Brazil, and Cardoso personally, led regional efforts to condemn and isolate the coup leaders, who fled or were arrested within days of their claim to power. Notably, Brazil relied principally on the Rio Group rather than the OAS for diplomatic action, a subtle but important way to shoulder aside the United States, which had signaled early support for the coup.

As regional trends shifted away from overt ruptures of democratically elected governments toward more sophisticated attempts by executives to accumulate power through both constitutional and extra-constitutional means, Brazil fell back to a more noninterventionist position. The emblematic case was Brazil's cautious response to antidemocratic moves by Peru's president Fujimori after his "auto-golpe" in 1992, and again in 2000, when Fujimori sought to manipulate elections to win a third term, a case that did not clearly trigger the anti-coup mechanism of the OAS. Consistent with its attachment to the principle of noninterference in domestic affairs, Brazil argued against collective action at the OAS. While Cardoso pointedly did not attend Fujimori's inauguration, and politely called for greater political pluralism and institutional reforms, he nonetheless invited Fujimori to the first ever summit of South American presidents a few months after the flawed elections, demonstrating Brazil's overriding priority to build a united South American pole of influence.[30] Just three months after the summit, Fujimori was forced to resign in the face of new revelations of bribery schemes by his chief intelligence and political adviser, and both men remain in jail on charges of corruption and human rights abuses. In this case, at least, history suggests that Brazil's preference for nonintervention and regional leadership led it astray from its purported commitment to democracy.

LULA AND THE RETURN OF GRANDEZA

Under Lula's presidency, the shift away from an activist approach to democracy and human rights in the region and toward a predominant concern for Brazil's rise as an economic and political leader of the global South continued and accelerated. Lula's ambitious claim for both regional and global leadership, including a robust campaign for a permanent seat on the UN Security Council, set the tone early on and only grew as the Brazilian economy took off in 2004. At the regional level, Lula doubled down on Cardoso's bet on Mercosul and a union of South American states and further developed a new initiative for integrating infrastructure with neighbors.[31] He sought to co-opt Venezuela's oil-fueled claim for regional influence by including it in Mercosul, despite its questionable credentials for membership.[32] Lula even went as far as praising Hugo Chávez as Venezuela's "best" president.[33] This friendly attitude toward its increasingly authoritarian neighbor was driven principally by commercial and economic objectives, which reached new heights during the Lula/Chávez era. A strategic alliance was signed in 2005 to manage more intense relations, which led to an 858 percent increase in Brazilian exports to Venezuela and a sevenfold increase in total bilateral trade from 2003 to 2012.[34] While sympathies on ideological matters were strong, Brazil did not sign up for Chávez's anti-West Bolivarian Alliance for the Peoples of our America (ALBA), preferring instead to work mainly within existing institutions to balance the United States. More recently, President Rousseff, Lula's handpicked successor who won elections in 2010 and again in 2014, has distanced herself from Chávez's replacement, President Maduro, whose harsh tactics against the opposition have drawn scorn from critics in the region and quiet criticism from Brazil but little in the way of concrete action.[35]

As with Chávez, the Lula administration parlayed its leftist credentials to influence other leftist politicians in the region. Ollanta Humala, who won the presidency of Peru in 2011, relied on Lula's party leaders for campaign advice.[36] Much of this more ideological agenda was managed by Marco Aurelio Garcia, a Workers Party intellectual who has served as special foreign affairs adviser to both Presidents Lula and Rousseff. Consistent with this approach, Brazil prioritized relations with other leftist governments, with modest support for democratic stability. For example, it took moderate steps to support peaceful resolution of political crises in Ecuador in 2005 and in Bolivia in 2008.[37] Brazil also supported an OAS mission to mediate a political crisis and monitor municipal elections in Sandinista-led Nicaragua in 2005.[38] That same year, however, it successfully blocked U.S. efforts to create a more robust OAS mechanism for collective responses to erosions of democratic standards under the

Inter-American Democratic Charter, highlighting its preference for dialogue over (U.S.-style) intervention.[39] By 2010, UNASUL had adopted a protocol to manage threats or breaches against democratic rule on par with the OAS mechanisms, but in practice these instruments generally have been left on the shelf.

Two cases in particular illustrate Brazil's strategy to build alliances with like-minded governments in the region during the Lula and Rousseff period and put Brazil's commitment to democratic principles to the test: Honduras and Paraguay. In June 2009, the leftist president Manuel Zelaya of Honduras sought to hold a referendum to amend the constitution to allow him to run for another term in office, a move that raised serious questions about constitutional procedures and abuse of power. In short order, the Supreme Court annulled the referendum, which Zelaya ignored, Congress voted to expel Zelaya, and the Honduran armed forces flew him in his pajamas to Costa Rica, allowing Roberto Micheletti, the opposition head of the Congress, to assume the presidency. Not surprisingly, the OAS and other regional bodies including UNASUL concluded it was a coup and refused to recognize the new government.

Brazil quickly condemned the illegitimate transfer of power, demanded Zelaya's return, and suspended its aid projects and military cooperation with Honduras; it later took additional measures, including canceling a visa-waiver program and meeting with Zelaya in a show of support. Events took an awkward turn, however, when Zelaya, his wife, and a small band of supporters showed up at the Brazilian embassy in Tegucigalpa seeking shelter, which Lula approved. In response, the Honduran government cut off food, electricity, and telephone transmission to the compound; rather than backing down, Brazil dug in its heels as it sought OAS and UN support for a resolution that would allow Zelaya to return to office to complete his term. The United States, on the other hand, concluded that the better exit to the crisis was to hold new elections that excluded both Zelaya and Micheletti, a process Honduras chose to follow. Elections held in November 2009 were free of violence but international election observers withdrew from the country, citing concerns about the fairness of the elections because of the Micheletti government's suppression of opposition media and demonstrators.[40] Nevertheless, they led to a "government of national unity" under Porfirio Lobo and the departure of Zelaya from the Brazilian embassy to the Dominican Republic to live in temporary exile.[41] Brazil refused to recognize the new government until May 2011, when Zelaya was allowed to return to the country.

The Honduras case illustrates what now appears to have been a spirited though unsuccessful attempt by Brazil to demand restoration of the status quo ante. It did so even after key factions in Honduras agreed to a viable if imperfect U.S.-led alternative, which sought to get beyond the crisis through a democratic process to sideline both the elected but controversial Zelaya and the coup supporter Micheletti in favor of a government of national reconciliation. Contrary to its usual practice of staying out of other countries' domestic politics in order to preserve a mediating role, Brazil's decision to open its embassy to the deposed president put it in the middle of the crisis and prevented it from playing the honest broker. It raised questions about whether Lula was more interested in return of a leftist anti-U.S. ally than a peaceful mediated outcome that reinforced democratic principles and multilateralism.

In the case of neighboring Paraguay, Brazil had for many years taken an activist and positive approach to diplomatic intervention to support its rocky transition to democracy. In June 2012, the democratically elected president, Fernando Lugo, was summarily impeached in a move characterized by his supporters as a "parliamentary coup." President Rousseff quickly won agreement to suspend Paraguay from both Mercosul and UNASUL until new elections were held, the first time these bodies took such an action. The United States, on the other hand, decided to follow the OAS's lead and recognize Paraguay's new government despite the questionable impeachment process.[42] At face value, it looked like a robust and constructive episode of Brazilian leadership in favor of democratic principles in the region. Shortly thereafter, however, Brazil took advantage of Paraguay's absence from Mercosul to push through a vote to admit Venezuela to the group, a long-delayed step opposed by Paraguay. As one observer noted, Brazil appeared "opportunistic and unconcerned about violating Mercosul's rule of consensus for adding new members."[43] More damning, it came at a time when Hugo Chávez was being roundly criticized for an ongoing series of antidemocratic actions, including repression of the media and opposition parties.[44] In the end, Brazil's principled leadership was sullied by a rather naked attempt to secure more important business and political interests in Venezuela. "Brazil wants a stable Venezuela to advance its goal of an integrated South America," explained a senior U.S. diplomat.[45]

Elsewhere in the region, Brazil under Lula showed no hesitation in embracing Cuba's regime despite its poor record of political and civil rights. This was a break from the polite but cool relations under Cardoso, who acknowledged once being inspired by Fidel Castro's revolution but ultimately concluded that "he had replaced one authoritarian regime with another."[46] In a colorful passage from his memoirs, Cardoso recounts visiting Cuba in the 1980s, "a country in the tropics, full of warm and spontaneous people, but living a life as gray and threadbare as I remembered it being in Warsaw Pact Romania and East Germany."[47] "Since then," he continued, "nothing much has changed. [Fidel Castro] still believes he is living in 1985, and that is the way he runs Cuba. . . . He never allows open debate of his policies." In private, according to Cardoso, other Latin American leaders criticized Fidel for running "a lousy, piece-of-shit island. . . . We're sick of apologizing for you all the time." Cardoso, on the other hand, kept quiet, reflecting his strong opposition to the U.S. embargo.[48] He instructed his foreign minister, nonetheless, to meet with Cuba's human rights activists when visiting the island. By the end of his term, and in particular in the wake of Cuba's crackdown on dissidents in 2003, Cardoso had given up on Castro and Cuban socialism as a viable path for Brazil, Cuba, or the region.

Lula, however, who won election as a leftist sympathetic to the social rights aspects of the Cuban model, was quick to extend a helping hand to Havana. On his first visit to Cuba, Lula praised the warming ties between the two countries and pledged to support Cuba's dire need for foreign assistance and investment.[49] In the ensuing years, Brazil's National Development Bank agreed to extend loans worth nearly $700 million to Brazilian construction giants like Odebrecht to develop a new modern port at Mariel, the anchor for Cuba's special economic development zone.[50] It also lent important assistance to Cuba's quest for deep-sea oil exploration and provided loans, training, and technical assistance to other projects on the island; Brazilian firms in the tobacco and sugar ethanol business have benefited from closer ties, as well.[51] Lula ignored, however, Cuba's human rights record and went so far as to deride activists for challenging the Communist Party's monopoly on power by belittling Cuban political prisoners on hunger strike.[52] On his third and final official visit to Cuba in 2010, in which he shared an "emotional" reunion with the ailing Fidel Castro, Lula had nothing to say about the hunger strike of political prisoner Orlando Zapata Tamayo, who died during the visit.[53] When he returned to Brazil, Lula, who once was a hunger striker himself, defended Cuba's actions: "Imagine if all the criminals in São Paulo went on hunger strike to demand freedom," he said, in an apparent comparison between Cuban dissidents and common criminals.[54]

Lula's and Rousseff's advisers claim that they privately raise the need for political reforms at the highest levels of the Castro government,[55] and that Brazil maintains close contacts with Cuban civil society and the Catholic Church. Publicly, however, Brazil plays to domestic and international audiences sympathetic to Cuba's predicament as a "victim" of the U.S. embargo. Brazil fought, for example, for lifting Cuba's suspension from the OAS in 2009 and for its inclusion in the Summit of the Americas, despite Cuba's lack of democratic credentials. President Obama's historic decision in December 2014 to begin normalizing relations with Cuba offers a test of Brazil's willingness to increase pressure on Havana's human rights performance. An increase in Brazil's criticism of Cuba's ongoing harassment of civil society activists, however, is unlikely. In addition to its growing economic interests on the island, Brazil imports 20,000 Cuban medical workers to Brazilian towns and villages, reaching 48 million residents, a highly popular program that is politically and financially beneficial to both countries.[56]

With Dilma Rousseff's election in 2010 as successor to Lula's ambitious and pragmatic foreign policy, Brazil more or less continued on course, though with less drive and skill. Given her own history as a former guerrilla and victim of torture, expectations were high that her administration would speak out on human rights, a sentiment fed by her early statements in favor of changing Brazil's position on human rights in Iran (see below). In the region, however, Rousseff's policy took a dramatic turn in the other direction when the Inter-American Commission on Human Rights (IACHR) issued a decision in April 2011 demanding Brazil suspend its signature Belo Monte hydroelectric dam construction project until it engaged in further consultations with local indigenous communities. Outraged by the external interference in one of Rousseff's priority development projects, the government condemned the decision, withdrew its candidate to the IACHR and its ambassador to the OAS, and refused to pay its dues. It also joined Ecuador and other ALBA states in an effort to weaken the inter-American human rights system, a process that absorbed two years of political debate and ultimately resulted in little change to the system. In 2012, Brazil began softening its position; it returned to paying its dues and in 2014 backed election of a strong Brazilian candidate to the IACHR; in 2015, it finally appointed a new ambassador to the regional body. The incident illustrates Brazil's willingness to abandon its stated commitment to human rights when international judgments threaten other national and foreign policy interests, including its not-so-subtle efforts to undermine the OAS.

Regarding Venezuela's continued slide toward illiberal democracy and economic crisis, Brazil has mainly worked behind the scenes to urge a mediated solution to the political crisis. As repression increased in 2014 and 2015, and with growing attention and pressure from political forces within and outside Brazil, its foreign minister called on Caracas to set a date for parliamentary elections as soon as possible and to adhere to prescribed timelines.[57] "The path Maduro is on is full of risks," one unnamed Brazilian official told Reuters. "We've been trying to encourage him to change."[58] Brazil's quiet approach is intended to avoid falling into the U.S. trap as a scapegoat for Venezuela's dire economic situation as it tries to protect the billions Venezuela still owes to Brazilian companies.

BRAZIL AND THE WORLD

Looking beyond its own neighborhood, Brazil's foreign policy over time evolved from a Eurocentric and North-centric orientation to a more diversified strategy that offered more options for its expanding economy and aspirations for global influence. Under President Lula, this autonomy-through-diversification policy accelerated at a time when a weakened United States and Europe, reeling from the 2008 financial crisis, fueled the post–Cold War demand for a more multipolar world. Building on its earlier investments in developing the BRICS group and IBSA, and less affected by the global recession, Brazil effectively maneuvered itself to an ever-more-important place on the world stage, particularly at the G-20, the climate change negotiations, and at the WTO trade talks. Tactically, Brazil doubled down on its efforts to build a South-South coalition of states that would both advance its economic interests and its demands for a greater voice in global governance. South-South cooperation, according to then foreign minister Celso Amorim, "reinforces our stature and strengthens our position in trade, finance and climate negotiations . . . building coalitions with developing countries is also a way of engaging the reform of global governance in order to make international institutions fairer and more democratic."⁵⁹ Vague concepts like "solidarity" with less developed countries facing similar challenges and "non-indifference" to their challenges became watchwords of the expanded approach. Human rights broadly defined remained at the heart of Brazilian foreign policy, Amorim insisted, consistent with Brazil's core interests in peace and security:

> The exercise of solidarity with those who are more in need has been one of the tenets of President Lula's foreign policy . . . Such attitude of *non-indifference* is not contradictory with the defense of our own interests. We are convinced that in the long run an attitude based on a sense of humanity that favours the promotion of development of the poorest and most vulnerable will not only be good to peace and prosperity around the world. It will bring benefits to Brazil herself, in political as well as economic terms.⁶⁰

Through multilateral fora and a widening array of bilateral relations, Brazil pursued a nuanced strategy of promoting peaceful settlements of disputes in ways that reflected its core values while still protecting other national interests. "The concept that a sound political environment—where democracy, the rule of law as well as good social practices prevail—is essential to avoid armed conflict is very dear to Brazil," explained Amorim.⁶¹ In practice, however, Brazil picked its battles at the international level in varied ways, at times going big, as in the case of Iran, where human rights was an afterthought, and at other times choosing smaller theaters, as in Haiti and Guinea-Bissau.

Brazil's choice of partners in its renewed push for global influence reflects its wish for maximum flexibility in advancing its interests. On the economic front, Brazil reinforced its role in the BRICS group (Brazil, Russia, India, China, and South Africa) as a way to establish distance from and balance against the United States and reinforce ties to China, its largest trading partner. As BRICS has added more substance to its agenda, including the creation of a BRICS New Development Bank underwritten mostly by deep-pocketed China, Brazil has enhanced its own stature, as well. On a parallel but overlapping track, Brazil invested some of its political capital in the IBSA group, which wore its democratic credentials on its sleeve when it emerged in 2003 as an informal consultation mechanism, including multiple leaders' summits. Its collaborative fund for poverty and hunger alleviation has received approximately $27 million since its establishment in 2006 for development projects in low-income and post-conflict countries that emphasize social inclusion and capacity building.[62] As in Brazil's other development aid projects, little if anything is targeted to address deficits in democratic governance and human rights. More recently, Brazil has emphasized BRICS "at the expense" of IBSA,[63] which does not convene at the leaders level as frequently as BRICS does.[64] On other fronts, it has been an active supporter of the UN Peacebuilding Commission, which it chaired in 2014, and lobbied successfully for the election of Brazilians to head the Food and Agriculture Organization and the World Trade Organization.

In the arc of modern Brazilian foreign policy, the Iran case demonstrated a newfound sense of Brazilian self-confidence that it could broker a nuclear deal between the traditional powers and Tehran, thereby advancing its larger claim for international leadership and its rising interests in trade and economic relations with Iran. It was a bold attempt to show that middle powers, in this case Brazil and Turkey, could slow if not reverse the march to potential conflict with Iran, which looked increasingly likely at the time. Unfortunately, the gambit failed, prompting serious criticism of the Lula administration both internationally and domestically.

Within Brazil, Lula came under attack in part because of his disheartening embrace of President Mahmoud Ahmadinejad, who made an official visit to Brazil in November 2009, just months after winning reelection in flawed balloting followed by violent suppression of protesters in Iran.[65] During the visit, Lula reiterated Brazil's support for Iran's right to a civilian nuclear program and criticized potential sanctions by the West; he also asserted Brazil's interest in peacemaking in the Middle East and promoted its growing commercial and trade ties with Iran. He failed, however, to say anything about Iran's notorious human rights record in part out of concern, apparently, for winning Iran's support for Brazil's bid for a seat on the UN Security Council. Brazil also continued to abstain from UN resolutions criticizing Iran's human rights record. The nuclear proposal by Turkey and Brazil, represented by images of Lula, Erdoğan, and Ahmadinejad raising their fists in victory, was roundly rejected by the UN Security Council, sidelining Brazil in the process and dampening its ambitious campaign for global credibility.

Notably, the domestic and international criticism of Brazil's indifference to Iran's human rights violations only grew when news broke in 2010 of Iran's intention to punish a woman for adultery by stoning.[66]

This time, Lula spoke up: "If my friendship and affection for the president of Iran matters, and if this woman is causing problems there, we will welcome her here in Brazil," he said while campaigning for his successor, Dilma Rousseff.[67] Shortly after her election in 2010, Rousseff told the *Washington Post* she would change Brazil's vote on the annual Iran human rights resolution at the UN from abstention to affirmative: "I would feel uncomfortable as a woman president-elect not to say anything against stoning. My position will not change when I take office."[68] Her adviser reassured the public that the Rousseff presidency would "emphasize human rights" as part of its foreign policy, and shortly thereafter Brazil voted for the first time in favor of a UN Human Rights Council resolution appointing a special rapporteur to monitor Iran's human rights situation.[69] Just months later, however, Brazil reverted to its traditional ways when it abstained on similar UN resolutions critical of Iran in the General Assembly and Third Committee; this pattern of alternating yes votes in Geneva with abstentions in New York continued until March 2015, when Brazil abstained on a Human Rights Council resolution on Iran in Geneva.[70] It has, however, played a quietly helpful role on some specific human rights cases in Iran of concern to the United States and France.

In similar though much less dramatic fashion, Brazil treated other country-specific human rights situations with an air of detached concern and ambivalence. In one of the more serious cases, North Korea (DPRK), Brazil alternated between affirmative votes at the UN and abstentions, including abstaining on an important resolution in 2009 extending the mandate of the special rapporteur to monitor and document violations in the country. It claimed at the time that dialogue with Pyongyang would have a better chance of yielding results. But after North Korea refused to accept any recommendations (including Brazil's) presented at the United Nations' universal human rights peer review session, and a concerted public campaign led by the Brazilian NGO Conectas Direitos Humanos to get the Foreign Ministry to take a stand, Brazil joined consensus to establish a UN Commission of Inquiry.[71] The commission has since issued a devastating report on North Korea's human rights situation, including allegations of crimes against humanity, with pressure mounting for a referral to the International Criminal Court.[72] In contrast to its earlier posture of indifference, Brazil this time supported referring North Korea to the ICC, voting yes on the November 2014 resolution in the Third Committee.[73]

In Brazil's quest to ascend the ladder of international power politics and make new friends in the global South, the small and turbulent nation of Haiti has played a surprisingly important role. Amid general disorder and armed rebellion in 2004, President Jean-Bertrand Aristide was forced to step down in disputed circumstances and transported to exile in South Africa. The successor government, led by Supreme Court Justice Boniface Alexandre, invited the UN Security Council to send an international peacekeeping force to calm the outbreak of violence and create a secure environment for new elections. By June 2004, a UN peacekeeping mission known as MINUSTAH was dispatched, comprising 7,000 troops led by Brazil. Brazil had no compelling national interest in Haiti other than as a sister American republic struggling for democratic stability, but it did have a vital interest in demonstrating its will and capacity to lead a UN mission and thereby prove its bona fides for Security Council membership. Brazilian generals have commanded the forces almost every year since then, and Brazilian troops and police personnel comprise the largest contingent. Brazil is rightfully proud of its decision to bear primary responsibility for the mission; it suffered the consequences of such leadership when twenty Brazilian personnel were killed in the brutal earthquake that struck Haiti in January 2010, including the UN deputy special representative to Haiti.[74] President Rousseff described Brazil's approach to MINUSTAH as a leading example of its determination to integrate peace, development, and security. "With deep respect for Haitian sovereignty, Brazil is proud to contribute to the consolidation of democracy in that country," she told the UN General Assembly in 2011.[75]

Africa, from which some 4 million people came to Brazil to labor as slaves until slavery was finally abolished in 1888, became a much higher priority under Lula for both political and economic reasons.[76] Today more than 90 million Brazilians share African roots.[77] From 2002 to 2012, the number of Brazilian embassies in Africa jumped from seventeen to thirty-seven,[78] a measure of expanding trade ties and the need to win African votes for Brazil's quest for UN Security Council membership. Over the same period, trade with Africa rose from $4.2 billion to $27.6 billion.[79] Loans from Brazil's National Development Bank to African projects also expanded dramatically, a boon to Brazilian transportation and construction businesses that benefit directly from preferential loans and tie-back conditions in which recipient countries must spend Brazilian foreign aid on Brazilian goods and services. The outreach to

Africa has continued under Rousseff, who emphasized Brazil's historic obligation to contribute to Africa's development "and to extend to African countries the social technologies of inclusion, which in Brazil have helped millions to climb into the middle class and even more millions to leave behind extreme poverty."[80] Brazil's investments focus principally on raw materials like oil, coal, and tropical agriculture,[81] raising questions of whether Brazil will behave in Africa any differently than China or the colonial masters of a previous era.

Despite the democracy and peace challenges on the African continent, including major conflicts displacing millions of people in places like Sudan, Democratic Republic of Congo, Central African Republic, and Mali, Brazil has shown little interest in using its newfound diplomatic and assistance leverage to advocate for political reforms. One exception can be found in Guinea-Bissau, a small former Portuguese colony facing political turmoil in 2010–12.[82] Interruption of elections and a military coup prompted Brazil and its cohorts in the Community of Portuguese Language Speaking Countries (CPLP), along with the African Union and ECOWAS, to coordinate UN efforts to demand the restoration of constitutional order and civilian control of the military. These states supported Security Council action to impose sanctions on military officers and establish a peace-building office in the country. Brazil even advocated through CPLP for a UN-authorized peacekeeping force to help restore democracy in the country, which runs counter to Brazil's usual reticence against the use of force to resolve political crises.[83] The exception in this case appears to prove the rule: a robust democracy promotion policy for small friendly states in its sphere of influence, and reticence (if not opposition) to intervention in more complicated cases, particularly if the United States is involved.

In the arena of human rights diplomacy, Brazil has played an increasingly positive role at the UN's Human Rights Council and General Assembly, shifting from abstentions on most country-specific resolutions to a strong pattern of yes votes in some of the most compelling cases. During most of the Lula period, Brazil generally abstained on country-specific situations, including those in Belarus, Burma, Cuba, the Democratic Republic of Congo (DRC), Iran, North Korea, and Uzbekistan. On the troubles in Sri Lanka, Brazil avoided taking a position on whether to hold a special session, then voted in 2009 in favor of a damaging resolution that defended the principle of noninterference in Sri Lanka's internal affairs. On freedom of expression, Brazil abstained twice from voting on the successful efforts of the Organization of Islamic Cooperation (OIC) to condemn "defamation of religion," a concept that threatened international standards of free expression. On the other hand, Brazil voted for closer scrutiny of Israel (three times), North Korea (three times), and Sudan (twice); supported resolutions to insert independent voices in the universal peer review process; and led the successful effort to convene a special session on the right to food, one of President Lula's signature initiatives.[84]

More recently, in response to her commitment to give greater attention to human rights in Brazil's foreign policy, President Rousseff's administration has tilted toward more principled positions at the UN's human rights bodies. During the first two years of its three-year term on the Human Rights Council (2013–15), for example, Brazil voted in favor of all the country resolutions that were put to a vote and, according to Human Rights Watch, played a key role in the renewal of the mandate on Haiti.[85] In 2014, Brazil broke from its BRICS partners and voted for resolutions to establish an international investigation into crimes committed during Sri Lanka's civil war, to recommend UNGA action on a report documenting crimes against humanity in North Korea, to renew the mandate of the UN special rapporteur on Iran,[86] and to protect the rights of peaceful protesters.[87] On the other hand, it tends to hang back from taking leadership positions as an active participant in country-specific debates or as cosponsor of resolutions, vacillated on a joint statement on Bahrain, and demurred on a call for referring Syria to the ICC.[88]

Brazil's strong preference is to use its human rights diplomacy to advance thematic issues that are close to its own domestic priorities on social issues and good governance. The UN's special mandate on the right to health, for example, was created on the initiative of Brazil in 2002.[89] It has also played a positive role in advancing the debate on the rights of sexual minorities, including sponsorship of a pathbreaking resolution in 2011 "expressing grave concern at acts of violence and discrimination, in all regions of the world, committed against individuals because of their sexual orientation and gender identity," which led to the first ever OHCHR report on the topic of discrimination against lesbians, gays, bisexuals, and transgender people.[90] In 2014, it led the effort to put the issue of sexual orientation back on the HRC's agenda and helped defeat amendments that would have diluted the resolution further.[91] In a similar vein, Brazil is often willing to play a leading role in less politicized good governance and anticorruption initiatives, for example, in partnering with the United States to launch the Open Government Partnership, a sixty-five-nation platform to encourage more accountable and responsive governance.

In the wake of revelations that U.S. spy agencies were tapping her phone, Rousseff told the UN General Assembly that "the right to safety of citizens of one country can never be guaranteed by violating fundamental human rights of citizens of another country."[92] She urged the United Nations to play a leading role in creating international regulatory frameworks to govern the Internet in a way that would protect privacy and freedom of expression, open and democratic governance, and net neutrality. Since then, Brazil, in partnership with Germany, has tabled resolutions on the right to privacy to address growing concerns about mass surveillance and the collection of personal data (including metadata). In March 2015, Brazil led a successful effort at the UN Human Rights Council to establish a special rapporteur to promote and protect the right to privacy in the digital age.[93]

A swing state on this issue, as with so many others, Brazil's policies do not fit squarely within the multilateral government-controlled model of Internet governance or the multistakeholder model (government, civil society, and private sector). It sides at times with both camps though domestic activism on the issue has shifted Brazil increasingly toward the more progressive approach to the issue. In 2014, after much public debate, Brazil adopted a "digital bill of rights" (Marco Civil da Internet) that protects rights to privacy and expression online and establishes net neutrality as the guiding principle of Brazil's digital policies. Internationally, Brazil hosted the multistakeholder NETmundial conference in April 2014, which identified a set of governance principles that prioritizes human rights, and leads the NETmundial Initiative. It also established a multistakeholder governance body called the Comité Gestor da Internet (CGI.br), which has been held up as a model for how governments can bridge the gaps between domestic interests and foreign policy with regard to Internet governance.[94]

BRAZIL AND THE ARAB SPRING

In the context of the Arab Spring, Brazil has taken a largely hands-off, noninterventionist approach. Any action Brazil has taken or endorsed has been multilateral in nature, with a strong preference for South-South cooperation and against external interventions. When uprisings began in January 2011, Itamaraty (the Foreign Ministry) took a soft, nuanced stance, expressing hope that states experiencing protests "will follow a path of political evolution that meets the expectations of their people in a peaceful environment, bereft of foreign interference, so as to foster the ongoing economic and social development."[95] From the outset, Brazil made it clear that political transitions should reflect popular will and not be dictated by foreign intervention. In the same statement, Itamaraty emphasized its economic interests, concluding that "Egypt is an important Mercosul partner (a free trade agreement was signed in 2010)."[96] Policy statements out of Brazil did not mention the word democracy until it was clear that Mubarak's days as leader were numbered.[97] President Rousseff signaled that Brazil supported the democratic movement, saying that the government "looks upon the Egyptian issue with much expectation, and hopes that it may become a democratic country."[98] After Mubarak relinquished power, Itamaraty declared that Brazil "expects the political transition in that country to be carried out while upholding the political and civil liberties and human rights of the population."[99]

When Brazil's foreign minister Antonio de Aguiar de Patriota visited Cairo in May 2011, however, Egypt's transition seemed to be a footnote to other economic and diplomatic discussions. The foreign ministers reportedly discussed ongoing events in the region but Patriota, unlike his counterparts from India or Turkey, met only with Egyptian government officials and not leaders of the opposition or civil society. The Brazilian foreign minister reportedly sought support from the Egyptian government, as well as from the Arab League, for Brazil's candidate to head the UN Food and Agriculture Organization (FAO). Itamaraty expressed solidarity with Egypt's transition, explaining that "Brazil is Arab, as it houses many representatives of the Arab community. We went to Egypt to support the transition process. We made contact so that Brazil may cooperate more with Egypt."[100]

Brazil's unwillingness publicly to raise democracy and human rights in the context of this visit is consistent with its generally low-profile and skeptical approach on these issues. In the Egyptian case, this reticence is at least in part due to Egypt's growing economic significance for Brazil. In 2010, Egypt became the second non–Latin American partner to sign a free trade agreement with Mercosul and rose to become Brazil's third largest African trading partner overall and the single largest African consumer of Brazilian goods.[101] Following the coup against Mohamed

Morsi in 2013, the Brazilian government called for dialogue and reconciliation. Ambassador Cesario Melantonio Neto, Brazil's emissary to the Middle East, Turkey, and Iran at that time, expressed the hope that the Egyptian government, opposition, and armed forces would come to a "negotiated accommodation."[102]

In the tumult of 2011, Brazil tried to walk a line between supporting UN actions intended to protect civilians while resisting the authorization of use of force. Brazil initially supported UN actions in Libya, for example, then abstained on endorsing the use of force, a position that has intensified in the case of Syria. In between these two episodes, however, it did join unanimous consent by the Security Council for UN forces in Côte d'Ivoire to use "all necessary means" to protect civilians caught up in post-election violence.[103] In line with its preference for regionally led efforts, Brazil emphasized during the vote that "efforts by the African Union and other regional actors in [Côte d'Ivoire] deserve our strong support."[104]

In the case of Libya, Brazil's explanation of the vote was carefully worded to say that it was not opposed to intervention in principle, but that it could not support the resolution's authorization of force. The statement further explained that Brazil understood and was sensitive to the Arab League's call for strong measures to stop the violence through a no-fly zone but was worried that armed force, as outlined in the resolution, could have "unintended effects of exacerbating tensions on the ground and causing more harm than good to the very same civilians we are committed to protecting."[105] Of special concern were large construction contracts with Brazilian companies and the evacuation of thousands of Brazilian laborers.[106] Furthermore, the statement explicitly cautioned that Brazil's abstention should not be interpreted as a "disregard for the need to protect civilians and respect their rights."[107] Brazil's noncommittal position fell short of its own earlier view, expressed by Foreign Minister Patriota during a trip to India just ten days before the Security Council passed the resolution, that Brazil "will support the international intervention in Libya only if UN approves" it.[108] In the end, however, Brazil's reluctance to back a forced collapse of the Qaddafi regime looks wise in the face of powerful evidence that both the strategy of eliminating Qaddafi and the absence of any serious plan to secure and rebuild the country have spawned nothing but more violence and terrorism, not only in Libya but in the wider Sahel region.

Like India, Brazil's objection to the NATO intervention in Libya, particularly the way in which it was interpreted as a mandate for regime change, largely influenced its unwillingness to condone UN intervention in Syria. It did, however, speak out clearly against Assad's behavior. As violence escalated in Syria in April 2011, the Brazilian Foreign Ministry "denounce[d] the use of force against unarmed demonstrators [and] note[d] that the legitimate desires of the peoples of the Arab world must be met with inclusive political processes and not with military force."[109] Furthermore, the Brazilian government reaffirmed that it was the responsibility of the UN Security Council and regional bodies like the African Union and the League of Arab States to address the impact of political crises in the Middle East and North Africa.[110] This reflects Brazil's preference for South-South solidarity, multilateral action, and an inclination to defer to regional bodies to resolve conflicts, a stance consistent with its own interests as a leader of UNASUL.

Brazil's message hardened slightly when Assad ramped up violence in July and August of that year. Aside from expressing "its repudiation of the use of force against civilian demonstrators," Brazil expressed concern "that Syria has not fulfilled commitments made publicly with regard to the right to demonstrate and the right of expression, and calls on the Syrian Government to move forward with the national dialogue and political reform process with utmost urgency."[111] In her September 2011 address to the UN General Assembly, President Rousseff, the first woman in history to open such a session, condemned the violence in Syria while reasserting Brazil's long-standing demand for diplomatic solutions from a reformed and more credible UN Security Council: "We vehemently repudiate the brutal repression of civilian populations. Yet we remain convinced that for the international community, the use of force must always be a last resort." In a swipe at Washington, she also recalled the "painful consequences of interventions that aggravated existing conflicts [and] allowed terrorism to penetrate into places where it previously did not exist, gave rise to new cycles of violence and multiplied the number of civilian victims."[112]

Despite professed indignation over violence against civilians, Brazil failed to support a proposed Security Council resolution to condemn Syria. In fact, Brazil was largely seen as working to soften tough language proposed by European governments and even advocated for dropping a provision calling on the Assad regime to permit press freedom.[113] Its subsequent support for the first special session on Syria in the UN Human Rights Council in April 2011 underscored its preference for a non-military UN response. Moreover, in negotiating the final text of that session's resolution, Brazil joined several states in calling on "the international community to acknowledge the recent progressive steps and reforms undertaken by the Syrian government."[114] In a similar move, Brazil requested that the Security Council's presidential statement on Syria include a provision "expressing concern about violent reprisals against the Syrian government and attacks against Syrian institutions."[115] This Brazilian desire for balanced language studiously avoids condemnation, sanctions, and use of force in favor of dialogue and nonintervention. To that end, it joined India and South Africa in accepting Assad's invitation to visit Damascus, a move that relieved international pressure on the regime at a critical time and yielded no tangible progress toward resolving the crisis.

Brazil's opposition to a condemnatory Security Council resolution on Syria was not only the result of frustration in the way NATO managed the Libya resolution and an overall desire to maintain support from the global South. In recent years, Brazil and Syria began cultivating improved economic ties. Trade volume between the two states increased by 240 percent between 2002 and 2008 alone,[116] and the Assad government and Brazil established a joint business council in 2010 to encourage more private and public investment. Syria also signed a preliminary agreement with Mercosul in December 2010 to lay the foundation for a free trade agreement.

When it came to the upheaval in Bahrain, Brazil expressed muted concern. In February 2011, the Brazilian government called on all parties to seek a peaceful resolution and "expect[ed] that Bahraini officials refrain from resorting to violence and uphold the freedom of expression and the civil rights of the population."[117] A month later, and amid increased violence, the Brazilian Foreign Ministry largely reiterated its message. In a press statement, Itamaraty called on Bahraini authorities "to engage in dialogue with the protestors and the opposition with a view of breaking current political deadlock . . . [and] reaffirm[ed] the need to uphold civil and political rights, as well as the peaceful right of expression of the Bahraini citizens."[118] Unlike its other rising power counterparts, Brazil's willingness to speak up on Bahrain or Syria was not constrained by energy dependence on Saudi Arabia or Iran since Brazil is relatively energy self-sufficient.[119]

Beyond its defensive role in warding off U.S.-led initiatives to apply coercive tactics to deal with Arab conflicts, Brazil stepped forward in the fall of 2011 with an important new proposal—Responsibility while Protecting (RWP)—that sought to meld the emerging R2P concept with

existing principles of international humanitarian law. In light of the diplomatic storm over NATO intervention in Libya, the proposal sought to
constrain R2P military operations through a set of principles and guidelines such as do no harm, proportionality, precaution, monitoring of
military forces by the UN Security Council, and accountability.[120] While
the Brazilian paper did affirm their support for outside military intervention in defense of human rights in certain circumstances, and reinforced the importance of R2P's other pillars of preventive diplomacy
and technical assistance to states facing domestic conflict, the overall
message was clear: to prevent abuse of R2P for ulterior motives, the
United States and its allies should be tied down in a thicket of rules and
regulations in which use of force would only be authorized after all
other options had been thoroughly exhausted. The Americans quickly
"dismissed the concept out of hand."[121] Although U.S. diplomats came
to regret their initial rejection of the idea,[122] it gained little traction in the
polarizing struggle for UN action on Syria, and the matter was largely
dropped. Brazil, however, remained adamantly opposed to more robust
coercive action against dictators and depravity against civilians. And as
seen in its hands-off policy toward the conflict in Ukraine and its alignment with Moscow and Beijing on Syria, it is prepared to look the other
way to protect its growing ties with Russia and China.[123]

FOREIGN POLICY AND DOMESTIC POLITICS

For much of its modern history, Brazilian foreign policy was hermetic,
left wholly in the hands of Itamaraty, the common term used to refer to
Brazil's highly professional and well-regarded foreign ministry.[124] "Traditionally, Itamaraty had truth and autonomy, and no one challenged
it," explained Sergio Amaral, Brazil's former deputy foreign minister.[125]
Popular opinion toward Brazil's role in the world, to the extent it existed
at all, was one of parochialism and passivity. "The Brazilian people,"
according to former president José Sarney, "have always tended toward
patriotic complacency."[126] Left to their own devices, Brazil's diplomats
carved a relatively modest and benign role in the world. The founding
father of Brazil's modern diplomacy, José Maria da Silva Paranhos, the
Baron of Rio Branco, was known for consolidating regional peace by fi-
nalizing Brazil's borders. He built on this achievement and domestic
prosperity to encourage Brazil to take on a greater role in the region and
on the global stage; he increased Brazil's national prestige abroad; he

emphasized pan-Americanism; and he sought a close alignment with the United States.[127]

As democratic politics took hold in the 1980s and 1990s, presidentialization of foreign policy decisionmaking became a dominant trend.[128] Itamaraty lost some of its autonomy and prestige to the president's own advisers and other ministries. More public attention was paid to Brazil's foreign policy, but in general it remained secondary to larger domestic political and economic agendas. With Lula's ambitious gambit for a greater role on the world stage, however, foreign policy began to get the attention it deserved. "Lula made it high profile, not a sideshow," according to one Brazilian analyst. "It was central to his government's very identity."[129] With greater attention came more diversity of opinion and interest. The media, an important source of information and generally critical commentary on international affairs, is probably the most potent public voice in the growing internal debate on Brazil's role in the world. A high percentage of Brazilians polled in 2011 wanted their government to participate actively in international affairs and believed Brazil would continue to grow more important on the world stage.[130] Majorities also expressed interest in global affairs and favored globalization and foreign direct investment. Social media continues to expand with more than half the population considered active Internet users; average time spent accessing social media on any device rose to three hours and forty-seven minutes in 2014.[131]

As the middle classes have grown, human rights has become a higher-profile topic, and such concerns are often echoed by public intellectuals, nongovernmental organizations, and columnists.[132] Business and industrial groups, particularly in São Paolo, also have begun to mobilize as their own global interests have multiplied. Their influence is still mainly felt in the corridors of power and reflected in Brazil's substantial portfolio of development assistance projects abroad. Brazil's active and well-organized civil society members, including human rights, environment, and social development groups, are increasingly focusing their attention on Brazil's political, economic, and trade relations abroad and have had some tangible success in pressing Itamaraty to change positions on cases like Iran and North Korea. Remarkably, Parliament is largely absent and ineffectual, although there are signs it is becoming more involved in serving as a monitor and watchdog in areas like migration, humanitarian affairs, and Brazil's increasingly internationalized private sector.[133] Religious groups, which generally hold conservative positions on such issues as women's rights and abortion, are increasingly vocal in domestic politics, but are also largely absent from the debate.[134]

Under Presidents Lula and Rousseff, the Workers Party (PT) government has reached out to a wide range of civil society groups on domestic policy concerns in a "social mobilization campaign" that convened eighty conferences and engaged 5 million people, according to a senior adviser. Critics of this approach have complained that the public outreach campaign was a top-down cooptation of social sectors already close to the PT camp.[135] More independent voices emerged, however, in 2005 when the NGO Conectas Direitos Humanos launched a special project focused on human rights in Brazil's foreign policy. It has since become the leading example in the global South of how civil society can mobilize to influence a government's human rights policies. Its argument for tackling what was a traditionally closed space is to treat foreign policy not as a secretive domain for the privileged few, but as any public policy that demands independent scrutiny and public debate. It uses the Brazilian constitution and a new access to information law to provoke public and congressional debate and plays a key role in building an NGO network in the global South focused on human rights and foreign policy. In 2006, it succeeded in its campaign for a multistakeholder platform—the Brazilian Committee on Human Rights and Foreign Policy, composed of representatives from civil society, the Brazilian government, the Senate and House Foreign Relations Committees, and the federal prosecutor for citizen rights—as a tool to stimulate greater transparency and dialogue about Itamaraty's work.[136] In the run-up to the 2010 elections, the committee proposed a "minimum agenda" of ten commitments on human rights and foreign policy to which all presidential candidates publicly pledged and held a follow-up hearing in Congress to discuss implementation measures.[137] The committee put forward a similar agenda in preparation for the 2014 presidential elections and Foreign Minister Luiz Alberto Figueiredo reaffirmed his commitment to increase contact with civil society.[138]

Brazil's decision to change its vote on Iran's human rights record at the UN offers an interesting case study of how activist NGOs from Brazil, Iran, and the United States, media attention, and a more sympathetic Rousseff administration combined to move an issue.[139] In 2009, the controversial reelection of Ahmadinejad as president of Iran, and Lula's embrace of him, provoked much criticism in the Brazilian media. The Baha'i community in Brazil, which had been closely monitoring

Brazil's votes on Iran at the UN, expanded its efforts to engage other NGOs, opposition legislators, and the media to exert pressure on the government to change its approach. Congress agreed to hold a hearing on the situation, and a delegation of human rights defenders from Iran traveled to Brazil for meetings with government officials. Media interviews, op-eds, and online petitions followed. Shortly thereafter, President-elect Rousseff declared her intention to change Brazil's vote on creating a special UN human rights monitor on Iran. A similar strategy was followed on North Korea: testimony from a North Korean victim asking the government to vote in favor of UN monitoring was broadcast in Brazil, a campaign on Facebook and YouTube was launched, and a petition by the regional prosecutor for citizens' rights demanded an explanation from Itamaraty on its earlier abstention votes. Ultimately, Brazil supported the Human Rights Council's decision to create the pathbreaking UN Commission of Inquiry on North Korea.[140]

These cases illustrate the growing attention that key actors in Brazil are paying to the intersection of human rights and foreign policy at a time when its leaders are asserting Brazil's global ambitions in new ways.[141] This trend reflects a generational shift in favor of understanding and influencing Brazil's role in a globalizing world. More and more students are taking up foreign languages (mainly English and Chinese) and international careers with a strong boost from federal assistance programs designed to expand Brazilian capacity in science and technology.[142] Think tanks like Fundação Getulio Vargas, Centro Brasileiro de Relações Internacionais, and the Instituto Fernando Henrique Cardoso are becoming increasingly visible actors in the media and behind the scenes and rate highly in international surveys of think tanks.[143] Igarapé Institute, created in 2008 as a southern think tank offering "progressive alternatives for security and development," is particularly influential with the PT government and serves as the secretariat for a high-level global commission on drug policy that has catalyzed an important debate on reforming counternarcotics strategies.[144] "We Brazilians are just learning about the world now," said one former diplomat. "But it will take at least ten years to catch up."[145]

This is a common refrain among experts who lament Brazil's lack of readiness to take on the more ambitious leadership role promoted by Lula. "We have a good image in the world," explained former president Collor de Mello, who later became chairman of the Brazilian Senate's Foreign Relations Committee, "but we are not prepared yet to be an important player internationally."[146] While Brazil's diplomatic outreach has expanded dramatically over the past decade to 227 foreign post-ings,[147] the foreign ministry faced major budget challenges in 2015. On human rights, Itamaraty's human rights division has fewer than ten pro-fessionals and, until 2014, had no dedicated course on human rights at its diplomatic training academy.[148]

As Brazil prepares itself to play a larger role in the world, it faces its own internal debate about the meaning of democracy and human rights. For adherents of the PT, human rights is first and foremost economic and social rights, and on that score, they vigorously defend Brazil's impres-sive record of improving living standards for the poor while strengthen-ing democracy.[149] They refer to the PT's social mobilization campaigns as a "complement" to the system of representative democracy, which they allege is increasingly a captive of special economic interests.[150] Others contend that Brazil's relatively stable transition to democratic elections and political and civil rights should be the defining feature of Brazil's face to the world. The outbreak of mass protests in 2013 against deficient public services, and Rousseff's quick recognition of their griev-ances and mitigation of police violence (in contrast to Erdoğan's handling of a similar situation in Turkey), was emblematic of both Brazil's striv-ing and unsatisfied middle classes and its handling through democratic processes. While Brazil's leaders recognize the long list of pending human rights concerns at home—prison reform, women's rights, racism, and ac-countability for police violence, for example—and mostly cooperate with UN human rights monitors, they also assert that the country's ris-ing place in the world is due to its ongoing progress on internal reforms. Rousseff's reelection in 2014 largely reflects the public's willingness to bet on continuity of this approach, but her victory was narrow, and pub-lic opinion has turned highly negative in the wake of high-profile cor-ruption scandals and a weakening economy. Notably, foreign policy, let alone human rights, was little debated during the campaign. The leading opposition figure, Aécio Neves, the grandson of former president Tan-credo Neves, raised questions about Brazil's close relationship with Cuba, particularly the deal to import Cuban medical workers, but otherwise focused on domestic policy concerns.[151]

CONCLUSION

In sum, Brazil's traditional preoccupation with sovereignty and strategic autonomy, its ambitious claim for global leadership, and the priority it places on economic development override a growing concern for a more values-oriented approach to foreign policy. While important segments of Brazilian society pay attention to and speak out about Brazil's aloofness when it comes to democracy and human rights abroad, its leaders cling tightly to a different conception of its soft power in the world, one that insists on dialogue, nonintervention, and peaceful settlement of disputes, even when these precepts fail to prevent or mitigate grave violence against civilians or accountability for war crimes. Its current twin economic and political crises have dampened its drive for global leadership and call out for more reforms. But its fundamentals—separation of powers, a thriving press, and proactive civil society—bode well for staying on track as a rising democratic power. As it grows stronger and richer, and more confident on the global stage, Brazil has the potential to become a leader—by its own example at home and by its actions abroad—for a more effective international democracy and human rights order. Until then, its demands for democratization of global governance will continue to be met by reasonable doubts about how Brazil would behave once it got a more secure seat at the table.

CHAPTER FIVE

South Africa

A Conflicted Mediator

> Issues of human rights are central to international relations . . .
> human rights will be the light that guides our foreign affairs. . . .
> South Africa will therefore be at the forefront of global efforts to
> promote and foster democratic systems of government.
>
> NELSON MANDELA, in *Foreign Affairs*,
> November/December 1993

TO UNDERSTAND THE ORIGINS of democratic South Africa's foreign policy, one must begin with its polar opposite—the history of its apartheid
system. The nature of South Africa's regime and its role in the world
changed so fundamentally in 1994 that the tainted vision of an independent racist state serves mainly as a guide for everything the new South
Africa is not.

When South Africa's white rulers declared the separation of the races
as official state doctrine in 1948, the country marked itself as a uniquely
illegitimate power whose system of government flew in the face of the
victory of civilized forces over fascism in World War II. It presented the
first real test of the newly founded United Nations' ability to speak with
one voice against a grave threat to its core values of peace, development,
and human rights. Starting with the activist leadership of independent and
democratic India, which strongly opposed laws South Africa adopted in
1946 discriminating against Indian nationals,[1] the world organization
began a long and ultimately successful effort to use its moral, political,

and economic leverage to pressure apartheid South Africa to change its
ways.

Through a series of measures designed to isolate and punish the apartheid regime for its systematic discrimination against nonwhites, particularly its forced segregation of blacks and whites in 1950, the United
Nations set an early precedent that certain sovereign actions were not
shielded from international opprobrium.[2] After the Sharpeville massacre in 1960, in which sixty-nine blacks were killed by government forces,
and the arrest of African National Congress (ANC) leader Nelson
Mandela in 1962, international momentum built quickly to cut off diplomatic, trade, military, and transport relations with Pretoria. This early
case of UN intervention against the so-called privileged immunity of domestic affairs paved the way for subsequent actions that over time have
continued to erode state sovereignty in the name of human rights. The
sentencing of Mandela and other ANC leaders to life imprisonment in
1964 further galvanized an international solidarity campaign that, to this
day, stands as a high-water mark in global activism for human rights.[3]
The weight of South Africa's history in the international human rights
and democracy order, therefore, is particularly heavy.

The struggle against apartheid also provoked some important line
drawing in international geopolitics that resonates in South African foreign policy today. As global opposition to the racist regime grew, South
Africans in exile mobilized to present themselves as the legitimate representatives of the country in international fora and demanded the expulsion of the white Pretoria government from the United Nations. This
campaign succeeded when the UN General Assembly refused to accept
the credentials of the South African delegation in 1974. But when the UN
Security Council cast its vote on the issue later that year, three permanent members voted against expulsion of South Africa—the United States,
the United Kingdom, and France. As wars for liberation heated up across
southern Africa, China and the Soviet Union sent military and financial
aid to the independence movement. Cuba also jumped into the fray,
sending more than 30,000 soldiers to train, equip, and fight alongside
opposition forces on the continent, particularly in Angola.[4] After many
years of growing pressure, and ongoing human rights violations by
South Africa against its citizens, the Security Council decided by a vote
of 13-0-2 (United States and United Kingdom abstaining) to declare the
new racist constitution of South Africa null and void and urged governments to disregard the results of elections held pursuant to the constitution.[5] The Reagan administration, however, opposed economic sanctions

against South Africa, and in 1986 Reagan vetoed the Comprehensive Anti-Apartheid Act.[6] Such actions are not easily forgotten by today's policymakers in Pretoria.

Elections in South Africa ultimately brought F. W. de Klerk to power as president in 1989. Under the growing weight of comprehensive international sanctions, de Klerk moved quickly to desegregate public facilities, suspend the death penalty, lift some restrictions on the media, and, in 1990, release Nelson Mandela after twenty-seven years in prison. The following year, de Klerk entered multiparty talks, repealed the apartheid laws, and negotiated the transition to democratic elections, which led to the victory of the ANC in free and fair elections in 1994. In response, international sanctions were lifted, and South Africa was welcomed back to the international community. When Mandela spoke from the podium of the UN General Assembly later that year as the first postapartheid president of South Africa, he not only reminded his colleagues of the UN's core purpose but also set the tone for the remainder of his government's foreign policy: "Everywhere on our globe there is an unmistakable process leading to the entrenchment of democratic systems of government. The empowerment of the ordinary people of our world freely to determine their destiny, unhindered by tyrants and dictators, is at the very heart of the reason for the existence of this Organisation."[7]

In his first and only term in power, President Mandela and his ANC colleagues imprinted these overlapping themes of democracy, human rights, and multilateralism onto South Africa's foreign policy. In addition to announcing South Africa's intention to subscribe to the Universal Declaration of Human Rights and other international human rights instruments, Mandela spoke of a values-based agenda that, consonant with the new South African constitution, held out human rights as a central tenet of its foreign policy. "Human rights are the cornerstone of our government policy and we shall not hesitate to carry the message to the far corners of the world," declared then foreign minister Alfred Nzo to the Nonaligned Movement in June 1994. "We have suffered too much ourselves not to do so."[8] Thabo Mbeki, who once served as the ANC's director of international relations and succeeded Mandela as president, went further, calling on African peoples to resist all tyranny in favor of popular rule.[9]

This values-based foreign policy was also a response to the geopolitical context in which the ANC came to power, a time of tectonic shifts in the world—the collapse of the USSR, the liberation of Africa from colonialism, and the expansion of multiparty democracy around the world.[10]

As an early postapartheid government document on South African foreign relations suggested, South Africa sought to grasp the newfound opportunity of the end of isolation and of the bipolar order to flex its new muscles, at once promoting the interests of southern Africa, the broader African continent, and even the entire Southern Hemisphere.[11]

Consistent with postapartheid South Africa's elevation of human rights and democracy in its diplomacy, Mandela and Mbeki embraced their own experiences of a negotiated settlement of disputes, a transitional national unity government, and a truth and reconciliation process as South Africa's calling card abroad. The country's successful transition from civil conflict to democracy, they believed, offered important lessons for others suffering from war and autocratic regimes. Preventive diplomacy and mediation became the operational watchwords of South Africa's efforts to settle a series of conflicts from neighboring Lesotho and Swaziland to Angola, Nigeria, Sudan, and the Democratic Republic of the Congo.[12] Its vision of Africans helping Africans establish a zone of peace through stable democratic systems,[13] a process under way in fits and starts in the 1990s, led it to take a hands-on role in conflict resolution, a priority it continues to follow to this day. As explained by Ambassador Ebrahim Rasool, an ANC activist whose family was forcibly relocated from a whites-only district and later became premier of the Western Cape Province, reconciliation among opposing forces was "the endgame" for South Africa's battle with apartheid and the birth of its democracy. "So we understand that it takes dialogue and negotiation to get there."[14]

A key element of South Africa's goal to promote a more integrated and peaceful continent was the assertion of a rules-based regional order that sought to bring good governance, accountability, and transparency to the fore. At the OAU Summit in 2000, for example, Mbeki actively supported a resolution that denounced coups and barred military leaders from future summits.[15] Mbeki was also instrumental in promoting the concept of an African Renaissance that led to adoption by the region of the New Partnership for Africa's Development (NEPAD)—a strategic framework for Africa's sustainable development, with a special emphasis on women's empowerment. To address Africa's governance challenges, South Africa also lobbied the African Union to adopt the African Peer Review Mechanism (APRM) as a voluntary tool to assess performance in such areas as democracy and political governance. It played a similar role in the Commonwealth, where it supported mandates for the collective protection and promotion of democracy. It deliberately aimed for creating a multilateral system that would reflect both its values and interests in a democratic peace and sustainable development on the continent. It also sought to rebrand Africa on the global stage as an attractive and stable investment for foreign donors. For a region beset with autocrats, civil wars, corruption, and ethnic conflict, this emphasis on human rights, rule of law, and good governance was a deliberate bid for legitimacy in the post–Cold War order and a clear break from the prior emphasis on national sovereignty and pan-African solidarity. Unsurprisingly, it also raised high expectations for postapartheid South Africa's leadership on the regional and global stage.

South Africa's early attempts to apply Mandela's idealistic vision of foreign policy to the continent soon ran into some strong headwinds from Africa's stable of authoritarian rulers. The leading example involved Mandela's decision in 1995 to shift South Africa's approach to the Sani Abacha dictatorship in Nigeria from diplomatic engagement to sanctions and isolation. Mandela spearheaded regional efforts to impose economic sanctions and expel Nigeria from the Commonwealth after Abacha, despite international appeals, executed the leader of the marginalized Ogoni people, Ken Saro-Wiwa. South Africa also exerted diplomatic pressure on the military government to release political prisoners and launch a genuine transition process. After Abacha's death in 1998, both Mandela and Mbeki played critical diplomatic roles in nudging the military to introduce democratic elections, release political prisoners, and recognize political parties.[16]

While these valiant attempts to steer Nigeria toward democracy may have had some effect, they drew a sharp response from other countries in Africa wary of Mandela's perceived moves to regain regional hegemony. Increasingly, senior South African officials were heard bemoaning their limited influence when it came to promoting human rights. "We start from the premise that South Africa is committed to human rights," explained then deputy foreign minister Aziz Pahad. "The problem we face in this regard is the issue of possibilities and limitations on South Africa in the real world. How do we get human rights enforced and implemented in the international environment? There must be a possible contradiction between South-South cooperation and the values which we may want to project."[17] Others complained South Africa was not African enough, too beholden to Western interests, and too arrogant in pushing its own inflated model of democracy.[18]

Over time, South Africa learned some hard lessons about its ability to drive the regional integration agenda toward democratic peace while simultaneously addressing its urgent needs for economic development and greater socioeconomic equity. Its much-criticized handling of the political and economic crisis in neighboring Zimbabwe has left it with a migration crisis on its hands and a damaged reputation in the eyes of both pro-democracy and pro-sovereignty constituencies. It misplayed its hand on the UN Security Council by shielding Zimbabwe and military-ruled Myanmar from scrutiny in 2007–08 and reversing positions on the military intervention against Mu'ammar Qaddafi in Libya in 2011. While development assistance to South Africa and other states in sub-Saharan Africa (primarily from Western donors) markedly increased in the wake of the AU's adoption of NEPAD, South Africa relied primarily on foreign direct investment to meet its goals of faster economic growth and increasingly found itself drawn to the growing allure of China's booming economy. China, in turn, saw South Africa as the route to better access to the rest of Africa. From 2003 to 2012, Chinese foreign direct investment in South Africa jumped a hundredfold, from $44.7 million to $4.7 billion.[19] By the time it joined the BRICS group in 2010, with China's sponsorship, South Africa under President Jacob Zuma (2009–present) had definitively moved to a position of pragmatic realism in which economic development, particularly its beneficial relationship with China, prevailed over its earlier embrace of human rights and democracy as a central pillar of its foreign policy.

South Africa's slow but pronounced shift away from a leadership role on liberal norms was presaged years earlier by Mandela's government as it searched for a redefinition of its national interests. At the time, Foreign Minister Alfred Nzo realistically considered the demands of matching Mandela's ambitions to South Africa's limited capacities: "We are not a great power, and therefore our foreign policy costume, as it were, should be cut according to our cloth."[20] A similar sentiment was expressed by Mandela himself when he urged his fellow leaders at the United Nations to remember South Africans' demands to address the decades of poverty and inequality left in apartheid's wake: "We cannot rest while millions of our people suffer the pain and indignity of poverty in all its forms. At the same time, we turn once more to this world body to say we are going to need your continued support to achieve the goal of the betterment of the conditions of life of the people."[21] This pragmatic mood reflected the ANC government's principal preoccupation with economic growth and job creation as the sine qua non of its program to make good on the ANC's vision of a more equitable country and thereby dominate electoral politics for years to come. Its ongoing underperformance in these areas has increased the pressure for pragmatic short-term measures to close the yawning gap in poverty and inequality, with less concern for the longer-term growth that comes from more open and accountable neighbors and trading partners.

More recent pronouncements of South Africa's foreign policy strategy confirm this softening of an earlier preoccupation with its moral example to the world in favor of a more hard-nosed focus on economic diplomacy and pan-Africanism cloaked in the rhetoric of "a better Africa for a better world." In 2011, its newly named Department of International Relations and Cooperation (DIRCO) adopted a White Paper proclaiming Ubuntu—"the idea that we affirm our humanity when we affirm the humanity of others"—as the central value supporting its focus on South-South solidarity.[22] In foreign policy terms, Ubuntu means a greater emphasis on collaboration, cooperation, and partnership over conflict and competition. Domestic priorities of economic growth, job creation, and competitiveness were placed at the heart of its international strategy, with a consequent focus on actively promoting trade, attracting foreign investments and tourism, and leveraging South Africa's long experience in the global marketplace. Africa's socioeconomic development and political unity are seen as critical to South Africa's own prosperity and security and therefore at the center of its foreign policy. Asia is cited as of growing importance, and Gulf states as key sources for financing infrastructure development, while Europe remains of critical strategic and trade interest. President Zuma's 2015 "state of the nation" address to Parliament almost exclusively spoke of domestic socioeconomic issues and on foreign policy stressed conflict resolution and regional economic integration.[23]

Notably, recent official statements mention democracy not as an aspiration for its neighbors but as a key principle for reforming global governance. The ANC's own policy document released in 2012 echoes and amplifies these themes of "progressive internationalism." Its demands for reform of the global economic and political order and an end to neoconservative unilateralism are couched in the spirit of "revolutionary transformation of society through the power of reason and mass mobilization."[24] On more specific issues like South Africa's denial of visas to the Dalai Lama and support for self-determination for Palestine and the western Sahara, the ANC document defensively states: "The use of independent South Africa's foreign policy choices that coincide with that of the East to cast us as stooges of China and Russia are part of this ideological onslaught on pro-reform stance misconstrued as anti-west behavior."[25] The global economic crisis of 2008, the ANC's guidance document argues, demonstrates the crisis of capitalism and opens opportunities for long-awaited creation of a new international economic order. Such views are not just rhetorical talking points for the party faithful but important principles that influence South Africa's reflexive desire to align itself on the side of upending the status quo in favor of a more balanced global governance system. Only once power imbalances of international organizations are corrected should developing democracies assume greater responsibilities.[26] It is these sentiments that currently seem to have the upper hand in South Africa's international diplomacy.

The many faces of democratic South Africa's foreign policy heritage, rooted in a complex international struggle for liberation from apartheid, allow its leaders to emphasize different strands to suit the circumstances. Currently, it prefers to underscore a flexible and open approach to constructing "a better world." As Foreign Minister Nkoana Mashabane stated in 2012, South Africa's foreign policy is guided by the words of Oliver Tambo, one of South Africa's most revered independence leaders. "We will have a South Africa which will live in peace with its neighbours and with the rest of the world," declared Tambo in 1976.[27] "It will base its foreign relations on the principles of non-interference and mutually advantageous assistance among the peoples of the world."[28]

While the political structure of South Africa gives the president the predominant role in designing and executing its multifaceted foreign policy agenda, its main lines are not drawn in a presidential vacuum. In addition to the significant voice ANC party leaders have in shaping the style and substance of the government's policies, expert voices from academia and think tanks, members of Parliament, nongovernmental organizations, labor unions, and the media are increasingly consulted and heard. These actors have provoked a lively debate on the tensions inherent in Mandela's earlier quest for moral realism and have had some influence in a limited number of cases in steering its policies toward more normative causes. But the central trend of the country's current international relations is clear: foreign policy is driven by the demand for economic growth and good jobs at home, and this means ever closer ties to China and the BRICS while also maintaining strong ties with the West.

A recent public opinion survey on South Africa's role in the world strongly supports the government's current approach. A combined total of 60 percent of respondents said promoting economic growth in South Africa and attracting foreign investment should be the country's main goals in its relations abroad.[29] Interestingly, another 24 percent wanted the government to promote a more equal distribution of power and wealth in the world, while only 16 percent cited promoting human rights as a top goal. The survey also showed that a strong majority of South Africans want the nation to play a more active role in world affairs, particularly in resolving conflicts and giving aid to other countries in Africa, and identify the African Union as more important to South Africa than the United Nations.[30] China came out on top as the country South Africa should pursue as a close partner, above the United States and Europe.[31] How South Africa reconciles these varied identities and goals while remaining faithful to its founders' concern for human rights will determine its credibility as a leading voice for international liberal norms.

SOUTH AFRICA IN ITS NEIGHBORHOOD

The pattern of early support for democratic trends in Africa followed by a more realistic strategy emphasizing conflict resolution, multilateralism, and economic integration is particularly evident in democratic South Africa's behavior in its region. As noted earlier, Mandela's demands for human rights and democratic accountability in military-run Nigeria, while faithful to the new South Africa's ideals, were met with derision and concerted opposition from others in the region. In neighboring Lesotho, it took the lead in constructing a coalition of Southern African Development Community states (SADC) to exert diplomatic pressure in 1994 to head off a reversal of democratic gains. When conditions deteriorated into civil violence in 1998, South Africa ramped up its involvement, this time with military force and joined only by Botswana, and stayed until elections were held in May 2002. Throughout the Lesotho intervention, South Africa contended it was "inspired" by SADC principles of responding to a neighbor facing threats to its democracy.[32] These principles, which later included a commitment to collective electoral observation, were established at the initiative of Pretoria.[33] After another round of political conflict in Lesotho in 2014, South Africa, conscious of past charges of hegemonic intervention in its neighbor, chose a less confrontational approach. Deputy President Cyril Ramaphosa, serving as special envoy on SADC's behalf, was dispatched to help facilitate a negotiated resolution that led to elections that SADC's observation mission, led by the South African foreign minister, declared free and fair.[34]

Zimbabwe, long under the thumb of liberation hero Robert Mugabe, presents a particularly revealing case for South Africa's proclaimed roles as a champion of both democracy and conflict resolution in the region. As South Africa began to assert greater leadership in SADC, which included an effort to integrate military and human security and promote democratization in the region, it was also involved in mediating the spreading conflict in the Democratic Republic of the Congo (DRC). Infighting over SADC's mission soon flared between Mandela and Mugabe who had taken opposing sides in the DRC, stalemating the initiative.[35] Pretoria's decision to abstain from the Zimbabwe-Angola-Namibia military alliance supporting Laurent Kabila's leadership in the DRC weakened its influence as a mediator in Kinshasa. Kabila went so far as to call South Africans "puppets of the aggressors."[36] In its defense, Foreign Minister Nzo stressed Pretoria's wish for a government of national unity in the DRC, as it was able to secure for itself.[37]

When regional and global attention then turned to Mugabe's own behavior in Zimbabwe, the inherent tensions in South Africa's strategy quickly became apparent. It joined SADC in sending electoral observers to parliamentary elections in 2001 but remained largely silent in the face of electoral violence and intimidation perpetrated by the Mugabe government. In March 2002, Mbeki, joined by the leaders of Malawi and Mozambique, became more vocal in chastising Mugabe's rough treatment of the opposition ahead of the presidential elections. Although SADC declared the elections "substantially free and fair," other independent observers saw it differently,[38] pressuring a reluctant South Africa to concede to a one-year suspension of Zimbabwe from the Commonwealth.

South Africa, however, remained avowedly opposed to the economic sanctions against Zimbabwe advocated by a growing domestic constituency and Western countries.[39] Instead it joined Nigeria in an effort to mediate between Mugabe and the opposition for a government of national unity. This was part of a deliberate strategy by Mbeki to deploy soft behind-the-scenes diplomacy with Mugabe, who made some nods toward accepting international observers and lowering the violence but generally became more obstructionist at each step down the authoritarian ladder. Torn between its image as a beacon for democracy in Africa and its fear of being labeled as a regional hegemon, Pretoria chose "strategic ambiguity," in the words of Christopher Landsberg. Mbeki was "pursuing a prudent two-pronged strategy. On the one hand, he is sending a tough, unwavering message that the new game in town is democratization." On the other, to avoid South Africa becoming isolated, Mbeki was forging partnerships with neighbors and building up regional institutions to help lift Africa closer to international standards of economic growth and development.[40]

As developments in Zimbabwe went from bad to worse, and criticism of South Africa's soft touch got louder, Mbeki became more intransigent. When the Commonwealth moved to suspend Zimbabwe again in 2003, Mbeki tried unsuccessfully to orchestrate the removal of the organization's secretary general in protest. When it sat on the UN Security Council in 2006–08, South Africa worked with Russia and China to block measures to condemn Zimbabwe's ongoing crackdown on opposition activists. After the 2008 elections, which SADC and AU electoral observers judged as neither free nor fair owing to serious violence and irregularities, Mbeki was forced to step up his mediation efforts. He managed to help the parties negotiate a weak national unity government that ultimately failed (some say in part because of South Africa's unwillingness to enforce key provisions; others blame Mugabe, who even refused to accept a generous financial package because it had political conditions attached).[41] As the situation continued to deteriorate, an obviously frustrated ANC declared in 2012 that it is "imperative that we do not begin to think that the challenges facing Zimbabwe can only be overcome by elections." It went on to insist, nonetheless, that the Pretoria government play "a pivotal role in constructing an international consensus on the conditions for a democratic election in Zimbabwe," both by pushing for a change of policy on sanctions and on better cooperation from Mugabe, under the direction of SADC.[42] Ultimately, Mugabe went his own way, managing to win reelection to his seventh term in office in 2013 despite opposition and international charges of misconduct, inflated voter rolls, disenfranchisement of urban voters, and state media bias. President Zuma congratulated the ninety-one-year-old Mugabe on his victory and urged all parties to accept an outcome that observers (chosen by the government) declared "an expression of the will of the people."[43]

The failure of SADC to resolve the Zimbabwe situation in accordance with the organization's own principles of democracy and human rights points to a larger challenge in consolidating southern Africa as a political, economic, security, and development community. Disagreements on how to integrate SADC's security cooperation and democratization agendas, exacerbated by the conflict in the DRC, led to compromises that marginalized the latter, leaving no detailed provisions for promoting democracy and human rights.[44] While significant progress has been made on the economic front with the implementation of the SADC free trade area, the larger SADC integration agenda, including targets of a monetary union in 2016 and a single currency in 2018, remains behind schedule. South Africa, which represents a quarter of Africa's gross domestic product and the gateway to southern Africa's 160 million people, is a natural leader of the group but feels a sense of debt to the bloc of former "frontline states" that provided critical support to the antiapartheid movement. A 1969 revenue-sharing agreement to compensate Botswana, Lesotho, Swaziland, and Namibia for the trade-diverting effects of apartheid South Africa's protectionist tariff structure, although revised in 2002, still provides important benefits to these states, benefits some believe are too heavy a drain on South Africa's treasury. The situation leaves South Africa divided between its own economic interests and its role as a benevolent hegemon still paying off debts for the sins of its predecessor regime.[45]

In terms of its foreign policy in the region, this dilemma has made it harder for South Africa to play a more robust role as an overt promoter of democracy and human rights. Mugabe's ability to cast his aggressive and at times violent campaign for land redistribution as the final stage of Zimbabwe's liberation struggle, and to link human rights to a Western plot to disempower black Africans through sanctions and pressure, put South Africa and SADC on the defensive. They downplayed Zimbabwe's human rights violations in favor of dialogue (national and international), leading Western governments to accuse their African counterparts of betraying their AU and NEPAD commitments to democratic governance. Democratic backsliding in traditionally stable Botswana, and South Africa's silence in response, is a more recent example of this tension.[46] The incomplete democratization process in several SADC states and authoritarian character of regimes like Swaziland mean that, in the end, prospects for SADC's cohesiveness as a group of self-identified democracies concerned as much with human security as national security and economic integration appear bleak.[47]

Outside the immediate zone of southern Africa, Pretoria has engaged in a range of activities that in broad strokes support democratization as an instrumental component of peace and stability. Under both Mandela and Mbeki, it led initiatives at the continental level to establish norms that characterized democratic governance and human rights as essential conditions for regional integration. These norms were put to the test after the military coup against the elected government of Côte d'Ivoire in December 1999. South Africa, in partnership with the newly elected government of Olusegun Obasanjo in Nigeria, joined a ten-nation OAU committee to increase pressure on the military regime to resign in favor of an inclusive government that would organize elections. South Africa's response to a military coup in Niger that same year, however, was less evident.

In response to this spate of coups, an OAU Summit in 2000 formally adopted a South African–led resolution barring from future summits any government that came to power through unconstitutional means, which later was ratified in the AU's Constitutive Act.[48] The AU's founding charter also commits African governments to intervene in cases of war crimes, genocide, or crimes against humanity. In the same vein, South Africa subsequently led the effort to establish an AU Charter on Democracy, Elections, and Governance, a document that commits African governments to a long list of core democratic principles and practices, including mandatory invitations to AU electoral observation missions, cooperation to prosecute coup plotters nationally or in the AU courts, and mandatory sanctions on any state that is proved to have instigated or supported an unconstitutional change of government in another state.[49] Adoption of the charter by all African states, however, is lagging behind the impressive number that have ratified the African Charter on Human and People's Rights.[50]

Despite repeated efforts to mediate the conflict in Côte d'Ivoire, political stability there remained elusive. In 2005, after years of conflict that killed thousands of people and left millions homeless, the United Nations imposed an arms and diamond sales embargo while Mbeki helped broker a peace deal through a series of talks hosted in Pretoria. One of the thorniest issues in the negotiations was the eligibility of opposition politician Alassane Ouattara to compete for the presidency against President Laurent Gbagbo. The United Nations, prodded by France (Côte d'Ivoire's former occupier), later dispatched a large contingent of peacekeeping forces to provide security for another round of elections that eventually were held in December 2010. During South Africa's tenure on the UN Security Council in 2007–08, it endorsed all eight resolutions on Côte d'Ivoire condemning human rights violations, extending sanctions, and renewing the UN's peacekeeping mission. Despite these efforts to prevent conflict, Côte d'Ivoire again erupted in flames after the 2010 elections that UN, African, and other international observers declared Ouattara won. By contrast, South Africa, faithful to its preference to remain as a neutral arbiter, claimed the elections were "inconclusive." "Our view is that we don't demand that one leader should go," stated Foreign Minister Maite Nkoana-Mashabane in an effort to protect South Africa's role as a leading mediator in the crisis. South Africa, represented on the AU mediation body by former president Mbeki and President Zuma, then placed a warship off Côte d'Ivoire's shores and put forward proposals that departed from the West African, EU, and UN consensus that Ouattara be declared the winner, drawing criticism from the Economic Community of West African States (ECOWAS) and human rights groups.[51] "South Africa's involvement thus far—in mediating the Ivorian conflict—raises profound questions about whose interests it is pursuing . . . Sadly the evidence suggests that Pretoria's sympathies are ambiguous at best, and at times publicly lean toward defending Gbagbo," according to Human Rights Watch.[52]

Its rivalry with Nigeria for regional leadership was also a factor in South Africa's demand for a negotiated settlement in Côte d'Ivoire. In addition, it strongly objected to France's ongoing intervention in the conflict. "The UN," according to an ANC policy document, "was turned into a partisan player working in cahoots with a former colonial power to unseat the incumbent president before the electoral disputes were resolved."[53] In the face of overwhelming pressure to address the spreading conflict, including from other African states, South Africa reluctantly voted for the UN Security Council resolution authorizing use of force to protect civilians, which ultimately led to Gbagbo's forcible removal from his heavily guarded hotel room by French forces and transfer to the International Criminal Court (ICC) in The Hague for prosecution on charges of crimes against humanity.[54]

As evidenced by these two prominent episodes on the continent, South Africa strongly prefers playing the role of arbiter of Africa's conflicts, and avoids taking sides in others' domestic disputes in favor of negotiated settlements and national unity pacts, similar to its own rational experience. It continues to invest significant capital in conflict mediation in the region, serving as SADC's official liaison to deal with political crises in Madagascar and Lesotho, as well as Zimbabwe; SADC has also allocated responsibility to South Africa for helping settle conflicts in south

Sudan and Sri Lanka, efforts led by Deputy President Cyril Ramaphosa.[55] Since Mandela's election, South African presidents have appointed no fewer than thirteen special envoys to seek negotiated settlements in fifteen different conflicts in and outside the region.[56] To protect its leadership role at the AU level, South Africa lobbied hard for the election of Nkosazana Dlamini-Zuma, its former foreign minister and ex-wife of President Jacob Zuma, to head up the AU Commission in July 2012. It also continues to invest diplomatic and financial resources in consolidating the region's efforts to upgrade democratic governance through NEPAD and the African Peer Review Mechanism.

SOUTH AFRICA IN THE WORLD

We have learned from our own experience domestically, as well as in our efforts on the Continent, that the peaceful resolution of disputes is preferable to the destruction and furies unleashed by military interventions . . . as uncomfortable as it is, parties should engage with their enemies to find solutions as the zero-sum approach to conflict has an expensive and bloody price tag paid by the people on the ground.

DEPUTY FOREIGN MINISTER EBRAHIM EBRAHIM, in
"Celebrating 19 Years of South Africa's
Foreign Policy," July 8, 2013

As the postapartheid governments looked beyond South Africa's own complicated neighborhood, they found more hospitable terrain for its global ambitions elsewhere. It discovered in Europe and North America a high degree of sympathy and moral indebtedness to Mandela's vision of a nonracial democracy to lead the continent and willing donors to help underwrite the African Renaissance project. In the global South, particularly with partners Brazil and India but also increasingly with China and Russia, South Africa secured new friendships allied around the goal of a more multipolar world. With a relatively peaceful transition to democracy and the most advanced economy in the region, South Africa had an enviable path to greater global prominence. As it entered powerful chambers like the UN Security Council (2007–08 and 2010–12), and as the only African country in the G-20 and the BRICS, South Africa touted its "unique historic political transformation process to become a constitutional democracy . . . as a unique contribution to the world."[57] In preparation for its hosting of the fifth BRICS Summit in Durban in 2013, South Africa also projected itself as the world's gateway to Africa and vice versa. It promoted its ranking as the world's richest country in terms of mineral reserves, "contributing significantly to the BRICS resource pool," and its sophisticated financial markets.[58]

In light of this ambitious geostrategic approach, it comes as little surprise that South Africa has had a difficult time adhering to Mandela's vision of human rights and democracy as central to its foreign policy. To its credit, South Africa has taken many positions that contribute positively to the international peace and human rights order. In addition to its leadership in conflict resolution and peacekeeping, it has won praise for its role in advancing the Arms Trade Treaty, which regulates the international trade in conventional weapons,[59] and played a prominent role in the successful 1997 Ottawa anti-land-mines talks. Although it hosted a controversial UN conference against racism in 2001 in Durban and the Durban review conference in 2009 (which drew boycotts from nine countries for allowing Iran to declare Zionism as tantamount to racism), it has on balance championed progressive norms to address racial discrimination, including the UN Convention to Eliminate Racial Discrimination. It consistently supported the ICC, adopted progressive implementing legislation giving force to the Rome Statute domestically,[60] and refused to sign a bilateral agreement with the United States that would give its personnel immunity from ICC prosecution. On the Israel-Palestine conflict, an issue with domestic advocates on both sides, it comes down squarely in favor of the Palestinian cause for statehood in peace with Israel based on pre-1967 borders, with East Jerusalem as its capital. In response to Israel's punishing treatment of Gaza in 2014, South Africa urged immediate cessation of air strikes and pledged $1 million for humanitarian relief after the conflict subsided.

On the difficult question of enforcing the ICC's arrest warrant for Sudanese president al-Bashir, South Africa initially walked a fine line. It invited al-Bashir to President Zuma's inauguration in 2009 but later advised that an arrest warrant had been issued and would be served if he entered South Africa.[61] More recently, however, as the regional mood toward the ICC's perceived targeting of African cases has turned sour, Zuma has made clear that he roundly disapproves of the ICC's prosecution of al-Bashir—or any other sitting African leader suspected of atrocities.[62] When the African Union adopted a resolution against criminal charges for any serving African head of state, largely a result of the uproar over the ICC indictment of Kenyan president Uhuru Kenyatta, South Africa was silent; Zuma later defended the action in the name of promoting stability.[63] In June 2015, South Africa welcomed al-Bashir to an African Union Summit in Johannesburg and let him leave the country despite the ICC's arrest warrant and a High Court order to bar him from leaving the country while it considered arguments on the matter.

At the UN Human Rights Council, South Africa has preferred to complain more about selectivity and hypocrisy of Western powers than about human rights violations committed in specific countries. It sided with India, Indonesia, and its colleagues in the NAM, OIC, and Africa Group against country-specific scrutiny in principle and in practice. Except for the HRC's special treatment of Israel's occupation of Palestine, South Africa consistently has voted against or abstained on most country-specific situations, including whether to hold special sessions on Myanmar, the DRC, and Sri Lanka.[64] An in-depth study of South Africa's positions at the HRC concluded that South Africa falls in line closely with its Africa Group colleagues Algeria and Egypt as "a defender of oppressive regimes and an obstacle to the international promotion of human rights."[65] In HRC sessions in March and September 2014, South Africa sided with Belarus in tabling damaging amendments to resolutions on peaceful protest and civil society protection.[66]

On other thematic issues, South Africa repeatedly joined OIC in support of resolutions on defamation of religions that undermined core values of freedom of expression and religion;[67] the resolution has since been sidelined by a more balanced series of resolutions on containing hate speech. In defending its stance, a senior South African diplomat explained, "We supported the resolution because the West was painting Islam as a religion of terrorism and extremism. We didn't want to align with this bias." Unfortunately, he added, OIC eventually "fell apart on this issue."[68] South Africa was alone in voting against a resolution on protection of religious minorities because the resolution failed to criticize the media's role in fostering negative stereotypes, and supported other resolutions that weakened freedom of expression.[69] Exceptionally, South Africa in 2001 played a leading role with Brazil in a pathbreaking HRC resolution on rights of LGBT persons, a step it took under significant domestic and international pressure; subsequently it suffered blowback from its African colleagues. It then avoided taking up the mantle on a follow-up resolution, eventually ceding sponsorship to Brazil and Chile in 2014.[70] As one critic put it, South Africa "must stop playing geopolitics . . . move beyond fingerpointing" and "show true human rights leadership" at the UN.[71]

South Africa's tricky balancing act between values and practices was put to the test during the Arab awakening, a time of initial enthusiasm for international action to promote the region's aspirations for democratization followed by skepticism and outright opposition to the use of force to save lives. South Africa at first showed its preference for African-led mediation efforts while also supporting, reluctantly, UN-sanctioned intervention. However, when these two approaches were at odds—as they were in Libya—the pan-African solidarity instinct won out.

As popular protests unfolded in Tunisia and Egypt, South Africa remained largely on the sidelines. Unwilling to take a position before Mubarak relinquished power, the South African foreign ministry issued a statement calling on the "government and people of Egypt to seek a speedy and peaceful resolution to the current crisis."[72] After Mubarak stepped down, President Zuma endorsed the decision, saying that the Egyptian strongman's departure showed he had "thought like a leader" and would allow Egyptians to "pick up the situation and build a government that will be based on the will of the people."[73] He reiterated South Africa's support for homegrown political transitions in his state of the nation address later that month, explaining that "we firmly believe that the course and the content of the transition as well as the destiny that these sister countries choose, should be authored by them," while also offering support to the political reform movements.[74] When the elected government in Cairo collapsed in the face of a military-led coup in 2013, South Africa supported Egypt's suspension from the African Union, urged its cooperation with an AU high-level panel commissioned to support restoration of the constitutional order, and offered to share the lessons it learned from its own transition from apartheid to multiparty democracy.[75]

South Africa's response to the crisis in Libya illustrated its inconsistent approach to popular uprisings and regime change in the Arab world. South Africa initially joined international condemnation of Qaddafi's threats against civilians and supported UN intervention under the emerging responsibility to protect doctrine. As violence escalated, the South African foreign ministry called on "the government and people of Libya to seek a speedy and peaceful resolution to the current crisis in accordance with the will of the people."[76] A few days later, South Africa joined unanimous support for Security Council resolution 1970, which extended sanctions on Libya and reiterated its support for the "will of the people."[77] Unlike India and Brazil, South Africa also voted for the Security Council's second resolution on Libya authorizing the use of force to protect civilians and the implementation of a no-fly zone. Its explanation of vote illustrated South Africa's concern for both protecting democracy and human rights and ensuring the sovereign integrity of a nation. "[A] holistic political solution must be found that would respect democracy; political reform; justice; human rights as well as the socio-economic development needs of the people of Libya; in order to ensure long-term peace and stability" in Libya.[78] The statement considered the Security Council resolution appropriate in order to implement the previous resolution but added that its support came "with the necessary caveats to preserve the sovereignty and territorial integrity of Libya; and rejecting any foreign occupation or unilateral military intervention under the pretext of protection of civilians."[79]

As the NATO military intervention proceeded alongside a growing chorus of statements that "Qaddafi must go," South Africa reversed course and became highly critical of Western powers' alleged contravention of the UNSC's original mandate. In part, the government was responding to domestic criticism, including within the ANC, about authorizing the use of force. Parliamentary members of the United Democratic Movement accused the government of being "duped into supporting military intervention by the [NATO]" and insisted the resolution "had now become about regime change and not about saving civilian lives."[80] The government also faced criticism from civil society: thousands of union-organized protesters gathered in Pretoria to object to the NATO intervention in early July.[81]

South Africa was particularly incensed that the NATO intervention sidelined any chance of it playing a leadership role in the AU-led mediation effort in Libya. Established on March 10, 2011, the AU ad hoc high-level Committee on Libya was cochaired by President Zuma and the presidents of Mauritania, Congo, Mali, and Uganda. In line with its mandate to "engage with all parties in Libya and continuously assess the evolution of the situation on the ground [and] facilitate an inclusive dialogue among the Libyan parties on the appropriate reforms," the committee met with Qaddafi, the Libyan Transnational Council (TNC), and rebels in Benghazi during two trips to Libya.[82] In addition, the committee was mandated to engage other multilateral partners like the League of Arab States, the United Nations, the OIC, and the European Union in

an effort to find a resolution to the crisis. The text of the AU communiqué deplored violence in Libya but also reaffirmed the AU's "strong commitment to the respect of the unity and territorial integrity of Libya, as
well as its rejection of any foreign military intervention, whatever its
form."[83]

As the NATO intervention in Libya escalated, Zuma distanced South
Africa from its vote in favor of the Security Council resolution and insisted on an African-led solution. Zuma concluded that the NATO intervention had overstepped its mandate and "undermine[d] the efforts of
the African Union in finding solutions to the problems facing its member
states."[84] The AU's efforts to resolve the conflict, however, were not finding much traction. Qaddafi had accepted the AU road map but the TNC
rejected the five-point proposal because it failed to demand that Qaddafi
relinquish power.[85] By the sixth meeting of the high-level committee in
June 2011, the AU continued to call on the United Nations to work with
the regional body to implement its road map, demanded a political solution to the conflict, and insisted that the Security Council resolution was
adopted to protect civilians and was "not about regime change and as-
sassinations . . . [and] believed the implementation [of the resolution]
should NOT go against the letter and spirit" of its original intention.[86]

Even when Qaddafi's exit was imminent in October 2011, and the
NATO mission was claiming victory, South Africa continued to condemn the intervention. In an effort to ease domestic criticism for inconsistency and hypocrisy, South Africa began to insist that it supported
humanitarian intervention in principle but opposed member state manip-
ulation of the SC mandate.[87] During a public speech on the topic, Deputy Foreign Minister Ebrahim Ebrahim explained that "NATO misused
the UN resolution to carry out bombing escapades on a defenseless African country . . . this action completely ignored the other important aspects of the resolution."[88] Invoking deep frustration at letting NATO's
actions torpedo its own efforts to resolve the matter through negotiations, Ebrahim bemoaned that "it is unfortunate that right from the
start the AU was never given an opportunity to lead in finding a solution
in Libya. The African Leadership, against all odds, continued to seek to
engage all parties . . . All of this never worked because powers outside
the continent were determining the future of Libya, and ceaselessly
worked not for a political solution but regime change."[89] Ebrahim also
pinned blame on the failure to transform the global system of governance: "Powerful states remain dominant and imposing over the power-

less."[90] South Africa—like other rising democracies—used the Libya episode to justify criticism of the Northern-dominated system and to demand its own seat at the table.[91] In contrast, the ANC's international relations statement found fault with "the slow response by the African Union [to the crisis in Libya] and its inability to get its point across cannot be excused."[92]

Similar to India and Brazil, South Africa's concern with NATO's overstep in Libya directly influenced its unwillingness to endorse Security Council action on Syria. After the Hama massacres of July 31, 2011, the South African foreign ministry declared that "the only solution to the current crisis is through a Syrian-led political process that is inclusive, with the aim of effectively addressing the legitimate aspirations and concerns of the population which will allow for the full exercise of fundamental freedoms, including that of expression and peaceful assembly."[93] Furthermore, the statement expressed appreciation for "the actions already taken by the Syrian Government in launching dialogue as well as the reform measures already announced" and called on the government to implement said reforms.[94] Deputy Minister Ebrahim Ebrahim hosted his Syrian counterpart later that week, when he was briefed on the ongoing situation. According to Ebrahim, South Africa took the opportunity to "welcome the announcement by President Assad to allow for multi-party democracy in Syria, and urge the government to speed up the reform process."[95] In line with South Africa's preference for multilateral diplomacy, Ebrahim reiterated its endorsement of the Security Council's presidential statement on Syria and suggested, ironically, that the UN Human Rights Council would be the appropriate place to continue the discussion (South Africa routinely voted against country-specific resolutions at the Council).

In subsequent efforts to reach UNSC consensus on Syria, South Africa consistently abstained or sided with Russia and China in opposing more consequential actions. When explaining its abstention on an October 2011 Security Council vote that would have condemned Syrian authorities for their violent crackdown but drew vetoes from China and Russia, South Africa expressed concern over recent Security Council "resolutions [that] have been abused and [whose] implementation went far beyond the mandate of what was intended . . . this [Syria] resolution should not be part of a hidden agenda to yet again institute regime change."[96] South Africa maintained its neutral position in November 2011 at the UNGA's Third Committee when it abstained on a resolution condemning Syria's human rights abuses.[97] Likewise, it has consistently abstained on resolutions on Syria at the UN Human Rights Council. South Africa did, however, publicly announce that it was "alarmed at the escalations that took place" in Syria and "condemned the use of chemical weapons," welcoming Syria's accession to the Chemical Weapons Convention in 2013.[98] As one senior South African diplomat explained it, the debacle in Libya and the failure of President Obama to enforce his supposed red line in Syria "is a delicious moment for us. It allows a real discussion on tactics and strategy. We gave the United States the benefit of the doubt on UN intervention in Libya. This has had an inhibiting effect on South African policy going forward."[99]

As on Syria, South Africa has been silent on Bahrain's repression of the majority Shi'ite opposition. There were isolated reports of South African protesters gathering at the Saudi Arabian embassy in Pretoria to oppose the use of violence by Bahraini and Saudi troops. The demonstrators also "demanded that the South African government make clear its position on the crackdown in Bahrain."[100] But their demands led to no apparent action. Not surprisingly, South Africa's silence on Bahrain is likely rooted in its concern for stable relations with its major trading partner, Saudi Arabia. South Africa imports 67 percent of the oil it consumes and nearly a third of it comes from Saudi Arabia, a key ally of Bahrain's.[101] South Africa's trade with the Gulf nation grew nearly 30 percent from 2010 to 2011.[102] Similar circumstances are probably influencing South Africa's reticence on Syria. In 2011, South Africa imported more than a quarter of its oil from Syria's closest regional ally, Iran—South Africa's largest supplier of oil and sixth largest supplier of goods overall at the time.[103] Iran's role as supplier to South Africa grew more than 10 percent in recent years.[104] Following U.S. and EU sanctions against Iran in 2012, South Africa halted imports from Iran (substituting with oil from Saudi Arabia, Nigeria, Angola, and others) and as of April 2015 had still not resumed imports from Iran.[105]

While Egypt and Libya have no major trading relationships with South Africa, their economic livelihood is essential to ongoing plans to create an African free trade zone. Originally launched in 2008, the "Cape to Cairo" trade bloc plans to integrate the twenty-six nations, 600 million people, and nearly $1 trillion market of the Southern African Development Community (SADC), East African Community (EAC), and Common Market for Eastern and Southern Africa (COMESA) into one free trade zone. South Africa is the leading driver of this effort and forged ahead with its second meeting in June 2011 amid revolutions in the region. After years of discussions, an agreement was reached in June 2015 to establish the Tripartite Free Trade Area (TFTA), although parliaments in each member country must approve the deal, which is expected to take until at least 2017.[106] This long-term pan-African plan further contributes to South Africa's preference for mediation and continental unity.

Despite South Africa's decision to champion mediation and neutrality over more decisive action to protect human rights during the Arab awakening, its foreign policy practitioners continued to insist that these values play a central role in the formulation of its policy. In a March 2011 discussion at the University of Pretoria on South Africa's goals as a member of the UN Security Council, Marius Fransman, deputy minister of international relations and cooperation, said South Africa's work at the body would "be built on our domestic priorities and on our country's vision of an African continent that is prosperous, peaceful, democratic, non-racial, non-sexist and united and which contributes to a world that is just and equitable."[107] In another speech a few months later, the same official again declared that "the advancement of human rights and the promotion of democracy are pillars on which South Africa's foreign policy rests."[108] Another senior South African diplomat put it differently: When it comes to foreign policy and human rights, he said, "there will always be double standards. The question is how to manage them. We need to say that human rights matter and have a global compact on how to do it. But it cannot be done in the current system, especially after Libya and Côte d'Ivoire."[109]

South Africa's pragmatic approach to its climb up the international ladder is most evident in its ever-closer ties to China. Currently its number one trading partner, China has become a critical export market for South Africa's abundance of coal, gold, and other commodities. Even before the explosive growth in economic ties, the postapartheid government aimed for closer political and diplomatic ties. It was Mandela who shifted official recognition of China from Taiwan to Beijing in 1997 in part as recognition of China's support for the antiapartheid movement.[110] Since then, Pretoria initially was cautious and more recently opposed to any outright criticism of China's human rights record. It notoriously denied a visa to the Dalai Lama to attend Archbishop Desmond Tutu's eightieth birthday in 2011, a move that led Tutu, a hero of South Africa's democratic transition, to claim the government was "worse than the apartheid government."[111] When Tutu sought to organize a meeting in

2014 for other Nobel Peace Prize winners in Cape Town, the Dalai Lama was denied a visa again, forcing the meeting's cancellation.[112] In both cases, the government remained silent, leading skeptics to assume that the denial was due to pressure from Beijing. As one former diplomat put it, "Why not just tell the truth: China is the priority."[113] In a similar episode, when human rights defenders staged a moment of silence for Chinese activist Cao Shunli at China's appearance before the Human Rights Council's peer review, South Africa joined China in decrying the protest, calling it a "dangerous precedent" incompatible with the rules of procedure.[114] On Myanmar, South Africa joined China at the UN Security Council in blocking consideration of the political, security, and human rights crisis in the country; China had made major inroads in Myanmar in the wake of a Western-led sanctions regime against the military government.

Cuba has similarly benefited from South Africa's willingness to avoid criticizing its human rights record. Fidel Castro was a strong supporter of the ANC's fight against the apartheid government and the roots of solidarity run deep. Upon his visit to Cuba in 1991, shortly after his release from prison, Nelson Mandela declared:

> The Cuban people hold a special place in the hearts of the people of Africa. The Cuban internationalists have made a contribution to African independence, freedom, and justice, unparalleled for its principled and selfless character. From its earliest day, the Cuban revolution has itself been a source of inspiration to all freedom-loving peoples . . . We in Africa are used to being victims of countries wanting to carve up our territory or subvert our sovereignty. It is unparalleled in African history to have another people rise to the defence of one of us . . . For the Cuban people internationalism is not merely a word but something that we have seen practiced to the benefit of large sections of humankind![115]

Under President Zuma, South Africa offered an economic aid package to Havana in 2010 with no apparent political conditions; it also provided 24 million rand to Sierra Leone to fund Cuban doctors involved in medical services.[116] In 2014, South Africa committed a further $31 million of economic assistance for Cuba to buy seeds, purchase goods from South Africa, and establish an $18.75 million line of credit. In response, one opposition MP pointed out the "tragic irony" that the funds were going to a "regime that denies its citizens the same democratic freedoms that were so hard won in South Africa," but South Africa's official policy is still one of support of (or at least nonopposition to) Cuba.[117]

Beyond the mixed diplomatic record, South Africa under Mbeki began to establish development assistance schemes to lend technical assistance and other forms of cooperation to its neighbors interested in learning from its own transition experience. In 2000, Mbeki established the African Renaissance and International Cooperation Fund with $30 million for projects to promote democracy and good governance, conflict prevention, socioeconomic development, and humanitarian assistance. One expert likened it to South Africa's version of the U.S. National Endowment for Democracy.[118] Expenditures for the democracy and governance pillar of the fund amount to more than $56 million from 2011 to 2014.[119] South Africa's Independent Electoral Commission has played an active role in competent administration of free and fair elections, a strong suit for the country, and the government provided substantial financial assistance to the DRC, Zambia, and the Seychelles for their respective elections.[120] The South African Development and Partnership Agency is expected to replace the African Renaissance and International Cooperation Fund and operate autonomously under the strategic oversight of the minister of international relations and cooperation, but the process has been repeatedly delayed. In the meantime, the fund has been reorganized with greater attention and resources expected to be given to the prevention and resolution of conflict.[121] South Africa also contributes $1 million annually to the IBSA fund, which funds projects aimed at alleviating poverty and hunger.[122]

FOREIGN POLICY AND DOMESTIC POLITICS

To a greater degree than other rising democracies, postapartheid South Africa under the leadership and legacy of Nelson Mandela traveled from a cold corner of international isolation and defensiveness to a higher plateau of regional and global prominence. It has come as far as it has in large part because of the international notoriety of the apartheid regime. When the ANC took power in 1994, for example, it was not a parochial actor. By the mid-1980s, the ANC had representation in more countries around the world than the apartheid government—twenty offices in Africa, fourteen in Europe, four in North America, and four in Asia.[123] Its leaders maintained an extensive network not only in Africa but in capitals from Moscow to Beijing to New Delhi, and they were well schooled in the politics of foreign policy and the impact of globalized communications and mobilization for a cause. In exile, they constructed the key tenets of a values-based vision for domestic and international peace articulated as far back as the Freedom Charter of 1955.[124] Once in power, Mandela and his liberation colleagues immediately faced the challenge of building a new inclusive government and foreign ministry, requiring major investments in education, management, diplomatic, and language training. As a highly diverse and stratified society composed of multiple black identities, whites, coloureds, Indians, and Asians speaking eleven official languages (the third highest in the world), and a magnet for migrants from Zimbabwe, Mozambique, and elsewhere, South Africa faced a particularly daunting gap between ambitions and capacity.

As a matter of constitutional law and political consensus, foreign policy decisionmaking after 1994 quickly consolidated in the hands of the president, who relied on a small circle of advisers within government and in the ANC. With his outsize international stature, Mandela devoted himself to building South Africa's new image, attracting foreign investment and aid, and repaying old debts to those, particularly in the global South, who supported the liberation movement. By his side, and increasingly as the lead actor on foreign policy matters, was Thabo Mbeki, his deputy president, who once served as the ANC's international relations director. When he became president in 1999, Mbeki built on and expanded South Africa's foreign policy ambitions with a heavy focus on upgrading Africa's performance, solving conflicts, and maintaining good relations with the West. He relied mainly on a small coterie of advisers who were dispatched as envoys to help mediate disputes in the region and on his activist foreign minister, Nkosazana Dlamini-Zuma, who led Mbeki's march to reconstruct the African Union and project a more hopeful image for the continent. Under Mbeki, the foreign ministry's task of internal reform and rationalization continued to preoccupy the bureaucracy, leaving a void for the president, Dlamini-Zuma, and other senior party officials to fill. The departments of defense, trade and industry, and national intelligence also contributed to shaping and executing foreign policy under the president's centralizing direction. Some analysts also note the informal role of provincial and local governments in designing their own sphere of international relations.[125]

Notably, the ANC, through its forty-member International Relations Committee, has continued to play a key role in shaping foreign policy positions in both the Mbeki and Zuma governments and in conducting party-to-party relations around the region.[126] Its 2012 International Relations Policy Discussion Document has become a touchstone for understanding the main priorities of South Africa's foreign policy. The ANC's style of governance in exile—"centralization of power, emphasis on party discipline, the pre-ordained election of leaders and the closing down of democratic space"—carried over to its modus vivendi in government, according to a study of the structure of South Africa's foreign policy decisionmaking by Lesley McMasters,[127] adding further complexity to the foreign policy decisionmaking process.

Mbeki, however, did not limit his circle of advisers to the anointed party elite. A number of other foreign policy stakeholders have emerged including trade unions, black-owned businesses, large corporations, agricultural interests, youth, academia, and a national forum of religious leaders.[128] By 2011, the newly named DIRCO had developed a draft White Paper on Foreign Policy with input from civil society, business, academia, and labor; its main message was that national interests and domestic priorities—the "developmental imperative"—would drive external relations.[129] Despite the effort to consult more widely, the end result was largely panned as a laundry list of objectives and concepts with little strategic vision. That same year, the Cabinet approved creation of a Council on International Relations (SACOIR) to generate greater public debate and transparency around South Africa's foreign policy. Through two annual plenary meetings and two thematic Working Group meetings, the twenty-five members representing business, academia, labor, and civil society were expected to weigh in on key foreign policy issues with internal and external actors. But four years after it was approved, representatives had still not been appointed.[130]

Despite South Africa's strong features of procedural democracy, its Parliament, which is controlled by the ANC, plays only a minor role in shaping foreign policy decisions. It has the power to ratify treaties, authorize deployment of troops, monitor and evaluate policies, and allocate monies to DIRCO, but it has not translated these functions into much leverage. It was not involved, for example, in the decision to send peacekeeping troops to Burundi in 2003.[131] It adopted only one piece of legislation related to international relations in 2012, an important bill implementing the four Geneva Conventions of 1949 and additional Protocols of 1977.[132] That same year, the ANC called for a more "activist" parliament to give the people it represents a greater voice at the international level, and suggested it take on democratization of global governance and the consolidation of the Africa agenda.[133] Nonetheless, the Parliament's International Relations Committee responsible for oversight of South Africa's foreign policy did not get around to receiving a briefing on DIRCO's White Paper until March 2014, almost three years after its release.[134] There is no official record publicly available of parliamentary committee meetings, limiting outside monitoring or influence on the proceedings, but interested groups can pay for a subscription to access relevant committee documents.[135]

While the circles of influence are relatively limited, civil society organizations of various stripes have become increasingly active in monitoring, critiquing, and influencing South Africa's foreign policy. The think tank and academic communities are considered the leading edge of reflection and input to policymakers, and are expanding their networks to other domains in the global South, particularly around the BRICS meetings.[136] The Congress of South African Trade Unions (COSATU), historically close to the ANC and representing more than 2 million workers, has on occasion broken away from the party line to mobilize opinion and direct action on human rights issues. It has been particularly active in criticizing trade deals with China that import cheap Chinese labor or goods. Notably, after the disputed elections in Zimbabwe in March 2008, COSATU worked with its Transport and Allied Workers Union affiliate and an ad hoc coalition of NGOs to stop delivery of a cargo of Chinese arms bound for Zimbabwe. "South Africa cannot be seen to be facilitating the flow of weapons into Zimbabwe at a time where there is a political dispute and a volatile situation" in the country, it argued.[137] The coalition mobilized efforts around the Horn of Africa to track the ship as it looked, unsuccessfully, for alternative sites for unloading the weapons. Attempts to sustain or replicate this initiative to other areas of concern, however, have faltered.

Nongovernmental organizations, supported by a number of donors in Europe and the United States, have also become more vocal in lobbying for human rights–oriented policies. A coalition of like-minded groups from South Africa, Brazil, and India came together on the eve of the BRICS Summit in Durban in 2013 to lobby for humanitarian aid to flow into Syria, a position endorsed in the final summit communique.[138] The group failed, however, to get the BRICS leaders to incorporate any criteria for transparency and respect for human rights in the foundational principles of the BRICS New Development Bank. The LGBT community in South Africa had better luck in pushing South Africa to lead the effort at the UN Human Rights Council for a milestone resolution on LGBT rights, but has since watched South Africa go cold on the issue.[139] Earlier examples of NGO advocacy on issues like banning land mines and regulating conflict diamonds led South Africa's policymakers to become more active in the Ottawa Convention process and the Kimberly verification scheme.[140]

The Southern Africa Litigation Centre (SALC) is turning to the courts to hold the South African government's feet to the fire on its commitments to uphold rule of law and international justice principles. In 2008, it submitted evidence to the South African National Prosecuting Authority showing the involvement of eighteen Zimbabwean security officials in perpetrating torture and demanded it initiate an investigation. It argued that the South African authorities had an obligation under national and international law to investigate and prosecute anyone who commits a crime against humanity as defined by the International Criminal Court. After six years of litigation, the Constitutional Court determined in SALC's favor that the authorities did have a duty to investigate the charges and ordered immediate action.[141] SALC also led the effort to get the High Court to demand South Africa bar Sudanese president al-Bashir, wanted on ICC charges for war crimes, from leaving the country in June 2015, an order the government ignored, prompting a national and international outcry. Other civil society initiatives have had less success. Both the South Africa Foreign Policy Initiative, hosted by the Open Society Foundation of South Africa as a human rights–oriented information resource on South Africa's international relations, and the South Africa Forum for International Solidarity, a coalition advocacy group devoted to a more ethical foreign policy, have foundered and largely collapsed in the last two years.

NGOs in general are viewed with suspicion by many government officials. One of the more puzzling and damaging aspects of Mbeki's insular approach to South Africa's alarming HIV/AIDS crisis was its unwillingness to heed the call of its own civil society and academics to take action to stem the disease. Brazil's handling of its own HIV/AIDS situation offers a startling contrast, as described by President Cardoso in his memoirs. In 1990, according to Cardoso, Brazil had the same infection rate as South Africa, just over 1 percent of the adult population. It faced a stark choice—either tackle the problem head-on or hope, as many governments in Africa did, that if it was not discussed openly, the problem might go away.[142] Mbeki in particular was notorious for ignoring the scientific consensus about how to fight the spread of the virus and blamed poverty and malnutrition instead.[143] Brazil, on the other hand, launched a massive sex education campaign, handed out free condoms, and guaranteed Brazilians free access to antiretroviral AIDS drugs, prompting strong objections from the international pharmaceutical industry and the United States, which filed a complaint with the World Trade Organization. By 2002, Brazil had half the number of HIV cases as predicted by the UN a decade before and the annual number of AIDS deaths dropped by nearly two-thirds during Cardoso's time in office. In contrast, nearly 20 percent of adults in South Africa at one point were infected with HIV or have AIDS, by some estimates. "Their destiny," Cardoso wrote, "could have easily been ours."[144]

South Africa at the time did not lack for civil society activism around the issue. The Treatment Action Campaign, founded in 1998 to campaign for access to AIDS treatment, resorted to the courts and a sophisticated national and international publicity strategy to demand universal government provision of AIDS medicines. By the time it was implemented, however, the damage had been done: approximately 12 percent of South Africa's population is HIV-positive and for people aged fifteen to forty-nine, the rate is 17 percent.[145] South Africa thus provides two important lessons to the world—the grave harm caused by denial of sound health practices and the invaluable contributions that can be made by civil society activists, scientists, and the media. It is a classic case of how the horizontal accountability and transparency of democratic systems provide channels for organized publics to override bad decisions of their leaders.

Media coverage of South Africa's foreign policy agenda is robust and operates in a relatively progressive environment. At times, ANC-backed initiatives to restrict media freedoms have made some headway, but these have not yet interfered with critical coverage of the government's actions. Still, President Zuma, in the face of heavy criticism of lavish spending on his home estate, filed multiple defamation lawsuits against journalists but in 2013 decided to drop them.[146] The ANC's International Relations Committee complained in 2012 that the country "should not rely only on slanted reporting in the media, reporting that is designed to confuse and obfuscate issues" of foreign policy, and called for greater public education.[147]

In sum, the democratization of South Africa's decisionmaking on foreign policy is fairly advanced because of a strong civil society and media, internationalized business sector, and activist ANC and COSATU leadership. But it may take another decade or two before a sufficient critical mass of public awareness and interest in foreign policy issues, along with a more engaged Parliament and competitive electoral politics, is able to effect more direct influence on its foreign policy decisions.

CONCLUSION

The South Africa case presents a dramatic example of a democratic country that has come far in just two decades, but has much further to go to consolidate the vision of a "rainbow nation" committed to its founding principles. Given its heightened profile on the African and world stage, the fate of South Africa's democratic model carries special weight. On the positive side, it has become a more stable and inclusive society with reduced poverty, new economic opportunities, and expanded trade and investment. Recent studies suggest, however, that it should tackle substantial economic and political reforms to consolidate its leadership role as a "beacon" for democracy in Africa.[148] The fact that the ANC remains secure in its majority dominance of electoral politics is cause enough for concern about South Africa's ability to evolve toward truly competitive multiparty government. High crime rates, an unemployment rate of 25 percent and above 50 percent for youths aged fifteen to twenty-four, and rising xenophobia are just some of the indicators of the massive challenges that democratic South Africa must still tackle.

Backsliding during the government of Jacob Zuma—the lack of justice in the Marikana mines massacre and the abuse of public monies for upgrades to Zuma's personal residence and subsequent harsh criticism of the ombudsman who made the charges—has raised serious questions about South Africa's moral compass. The spate of violence carried out against migrants in 2015, which generated a combative round of finger-pointing in the region, further underscores this point.[149] A $25 million philanthropic fund announced in February 2015 to help South African civil society groups advance the country's progressive constitutionalism and open society is another indicator of the importance the international community places on the success of the South African experience and the long road yet to travel.[150]

On foreign policy, South Africa has proven disappointing and inconsistent in its support for demands for democracy and human rights on its continent and in the Middle East. Much of the disappointment lies in its failure to translate its strong constitutional and rhetorical endorsement of these values into actions. Its inconsistency can be explained in part by its overlapping and at times conflicting personalities—as an outspoken advocate for pan-African and South-South solidarity, its strong preference for mediation and conflict resolution through dialogue, and its desire to maintain close ties both to China (and derivatively to the BRICS group) and to the West. If and when it strengthens at home, South Africa's influence abroad will grow, but it will remain a conflicted mediator and wobbly defender of universal liberal values.

CHAPTER SIX

Turkey

A Questionable Model

We trained everyone to be democrats, and then we found ourselves really having to accept it.

İSMET İNÖNÜ, *president of Turkey (1938–50)*

Turkey is a country that believes in democracy, and where rules work and the supremacy of law and court rulings work. It's at Western standards.

ABDULLAH GÜL, *president of Turkey (2007–14), quoted in the context of the Gezi Park protests, June 3, 2013*

Democracy is a train that takes you to your destination, and then you get off.

RECEP TAYYIP ERDOĞAN, *then mayor of Istanbul (1994–98), former prime minister (2003–14), and president of Turkey (2014–)* *

OF THE FIVE RISING democracies, Turkey presents the most complicated case for the proposition that liberalizing states offer a powerful example to others seeking a democratic path to development. Its strong authoritarian

---

*Often quoted line made by Erdoğan at an election event, December 6, 1997, while mayor of Istanbul, where he also read a poem from nationalist figure Ziya Gökalp, for which he was sentenced to ten months in jail for "inciting ethnic and religious hatred."

legacy from Ottoman and post-Ottoman periods, personified by the presidency of modern Turkey's founder, Mustafa Kemal Atatürk, runs deep. Today it finds echoes in the behavior of President Tayyip Erdoğan, a strong-willed leader who has engineered Turkey's impressive rise on the world stage while leading his party toward multiple electoral victories. Despite demonstrable progress toward liberal norms, particularly during his first term as prime minister, Erdoğan's increasingly controversial behavior as a modern-day sultan in democratic clothing is seriously undermining Turkey's claim to be a positive example of liberal democratic norms.

Atatürk's quest after World War I to rebuild Turkey as a modern secular state out of the ashes of the Ottoman sultans' defeat and withdrawal from the Balkans, Central Asia, and the Middle East was largely accomplished through the suppression of religion, democracy, and human rights. To subjugate religion to the state bureaucracy, in 1924, Atatürk abolished the office of the caliph, closed Ottoman Sharia courts, and adopted the Swiss civil code as a model for the Turkish Civil Code of 1926. He replaced Islamic *medrese* schools with state schools, and the Ottoman-Arabic alphabet with Latin script. Atatürk banned the fez, and dissolved Sufi *tarikats* (networks) as well as their *tekkes* (lodges) and *türbes* (shrines). The Grand National Assembly made criticism of the president or Grand National Assembly punishable by imprisonment. Finally, he stifled opposition to *laiklik* (secularism) through the Press Law of 1931, which gave the government power to close down any newspaper that it deemed worked against the "general policies of the country."[1] He did not believe Turkey was ready to be governed democratically, and thus ruled an autocratic and highly patriarchal state. While some reforms were more progressive, particularly the granting of rights and political representation to women, Atatürk only grudgingly experimented with licensed and limited opposition, which he would ultimately violently suppress.[2]

A succession of civilian and military governments following Atatürk's death in 1938 revealed the profound conflict between strong popular desires for greater freedoms, including religious expression, and elite demands for order, secularism, and stability. The year 1945 proved catalytic for Turkey's democracy as World War II ended and Turkey became a founding member of the United Nations.[3] On August 15, 1945, when the United Nations Charter came before the Grand National Assembly for ratification, Deputy Adnan Menderes, a leading advocate for liberalization, argued, "Turkey, by signing the Charter, had definitely engaged to practice genuine democracy."[4] Martial law finally ended in December 1947, and freedom of expression and print media began to flourish.[5] When the ruling party under President İsmet İnönü decided to allow multiparty elections in 1950, the opposition Demokrat Parti (Democrat Party [DP]) won by a clear majority of 53.4 percent, ending the Cumhuriyet Halk Partisi's (CHP) twenty-seven years of political domination.[6]

This triumphant moment, however, was short-lived. The military, which viewed itself as the guardian of the secular Kemalist legacy, would continually intervene to "save democracy" through coups in 1960, 1971, 1980, and the "postmodern" coup in 1997. Throughout the 1950s to 1980s, the so-called guardian state—a mostly clandestine alliance between the military, judiciary, and bureaucracy—manipulated politics and used mass violence to destabilize civilian governments.[7] Still, during this time conservative democracy also emerged. The DP represented an alliance of social classes (the bourgeois industrialists and the conservative rural population) that would feed Turkey's succession of conservative democratic parties, from Süleyman Demirel's Adalet Partisi (Justice Party [AP]), to his and Tansu Çiller's Doğru Yol Partisi (Party of the True Path [DYP]), to Turgut Özal's Anavatan Partisi (Motherland [ANAP]), and finally to Tayyip Erdoğan's Adalet ve Kalkınma Partisi (Justice and Development Party [AKP]).[8] The economic restructuring under Özal unlocked the Turkish economy from its insular state-led model and fueled an explosion in the middle class that set the stage for later economic growth in the 2000s. Turkey's per capita income increased from approximately $1,400 in 1985 to $2,900 in 1995 to $10,400 in 2008.[9]

This burgeoning middle class, particularly the striving small and medium-size entrepreneurs from Turkey's heartland known as the Anatolian Tigers, ultimately served as the support base for the AKP in the 2000s. Further structural economic and political reforms following the 2001 financial crisis paved the way for significant growth in the 2000s under the government of Erdoğan, the charismatic former mayor of Istanbul once jailed for reciting a poem that the court said incited religious hatred.[10] As the Turkish economy weathered a major crisis and elections approached in 2001, Erdoğan campaigned on a promise to end corruption and poverty. His party won an absolute majority in the National Assembly. This was an important moment for the consolidation of Turkey's democracy, as it led to the first stable single-party government since 1987 and the first two-party parliament in forty-eight years.[11]

FOREIGN POLICY DOCTRINES: PRAGMATISM WITH A TWIST

After the collapse of the Ottoman Empire in 1923, Atatürk began his quest to secure the new Republic of Turkey's independence within defined and secure borders. He pursued a pragmatic foreign policy of neutrality, peace with neighbors, and nonalignment, while identifying mainly with the ideation of Western civilization. For most of the twentieth century, Turkish foreign policy functioned as an extension of Kemalism and was thus oriented toward the West and in pursuit of modernization, perceived as "Westernization." Guided by Atatürk's maxim, "peace at home, peace abroad," and fueled by a general suspicion of foreign powers (the "Sèvres Syndrome"),[12] Turkey was also strongly nationalist and largely self-isolated.[13] As World War II broke out, Turkey cautiously decided to align itself with the Allied powers, partly out of fear of Soviet expansionism and suspicion of nearby fascist Italy, but mainly stood on the sidelines militarily.[14]

As the Cold War took hold, Turkey concluded that its interests were better protected against Soviet encroachment as a member of the North Atlantic Treaty Organization (NATO), which it joined in 1952, anchoring it with many "institutional and ideological bridges" to the West. It joined allied forces in the Korean War and hosted nuclear weapons on its soil. After the fall of the Soviet Union, it supported NATO enlargement, which further buttressed stability in its northern neighborhood.[15] Turkey largely avoided getting too involved in Middle Eastern affairs other than through defensive moves like hosting a U.S. missile defense radar.[16] Normative concerns of democracy and human rights "played little if any role in its diplomacy" toward the region during this period.[17] With the end of the Cold War, however, and a loosening of the Western alliance, Turkey began proactively engaging its changing neighborhood and other regions from an interests-driven perspective focused mainly on economic, security, and energy considerations.[18]

When the AKP came to power in 2002, Ahmet Davutoğlu (Erdoğan's chief foreign policy adviser since 2002, foreign minister from 2009 to 2014, and current prime minister) provided a heuristic framework that would direct Turkish foreign policy for more than a decade. Davutoğlu outlined his foreign policy strategy in his 2001 seminal book *Stratejik Derinlik: Turkiye'nin Uluslararasi Konumu* (Strategic Depth, Turkey's International Position).[19] Davutoğlu argued that Turkey is an emerging power and central state, and that its "strategic depth" is derived from its geographic and historical position in the world—that is, its geostrategic location and historical legacy of the Ottoman Empire.[20] He set forth a number of principles—"Davutoğlu buzzwords"—to guide Turkish foreign policy: "zero problems with neighbors"; balance between freedom and security; multilateralism; rhythmic diplomacy; firm flexibility; strategic autonomy; high-level political dialogues; economic interdependency; multicultural coexistence; multidimensional foreign policy; and proactive and preemptive peace diplomacy.[21] Notably, his book did not address a concern for democracy and human rights in other countries.[22] As Senem Aydın-Düzgit and E. Fuat Keyman argue, "The party's motto, 'zero problems with neighbors,' reflected its desire to use Turkey's Ottoman legacy and its socioeconomic ties to the region to rekindle relations and avert tensions with both democratic and nondemocratic partners in the Middle East."[23] Others accused Davutoğlu of being neo-Ottoman or imperialist, an interpretation he firmly rejected: "Why are those who united the whole of Europe not called neo-Romans, but those who united the Middle East are labeled neo-Ottomans?"[24]

During this time, Turkey emerged as a self-confident actor who employed soft power in pursuit of "zero problems with neighbors," unafraid to act unilaterally in pursuit of strategic autonomy, security, and economic opportunities. Under Davutoğlu, Ankara improved relationships in the region through diplomatic engagement, trade, aid, and visa-free travel. In 2009 it was elected by 151 states as a nonpermanent member of the UN Security Council for the first time in forty-eight years. Turkey's diplomatic service (both recruitment and new embassies) also expanded during Davutoğlu's term: from 2003 to 2013 the number of embassies increased from 93 to 129 and foreign representation rose in Ankara from 162 to 221.[25]

A key component of Turkey's evolving strategy was to consolidate its relations with the transatlantic alliance and redouble efforts to secure accession to the European Union after a rocky period of relations. Turkey's formal application for EU membership was filed in 1987 but was rejected two years later because of "the problematic state of Turkish democracy," violence between the Kurds and the state, and because the European Union's predecessor entity was focused on consolidating its markets at the time.[26] In 1995 it agreed to a customs union that led to important trade and business ties to the continent. Ever since, Turkey and the Europeans have moved toward integration in a series of fits and starts that have generated mutual disappointments and, from the Turkish side, cries of European Islamophobia. In 2002, "when we came to power," Davutoğlu explained, "our choice was . . . full integration with EU as early as possible and to develop our vision—new vision—inside EU, together with EU."[27]

Most experts agree that the EU accession process did inspire important progress toward liberal democracy in Turkey—particularly between 2002 and 2005—as Ankara worked toward harmonization with European standards.[28] Notably, it made considerable advancements with regard to civilian control of the military, although some critics argue that Erdoğan exploited this criterion for EU accession as a tool for eliminating the military's threat to his plans to Islamicize Turkish politics.[29] Turkey also abolished the death penalty and state security courts; adopted a policy of zero tolerance toward torture; ratified the UN International Covenant on Civil and Political Rights as well as the International Covenant on Economic, Social, and Cultural Rights; introduced the right to information; expanded the right to counsel; advanced judicial independence; civilianized the National Security Council; broadened cultural rights by lifting bans on the use of the Kurdish language, restoring village names, and allowing citizens to give their children non-Turkish names; enacted structural economic reforms; and initiated a slew of important infrastructure and development projects.[30] But as French and German opposition to Turkey's bid for membership crystallized in the second half of the 2000s, and Turkey's own economy outpaced Europe's, Ankara grew increasingly wary and uninterested in the cause.

Subsequently, despite some progress in talks with the European Union,[31] Turkey under Erdoğan has moved backward in terms of political rights and civil liberties. In February 2014, the Turkish Grand National Assembly enacted a new law that restored many powers to the minister of justice, essentially subjugating the judiciary to executive influence.[32] In April 2014, a new law increased the surveillance powers of the National Intelligence Organization (Milli İstihbarat Teşkilatı [MİT]), threatened journalists who report on MİT activities with prison terms of up to nine years, exempted MİT agents from prosecution, and allowed official access to private data without a court order.[33] The AKP-controlled Grand National Assembly also passed a new "Internet law" that increased state control over the Internet by expanding the powers of the regulating body, the Presidency of Telecommunication and Communication (TIB). TIB now has the authority to require Turkish Internet providers to block access to online content and store users' online activ-

Figure 6-1. Political Cartoon Depicting Turkish Censorship of Twitter

EBERT

Source: Enrico Bertuccioli.

ities for two years, as well as remove content they feel violates privacy.[34] According to the *New York Times*, "In the first six months of 2013, Google was asked to delete more than 12,000 items, making Turkey the No. 1 country seeking to excise Google content."[35] Banning YouTube and Twitter (see figure 6-1) brought out the best of Erdoğan's bravado and international criticism: "We now have a court order. We'll eradicate Twitter. I don't care what the international community says. Everyone will witness the power of the Turkish Republic."[36] Not surprisingly, Turkey's standing in international rankings of press freedom has markedly declined.[37] According to the Committee to Protect Journalists, reporters face harassment, investigations, and prosecutions over social media posts and authorities repeatedly gag coverage of sensitive issues.

Furthermore, despite minor progress on the rights of religious minorities, authorities continue to use article 216 of the Turkish Penal Code, which bans "fomenting hatred and enmity among the public" and "insulting religious values," to silence critics of Islam. To name just one instance, in May 2013, Ertan P. received a fifteen-month prison sentence for tweets that made fun of Muslim believers under the name "Allah CC."[38]

As relations with Brussels and Washington cooled off, Turkey continued its robust outreach to its neighbors to the south and east. The situation grew more complicated for Turkey's "zero problems with neighbors" policy, however, when the Arab Spring protests erupted in 2011. Analysts pointed to Turkey as a potential model for countries that had recently overthrown their leaders, a role Turkey embraced as it began to shed the "zero problems" approach in favor of promoting democracy in the region in various ways. President Abdullah Gül bluntly explained that Turkey "is with people, not with regimes," while Foreign Minister Davutoğlu cited his country as a "source of inspiration" for the Arab people's demands for democracy and human rights.[39] He committed Turkey to become "a firm defender of universal values . . . in particular, human rights and such norms as democracy, good governance, transparency and rule of law. We will extend our assistance to the people who rise up to demand such values because given our belief in the principles of justice and equality, we are convinced that they also deserve to have the same rights and privileges enjoyed by our own people."[40]

Reflecting on the growing linkages among such issues as the global economic crisis, sectarian confrontations, Islamophobia and terrorism, and Turkey's place as the global crossroads, Davutoğlu told an audience at the Brookings Institution in 2013 that Turkey preferred a "visionary" approach to the international order based on principles, rather than ad hoc crisis containment. The "restoration" of Turkey's economy, politics, and foreign policy, he argued, rested on democratization and the concept of citizenship as the best formula for security and stability in Turkey and the region: "We believe that long-term stability will be granted only if there is a new consensual relation between leaders, state and citizens." Short-term thinking that favors stability over democratic change, "hoping that some autocratic leaders will bring security and stability in the Middle East, [is] a big, big mistake."[41] This was a far cry from the "zero problems" strategy articulated before the Arab revolts.

Even before the onset of its own democratic reforms, Turkey was a relatively constructive if quiet player in supporting democratic trends abroad, mainly because of its alignment with the United States, NATO, and the EU. Turkey participated in electoral monitoring missions, gave rhetorical support to democratic developments in its region, particularly in the Balkans, and "made significant contributions to peacekeeping and post-conflict reconstruction efforts that were essential in preparing the ground for establishing democratic regimes."[42] In July 2010, Turkey codified its more values-oriented foreign policy through adoption of a new law mandating the Foreign Ministry to "defend and promote human rights and democratic values . . . and fight against all sort of discrimination based on language, race, color, political thought, philosophical belief, religion, confession, etc." The law also created a new division in the foreign ministry on global and humanitarian affairs dealing explicitly with human rights issues.[43]

Domestic politics also have played a key role in shaping Turkey's professed concern for the fate of other peoples living under repressive rule while still pursuing its core national security and economic interests. Its complex demographic makeup and strong religious identity coupled with powerful business interests and legacies of secularism and European-oriented aspirations drive a multifaceted and ambitious foreign policy agenda. As Davutoğlu explained:

> Turkey's unique demographic realities also affect its foreign-policy vision. There are more Bosnians in Turkey than in Bosnia-Herzegovina, more Albanians than in Kosovo, more Chechens than in Chechnya, more Abkhazians than in the Abkhaz region in Georgia, and a significant number of Azeris and Georgians, in addition to considerable other ethnicities from neighboring regions . . . Because of this fact, Turkey experiences regional tensions at home and faces public demands to pursue an active foreign-policy to secure the peace and security of those communities.[44]

Turkey's volatile neighborhood and the demands of its diverse domestic constituencies present a complicated balancing act for Ankara's regional policy. Its long struggle to repress and more recently to accommodate demands for autonomy of its significant minority population of Kurds tends to constrain its projection of hard and soft power abroad, particularly in Syria and Iraq. Direct military intervention against forces in Syria (Assad or ISIL), for example, has provoked retaliatory attacks on Turkish soil, thereby jeopardizing the safe and secure environment it needs to attract the more than 30 million foreign tourists who generate annually more than $20 billion for Turkey's economy.[45] Turkey also continues to struggle with its historical legacy of conflict in its near abroad. Relations are especially polarized with Armenia, which charges Turkey with committing genocide and other crimes against humanity against Armenians during and after World War I.[46] On the other hand, it has become a generous donor of humanitarian assistance, ranking number three in the world, and boasts an active network of predominantly Islamic charities involved in humanitarian relief activities around the world.[47] The Turkish spirit of generosity is also reflected in its well-regarded refugee camps established to house the influx of more than one and a half million refugees from Syria.[48]

Ultimately, Turkey's ambitions to play a leading role as a voice for democratic stability and development in the Muslim world and beyond hinge directly on its ability to adhere to democratic standards at home. Its own rhetoric strongly supports this thesis: "Advances in our democracy and economy . . . made it possible for Turkey to pursue a foreign policy that is active, principled, visionary and multi-dimensional," the Foreign Ministry's annual statement declares. To accomplish this, Turkey's leaders have adopted a dual approach of opening new markets for Turkish exports and "comprehensive relations with other democracies [to] support our own democratic strides."[49] In the past few years, however, the AKP has chosen to adopt majoritarian/authoritarian measures that run counter to the country's traditional prescriptions for peace at home and peace abroad. Its once promising example as a rising democracy delivering both political and economic and social rights is badly tarnished by Erdoğan's insistent demands for greater control and his overheated rhetoric against his domestic and foreign critics. In June 2015 parliamentary elections, Erdoğan's aggressive campaign for AKP to win a supermajority of seats that would have allowed him to rewrite the constitution to consolidate power in his favor was dealt a stinging rebuke when voters left the party almost twenty seats short of the majority needed even to form a government. The Constitutional Court also issued rulings in 2014 and 2015 that went against the president,[50] suggesting at least some independent checks on executive power. As long as the increasingly autocratic Erdoğan remains in control, however, Turkey is unlikely to be able to fulfill earlier expectations as a principled leader for peace through democracy and human rights.[51]

TURKEY AND ITS NEAR ABROAD

Uniquely among the five rising democracies, Turkey sits astride a multitude of cultural, political, religious, and economic crosscurrents, allowing it to stretch its influence across multiple borders in its near abroad. With Europe to its west, the Balkans to its north, Russia and the Caucasus to its east along with the complex subregions of the Middle East and North Africa to the south, Turkey truly sits in one of the most difficult and turbulent geopolitical environments in the world. Its so-called Kurdish problem, which implicates Kurdish populations in northern Iraq and Syria, inextricably binds domestic and foreign policies. All the more reason why its own internal choices of governance, reconciliation, and coexistence, and its long experience seeking harmony between democracy and Islam, carry special weight as an example for other countries wrestling with their own internal ethnic divisions and sectarian conflicts.

In the pre–Arab Spring period, Turkey often aligned itself with various Western-led initiatives to stabilize such troubled countries as Iraq, Afghanistan, and Bosnia and Herzegovina. It played a pivotal role in supporting the international campaign to remove the Taliban in Afghanistan, deploying nearly 2,000 troops and committing almost $15 million since 2007 to support the NATO-ANA trust fund dedicated to equipping and sustaining the Afghan National Army (ANA).[52] Its development assistance agency, which has grown exponentially in the past ten years, spent 45 percent of its funds to support reconstruction in Afghanistan in 2008.[53] At other times, as in the case of the U.S. invasion of neighboring Iraq, Turkey went its own way, refusing, for example, to allow the U.S.-led coalition's planes to use Turkish airspace to sustain the operation. Its close ties with the Kurdish Regional Government in northern Iraq as a balancing force against domestic pro-Kurdish rebels and an expansionist Iran was a key factor in this decision, as well. Nonetheless, Turkey has engaged both bilaterally and multilaterally to support a variety of reconstruction, training, and democracy-building efforts in Iraq, including an effort to convince the Sunnis to participate in the post–Saddam Hussein elections in 2005.[54] It also supported the appointment of Haider al-Abadi to form a new government in Iraq over Shiite cleric Ali al-Sistani, openly supporting Abadi's efforts to assemble a functioning nonsectarian government that could maintain territorial integrity.[55] The main thrust of its approach to the region, however, was building economic and energy ties, border security, and stability. In keeping with its "zero problems" approach, as Soli Özel and Gencer Özcan point out, Ankara ignored the abuses of the Baathist regime in Syria and its alleged complicity in the murder of Lebanese leader Rafiq Hariri, the genocide charges against Omar al-Bashir in Sudan, and the bloody suppression of the Green Movement protests in neighboring Iran in 2009.[56]

During this period, Erdoğan and Davutoğlu also sought better relations with Israel as a means of advancing the cause of the Palestinians, a major recipient of Turkish donor assistance,[57] and as a broker between Israel and Syria. Relations soured, however, when Israel invaded Gaza in December 2008 without warning Ankara. In response, Erdoğan embarrassed Israeli president Shimon Peres in a celebrated walkout at the Davos World Economic Forum, earning him widespread plaudits on the vaunted Arab street.[58] Erdoğan also took a firm stand against Israel's attack on a Turkish humanitarian NGO flotilla aiming to break Israel's blockade of Gaza in May 2010. These incidents, and Turkey's progress toward stable democracy and high economic growth, generated positive views toward Turkey in the region. For example, in a post-flotilla 2010 survey of Arab public opinion, an overwhelming majority of respondents said they had a positive image of Turkey, while 66 percent said they looked at Turkey as a model for countries of the region.[59]

As the Arab Spring unfolded in 2011, Turkey's image in the region remained highly positive. A similar regional survey of 2,323 people gave Turkey a 78 percent favorability rating, the highest in the region, with high marks for contributing the most to peace and conflict resolution; it also earned the highest ratings as the region's future economic leader.[60] Turkey, moreover, was regarded by 56 percent of the regional average as having had a positive effect on the events of the Arab Spring.[61] Correspondingly, a high majority of Turks surveyed in 2011 supported the concept of Turkey as a positive political model for the region.[62]

As the wave of demands for democracy swept across the Arab world, Turkey made a decisive shift away from its more traditional attitude of cautious ad hoc measures of mediation toward outright calls for political change cloaked in the language of universal rights to freedom and popular sovereignty. Its condemnation of repressive secularist regimes in Syria, Egypt, Tunisia, and Libya also aligned nicely with a more sectarian aim of supporting Islamist (Sunni) parties that, if given the chance, would likely do well in free and fair elections and solidify Turkey's alliances in the region. This attitude was reflected earlier in Turkey's full-throated support for the electoral victories of Hamas in Gaza in 2006.

Amid widespread protests in Egypt in 2011, Prime Minister Erdoğan was among the first world leaders to call on President Hosni Mubarak to step down. He urged him to "meet the people's desire for change with no hesitation" and went on to say that "in our world today, freedoms can no longer be postponed or ignored."[63] Erdoğan further announced that "no government can survive against the will of its people. The era of governments persisting on pressure and repression is over."[64] A few weeks later the prime minister's office confidently announced that "since the start of the mass demonstrations in Egypt, Turkey has supported the Egyptian public's legitimate demands for democracy and freedom."[65] As Western powers hesitated to support the protesters and urged all to eschew violence, Erdoğan took an unequivocal stance in support of the Egyptians on the street. As one leading European politician put it, Erdoğan "was backing the masses and their appeals for more democracy 100 percent, without hesitation, without 'ifs' and 'buts.'"[66] A senior adviser to the Foreign Ministry added, "We believe that the people will choose tolerance and peace if they are given the chance."[67] After Muslim Brotherhood leader Mohamed Morsi won elections in Egypt, Erdoğan received a hero's welcome on a victory lap visit to Cairo in September 2011 and was dubbed the "king of the Arab Street."[68]

Despite its appeal to universal norms, Turkey's quick support to the elected Muslim Brotherhood government of Mohamed Morsi reinforced the perception that the AKP was skewing democracy promotion to its own particular, largely sectarian ends. During a visit to Ankara in September 2012, Morsi and Erdoğan signed an agreement for a $1 billion loan to Egypt, reportedly part of a $2 billion total aid package.[69] Upon the military's overthrow of Morsi in July 2013, Ankara immediately called the move "unacceptable" and demanded his unconditional release from house arrest and return to power.[70] Erdoğan defended this approach in an address to foreign ambassadors in Ankara: "As Turkey, we don't follow a policy regarding Egypt that defends or looks after certain people or institutions. We follow a policy that looks after universal values and principles."[71] He then scolded "countries which embrace and care about democracy" for their "double standards," adding "we want to see their backbones."[72] The harsh criticism of the military's takeover in Cairo, which stirred up ongoing tensions between Erdoğan and his own military establishment, led both countries to withdraw their ambassadors. As the al-Sisi regime in Cairo has doubled down on repression, jailings, and executions of Muslim Brotherhood leaders and supporters, Ankara has grown even more despondent toward its erstwhile ally. Erdoğan condemned the death penalty judgment against Morsi as a return to "ancient Egypt" and again criticized Western nations for failing to do enough to oppose Morsi's ouster.[73]

Turkey's reaction to the first uprising in the region, however, was not as quick and unambiguous. In Tunisia, Turkey was largely caught off guard and did not take an official stance in support of democratic demands until President Ben Ali fled the country. Instead, Foreign Minister Davutoğlu neutrally observed amid protests that "social explosions are common in societies absent of democracy and free elections."[74] In the aftermath, Davutoğlu took great offense at criticism that Turkey remained silent during Tunisia's uprisings, insisting that the government supported a principled policy and that it attached great importance to democratic values as well as to stability and internal peace in friendly and neighboring countries.[75] Turkey continues to affirm its rhetorical support for Tunisia's democratization efforts regularly in press releases, including during the 2014 presidential elections.[76]

Whether loud and definitive as in the Egyptian case or more muted as in the Tunisian case, Turkish support for protesters in both countries posed no great challenge to Turkey's core national security interests. In the case of Tunisia, though Ben Ali had been an ally and economic relations with Tunisia had improved under the AKP government, the relationship was by no means a critical one.[77] Moreover, it was consistent with AKP ideology to support Tunisian protesters against Ben Ali, a staunch secularist similar to AKP's domestic opponents. In Egypt, on the other hand, the bilateral relationship was stronger and the economic stakes higher. Turkish investments alone in Egypt rose to $1.5 billion in 2010 from $60 million in 2005. After signing a free trade agreement in 2007, the volume of trade between the countries more than doubled from $1.5 billion annually to $3.2 billion in 2010.[78] Despite these stakes, Mubarak's exit represented an auspicious opportunity for Turkey to expand its regional leadership and, more parochially, agitate for its ideological cohort, the Muslim Brotherhood.

In the cases of Libya and Syria, Turkey similarly supported opposition forces but its vital security and economic interests strongly influenced the timing and nature of the support. At the onset of protests in Benghazi, Turkey was benefiting from $2.4 billion in annual trade with the Qaddafi regime and that number was expected to increase to $10 billion in the near future, according to the Foreign Ministry. In all, Turkish companies had conducted more than $20 billion worth of construction projects in Libya, second only to Russia in Libyan construction investment.[79] In addition, more than 25,000 Turkish citizens were living in Libya as the crisis unfolded. Turkey's initial silence and refusal to criticize the Qaddafi regime coincided with intensive efforts to rescue its expatriates and mediate the conflict. Accordingly, Turkey at first opposed the UN Security Council's resolution to establish a no-fly zone and the subsequent NATO intervention, unlike some of the other rising democracies.[80]

Eventually, however, Turkey decided to support NATO's efforts to dislodge Qaddafi. After reaching a compromise with fellow NATO governments, Turkey agreed to transition the mission from U.S.-led forces to NATO in March 2011 and sent five naval vessels to assist the international maritime quarantine against Qaddafi.[81] In May, Prime Minister Erdoğan finally called on Qaddafi to step down, saying that "one cannot establish future, liberty, stability, peace and justice on blood. Therefore we wish Libyan leader immediately pulls out from Libya and steps down for himself and for the future of the country."[82] A few months later, Turkey officially recognized the Libyan opposition, the Transitional National Council, as the rightful representative of Libya and pledged $300 million to it.[83] As its approach in Libya evolved from measured criticism to explicit support for the opposition, Turkey continued to position itself as a leader capable of mediating a negotiated transition to democracy. It cochaired with the United Arab Emirates the fourth meeting of the Libya Contact Group in Istanbul in July 2011, for instance, and presented its road map to resolve the conflict. More recently, however, Turkey has gotten bogged down in Libya's ongoing internal strife and appears to have little leverage to resolve the conflict.[84]

The uprisings and subsequent civil war in neighboring Syria represent the Arab Spring's most complicated and dangerous quagmire for Turkey. AKP leaders had invested precious time and resources in their relationship with the Assad government and the normalization of diplomatic and trade relations with Syria had been the crown jewel of Erdoğan's "zero problems" policy. The volume of trade between the two countries rose from $752 million in 2004 to $2.3 billion in 2010. The Foreign Ministry had hoped that the 2004 free trade agreement between the countries would increase trade volume to $5 billion in the near term.[85] Aside from these economic losses, chaos in neighboring Syria has had very tangible implications for Turkish security as an estimated one and a half million Syrians have sought refuge across the 822-kilometer border the two countries share, costing Turkey more than $5.5 billion as of April 2015.[86] The emergence of Daesh, the Islamic State of Iraq and the Levant, has further drawn Turkey into what has now become a regional nightmare of historic proportions.

Initially and with these interests in mind, Turkey tried to use its leverage to convince the Assad regime to pursue democratic reforms. In response to Assad's failure to implement meaningful changes, Erdoğan remarked: "He says, 'I will do it.' But I have a hard time understanding if he is being prevented from doing it or if he is hesitating."[87] Erdoğan went on to criticize the regime for its "savagery," adding that "sadly, they don't behave like humans."[88] Upon news of the July 2011 massacres in Hama on the eve of Ramadan, the Foreign Ministry first responded with a measured press statement that expressed "suspicions regarding the intention and sincerity of the Syrian administration to resolve the issue through peaceful methods" and called on the government "to end the operations and resort to political methods, dialogue and peaceful initiatives in order to reach a solution."[89] Ankara, however, grew increasingly exasperated as Assad failed to deliver on promised reforms while insisting on ramping up the violence. Deputy Prime Minister Bülent Arınç finally confessed that "what's going on in Hama today is an atrocity," and that those responsible "can't be our friend . . . they are making a big mistake."[90] In a seemingly last-ditch maneuver to influence the situation, Erdoğan sent Davutoğlu to Syria in August 2011 to "deliver a decisive message personally to Assad."[91] In the meantime, in addition to providing refuge for the thousands of Syrians fleeing violence, Turkey permitted Syrian opposition forces to meet on Turkish soil and began providing food aid across the border.

Having grown tired of Assad's unwillingness to reform, Erdoğan finally concluded that the Syrian leader should be the next Arab dictator ousted. Erdoğan declared in a September 2011 interview that Assad's days as leader "might be extended a little bit more, but sooner or later in Syria . . . people want to be free," further noting that "autocratic systems are getting eliminated once and for all to move toward democratic systems."[92] In perhaps his harshest words about his Syrian counterpart—in a speech to the Turkish Parliament—Erdoğan compared Assad with recent and historic madmen who notoriously violated their people's rights:

Assad is showing up and saying he would fight to the death. For God's Sake, against whom will you fight? Fighting against your own people is not heroism, but cowardice. If you want to see someone who has fought until death against his own people, just look at Nazi Germany, just look at Hitler, at [Benito] Mussolini, at Nicolae Ceauşescu in Romania. If you cannot draw any lessons from them, then look at the Libyan leader who was killed just 32 days ago in a manner none of us would wish for and who used the same expression you used.[93]

As the situation in Syria further deteriorated and the Arab League agreed to isolate and sanction the Assad regime, Erdoğan translated his critical rhetoric into action. The Turkish government announced in November 2011 that because the "Syrian Government gave more priority to security measures that falls into the spiral of violence than [to] democratic openings, in spite of our recommendations, warnings and convictions," it is necessary to "increase the regional and international pressure on the Syrian Administration and to take steps in order to curtail the capacity of this administration to engage in cruelty against its people."[94] Accordingly, the Turkish government announced economic sanctions and the suspension of the high-level strategic cooperation mechanism between Turkey and Syria "until a democratic administration comes to power."[95] Since then, Turkey has continued building up its material assistance to Syrian opposition forces, including training and supplying militias and facilitating their movements across the border, and engaging in direct armed confrontation against Syrian military forces. By the summer of 2015, after ISIL and other attacks against Turkish soldiers and civilians, Turkey stepped up its involvement with aerial bombings of ISIL-controlled territory in Syria, along with targeted attacks against armed Kurdish forces, as well as permitting U.S. and NATO planes to access Turkish bases.

Turkey's belligerent stance, however, has increased a variety of risks. Syria, with help from Iran, could mobilize its Kurdish insurgency to create a threatening safe haven on Turkey's border. The U.S. military withdrawal from Iraq and its implications for stability in the predominantly Kurdish north that borders Turkey further complicate matters. Meanwhile, its efforts to convince Syrian opposition groups to participate in U.S.-Russian-sponsored peace talks in Geneva have foundered, leading some critics to charge that Turkey's biased support to parties aligned with the Muslim Brotherhood at the expense of the country's Alawite, Christian, and Kurdish minorities have only worsened prospects for a negotiated peace.[96] Even the relatively successful U.S.-Russian effort to dismantle Syria's chemical weapons in 2013 was greeted warily by Ankara, with President Gül reasserting that only Assad's overthrow would bring an enduring solution to the threats posed by its neighbor.[97]

In Bahrain, where Shi'a majorities aligned with Iran seek a greater voice in politics, Turkey has been noticeably less willing to lead on democracy and human rights. Similar to other countries, Turkey reacted to oppression in Bahrain with foremost concern for broad stability in the Gulf and with little reference to democracy and human rights. As Foreign Minister Davutoğlu stated upon his visit to Manama, in April 2011, "Bahrain and the Gulf countries are the backbone of stability in this region; therefore we do not want any tension in this strategic and economically important part of the world."[98] Davutoğlu did make a point

to meet with opposition representatives in addition to government officials during his trip to the country.

In Yemen, prior to the Houthis takeover of Sanaa in 2015, Ankara
had been conspicuously silent on the ongoing political crisis. More recently, it has thrown its hat in with Saudi Arabia and other Gulf countries concerned about the Houthis' alliance with Iran and called for the
Houthis to withdraw from Yemen. This latest confrontation, according
to Bulent Aras, a senior adviser to the Turkish Foreign Ministry, represents Turkey and Iran's competing visions of the government systems
they want to have in their own countries in the context of a larger transformation of Iran and Turkey under the influence of the Arab Spring
tumult.[99]

Turkey's complex relations with neighboring Russia, which supplies
more than half of Turkey's natural gas and holds a major trade surplus,
have deteriorated owing to their opposing positions on the conflict in
Syria. In response to Russia's seizure of Crimea, where Turkic Muslims
(Tatars) represent 12 percent of the peninsula's population, Turkey has
called for respect for international law and voiced support for the
Ukrainian people and their demands for self-determination. Despite its
energy vulnerability and prior damaging experience from energy wars
between Russia and Ukraine, Davutoğlu told Tatar leaders that Turkey
is in " 'mobilization' to defend the rights of our kin in Crimea by doing
whatever is necessary."[100] Decisive action against Russia, however, has
been lacking; Turkey, for example, did not join U.S. and EU moves to
sanction Russia for its provocations toward Ukraine.[101] Similarly, it
downplayed Russia's attacks against Georgia in 2008 in favor of pushing for a multilateral regional security framework and initially blocked
American pleas to send ships through the Turkish Straits into the Black
Sea.[102] In Azerbaijan, another South Caucasus neighbor undergoing
political turmoil, Turkey has chosen the path of close economic, political,
and cultural engagement with little to no apparent concern for Baku's increasing repression of opposition figures, NGO leaders, and journalists.[103]
Turkey has amassed considerable soft power in Azerbaijan through cultural diplomacy, reciprocal tourism, and religious and educational activities.[104] Influence runs both ways. As the supplier of natural gas from the
Caspian basin through a new pipeline crossing Turkey, and one of the
largest investors in its economy, Baku has considerable leverage over
Ankara. Here, Davutoğlu's "zero problems" policy, with its attendant
silence on the Aliyev regime's crackdown on civil society, is on full
display.

When casting its eyes to Central Asia and the millions of citizens of Turkic descent in former Soviet republics, officials in Ankara have debated competing impulses toward democratization, especially in light of the Arab revolts. As Richard Weitz chronicles,[105] one group of Turkish officials believed Central Asia may be ready for political change, which would benefit Turkey by replacing closed and corrupt authoritarian governments with more transparent, stable, and prosperous societies. Other officials believe the region's governments will not change in the short term and fear that democratization could backfire and lead to greater repression. Both sides agree that Turkey can play a soft power role to promote Turkic culture, business investments,[106] and the rule of law in the hopes "modernization trends would eventually lead to more democratic governments in the region."[107] In this vein, during a recent visit to Kazakhstan, Erdoğan and Kazakh president Nursultan Nazarbayev recommitted to expanding trade volume from $3.1 billion in 2012 to $10 billion, and heralded their role as "symbols of stability, security and prosperity in their regions, to act together against the circle of fire today."[108] With $20 billion in projects with some 1,600 Turkish companies, Turkey has much to lose by pressing for political change in Kazakhstan that could upset the status quo.

In sum, Turkey's response to protests in the Arab world, while cloaked in universal demands for justice and freedom, conveniently aligns with its more ambitious claims of leadership of Islamist and, more specifically, Sunni expansionism in Arab politics. Its desire to lead the region in this direction was best articulated during parliamentary elections in June 2011 when AKP politicians explained the benefits of Turkish leadership and the inextricable link between foreign policy and domestic politics. When delivering the party's victory address, Erdoğan alluded to Turkey's aspiration to be a voice in the West for the Middle East and the Muslim world, saying, "Sarajevo won today as much as Istanbul, Beirut won as much as Izmir, Damascus won as much as Ankara, Ramallah, Nablus, Jenin, and the West Bank, Jerusalem won as much as Diyarbikir."[109] Having built up credibility as a reforming and advancing democratizer during the 2000s, Erdoğan's Turkey opportunistically sought to grasp the brass ring of preeminence at a moment of turbulence and political change in the neighborhood. The results of this approach, however, have been, in the eyes of many observers, disastrous for Turkey's own economic and national security. By forsaking its more traditionally cautious and even isolationist approach to the region, and its quest for EU accession, in favor of activist support for democratic change that favors Islamist parties, Turkey has gotten badly burned.[110] Its relations with neighbors to the east, on the other hand, have toed the "zero problems" approach, eschewing direct criticism of antidemocratic behavior in favor of advantageous trade, commercial, and energy ties.

TURKEY IN THE WORLD

Turkey's ambitious claims for a restoration and extension of its influence in the world lie principally in Africa, where relatively positive trends toward conflict resolution, democratization, and economic growth have solidified over the last decade. In many ways, Africa has become the laboratory for Turkey's soft power agenda, explicitly reminding others of the Ottoman Empire's benevolent rule in parts of the region and offering itself as an example of democratic development.[111] It has tried also to position itself as "the voice of Africa" in the G-20 and other multilateral and bilateral fora, and touts its humanitarian and development assistance, educational scholarships, medical diplomacy, training for diplomats, and technical support for democracy and good governance.[112] As a country facing its own transition challenges, Turkey says it offers more relevant expertise and solutions for Africa's problems, what it calls the "shared experience effect."[113] Turkey's activist business class, which is thirsty for export markets for its industrial goods and construction services, has worked closely with the AKP government to ramp up its presence on the continent, particularly in Ethiopia, Somalia, Nigeria, and South Africa.

The growth in Turkey's activism in Africa over the past decade is remarkable. According to the Turkish Foreign Ministry, diplomatic outposts have grown from twelve in 2009 (five of them in North Africa) to thirty-nine in 2014, with a comparable jump in African embassies in Ankara. Tourism, travel, trade, and investment have all expanded significantly. Bilateral trade with sub-Saharan Africa, for example, grew from $750 million in 2000 to $8.4 billion in 2014, a tenfold increase. Turkey provides personnel and funding to six of the existing nine UN missions in Africa, led the multinational command task force to combat piracy in the Gulf of Aden in 2010, and in 2014 sent a naval flotilla on a twenty-eight-country circumnavigation of Africa to participate in joint training and humanitarian exercises, the first time since 1866 that Turkish ships have plied such waters.[114] It is a nonregional member of the African Development Bank and makes an annual contribution of $1 million to the

African Union, which agreed to a strategic partnership in 2008. Its humanitarian and development assistance to Africa has increased from $28 million in 2006 to $772 million in 2012. In U.S. parlance, this is known as "putting your money where your mouth is." Apart from official government activities, it is worth noting the active presence of Turkey's Gülen movement, which has established nearly forty Turkish schools throughout the continent.[115]

Nowhere has Turkey invested more political and financial capital than in Somalia, a hotbed of instability, piracy, and terrorism for years. As part of a nationwide campaign to support the country, then prime minister Erdoğan made a celebrated visit to Mogadishu in August 2011 to demonstrate Turkey's determination to make a difference where the rest of the international community had failed. Despite the ongoing violence, more than 500 Turkish relief workers and volunteers traveled to the capital to participate in humanitarian and construction projects.[116] The Turkish International Cooperation and Coordination Agency (TIKA) launched projects across the country in education, health, agriculture, and water management.

Turkey, however, has paid a price for its generosity toward the conflict-plagued country. A suicide bombing at the Turkish embassy in July 2013, which the al-Shabab terrorist group sponsored, killed three people, including a Turkish security agent. Moreover, corruption allegations emerged in Ankara that suggested millions of dollars in budgetary support destined for Somalia were found stashed in shoe boxes in the home of Halkbank CEO Süleyman Aslan.[117] By the end of 2013, Turkey abruptly halted financial contributions to Somalia but denied any connection to the allegations. By January 2015, however, Erdoğan was back in Mogadishu promising more assistance, despite the notorious infighting and corruption among Somalia's many clans.[118] Turkey's generous commitment to rebuilding Somalia, and Erdoğan's personal involvement in the cause, speaks volumes about his determination to carve a distinctive leadership role for Turkey on the world stage.

Turkey under Erdoğan and Davutoğlu has stretched its wings to other regions not in its traditional bandwidth. It has expanded its bilateral and multilateral presence in the Asia-Pacific region, joined the China-led Shanghai Cooperation Organization as a "dialogue partner" in 2012,[119] and elevated its ties to China and the Republic of Korea, among others. Its economic diplomacy has also reached Latin America and the Caribbean, where trade volume has increased ninefold in the past decade.[120]

In special cases, like the attacks against the Muslim Rohingya community in Myanmar in 2013, Turkey's leaders have condemned human rights violations, delivered humanitarian aid to victims, and urged dialogue and reconciliation with the Buddhist majority.[121] Its overarching priority, however, is to promote Turkey's economic interests far and wide, deploying diplomatic tools, development aid, cultural products, and humanitarian assistance to introduce itself as a benevolent middle power or, in Davutoğlu's words, a "central state" indispensable to global order.

As part of its strategy to project itself as a responsible global partner, Turkey has jumped into a variety of leadership positions over the past decade. In 2004, it launched the Alliance of Civilizations initiative with Spain to promote tolerance and diversity and reject extremism. It has played an outsize role in the Organization of Islamic Cooperation (OIC) and was an early advocate for democratic reforms among its members. In 2011, it hosted the UN Conference on the Least Developed Countries in Istanbul, where Davutoğlu made a concerted effort to recast the forum as a way to support "future developing countries" in their struggles to escape high levels of poverty, with Turkey as its inspiration and champion. In casting its claim for leadership, Davutoğlu pointed to Turkey's own experience addressing poverty at home as giving it "a certain distinctive credibility" with the LDC states.[122] To his credit, Davutoğlu argued for greater emphasis in development aid on accountability of governments to their own societies, both people and legislative institutions, and only secondarily to international donors.[123]

Curiously, such a position runs counter to Turkey's own interests as one of the largest development and humanitarian donors in the world. Between 2002 and 2012, Turkey's total development assistance increased almost twenty-seven-fold, rising to $3.3 billion in 2013, or 0.42 percent of its gross national income.[124] It is the fourth largest donor of humanitarian assistance in the world and joined the ranks of the top twenty donors to the United Nations in 2014. Unlike the other rising democracies, Turkey has used its impressive economic growth to make substantial investments in the international liberal order and, despite multiple setbacks in its neighborhood, continues to provide generous amounts of aid, particularly in favored states like Pakistan, Somalia, Palestine, the Balkans, the Caucasus, and Central Asia.

Turkey's campaign for leadership at the international level, including its assumption of the G-20 presidency in 2015 and its hosting of the first World Humanitarian Summit in 2016, hit a major speed bump, however, when it badly lost its second bid in five years for a nonpermanent seat on the UN Security Council in October 2014, garnering only sixty votes.[125] Despite its proactive diplomacy and generous aid policies, Turkey appears to have reached too far in its frenzied reach for global influence.

On human rights, Turkey for years has studiously avoided running for a seat on the Human Rights Council out of concern that it would face too many difficult trade-offs when voting on resolutions that condemned countries' human rights behavior. In the General Assembly, however, it has more often than not taken positions in favor of important human rights resolutions,[126] while regularly avoiding taking sides on Iran.

FOREIGN POLICY AND DOMESTIC POLITICS

The ascension of the AKP with Erdoğan at the helm lent a dramatically new flavor to the tone and substance of Turkey's foreign policy. A charismatic and strong-willed man of the street, Erdoğan played to mass public opinion in ways that tilted favorably toward populist causes like Palestine and negatively away from Israel and its chief sponsor, the United States, both seen by most Turkish citizens as threats to Turkey's peace and stability.[127] The rise of the middle classes, particularly the conservative business groups known as the Anatolian Tigers, drove a pragmatic orientation toward opening new markets around the world. While foreign policy issues are generally not of much concern to the average voter, AKP leaders understood that it would perform well electorally as long as the increasingly export-oriented economy went well. The expanding space for religion in public affairs inspired greater attention to religious and humanitarian issues abroad, as seen in Turkey's response to Somalia and the Arab revolts against secular regimes. After decades of a top-down focus on relations with Europe and the West, and away from neighbors perceived as hostile, "Turkey is paying attention to its own citizens now."[128] As the economy grew and expanded to other regions, Turks became more self-confident about their new identity as modern, prosperous, and pious Muslim citizens capable of inspiring other countries to embark on a more openly democratic path. In a survey of Turks in May 2011, for example, 72 percent supported the concept of Turkey as a political model for others.[129]

As the Arab Spring unfolded, such public sentiments pushed government officials to take sides in the battle between the people on the Arab street protesting the authoritarian status quo and otherwise friendly regimes. "It was impossible for a democratic Turkey not to take the side of the people," according to one senior journalist.[130] Formal contacts between AKP leaders and other Islamist-oriented parties in the region led to practical democracy and party-building activities. More important, Turks directly affected by the collapse in business and trade with Syria and other neighbors were relatively patient about suffering the consequences of Ankara's pro-democracy policy. After years of being told that Syrians were Turkey's enemies, the period of rapprochement with Damascus opened new doors "and we see they are not to be feared," said one businessman in Hatay, near the border with Syria. Now "they are killing our brothers and sisters in Syria, and this is unacceptable."[131] The local mayor added, "We have already lost tourism business from the unrest in Syria but we can live with that." People's rights and freedom come first, profits second, he said. In the spirit of Turkish generosity, local citizens welcome Syrians not as refugees but as guests. The intransigence of the conflict, however, and its spread to Turkish territory, are wearing down this tolerance and forcing a more activist posture to stop the bleeding.

The gradual democratization of foreign policy debate and decision-making, particularly in the era of Turkey's concerted efforts to prioritize accession to the European Union, has opened new doors for a range of actors to influence public policy. A greater willingness to consider alternatives to official policy and to tackle previously taboo subjects like the Kurdish question allowed business groups, think tanks, NGOs, and the media to generate new ideas and proposals. The rapid expansion of technology and transparency of government affairs means officials "cannot pretend that we are not accountable," according to the governor of Hatay.[132] Although Turkey's large and diverse network of more than 85,000 NGOs deals mainly with domestic issues and can be highly polarized between secularists and Islamists, Muslim organizations are increasingly active on international matters and taking on human rights and humanitarian issues.[133] Many think tanks have direct access to senior government officials but because of their reliance on state funding are reticent to criticize government policy publicly. The intellectual infrastructure to support Turkey's ambitious foreign policy agenda, however, is underdeveloped. According to several experts, higher education is only recently turning its attention to international relations and has a long way to go in preparing its students for Turkey's amplified role on the global stage.[134]

Unlike other rising democracies, Turkey suffers from a highly polarized media environment that increasingly faces outright attacks from the highest levels of government (particularly the thin-skinned Erdoğan) and self-censorship. Press freedom, according to watchdog groups, has reached a crisis point, with Turkey falling from 98 to 154 since 2007 in global rankings, according to Reporters without Borders. Coverage of international affairs is limited mainly to events in Turkey's neighborhood, although antigovernment outlets regularly broadcast Western criticism of the Erdoğan government's tactics of repression. Parliament, which remains under the control of AKP leadership, offers little check on executive powers in national security; its denial of Erdoğan's request to grant U.S. warplanes access to Turkish airspace during the invasion of Iraq in 2003 is a noteworthy exception.

While government pressure on the media is not new, allegations of "deep state" coup-mongering by the military in cahoots with other hardline nationalist and Kemalist figures and operated through the press cast a long shadow of official suspicion and hostility toward the sector. These issues came to a head with the arrest and imprisonment in 2008–10 of dozens of journalists and retired military officers caught up in the alleged Ergenekon plot to topple the AKP government.[135] Revelations of a related coup plot under the name of Sledgehammer in 2010 and the subsequent arrest of military officers, journalists, and others opposed to the AKP government led to questionable trials and long prison sentences for nearly 300 defendants.[136] While the cases underscore the ongoing challenge of asserting civilian control of Turkey's traditionally nationalist and antidemocratic military establishment, they also raise serious concerns about the quality and independence of the country's prosecutorial and judicial institutions.

One of the more divisive factors in Turkey's domestic and international politics is the role of the Gülen movement, a transnational religious and social action community of approximately 4.5 million people inspired by Turkish Islamic scholar and preacher Fethullah Gülen. Currently living in exile in Pennsylvania, Fethullah Gülen is considered a leader in moderate Islam, interfaith dialogue, multiparty democracy, scientific inquiry, and private education services around the world. An estimated 2,000 Gülen schools can be found in Turkey, Africa, Central Asia, the Balkans, and the United States. Gülen movement followers are active in major media outlets, law enforcement, and judicial circles in Turkey, and its leading charity organization, Kimse Yok Mu, carries out humanitarian and development projects around the world. Gülen and Erdoğan had a political alliance of convenience until December 2013 when an explosive investigation into alleged corruption named top members of the Erdoğan government and members of his family. In response, Erdoğan accused Gülen and its followers of creating a parallel state of prosecutors, judges, and police devoted to his overthrow and petitioned the United States for his extradition. A crackdown against journalists, prosecutors, and police officials charged with illegally eavesdropping on Erdoğan and his cohorts followed in late 2014 and into 2015, drawing criticism from U.S. and EU officials. The episode sharpened divisions in the country, weakened efforts to tackle official corruption, and intensified Erdoğan's drive to expel any challengers to his political dominance.[137] It also raises serious doubts that Turkey's reputation as a modern country devoted to liberal principles and tolerance, and its influence as an "inspiring" example of democracy, can be recovered.

CONCLUSION

Turkey's troubled path toward liberal democracy and its erratic and overly ambitious reach for influence in its chaotic neighborhood and beyond have hobbled its otherwise positive embrace of the foreign policy principles of a democratic peace. The June 2015 parliamentary elections, in which the AKP temporarily lost its thirteen-year majority and the pro-Kurdish HDP party crossed the 10 percent threshold to enter Parliament for the first time, dealt an important blow to Erdoğan's determined quest for centralizing power in the presidency and bodes well for the consolidation of Turkey's fragile democracy. But given new election results in late 2015 favorable to Erdoğan, it is clearly not out of the woods yet.

In contrast to Turkey's unfinished business on the democracy and human rights front at home, which at times appears to be headed off the rails, Turkey's economy continues to grow at a healthy pace despite regional turmoil and a weak European market. Its activist posture as a leading humanitarian donor around the world and its welcoming of hundreds of thousands of Syrians fleeing war next door mark it as a standout contributor to the international liberal order. It has also played a leading role as an outspoken if selective critic of authoritarians in the Arab world while holding back on supporting pro-democracy forces in neighboring Russia, the Caucasus, and Central Asia. It has sought to carve out a leadership role in bridging East-West divides and supporting moderate Islamist movements but has played a weak hand on human rights issues at the United Nations. In effect, Turkey, like its bespoken geographic location and its chaotic internal politics, is all over the map when it comes to its role in the international human rights and democracy order. Resolution of the Syrian conflict and of Turkey's long fight against the Kurds present its overriding short- and medium-term challenges. The real test, however, will come if and when Erdoğan is pushed aside in favor of new leadership—of his own party and the nation. Only then will Turkey be able to resolve its long hangover of authoritarian tendencies and embed itself firmly on the democratic path.

CHAPTER SEVEN

Indonesia

A Quiet Player

Gandhi said, "I am a nationalist, but my nationalism is humanity." The nationalism we advocate is not the nationalism of isolation, not chauvinism . . . do not let us say that the Indonesian nation is the noblest and most perfect, whilst belittling other people. We should aim at the unity and brotherhood of the whole world.

> PRESIDENT SUKARNO, in "The Birth of *Pancasila*" speech, June 1, 1945, outlining Indonesia's future political philosophy

Indonesia is facing a strategic environment where no country perceives Indonesia as an enemy and there is no country which Indonesia considers an enemy. Thus Indonesia can exercise its foreign policy freely in all directions, having a million friends and zero enemies.

> PRESIDENT SUSILO BAMBANG YUDHOYONO, *inaugural speech, October 20, 2009*

INDONESIA, LIKE INDIA, OFFERS the world a compelling example of a large, diverse, and modernizing society committed to principles of democracy, pluralism, and moderation. After four decades of revolutionary nationalism under President Sukarno and military-led economic nationalism under President Suharto, Indonesia transformed itself in just ten years into a multiparty democracy with strong economic growth, a remarkably speedy turnaround. As the world's largest Muslim-majority

democracy, its appeal is particularly powerful in an era of profound turbulence within the Islamic community and its relations with the rest of the
world. Its influence in constructing a stronger international liberal order,
however, is limited by a host of domestic and external factors that may
ultimately position Indonesia as a constructive but underwhelming player.

Spread across an expansive archipelago of more than 17,000 islands
in Southeast Asia, Indonesia's approximately 250 million residents
represent the fourth largest population in the world. With six officially
recognized religions,[1] some 300 different ethnic groups, and hundreds
more languages and dialects, Indonesia since Sukarno's declaration of
independence in 1945 has sought to construct a national identity around
the common language of Bahasa Indonesia, universal education, and
centralized administration. Not surprisingly, its national motto is Unity
in Diversity (*Bhinneka Tunggal Ika*). Despite terrifying episodes of violence in its relatively short national history—an estimated 500,000 Indonesians were killed during Sukarno's battle against Communists in
1965–66—it is now largely a country at peace with itself. Although the
movement for greater autonomy persists in West Papua, the country's
rating of internal conflicts is lower than three of the four other democracies covered in the book.[2] Its turnout of nearly 70 percent of voters
and public outcry against isolated attempts of military interference in
the national elections of 2014 are two recent examples of the preference
by elites and the public for resolving differences through free and fair
elections. Constitutional reforms since the *reformasi* period began in
1999 removed the military from appointed seats in the Parliament and
delegated more power to Indonesia's districts and provinces, allowing
greater flexibility in adapting national laws to local customs and Islamic
mores. Direct elections for governors and mayors, first introduced in
2005, opened the door to new politicians, including the country's latest
president, Joko Widodo (also known as Jokowi), who previously won
elections to serve as mayor and governor of Jakarta. An opposition
party attempt to reverse such elections shortly after Jokowi's election to
the presidency was strongly criticized by outgoing President Yudhoyono,
civil society, and the media, and ultimately failed in 2015.[3]

With economic growth rates of almost 4 percent a year on average
since the fall of Suharto in 1998, an expanding middle class, and a bal-
looning social media environment, Indonesia has broken out as a leading example of both economic and political liberalization in the Asia-
Pacific region. Incomes expanded by 640 percent from 1998 to 2013

with GDP per capita reaching $3,475, and the poverty headcount has been slashed nearly in half.[4] The Internet reached 16.7 percent of Indonesian homes in 2014—up from 2.6 percent just ten years ago—and as of summer 2014, there were 69 million active Facebook users in Indonesia (about 29 percent of the population), many of whom access social media from cheap smartphones.[5] It is the world's fourth most active country on Facebook and the third most active on Twitter; an astounding 10 percent of all tweets globally from November 2010 to May 2014 have originated from Indonesia.[6] Currently the world's sixteenth largest economy[7] and one of the top three fastest growing economies in G-20, Indonesia has risen in stature in a host of multilateral fora, including the G-20, the Asia Pacific Economic Cooperation forum (APEC), and the Organization of Islamic Cooperation (OIC).

Indonesia's successful transition from an autocratic and military-dominated regime to the world's third largest democracy has become a core feature of its national identity, proclaimed by senior government officials at every opportunity not merely as a point of pride but as a badge of global credibility and soft power. As then foreign minister Marty Natalegawa proclaimed upon the visit of President Obama to Jakarta, "I can find no greater contribution to the global cause for democracy and human rights than that which has been achieved in Indonesia, where nearly a quarter of a billion people now enjoy rights and liberties hitherto denied to them."[8] The turbulent but ultimately peaceful presidential elections of July 2014, won by a former furniture salesman turned technocrat who climbed the ranks of Indonesia's city and provincial governments to defeat a revanchist general from the Suharto era, add new luster to this auspicious narrative. The public gave outgoing President Yudhoyono approval ratings of more than 68 percent, have similarly high expectations for his successor, have relatively high levels of trust in the country's main institutions, and continue to express strong support for democracy in principle and in practice.[9] Nonetheless, Indonesia faces a host of daunting challenges—from widespread corruption, rising inequality, and poor access to health care to intolerance for minorities and questionable use of the death penalty—that underscore there is much more work to be done to consolidate its progress to date and, in conjunction, hold itself out as an attractive liberalizing reformer in the heart of Southeast Asia.

FROM INDEPENDENT NATIONALISM TO
MODEST INTERNATIONALISM

Born from a struggle against two centuries of European (mainly Dutch) colonialism followed by Japanese occupation during World War II, independent Indonesia sought quickly to define itself as a leader in Asia and spokesman for the global South. But it first had to consolidate its own standing as an independent and unified state in a chaotic postwar world. To that end, in June 1945, independence leader Sukarno laid down the core principles of the new state in a celebrated speech known as "the birth of Pancasila." In it, he articulated five foundational principles for Indonesia:

1. Nationalism based on one united archipelago "ordained by God Almighty to be a single entity between two continents and two oceans" governed by "all for all"

2. Internationalism of the type Gandhi advocated, a nationalism with humanity, in contrast to the chauvinism of Nazism and fascism

3. A style of representative government that required "conferring" and consulting with the people to allow Islam to flourish but not dictate to others

4. Social justice so that "every man has enough to eat, enough to wear, lives in [common] prosperity" unlike the capitalists of Europe

5. Belief in one supreme God worshiped in freedom with mutual respect, whether Muslim, Christian, or Buddhist

The decision in 1945 to create a multireligious rather than an Islamic state laid a solid foundation for Indonesia's eventual transition to democracy. [10]

While Sukarno and his allies initially accepted a quasi-parliamentary form of government in its settlement with the Netherlands, intractable disputes around local autonomy, economic policy, and political ideology ushered in a period of "guided democracy" in 1959 led by an alliance between President Sukarno and the military, which later formally adopted a dual function (*dwifungsi*) as a sociopolitical force as well as defender of national security. Both Sukarno and Suharto manipulated these principles to protect their own brands of autocratic rule and imposed heavy demands on key political and social actors to accept Pancasila as sacrosanct, a trend that persists even today.[11] Throughout these periods until today, however, leaders also have used Pancasila to foster Indonesian nationalism, one rooted in liberal concepts of representative democracy, social justice, freedom of religion, and tolerance that continues to animate and guide its transition to democracy and its cohesion as a diverse society.

In foreign policy terms, the Pancasila principles were accompanied by an early statement of Indonesia's "independent and active" foreign policy doctrine (*bebas dan aktif*) articulated by Prime Minister and Vice President Mohammed Hatta in 1948:

Should the Indonesia people who are fighting for their independence choose between the pro-Soviet and pro-American stand? Can we have any other stand in pursuit of our goal? The Government is of the view that Indonesia should not become an "object" in the international political struggle. On the contrary, it should become a "subject" which has the right to make its own choice, that is, to achieve our complete independence . . . But this independence should be gained through self-confidence.[12]

While proclaiming that it would "row between two reefs" rather than align itself with one or the other bloc, Indonesia's founding fathers in fact navigated a course throughout the Cold War that tacked in different directions depending on the prevailing internal and external winds. Indonesia, for example, vacillated between a close relationship with China under Sukarno, followed by a sudden rupture after an attempted coup in 1965 allegedly led by Communist Party loyalists allied with Beijing. The failed coup prompted a severe military-led crackdown that resulted in more than half a million deaths.[13] Two years later, Sukarno's tenure was terminated with the ascension of army chief of staff General Suharto in 1967.

Under Suharto, Jakarta prioritized economic development and relied extensively on foreign direct investment, loans from international financial institutions, and robust trade with the West. Economic growth during the three decades of Suharto's heavy-handed rule averaged 6.57 percent. A failure to adopt macroeconomic reforms sought by the IFIs, however, led to a major financial crisis in 1997 that forced Suharto from power and initiated a transition toward democracy. Its core international identity, however, remained as a non-aligned nation and champion of the developing world, as exemplified by its leadership at the Asia-Africa Conference at Bandung, Indonesia, in 1955 attended by twenty-nine countries, including cosponsor India. The ten Bandung Principles were a

declaration of independence from the West versus East blocs, emphasizing territorial sovereignty, non-interference in internal affairs, nonalignment, and peaceful settlement of disputes. Lost in Indonesia's drive
for nonalignment, however, was the first principle of Bandung—"respect
for fundamental human rights." Later, as part of democratic Indonesia's
constitutional reform process between 1999 and 2002, new language
was adopted that more explicitly addressed the importance of promoting
and protecting human rights.[14]

The initial post-Suharto transition period was rocky and difficult as
Indonesia sought to climb out of its economic crisis and stabilize relations with its neighbors. President B. J. Habibie inherited a slew of painful conditions from the International Monetary Fund (IMF) and acceded
to demands to withdraw from East Timor, a former Portuguese colony
Indonesia had invaded in 1975. Both episodes generated resentment
toward external pressure that had tangible effects on Indonesian politics
and foreign policy. According to one commentator, President Abdurrahman Wahid (1999–2001) "alienated the IMF by refusing to meet some
of its conditions. The IMF withheld disbursements and the perceived loss
of international support helped to speed up Wahid's downfall."[15]

Similarly, the wide international condemnation of Indonesia's human
rights abuses in East Timor along with the insertion of peacekeepers led
by Australia and subsequent restrictions on military assistance by the
United States and others fed sentiments in the military and other nationalist sectors against alignment with the West. Other episodes stoked a
simmering resistance to a pro-U.S. alignment. Shortly after the 9/11 attack on the United States, for example, Presidents Bush and Megawati
broke new ground by agreeing to work together against global terrorism, including attacks against al Qaeda in Afghanistan; Washington also
announced a $630 million aid package for Jakarta, including economic,
trade, and investment assistance, and lifted the prohibition on the sale of
nonlethal defense materials.[16] Reactions by pro-Islamist groups in Indonesia were swift and harsh, forcing Megawati to withhold her government's open support for the U.S. campaign in Afghanistan and to call
for a suspension of bombing during Ramadan.[17]

While democratizing Indonesia struggled through a period of chaotic
governance—four presidents in a span of six years, the rise of political
Islam, ongoing fallout from its occupation and subsequent relinquish-
ment of its former territory of East Timor, and accompanying demands
for accountability for human rights abuses committed by its forces—it

also began to project its democratic credentials abroad as a way to restore its reputation as a politically stable, economically dynamic state. After its first free and fair direct elections in 2004, President Susilo Bambang Yudhoyono (2004–14) and Foreign Minister Hassan Wirajuda (2001–09) quietly chipped away at the principles of nonalignment and noninterference, an article of faith for Indonesia for decades, and gingerly began to build international consensus for commitments to democracy and human rights. At the fiftieth anniversary of the 1955 Bandung Conference, the historic bosom of nonalignment, Indonesia and South Africa even engineered a final declaration that, while reinforcing the original ten principles of the Nonaligned Movement, adopted new commitments, including "promotion of a just, democratic, transparent, accountable and harmonious society; [and] promotion and protection of human rights and fundamental freedoms, including the right to development."[18] A similar effort, with varied success, was undertaken with regard to ASEAN and a new initiative known as the Bali Democracy Forum.

Indonesia's increasingly confident projection of its democratic identity is the latest manifestation of the "independent and active" foreign policy forged in the earliest years of independence. After the rapid fall of the New Order government led by President Suharto (1965–98), Indonesia's *reformasi* leaders quickly embraced a host of constitutional reforms that institutionalized a system of stronger checks and balances. This transformation was its new calling card on the international scene, offering its leaders a renewed sense of legitimacy and independence as democratic movements gained power throughout the world free from the narrow parameters of the Cold War. In the words of Dewi Fortuna Anwar, an important foreign policy adviser in Jakarta, "Indonesia's identity as the third largest democracy in the world needs to be constructed as the primary image of the country."[19]

Indonesia's emerging democratic legitimacy, along with its generally moderate and tolerant brand of Islam, had tangible economic rewards for the country as it continued to climb out of its financial crisis: Western donor countries were eager to help it consolidate its fragile democracy and Indonesia was able to accept their assistance without the countervailing constraints of the Cold War.[20] These investments have yielded substantial dividends—it moved in Freedom House rankings from not free in 1997 to free in 2005, for example—but Indonesia still has a long way to go to consolidate its leadership credentials as Southeast Asia's most stable and economically dynamic democracy. The question policymakers in Jakarta face now is whether it should continue to rest on its democratic laurels and modest efforts to promote democracy and human rights, or pursue a more assertive set of policies to establish its credentials as a leading example of democratization in Asia and more activist defender of the international liberal order.

BUILDING CONSENSUS FOR DEMOCRACY AND HUMAN RIGHTS IN SOUTHEAST ASIA

Since a democracy works best in a democratic environment, we should also like to see the further growth of democratic values in our own neighbourhood.

HASSAN WIRAJUDA, *Foreign Minister (2001–09)*,
as quoted in *Journal of Democracy*, October 2011

Indonesia has long looked to its neighborhood as the main priority in its relations with the world. As the largest country in the region, across multiple indicators, Indonesia naturally took as its area of influence the neighboring states of Malaysia, the Philippines, Thailand, and Singapore. These states, due largely to Indonesia's diplomatic efforts, came together informally as the Association of Southeast Asian Nations (ASEAN) in 1967. Yet it took more than three decades for the group to formalize its structure, expand its membership to ten,[21] and establish the formalities of a regional organization, including an ASEAN Charter and Secretariat that finally took effect in 2009. From the start, Indonesia and its four original partners in ASEAN each had their own national reasons for joining the club, none of which had anything to do with democracy and human rights.[22] Each of the nondemocratic members who joined later also had no reason or interest to associate ASEAN with a democratic identity.

Yet with the consolidation of Indonesia's democratic regime during the 2000s, ASEAN gradually, and with very modest results, has at least incorporated the language of democracy, good governance, rule of law, and promotion and protection of human rights as fundamental principles of the organization. This is striking. Unlike Europe, Latin America and the Caribbean, the Commonwealth and Africa, which is each composed of a majority of electoral democracies and has developed robust democracy and human rights mechanisms, ASEAN in 2014 can count only two members with the requisite attributes of liberal democracy—Indonesia and the Philippines—and recently lost Thailand, perhaps for many more years, from this short list. So what explains its adoption of the rhetoric of democracy and human rights in its foundational documents and the creation of an ASEAN Intergovernmental Commission on Human Rights in 2009?

The answer lies largely in the determination of Indonesia to steer ASEAN toward a vision of democracy and human rights as a shared norm of the region. This was both a projection of Indonesia's own trajectory and of its fundamental belief in the value of democratic stability in its neighborhood. "My approach to ASEAN was driven by my own political experience in changing Indonesia," remarked former foreign minister Hassan Wirajuda. "Once people are fed and educated, they will ask for freedom. So it's best that we prepare for that by paving the way for democracy. That's why I introduced the concept of political development as one of the main pillars of the ASEAN community."[23] Indonesia felt so strongly about this principle that it even delayed signing the ASEAN Charter until it received assurances that human rights and democratic institutions would be integral to regional integration.[24]

In 2009, due mainly to Indonesia's leadership, ASEAN, as part of its drive toward regional integration on multiple fronts, adopted a blueprint for an ASEAN Political-Security Community (APSC) founded on shared values and norms.[25] The APSC "shall promote political development in adherence to the principles of democracy, the rule of law and good governance, respect for and promotion and protection of human rights and fundamental freedoms as inscribed in the ASEAN Charter," the Universal Declaration of Human Rights and the Vienna Declaration on Human Rights.[26] Toward that end, it agreed to finalize terms for an intergovernmental human rights body by 2009, draft an instrument to promote and protect the rights of migrant workers, and establish a commission on the rights of women and children.[27]

Not surprisingly, progress on ASEAN's political development pillar, due to come to fruition in 2015, has been frustratingly slow and, in its current form, is likely to remain stunted given the largely nondemocratic composition of ASEAN. The ASEAN Intergovernmental Commission on Human Rights (AICHR), which was inaugurated in October 2009, is composed of representatives of the ten member governments, who explicitly do not serve as independent commissioners, as they do in other regional human rights bodies.[28] The commission has no independent secretariat and no mandate to go beyond promotion to protection of human rights, for example, to receive or act on individual complaints or undertake its own investigations. While Indonesia led the way in appointing a well-regarded human rights activist as its representative, the majority of the commission's members are former or current diplomats who toe the governments' status quo line. As a result, valiant efforts by Indonesia to negotiate a viable ASEAN Declaration on Human Rights to guide the body's work were largely undone by the insertion of relativist language that stymies the commission's work: "the realisation of human rights must be considered in the regional and national context bearing in mind different political, economic, legal, social, cultural, historical and religious backgrounds."[29] Other language allows governments to restrict basic rights based on cultural or historical grounds, or on "requirements of national security, public order, public health, public safety, public morality, as well as the general welfare of the peoples in a democratic society."[30]

Such broad constraints echo earlier assertions of "Asian values" that many believe challenge the core concept of the universality of human rights.[31] On the other hand, the insertion of human rights into the ASEAN agenda is a break from past practice and may herald a longer-term evolution toward liberal norms.[32] Human rights activists and thought leaders like former ASEAN secretary general Surin Pitsuwan of Thailand and former Indonesian diplomat Makarim Wibisono have pushed back against the relativistic rhetoric, arguing, for example, that the doctrine of responsibility to protect civilians "is consistent with and integral to the overall goals" of a "caring and sharing ASEAN Community."[33] In their report on R2P in Southeast Asia, they remind ASEAN states of their endorsement of R2P principles at the 2005 World Summit and outline a series of steps to mainstream genocide prevention in the region.[34] It is unlikely, however, that their arguments will carry much weight with their nondemocratic ASEAN neighbors.

A critical operating principle of ASEAN and AICHR is consultation and consensus. This is both a blessing and a curse. According to former foreign minister Wirajuda, Indonesia supported the consensus principle because it gave it the ability to block moves that would undermine human rights. Given the composition of ASEAN, "we would have lost completely on these issues if they came to a vote."[35] It also reflects the value Indonesian officials place on deliberation and dialogue as a form of democratic decisionmaking in their own society, a value they suggest is a key element of their soft power in the world. On the other hand, consensus usually results in interminable debates and watered-down statements (if any at all) that have little to no impact outside the closed halls of ASEAN. ASEAN's silence in the face of the 2014 military coup in Thailand is a recent example of this phenomenon.[36] Another obstacle is the outsize role the rotating chairman plays in setting ASEAN's agenda. A Laos, Cambodia, or Brunei chairmanship yields little to no leadership on the political development pillar. In sum, according to one expert, ASEAN lacks "organizational coherence and clarity of leadership," despite Indonesia's ongoing efforts to forge common positions.[37]

While Indonesia deserves some praise for its efforts to introduce democracy and human rights concepts in such inhospitable terrain, there is little room for optimism in the short to medium term.[38] Until the member states of ASEAN themselves adopt more liberal and open forms of governance, progress toward a more robust human rights agenda in the region—country visits by independent experts, a mechanism to receive individual complaints, and the power to issue precautionary measures, for example—is unlikely. And as long as Indonesia continues to favor ASEAN as its first and closest "concentric circle" of foreign policy, human rights and democracy will take a back seat to other interests.

INDONESIA'S ACTIVIST APPROACH TO MYANMAR

In the mid-1990s, a pro-regime Burmese newspaper referred to Myanmar and Indonesia as "two nations with a common identity."[39] From its shared history as former colonies of European powers with hybrid economic systems, early but failed attempts at parliamentary democracy, and an outsize role for the military, the two neighbors for many years learned from and supported each other's regimes.[40] Modeling its political development on the Suharto New Order system, however, appears to have done little for Burma other than entrench the military's elite role in politics and the economy.[41]

During this time, Myanmar was eager to become a member of ASEAN as a means to fend off the growing international condemnation of the junta,[42] while some ASEAN members wanted to wean it away from China. In 1996, Indonesia under Suharto agreed with Malaysia that Myanmar should become a member of ASEAN in two years, overriding fears that this would only encourage the junta to continue to ignore calls for the transfer of power to a civilian government and for improvement

in its human rights record.[43] In response to U.S. and European criticism
of the decision,[44] ASEAN states maintained that the association would
now have more influence on Myanmar's development and that socializa-
tion into the group would improve the junta's behavior.[45] Furthermore,
there were economic and geopolitical incentives to include Myanmar in
ASEAN, such as the creation of an ASEAN economic area and the shared
desire to check China's growing influence in the country.[46]

Indonesia's pro-engagement policy toward Myanmar quickly changed
after the fall of Suharto and the onset of Indonesia's democratic transition. Its first post-Suharto president, Abdurrahman Wahid, openly sym-
pathized with Aung San Suu Kyi, the Burmese opposition leader placed
under house arrest in 1989, thus breaking the ASEAN tradition of declining to comment on the domestic politics of neighboring countries.[47]
His successor, President Megawati Sukarnoputri, used Indonesia's chairmanship of ASEAN in 2003 to forge language critical of the junta and
demanding Suu Kyi's release, another departure from its strict adherence
to the principle of noninterference.[48] Indonesia's leaders, however, did
not take a strong public stand against Myanmar, preferring instead to
publicize the regime's "guarantee" that Suu Kyi's case would be dealt
with before the impending ASEAN summit in Bali.[49]

As Myanmar's turn to assume chairmanship of ASEAN in 2006 approached, Megawati became more forceful in her rhetoric, stating in
2004, "We should be able to hold dialogue among ourselves openly and
frankly even on internal or domestic issues that . . . can have a severe
impact on the region."[50] Other pressures began to emerge on Indonesia
to toughen its approach toward the military regime. In February 2005,
Indonesian parliamentarians announced the launch of the Indonesian
Parliamentary Caucus on Myanmar, part of a larger ASEAN Inter-
Parliamentary Myanmar Caucus (AIPMC), formed in Malaysia and
Thailand the year before.[51] The Indonesian foreign office, along with
Malaysia and Singapore, stepped up its expressions of disappointment
in the lack of political reform in Myanmar, and politicians in Indonesia
and other ASEAN states began calling on Myanmar either to undertake
real political reform or forfeit the upcoming chairmanship.[52] In July
2005, after American and European threats that they would boycott
ASEAN events if Myanmar did not either release Suu Kyi or give up the
chairmanship, Myanmar agreed to skip its turn to chair the association.[53] While a few ASEAN members—Indonesia included—continued
to push for reforms behind the scenes, other members groused about

Western pressure and remained committed to ASEAN's noninterference policy.[54]

Jakarta's newfound interest in Myanmar's democratization was likely motivated by two factors. The first was domestic: Indonesia's rocky democratic transformation, still in its early years during the controversy over Myanmar's chairmanship, depended on attracting external financial support and foreign investment.[55] Indonesia's ability to convince the international community of its commitment to democracy as both a national and regional norm would encourage these inflows.[56] Megawati Sukarnoputri took up the issue of Myanmar's democratic transition to demonstrate this commitment, especially during Indonesia's chairmanship of ASEAN in 2003.[57] The second factor was regional: Indonesia's stature as an ASEAN leader depended on its handling of the long-standing Myanmar issue. If Indonesia could persuade Myanmar to embrace democracy, Indonesia's regional, not to mention international, reputation would be greatly strengthened.[58] And its investment in a more credible ASEAN would be advanced, as well.

President Yudhoyono continued to build on Megawati's push for democratization in Myanmar through a policy of constructive engagement, in opposition to the European Union's and United States' policy of punitive sanctions. In preparation for Yudhoyono's first state visit to Myanmar, the foreign ministers of Indonesia and Myanmar signed a memorandum of understanding in March 2006 on the formation of a joint commission for bilateral cooperation (JCBC), a "realization of Indonesia's efforts to help Myanmar implement democratic principles successfully," according to the Foreign Ministry in Jakarta.[59] The first round of JCBC meetings, however, focused on economic matters, trade and investment, energy, mines, agriculture, fisheries, tourism, defense, and security, revealing Jakarta's other priorities.

Although officials in Jakarta continuously called on Myanmar to demonstrate progress,[60] politicians within Indonesia argued that it was not enough. Indonesia's decision to abstain on a UN Security Council resolution in 2007 criticizing the junta in Myanmar drew immediate criticism from many Indonesian legislators.[61] The resolution, which called for the adoption of a democratic process in Myanmar and an end to suppressive actions against Karen and Rohingya minorities, failed as a result of vetoes by Russia and China.[62] Djoko Susilo, coordinator of the Indonesian Parliamentary Caucus on Myanmar, called the decision "very regrettable," adding that "as a developing country moving toward a true democracy and showing respect to human rights, Indonesia should put its weight behind the U.S.-proposed draft resolution to see major changes on human rights in Myanmar."[63] Legislators from the AIPMC also criticized the abstention, arguing that it damaged Indonesia's international image as a supporter of human rights.[64] Indonesia once again was compelled to "row between two reefs"—friendly relations with the United States, which sponsored the resolution, on the one hand, and with China (an important trade partner and infrastructure investor) and Russia (a source of arms), on the other.[65]

Meanwhile, the pressure on Jakarta to do more to punish Myanmar for its actions continued to build. Later that same year, at the 116th Inter-Parliamentary Union (IPU) Conference in Bali, the Governing Council called on "parliaments of the countries which are members of the Security Council to press their governments to ensure full and continuing consideration of the situation in Myanmar by the Security Council."[66] On the sidelines of the conference, Agung Laksono, the Indonesian Parliament Speaker of the House of Representatives, argued that regional stability depended on Myanmar's democratic and human rights progress: "Regional stability . . . will always be threatened by the spill-over effects of Myanmar's Government misrule, whether it is an impact of human rights and democracy violation or economic mismanagement. It is very clear that our destinies as neighboring countries are to seriously address Myanmar's deteriorating crises without delay."[67]

Conditions in Myanmar, meanwhile, deteriorated. In August 2007, large-scale demonstrations led by Buddhist monks against the military regime's policies, which came to be known as the Saffron Revolution, triggered a harsh crackdown and an international outcry. The Indonesian Parliamentary Caucus on Myanmar encouraged Yudhoyono to draw attention to the protests in his annual speech to the UN General Assembly.[68] Yudhoyono said nothing,[69] but he sent retired general Agus Widjojo, a key figure in Indonesia's own process of military reform, to Myanmar ostensibly to press the generals on the need for a democratic transition.[70] Yudhoyono also struck up a private correspondence with military junta leader Than Shwe "to share their thoughts in a no pressure format away from the media spotlight," according to one senior diplomat.[71] President Bush, on the other hand, announced new sanctions in response to the repression and the United Nations dispatched Special Envoy on Myanmar Ibrahim Gambari for a round of shuttle diplomacy to resolve the crisis.

By 2009, Myanmar's intransigence led the AIPMC, including its Indonesian parliamentarian members, to call on ASEAN to suspend Myanmar's membership if it failed to release Suu Kyi, and to consider sanctions in order to increase pressure for democratic reform.[72] In November 2010, the crisis finally broke when a new military-backed civilian government replaced the military junta through questionable elections, followed by the release of Aung San Suu Kyi a week later. The following May and October, the newly installed Thein Sein government freed several political prisoners; it also met with Aung San Suu Kyi and relaxed restrictions on peaceful demonstrations. By October 2011, Indonesian foreign minister Marty Natalegawa said enough democratic progress had been made to permit Myanmar's assumption of the ASEAN chair in 2014.[73] "It's not about the past, it's about the future, what leaders are doing now. We're trying to ensure the process of change continues," he told BBC News.[74] Despite attacks against the Rohingya minority in Burma's Rakhine State in 2012 and Indonesian support for reconciliation there,[75] Yudhoyono said in April 2013 that he saw significant progress toward democracy in Myanmar after the opposition won the vast majority of seats in parliamentary by-elections,[76] and reaffirmed support for Myanmar's assumption of the ASEAN chairmanship in 2014.[77] Indonesia's policy of constructive and critical engagement with a neighboring state in transition appeared to have been vindicated.

As key international stakeholders involved in Myanmar quickly adjusted their policies toward engagement with the Thein Sein government, including high-level visits from Secretary Clinton and President Obama and a sidelining of China,[78] Indonesia was well placed to lead external efforts to support the transition. Shortly after Yudhoyono's second state visit to Myanmar in April 2013, the third ministerial meeting of the joint cabinet group was held in Bali, preceded by a visit by the Myanmar delegation to the Institute for Peace and Democracy in Bali.[79] An Indonesian delegation then traveled to Yangon to initiate a three-year capacity-building partnership program aimed at strengthening cooperation to promote democracy, national reconciliation, social and economic development, and resilience.[80] Later that year, members of Myanmar's Presidential Advisory Council visited Aceh to observe the reconciliation process there.[81] Indonesia also extended asylum to some members of the Rohingya, a persecuted Muslim minority in Myanmar (with mixed results),[82] and has sought to deliver aid to the Rohingya community in Rakhine State.[83] At first, Indonesia refused to accept Rohingya refugees, fearing an influx of migrants they could not handle. However, following a two-week migration crisis in May 2015 in which migrants trapped at sea for two weeks were being bounced from country to country, Indonesia responded to international pressure and agreed to temporarily house some of the 7,000 "irregular migrants," which included Rohingya Muslims fleeing Myanmar.[84] It is only a temporary solution and the country signatories to the agreement (Indonesia, Malaysia, and Thailand) called on the international community to handle the resettlement and repatriation process within a year.

In contrast to Indonesia's deliberate and relatively progressive stance on democratic reforms in Myanmar, it mostly has been missing in action when it comes to democratic and human rights problems in other ASEAN states like Vietnam, Cambodia, and Laos. All three states joined ASEAN around the same time and all three have been obstacles to ASEAN's political reform and human rights commitments ever since.[85] Indonesia's principal role in Cambodia has been to mediate a long-standing border dispute between it and Thailand, including the dispatch of up to forty civilian and military observers to the disputed zone.

Ongoing political instability in Thailand, which reached a peak in May 2014 when the Thai army declared martial law and seized power from the democratically elected civilian government, has largely escaped Jakarta's attention. Initially, Foreign Minister Natalegawa called for "respect of constitutional process and democratic principles in order to promote national reconciliation and unity, reflecting the wishes of the Thai people. . . . It is our hope that this latest development will not detract from such principles and normalcy can quickly be restored."[86] When the Thai army seized full power soon after, Foreign Minister Natalegawa issued a tepid statement: "Without intending to interfere in the internal affairs of Thailand, as part of the ASEAN Community, in particular [the] ASEAN Political and Security Community, and in accordance with the Charter of ASEAN which emphasizes adherence to democratic principles and constitutional government, the developments in Thailand merit Indonesia's and ASEAN's attention."[87] Indonesia should have a particularly strong interest in seeing a return to democracy in Thailand as Bangkok has been a relatively reliable pro-democracy partner in ASEAN, including on the activist approach to Myanmar, Thailand's neighbor.[88] Although ASEAN issued a statement in December 2013 calling "on all parties concerned to resolve the current situation through dialogue and consultations in a peaceful and democratic manner,"[89] it has stood by its traditional doctrine of noninterference and has not responded to the May coup.[90]

INDONESIA AND THE WORLD

> We in Indonesia have shown, by example, that Islam, democracy and modernity can grow together. We are a living example that there is no conflict between a Muslim's spiritual obligation to Allah SWT, his civic responsibility as a citizen in a pluralist society, and his capacity to succeed in the modern world.
> PRESIDENT SUSILO BAMBANG YUDHOYONO, World Movement for Democracy, Jakarta, April 12, 2010

Indonesia's ambitions to improve the international climate to both protect and promote its own democratization process did not stop at the water's edge of Southeast Asia. On December 10, 2008, the sixtieth anniversary of the Universal Declaration of Human Rights, President Yudhoyono inaugurated the Bali Democracy Forum (BDF), the first intergovernmental dialogue on democracy in Asia. Yudhoyono artfully packaged the initiative as an effort to break away from the exclusive invitation-only format of the Community of Democracies and other clubs of democracies in favor of an inclusive approach that accepted all Asian states, from Beirut to Beijing, regardless of their political system. But Yudhoyono's core message was clear: as Asia rises, he asserted, its fate will depend on "our collective ability to advance democracy. . . . Our ability to meet this democratic challenge will be critical because unlike the 20th century, which was the century of hard power, the 21st century will be the century of soft power. And much of this soft power will be sourced in our democratic development."[91] He also rejected claims that democracy was a Western imposition alien to Asian or Islamic culture and history while acknowledging Indonesia's own struggles to connect democracy to good governance. He called on the thirty-two participating governments (including senior representatives from China, Saudi Arabia, and Syria) to join "an organized learning process" on practical issues of democratic governance, from elections to independent judiciaries, dynamic civil societies, and professional apolitical militaries.

By 2014, participation in the annual Bali ministerial had grown to eighty-five countries plus eight international organizations. In the closing ceremony of the 2014 forum, which examined themes of political development, socioeconomic progress, and public participation, Deputy Minister of Foreign Affairs Dino Patti Djalal noted a shift in understanding of the relationship between economic and political development. "Several decades ago," he said, "we assumed that democracy and economics could not be developed hand in hand. But today, all participants agree that politics and economics can be developed simultaneously in different ways."[92]

While observers are quick to point out that the BDF is little more than a talk shop for democrats and autocrats alike to make claims of fidelity to democratic values, Indonesia has not shied away from using the forum to promote core values familiar to any promoter of democracy. More important, Yudhoyono put institutional momentum behind the effort through creation of the Institute for Peace and Democracy (IPD), an independent implementing agency of the BDF charged with organizing workshops, trainings, and research on democratic governance. In its first five years, IPD has operated under the umbrella of legitimacy provided by BDF to engage in some important activities. It has carried out programs to promote constitutional reform in Tunisia and free and fair elections with Egypt, Tunisia, Fiji, and Myanmar, including bringing delegations from several countries to Indonesia to observe its 2009 and 2014 elections. Civilian control of the military has been an important theme in its work with Myanmar. In all such activities, IPD's approach relies principally on the political will of the relevant parties to learn from Indonesia's own experience, starting with its own mistakes. This more humble "peer learning" style is intentionally distinct from the preachier version of U.S.-style democracy promotion; however, its results are still unclear. Indonesia, for example, rarely criticizes other countries publicly and rejects placing human rights or good governance conditions on development and trade cooperation.[93]

In contrast to its democracy promotion profile, at the United Nations, Indonesia's tradition of noninterference in internal affairs runs strong and deep. It studiously avoids voting for resolutions that criticize specific countries, regardless of the intensity of the violations at stake. In a study comparing the votes of five rising democracies on human rights resolutions at the UN Human Rights Council and General Assembly from 2005 to 2010, Indonesia scored lowest.[94] On resolutions criticizing human rights situations in countries such as Belarus, Cuba, North Korea, and Sudan, Indonesia consistently voted no or, in special cases, abstained. An exception to its adherence to noninterference is Israel-Palestine; Indonesia regularly aligns itself with OIC to condemn the occupation and the conflict in Gaza. During Indonesia's tenure on the UN Security Council (2007–08), Indonesia largely joined consensus on such country-specific texts as Afghanistan, Côte d'Ivoire, Iraq, and Somalia, but abstained on important resolutions regarding Myanmar, Zimbabwe, and Lebanon. In each of those cases, its diplomats acknowledged the deteriorating human rights situation but demurred on elevating it as a threat to international peace and security, as required by chapter VII, calling instead for greater dialogue and mediation.[95]

Since 2011, Indonesia has slightly improved its voting record at the Human Rights Council, voting for eleven of thirteen resolutions on the human rights crisis in Syria and abstaining on resolutions critical of Belarus, rather than voting no. On Sri Lanka, however, Indonesia voted against a series of resolutions calling for greater accountability for the human rights violations committed during the final battles against Tamil separatists. Similarly, it has abstained on recent resolutions that would have offered technical assistance to Ukraine following Russia's incursion into Crimea in 2014. Indonesia showed no support for joint statements on Eritrea, Bahrain, or Egypt and tried to water down resolutions critical of its neighbors Myanmar and Cambodia. It also either abstained or voted against all six UNHRC resolutions condemning violations in North Korea, and backtracked somewhat in its voting patterns toward human rights violations in Iran, voting no on two recent resolutions instead of abstaining as it had previously.[96] At the UN, at least, Indonesia's record remains beholden to the noninterference doctrine.

In other cases of democratic backsliding in Asia, and more high-profile cases of egregious human rights violations such as during the Arab awakening, Indonesia has sought to engage, if at all, in ways that reflect its low-profile, cooperative approach. In Fiji, for example, repeated coups and stalled elections have led neighboring states like Australia and New Zealand to sever relations and impose heavy sanctions along with suspension from the Commonwealth. Despite Fiji's failure to meet a 2010 deadline on elections, Indonesia invited Fiji for the first time to the Third Bali Democracy Forum in December 2010.[97] Indonesia had a larger goal in mind when it reached out to the island nation: it sought to influence the emerging Melanesian Spearhead Group (MSG), which had admitted a political group sympathetic to separatist forces seeking independence for the Indonesian half of Papua.[98] The indigenous population of the two

Indonesian provinces on Papua is mainly Melanesian and Christian. The separatists would like to gain membership in the MSG to strengthen their bid for international recognition. Indonesia wanted observer status in the MSG and Fiji was interested in observer status at ASEAN.[99] Bilateral ties were further strengthened with the opening of a Fijian embassy in Indonesia in April 2011.[100]

Soon thereafter, in 2012, as Fiji undertook a process of public consultation for constitutional reform, the two governments agreed on a strategy to help Fiji prepare for the 2014 elections, to be implemented by Indonesia's Institute for Peace and Democracy (IPD).[101] Ketut Erawan, the executive director of the IPD, during a March 2013 visit, cited three lessons in particular that Indonesia could share with Fiji:

1. How to create "a sense of nation," "a set of proposals of oneism," for a country in which so many different ethnic groups and histories exist.

2. How to design rule of law and create a legal and political system on which to base the democratic process.

3. How to conceive of the democratic process—which is "not a short game," but, in his words, "continuous [and] long."[102]

As part of Indonesia's renewed interest in its Pacific Island neighbors,[103] President Yudhoyono traveled to Fiji in June 2014 to accept its invitation to co-lead the multinational group of observers of Fiji's September election.[104] Although five political parties told journalists they were concerned about ballot tampering, the Multinational Observer Group did "not [observe] any significant irregularities in the counting process" and issued a preliminary statement declaring the election credible.[105] Shortly thereafter, the Commonwealth readmitted Fiji and its leading member, Australia, dropped sanctions.

Consistent with its modest, incremental approach, Indonesia quietly reached out to governments in the Arab world to offer assistance as they coped with the tumultuous demands for political and economic change in the region. Officially, Indonesia carefully maintained a neutral stance toward the uprisings to protect its otherwise amicable relations with its Arab Muslim cohorts, many of whom receive hundreds of thousands of Indonesian migrant workers. It is also concerned, reasonably so, that extremist forces fighting in the region not find a foothold in Indonesia, through recruits, financing, or alliances with domestic forces. Humanitarian missions to Syria carried out by Indonesian Islamic organizations providing cash and medical assistance to extremist Islamist fighters have provided a gateway for direct participation by Indonesian citizens in the fighting, despite government efforts to rein them in.[106]

Wary of appearing preachy or interventionist, especially after the U.S. war to topple Saddam Hussein in Iraq, Indonesian officials are quick to point out to Arab audiences that democracy must be a homegrown affair. "Our role is to compare notes and share lessons learned, especially problems we've encountered so they don't necessarily have to re-invent the wheel," explained Foreign Minister Natalegawa.[107] Transitional governments in Tunisia and Egypt were quick to take up the offer of assistance. In May 2013, for example, Indonesia hosted a Tunisian delegation to observe elections and attend a workshop on holding free and fair elections, the need for professional judges to deal with election irregularities, the role of the military in elections and in politics in general, and the role of Islam in politics.[108] In the case of Egypt, which under Hosni Mubarak shared many characteristics of Suharto's regime in Indonesia,[109] President Yudhoyono sent a message to the ruling military council acknowledging the similarities of experience and expressing interest in sharing "messages, views, and recommendations."[110] Over the next eighteen months, Indonesian and Egyptian representatives from political parties, think tanks, academia, media, and civil society engaged in a series of five workshops organized by the Institute for Peace and Democracy on topics ranging from constitutional and judicial reform and minority rights to the role of women and Islam in politics.[111] Apparently, neither the Muslim Brotherhood government under President Morsi nor the Egyptian military absorbed the lessons of the Indonesian transition: as the democratization process collapsed in Cairo and the military ruthlessly retook the reins of power in July 2013, Indonesia's leaders were left on the sidelines to protest the use of force against protesters and call for reconciliation with the Muslim Brotherhood, while not condemning the coup, per se.[112]

On Syria, the Indonesian government was relatively quiet as protests against the regime emerged. After the Hama massacres in August 2011, however, the government issued a statement condemning the use of force and expressing a need for dialogue. That year it also supported the UN Human Rights Council's special session on Syria and its appointment of a Special Rapporteur for the crisis, a break from its traditional practice of abstention on resolutions critical of specific countries.[113] Despite his previous silence on the civil war in Syria, Yudhoyono went further in early 2013, urging President Bashar al-Assad to step down.[114] The statement was made during a private discussion with seven syeikh (Islamic scholars) about how to bring about an end to the Syrian conflict. Yudhoyono expressed the view that Assad's resignation would do just that.[115] The presidential spokesman for international affairs later said Indonesia would not sever all ties with the Assad regime, as Indonesia tries to maintain contact with all relevant parties so as to more effectively seek a resolution.[116] When it came time to vote in May 2014 on a UN General Assembly resolution condemning the Assad regime and accepting the opposition Syrian National Coalition group as a party to a political transition, Indonesia demurred, arguing that it did not want to take sides with certain parties in the conflict. "For Indonesia," Foreign Minister Natalegawa explained, "the legitimate government of Syria is for Syrian people themselves to decide, not outside parties."[117] Noninterference and other interests once again prevailed.

During the HRC special session on Libya in February 2011, Indonesia's delegation spoke out against the violence and encouraged dialogue between the people and the authorities to turn the situation into "an opportunity for democracy, progress and a prosperous future for the country."[118] When the UN General Assembly suspended Libya from the Human Rights Council a month later by consensus resolution, Indonesia spoke about the importance of respecting international human rights and humanitarian law and providing relief to the Libyan people to "ensure conditions conducive to a democratic political process."[119]

FOREIGN POLICY AND DOMESTIC POLITICS

The success of Indonesia's strategic projection of its modern identity as a pluralist, democratic society depends, of course, on the quality and depth of its own behavior at home. For a country with a shortage of hard power resources—Indonesia spends only 0.83 percent of its GDP on its military[120]—soft power, defined by Indonesia's leaders as its identity as the world's third largest democracy, is critical to its influence abroad. By most accounts, its reputation as a democratizing reformer continues to rise, although some serious weak spots may dint the glow the Yudhoyono administration has tried so hard to create. Jokowi inherits, for example, a declining rate of poverty reduction (93 million Indonesians live on under $2 a day), low capital investments in much-needed infrastructure, low student achievement scores, and the fifth lowest level of public spending on health in the world.[121]

Unlike India, which is preoccupied with tackling its own daunting development challenges while competing with rivals China and Pakistan, Indonesia projects a nonthreatening self-confidence about its trajectory as a prosperous and stable democracy. In his final address to the UN General Assembly in September 2014, President Yudhoyono noted that Indonesia had increased national income per capita by 400 percent in ten years and cited "smart governance"—innovative leadership and public participation—as the most important driver of change.[122] Yudhoyono also left power in the wake of a third set of free, fair, and highly competitive elections that brought more than 133 million Indonesians (69.58 percent) to the polls to choose between candidates with starkly different histories and platforms. When the losing candidate, former general Subianto Prabowo, contested the results, constitutional and legal norms and mechanisms were used to handle the dispute and the Constitutional Court's decision to uphold the victory of Jokowi was widely accepted. A majority of voters polled after the elections said they were happy with the direction of the country, preferred democracy, and were optimistic about the condition of the economy.[123]

In a maneuver designed to weaken Jokowi's mandate, opposition forces led by Prabowo pushed the legislature to eliminate direct elections of governors, mayors, and other local officials. This move was widely rejected by the public,[124] another sign that Indonesian citizens, if not their political leaders, take seriously their rights to have a voice in public affairs, despite a fair measure of electoral fatigue and rising corruption in electoral politics. President Yudhoyono, who told BDF the bill was a "step backward for Indonesia's democracy,"[125] issued two emergency decrees (*Perppu*) the next week, one that repealed the law and another that revoked the Regional Legislative Council's right to elect regional leaders.[126] A few months later, Parliament reached consensus to restore direct elections, a major win for the new president and his predecessor and an important nod to public opinion.

Even ardent defenders of Indonesia's progress acknowledge, however, that its ability to promote democracy and human rights abroad is weakened by its troubling record on issues of religious rights, police torture, impunity for violations by security forces, the death penalty, and restrictions on civil society, especially in the restive region of Papua. New law adopted in 2013 covering all civic and religious NGOs, including media, empowers the government to dissolve organizations that do not avow the principles of Pancasila, narrows the types of activities they can undertake, and increases bureaucratic controls; foreign groups are restricted, as well.[127] Its ambitious process of decentralization, launched in 1999 as a means of tamping down secessionist threats in Aceh and Papua, has proven particularly challenging to basic governance and a threat to the rule of law and human rights. Local officials often ignore edicts from Jakarta, engage in corrupt practices, or impose restrictions on civil liberties in the name of Sharia. Democracy promoters in Indonesia recognize that its experience with decentralization to date "caused a lot of headaches, so [we] are very cautious in adding it" to the democracy agenda with other countries.[128]

Other factors of Indonesia's national history cast a shadow on its willingness and ability to be a serious advocate for democracy and human rights in other countries. From its earliest days of independence, it struggled to create a unified state, fighting and ultimately beating Dutch attempts to impose a weak federal system.[129] The army's defeat of the 1958 rebellions in the "Outer Islands," which some historians claim were manipulated by the United States to prevent Sukarno from forging an alliance with communist forces, was another milestone in Indonesia's nationhood and its historical preoccupation with territorial integrity and sovereignty.[130] Its decision to annex East Timor in 1976 and the subsequent twenty-year period of "integration as Indonesian brothers" was a particularly aggressive episode of Indonesian nationalism that ended badly for Jakarta. As Timorese nationalists dug in for a long campaign for independence, Indonesia sent "volunteers" to defend the province, prompting criticism both from developed countries opposed to Jakarta's heavy-handed tactics and from NAM colleagues in favor of self-determination. But it was not until the Cold War came to an end that Indonesia's behavior in East Timor garnered enough attention and pressure from the international community to force Jakarta to loosen the reins and ultimately let East Timor break away. This trauma, coupled with secessionist campaigns in other provinces (Aceh, Irian Jaya, and Maluku) and even events like the breakup of the former Yugoslavia, reinforced the importance for some leaders of maintaining the government's control of Indonesia's far-flung provinces.[131]

The legacy of violations committed by Indonesia's security forces in East Timor, particularly during the violent aftermath of the East Timorese independence referendum in 1999, continues to constrain its willingness to adopt international accountability instruments like the Rome Statute of the International Criminal Court (ICC). Although the

ICC's jurisdiction is not retroactive, Indonesia's troubled history of impunity, particularly stemming from the brutal and widespread crackdown on alleged communist sympathizers in 1964–65, gives Indonesian politicians pause.[132] As Defense Minister Purnomo Yusgiantoro put it, "We've already got a law on human rights, a law on human rights tribunals and the Constitution . . . So even without ratifying [the Rome Statute], we're already complying with the principles enshrined in it."[133] Indeed, some modest improvements have been made in prosecuting military and police officials charged with human rights violations.[134] But the presence of powerful politicians like Prabowo, former lieutenant general, who nearly won the presidency in 2014 despite serious allegations of his responsibility for human rights violations surrounding Suharto's downfall in 1998, are a fresh reminder that the country has unfinished business.

The terrorist attacks of September 11, 2001, followed by bombings in Bali in October 2002 and in Jakarta in 2003, provoked a new wave of anxiety among Indonesian elites that radical Islamist factions might get a foothold in Indonesia and disrupt its fragile democratization process. The country's Muslim majority population adheres mainly to moderate forms of Islam, and Islamic principles did not figure prominently in elite decisionmaking for years. The appointment of Abdurrahman Wahid, the president of the Nahdlatul Ulama Islamic organization and a forceful advocate of religious tolerance, to the presidency in 1999 was a breakthrough in terms of accommodating religious views in the political sphere. The al Qaeda–inspired attack by the Jemaah Islamiyah terrorist group against a tourist site in Bali, however, was a setback to this trend. It demonstrated the price Indonesia would have to pay for its support of the U.S.-led war against terrorism and the potential localization of global Islamist radicalism in Indonesia.

Indonesia has long struggled with its dual identity as a secular state whose society and domestic politics are shaped and guided by the values and norms of Islam. Tensions escalated in the wake of the September 11 attacks in the United States as the Indonesian government and public grappled with the issue of terrorism and its conflation with Islam. Anti-American demonstrations and other public pushback against President Megawati's reaction in the immediate aftermath of the attacks forced the government to walk back its support of the United States, a prime example of how domestic politics (and in this instance Islam) can hamstring foreign policy.[135] The intensification of conflict with Aceh separatists in 2002–03, which President Megawati tried to link to international terrorism, was another manifestation of the preoccupation with national sovereignty and noninterference, particularly in the military. As Susilo Bambang Yudhoyono took up the presidency in 2004, the Aceh conflict had subsided, due in part to the massive tsunami that hit the country in December 2004. A peace agreement was signed in August 2005, allowing Yudhoyono to turn his attention to projecting a new image for Indonesia as an aspiring democratic leader in the region and beyond.

More recent violence in the Middle East, stoked by the brutal tactics of ISIL and its armed campaign for an Islamic caliphate, is drawing recruits from around the world, including Indonesia, and provoking anxiety about Indonesia's ability to contain more radical elements on its own soil. Although Indonesia officially banned ISIL in August 2014 for espousing teachings "not in line with state ideology, Pancasila," apprehension about fighters returning from the Middle East conflicts also no doubt played a role in the decision as Indonesia continues to struggle with its dual identity as a secular state whose society is shaped and guided by the values and norms of Islam.[136]

As Indonesia became more confident in its democratization process, it opened doors to more voices in foreign policy decisionmaking, as well. Yudhoyono and his foreign policy team made a deliberate effort to engage actors outside the traditional foreign policy and military elite, first and foremost in the lower house of Parliament, the People's Representative Council (DPR). They did not really have a choice. Measures adopted early in the *reformasi* period expanded the DPR's powers dramatically, including in foreign policy and national security affairs. These included consultation on ambassadorial appointments (which in practice meant power to approve or reject the government's candidates) and, unusually, the right to approve ambassadors sent to Jakarta by other countries. The DPR also reasserted its traditional powers to ratify treaties and demand senior officials to testify, with results that often challenged the government's proposals.[137] For example, Indonesia's vote in 2007 for a UN Security Council resolution imposing sanctions on Iran for its nuclear program drew strong opposition from various constituencies and legislators, particularly from Islamist parties, for appearing to unfairly condemn a fellow Muslim country. Islamic leaders also complained that the government was bowing to demands from the West to defend the interests of Israel.[138] In addition, some political factions used the controversy to try to embarrass the president after losing seats in a disappointing cabinet reshuffle.[139] The DPR demanded President Yudhoyono appear for questioning on the matter and rejected the president's counteroffer of a delegation of ministers. While ultimately DPR relented after intensive lobbying by Yudhoyono, the episode had a chilling effect on Indonesian diplomats responsible for casting votes in international bodies on issues that might attract public controversy. Indonesia henceforth abstained on UNSC votes sanctioning Iran,[140] and for the most part has continued to keep a low profile on matters concerning Iran. Indonesia voted no on the two most recent UNHRC resolutions holding Iran accountable for human rights violations, indicated support for the Iran nuclear deal announced in July 2015, and hosted an Iranian delegation later that month to discuss bilateral cooperation on energy, nuclear technology, and banking.[141]

Another consistent feature of Indonesian foreign policy since the advent of democracy is the promotion of Palestine as an independent state free from Israeli occupation, a view widely supported by the Indonesian public. President Wahid, who came from the country's largest Islamic organization, learned the importance of this issue the hard way when he proposed opening trade relations between Israel and Indonesia, prompting a firestorm of criticism at home. Since then, Indonesian leaders have reliably highlighted their rhetorical support for the Palestinian cause at the UN and other fora, though with few substantive efforts beyond that, and by voting in favor of all UN resolutions supporting Palestine. When plans to establish an Indonesian representative office in Ramallah to manage relations with Israel fell through, Foreign Minister Natalegawa emphasized that "the problem is not with Palestine" but rather "Indonesia has yet to recognize Israel" and "we still don't want to open [diplomatic ties] with the occupying state."[142] Indonesia and Palestine retain a strong bilateral relationship, but Indonesia is far from one of the Palestinian authority's most vocal supporters at the international level. Jokowi promises to continue this general approach.

Beyond the obvious political imperative of addressing the concerns of Muslim groups, Indonesia's foreign policy leaders made a concerted effort to reach out to diverse segments of civil society to help democratize both the process and substance of its policies. Foreign Ministers Wirajuda and Natalegawa both have made a point of actively consulting with academics, think tanks, journalists, nongovernmental organizations, and the relatively free and open media through regular briefings and workshops.[143] At least one coalition of NGOs, the Human Rights Working Group, actively campaigns for greater attention to human rights in the country's foreign policy, particularly regarding ASEAN. Indonesia's burgeoning social media scene—Indonesians are among the world's most active users of Facebook and Twitter—adds another dynamic to the debate, and raises the pressure on reputation-sensitive government officials to react quickly to emerging issues.

Yudhoyono's ambitious drive to raise Indonesia's profile as a serious player on the international scene was accompanied by his foreign minister's leadership of a comprehensive reform process within the foreign ministry, building on the military's withdrawal from civilian posts across the government.[144] His "self-improvement process" sought to upgrade the ministry's information technology infrastructure and instill a more democratic decisionmaking culture. New resources were committed to upgrade its public diplomacy efforts as key to projecting its soft power attributes. A special Human Rights Directorate and Directorate for the Protection of Indonesian Nationals ramped up consular and other support to Indonesian migrant workers overseas, an important economic and political constituency for the government. Other observers have commented, however, that even with 132 missions abroad,[145] the government lacks the capacity to deliver on its ambitious vision and Natalegawa has been unable to persuade parliament not to cut the foreign ministry's budget. His new deputy, Dino Patti Djalal, recently called for greater creativity in the ministry's approach by moving beyond nostalgia for the past. He also acknowledged, however, that Indonesia "is a middle power with limited diplomatic, military and economic resources."[146] In addition to scarce diplomatic resources, Indonesia has one of the lowest development assistance budgets among middle power democracies as it slowly pivots from being a large recipient of foreign assistance to a modest donor of mainly South-South cooperation.

As President Jokowi seeks to consolidate the soft power gains made under his successor, he will have to address some of the most pressing deficits in Indonesia's democratic ledger at home. Initial signals were discouraging. A running battle between the police and the independent Corruption Eradication Commission (KPK), which has received high marks for its willingness to go after senior government officials and judges for corruption, intensified in 2014 when Jokowi named police General Budi Gunawan to head the national police service. The KPK responded by opening a graft case against Gunawan, forcing Jokowi to sideline him to the deputy police position, but at a cost. Two KPK commissioners were forced to resign and now face their own investigations.[147] Jokowi has an opportunity to defend the KPK against mounting attacks from the police and other power brokers swept up in its impressive dragnet (it has achieved a near 100 percent conviction rate) by appointing strong candidates to its board and allocating more resources to its threadbare budget. He will have the public's support in doing so—polls show KPK is one of the country's most trusted institutions.[148] Jokowi could also promote a next generation of political reforms to streamline the electoral system, get control of the decentralization process, and regulate the freewheeling flow of money into political campaigns. In foreign policy terms, he would be smart to build on Yudhoyono's successful drive to raise Indonesia's profile as a democratic reformer in the region, and pick one or two priorities for action, like tackling the unfinished business of Myanmar's democratization process and improving Indonesia's recalcitrant record on human rights matters at the UN.

CONCLUSION

In sum, Indonesia's transformation from its former authoritarian model to a competitive pluralist democratic state has had a direct effect on its decision to mainstream democracy and human rights in its foreign policy. In the Suharto era, Indonesia accepted UN human rights visits only as a way to deflect international pressure it was facing in Geneva. In contrast, during the early difficult years of its transition, it looked to international instruments like country visits by the UN's independent human rights experts, ratifications of treaties, and more recently the Universal Periodic Review (UPR) process as a means of catalyzing the reforms needed to consolidate civilian control of the military and a more open government.[149] "Diplomacy," according to former foreign minister Wirajuda, "is more than just projection of national interests. It is also about translating international norms to the national level."[150] Having experienced for itself the positive contribution of international norms and practices to its own reform process, Indonesia is more open to suggest such mechanisms for others, even in the inhospitable terrain of its ASEAN neighborhood. Its profile as a member of the international liberal order, however, reveals a distinctly Indonesian style. While it remains constrained by historical experiences that weaken support for a robust international order and by a dynamic political scene that includes nationalist and conservative Islamic voices, its founding Pancasila principles of "nationalism with humanity and social justice" provide the necessary foundation to help Indonesia become a quietly principled and constructive leader for democracy and human rights around the world.

CHAPTER EIGHT

Paths to Convergence

SINCE THE END OF the Cold War, the global democracy and human rights order has evolved, in fits and starts, toward greater activism on a widening array of issues, from water and sanitation to business and human rights to equality for all, regardless of sexual orientation. The rights of the elderly, people with albinism, people with disabilities, contemporary forms of slavery, climate change and the environment, truth and reconciliation, and rights affected by counterterrorism are some of the many new areas of special concern on the international human rights agenda. The language of rights has also broadened to include new concepts like human security and responsibility to protect civilians along with new mechanisms like international criminal courts, commissions of inquiry, and universal periodic review of every state's human rights record. The creation of a full-time UN Human Rights Council in 2006 and the burgeoning activity of regional human rights mechanisms and courts demonstrate a growing acceptance of monitoring and accountability for behavior that transgresses universal norms. Concepts of transparency, accountability, and rule of law are increasingly integrated in a range of "good governance" and development assistance projects around the world. It is fair to say the international human rights and democracy agenda is enormous and expanding.

None of these new developments would have been possible without a broadly shared consensus led by the world's democracies that these challenges demand not just national but international action of some kind—from research and debate on new norms to adoption of treaties, appointment of independent monitors, in-country investigations, and prosecution of alleged perpetrators. As the number of democratic governments has grown, so too has the public's interest in holding their governments to account for how they behave both inside and outside their borders. It also speaks to the enduring power that concepts like democracy and human rights hold over a state's national and international image and reputation and the ensuing battle over what defines them.

The democracy and human rights movement, nonetheless, faces a mounting crisis of confidence in the face of a string of major setbacks.[1] The traditional leading voices for the universality of democracy and human rights—the United States, Europe, and a scattering of like-minded allies such as Australia and Canada—are coping with their own internal challenges, both economic and political, that feed skepticism about the ability of democracies to meet the aspirations of rising middle classes and breed populist nationalism. Their leadership of the international order is being questioned by critics who charge that the promotion of human rights and democracy are tools of hegemonic powers bent on reshaping the world in their own images and pursuing their own geopolitical ends. They allege, for example, that the traditional champions of human rights have overreached, the global brand has been corrupted, the proliferation of norms and treaties has not led to real improvements on the ground, and we are now facing the messy reality of a multipolar world that does not share the same values.[2] They further complain that conventional powers promote a biased view that elevates political rights at the expense of economic and social rights and capitalist orthodoxy over socialist systems. The intense debate surrounding U.S.-led interventions in Iraq and Libya generated strong currents against armed interventions even when intended to protect civilians facing mass atrocities. Others reaffirm the value of a universal approach to human rights but assert that the more expansive notion of "human dignity" would take us further in a global dialogue meant to overcome profound historical, cultural, and religious differences.[3]

The behavior of the United States abroad, particularly after the attacks of 9/11, has probably hurt more than helped matters. From the "democratic imperialism" of the Iraq war to the hardline regime change approach to Libya and the collateral damage inflicted by U.S. warplanes and drones on unarmed civilians in places such as Pakistan, Yemen, and Iraq, to the brutal treatment of detainees at Abu Ghraib and Guantanamo Bay and the ongoing impunity and lack of transparency for such violations, the United States has lost moral standing as a champion for human rights in the eyes of millions of people around the world. In response to allegations of torture by U.S. personnel, documented in gross detail in a U.S. Senate report, UN High Commissioner for Human Rights Zeid Ra'ad Al Hussein remarked to the Human Rights Council in March 2015, "Under international law, the [Senate report's] recommendations must be followed through with real accountability. There is no prescription for torture, and torture cannot be amnestied. It should also lead to examination of the institutional and political causes that led the U.S. to violate the absolute prohibition on torture, and measures to ensure this can never recur."[4] Despite the clear legal obligations to prohibit, investigate, and prosecute alleged acts of torture,[5] action to hold U.S. individuals accountable for such acts looks unlikely. And while the Senate report on torture laid down an important marker for transparency, the Senate remains allergic to accepting other international human rights treaties, even those modeled on U.S. law, such as the UN Convention on the Rights of Persons with Disabilities.[6]

Fatigue from the long wars in Afghanistan and Iraq, and the painful scars carried home by U.S. forces, are constraining U.S. leadership, as well. President Obama's ambitious first-term efforts to right the wrongs of the "global war on terror," reach out to the Muslim world, protect civilians in Libya, and learn the lessons of Rwanda have faltered. The weak response to the horrific violence of the Bashar al-Assad regime in Syria and the spiraling explosion of warfare there is perhaps the most compelling example of what can go wrong when Washington looks away even as proclaimed red lines are crossed. While the Obama administration deserves credit for speaking out and acting on a variety of compelling human rights and humanitarian emergencies, such as the use of chemical weapons in Syria and the Ebola crisis in West Africa, a mood of paralysis and parsimony has prevailed.

The failure of the United States to lead by example at home is also exacerbating the crisis of confidence. The American political system, the purported "shining city on the hill" that politicians like to proclaim, has slid toward dysfunctional polarization as secret money, sanctioned by the Supreme Court, creeps its way into all levels of elections, including judicial races. The revelations by Edward Snowden and others of intrusive post-9/11 U.S. intelligence collection at home and abroad are another wake-up call that American civil liberties are at risk. The disastrous global recession of 2008, kick-started by the legal and ethical lapses of the U.S. financial system, added to the pervasive pessimism toward the U.S. ability to lead the global economy. The growing awareness of police violence toward minorities and entrenched impunity for such acts are yet more evidence that the United States is not so exceptional in world affairs,[7] at least in positive terms.[8] And despite some recent improvements in the U.S. economy, the continued decline of the American middle class and rising inequality suggest the vaunted American dream that has drawn millions of immigrants to U.S. shores is increasingly out of reach for younger generations.

The United States, a self-admittedly imperfect democracy, believes in and continues to show the world the value of self-correcting, if slow and inadequate, mechanisms. This was highlighted symbolically by the improbable election—twice—of Barack Hussein Obama to the White House, a moment that improved perceptions about the American model of social and political mobility and inclusion. Other recent examples include measures to rein in secret wiretapping, reduce harsh penalties for nonviolent drug offenses, and expand universal health care coverage. Nonetheless, most observers agree that Washington's wings have been clipped of late and argue the United States must correct its growing political dysfunction and rights record if it is to recover its moral standing and regain influence.[9]

The democratic and economic recessions in the United States and Europe are mirrored by a more generalized stalling and backsliding on the post–Cold War democracy wave. As documented by Freedom House, ratings of respect for political liberties and civil rights have declined annually for the past nine years.[10] Other indexes of democratic governance like the World Bank's Governance Index and the Bertelsmann Transformation Index echo and amplify these findings. Countries once thought to be solidly on the democratic path, like Thailand, Ecuador, and Hungary, are falling aside or wobbling. As documented in chapter 1, the IBSATI five are also underperforming on a range of democracy and human rights indicators. Most notably, the hopes of the Arab Spring, with the sole exception of Tunisia, have shattered into an orgy of violence and despair as secularists, monarchists, and the military battle against extremist violence by Islamist radicals bent on imposing a winner-take-all scheme that is the antithesis of human rights and democracy.

Within this turbulence, Russia and China are playing leading and complementary roles in undermining core principles of democracy and human rights at the national and international levels. Vladimir Putin's cynical and frontal attack on so-called Western imperialism allegedly disguised as support to civil society and digital freedom, combined with his aggressive moves to redraw boundaries with neighboring, and democratizing, Ukraine are particularly threatening. The ambitions of President Xi Jinping to assert China's leadership in Asia, its intensifying repression of human rights activists at home and in Hong Kong, and its no-strings approach to massive loans and investments in Africa and Latin America also pose serious challenges to the established liberal order. Its authoritarian capitalist model, in which economic prosperity is coupled with tight state control of political and civil freedoms, has, for some, a certain appeal.[11] China has been known to exact punishment when states cross important red lines regarding meetings with the Dalai Lama or awarding Nobel Peace prizes to Chinese human rights activists, and often exerts a negative influence at bodies like the Human Rights Council.[12] Russia and China have used their vetoes as permanent members of the UN Security Council to block a number of attempts to assert more forceful intervention in Syria. They also have aggressively entered the public diplomacy sphere through state-sponsored news channels beamed around the world with often one-sided and propagandistic renditions of their success, fanning the flames of an East versus West narrative.[13]

Of particular concern is the deliberate attack against the growing prevalence and effectiveness of civil society organizations, which rely extensively on donors from the West. Together, Russia and China, along with other like-minded authoritarian governments such as Vietnam, Cuba, Saudi Arabia, Syria, and Egypt, as well as elected autocrats in countries like Venezuela and Sri Lanka, are manipulating and blocking attempts by liberal forces to bolster and sustain the progress made over the past twenty years. These counterattacks are a testament, in part, to the effectiveness of these watchdogs, recent memories of the string of "color revolutions" that previously toppled autocratic regimes, and the resonance that conspiracy theories continue to have with elite and public opinion.

Unfortunately, as explained in previous chapters, this authoritarian coalition often includes swing state democracies like South Africa, India, and Indonesia. A "Like-Minded Group" of states led by Russia, China, Egypt, and Pakistan, often joined by Indonesia, South Africa, and India, is generally first in line at the UN to demand strict adherence to non-intervention principles, at the expense of unarmed civilians caught in the cross fire. These states opposed, for example, UN efforts to investigate Sri Lanka's heavy-handed termination of its civil war as intrusive and unwarranted.[14] The controversies over armed intervention in Libya led Brazil, India, and South Africa to side with Russia and China to put the brakes on using R2P to justify intervention in Syria. While armed interventions to save civilians can lead to their own human rights violations, a point Brazil and its colleagues in IBSA are quick to make, their suggested remedies often lead to nonaction; wholesale indifference to the slaughter of innocents in places like Syria and South Sudan damages the credibility of international commitments to prevent and respond to gross human rights violations and crimes against humanity.

On the bright side, while swing state democracies often seek to counter a power balance that still skews toward the West, they continue to vow allegiance to the fundamental norms of the international human rights and democracy order. As a matter of national and foreign policy identity, these states embrace democratic values of accountability, transparency, participation, and inclusion in ways that non-democracies do not. They partner with other democracies on a raft of initiatives that seek to improve open government, fight corruption and racism, and strengthen the rule of law. Nonetheless, and often for deep historical reasons, the politics of cooperation with the West continue to stir controversy and contradictions in their bodies politic. They also face their own daunting array of internal challenges, both political and economic, and are reluctant to strengthen an international system that they fear will turn a critical eye to their own checkered behavior. These deficiencies, in such areas as violence against women, religious intolerance, police violence and impunity, and profound corruption, constrain their willingness to invest in the rules of the international liberal order. When it comes to democracy and human rights, these contradictions persist on issues of both principles and methods.

As global power diffuses and shifts South and East, countries long devoted to a vision of an international liberal order composed of prosperous and rights-respecting democracies must find new ways to consolidate and modernize the global consensus around universal norms. The path toward convergence requires a recognition that old power dynamics are yielding to new actors with their own views on the role international actors should play in shaping demands for political reform.[15] These emerging voices, lost for years in the pitched battles between capitalism and communism and now benefiting from the opening of their own political and economic systems, sing a cacophonous tune: harmonious endorsement of progressive norms at the rhetorical level alongside heavy dissonance when it comes to applying those principles to concrete cases. These states, as they continue to leverage globalization for their own economic development, face complex trade-offs similar to those of more established players when it comes to weighing national interests and values. Business interests, energy dependency, migration flows and remittances, and aspirations for regional and global leadership all weigh significantly toward careful, cautious, and ad hoc policies concerning issues of norms and values.

In such a complex environment, the task for those who want to save the international liberal order is to find common ground where advocates for democracy and human rights from North and South, East and West can coalesce around both values and interests. This chapter outlines the conceptual basis on which convergence is possible, suggests some specific areas where prospects for international cooperation are greatest, and makes recommendations for strengthening cooperation for win-win outcomes. Rising democracies will play a pivotal role in determining whether such a convergence is possible, both by their example at home and their behavior abroad.

THE UNDERPINNINGS OF CONSENSUS

As earlier chapters show, the foreign policies of these five rising democracies as they relate to the global democracy and human rights order are in play and trending, albeit fitfully, toward liberal realism, that is, a hybrid mix of safe, soft power measures to support democracy and human rights when convenient, and opposition to more robust measures that in their view do more harm than good. In the meantime, more established democracies are confronting their own internal and external challenges, diminishing their ability to respond robustly to each and every human security crisis, and incentivizing them to find new partners interested in and capable of buttressing a democratic peace strategy. These intersecting trends suggest that established and rising democracies can work together in strategic areas of concern and thereby forge a more durable and credible path for the international human rights and democracy order.

How could this be done? First and foremost, all stakeholders involved need to reinforce their genuine acceptance and practice of the fundamental values of democracy and human rights. This must cover the full panoply of internationally recognized human rights and democracy standards. The North needs to address legitimate demands for economic and social rights rather than seeing them as a threat to their economic systems and private sectors, and the South needs to be more willing to put their voices and pocketbooks to work in defending political and civil rights rather than hiding behind the cloak of noninterventionism.

More important, all democracies need to redouble their own efforts to practice what they preach both at home and abroad. This should, in theory, not be so difficult given the more open, flexible, and resilient nature of democratic regimes. Like many established democracies, rising democracies have emerged from dark periods of authoritarian rule to make unequivocal commitments to democratic and human rights standards in domestic law and practice, both as ends in and of themselves and as instruments for attaining national development. They have also adopted these values as a general principle of their foreign policies. But implementation of these principles by established and rising democracies still falls far short of reasonable standards of behavior and of their own proclaimed benchmarks.

These shared starting points offer a number of advantages in finding common ground among both rising and more established democracies on strategies for addressing a range of scenarios where democracy and human rights are threatened. A like-minded group of democracies, such as the Community of Democracies and its caucus at the United Nations, is an important umbrella vehicle for reaffirming these shared values and facilitating cooperation across a multitude of platforms. States like India and South Africa, which were founding members of the Community of Democracies, along with Brazil and Indonesia, could do much more to support its myriad initiatives.[16] International IDEA, an intergovernmental grouping with observer status at the United Nations, offers another important forum for strengthening habits of cooperation between established and emerging democracies. Other complementary and more ad hoc coalitions on specific initiatives, like the Open Government Partnership, are readily available, as well as the universalist instruments of the United Nations. A new forum on human rights, democracy, and the rule of law proposed by a diverse coalition of established and newer democracies and approved by the Council's members in early 2015 without dissent presents another opportunity to reinforce a more progressive group of like-minded states.[17]

A wide gap exists, however, regarding the preferred means and methods of international action in this arena: The rising democracies have a strong preference for what they describe as constructive engagement (regardless of regime type), mediation, and quiet diplomacy as the primary tools of international intervention, while the established democracies are quicker to pursue condemnation, sanctions, and, in extreme cases, military action. With some goodwill, this gap can be closed. Swing states, for example, stand ready to provide help on democracy and human rights when requested by a transitioning state. Increasingly they have the resources and experience to contribute financially and through technical assistance to projects focused on bolstering democratic institutions. Established democracies, which have a long track record of experience in this field, should welcome this trend and encourage greater dialogue and collaboration among donors and recipients. They should propose win-win initiatives that give developing democracies more of a leadership role in reinforcing democratic governance, such as the Open Government Partnership led initially by Brazil and the United States, or trilateral partnerships in the field.

Emerging democracies should also learn lessons from mistakes of the developed democracies. These include staying neutral in contested national elections, supporting civilian nonviolent movements regardless of ideology, levying more targeted sanctions against wrongdoers, and leveraging development assistance to promote greater transparency, citizen participation, and accountability and to combat corruption. The Universal Periodic Review (UPR) process of the Human Rights Council offers a nonconfrontational way for democratic states to cooperate by both calling out laggards and helping them improve their performance through direct financial assistance and technical support linked to the recommendations made at the Council. When it comes to more robust approaches to defending universal norms, established democracies, particularly former colonial powers and the United States, need to better understand where the rising democracies are coming from when they ask them to join as partners. Each country's unique history of overcoming authoritarian, military, or colonial legacies that were directly supported or abetted by Western powers and establishing constitutional democracy (also, at times, with some help from the West) does not translate into automatic support for Western-led action to protect democracy and human rights. Not surprisingly, the memory of external impositions or endorsement of odious regimes runs deep.

This history leads policymakers in these countries to prioritize principles of national sovereignty and noninterference and to resist or oppose traditional means of "regime change" in favor of peaceful, mediated, or longer-term processes of change, even at the cost of short-term violence and instability. Other times, they stay out of the political fray entirely to pursue narrow national interests. The democratic peace theory is not well accepted in most of these countries, a problem that could be addressed through strategic dialogues with national security experts, support for academic exchanges with leading foreign policy thinkers and diplomats, and a review of curricula for diplomatic training. More broadly, Western powers ought to consider how best to acknowledge the mistakes of the past and their own imperfections and address them explicitly in their dealings with the rising five.

Another complicating factor for building cooperation with rising democracies is the current unbalanced distribution of power in the global order, which they all object to in varying degrees. This leads them to claim a greater voice in structures of global governance, such as the UN Security Council, and generally oppose more robust international actions on grounds of selectivity, double standards, and hypocrisy. To secure a permanent seat on the Security Council, states like Brazil and India seek to win as many friends as possible, thereby mitigating overt criticism of nondemocratic regimes and reinforcing the bonds of South-South solidarity. If they truly want a partnership with these states, established powers will have to find ways to expand the voice of the swing states in global decisionmaking while locking in commitments to those aspects of the liberal democratic order from which these swing states have benefited and discarding those that have disadvantaged them.

For their part, the rising democracies could show some leadership by forging their own democratic identity and voice for both protecting and updating the global democracy and human rights order. The India-Brazil-South Africa forum (IBSA), which unlike the BRICS group explicitly endorses democracy and human rights as a shared value proposition and boasts a proud history of democratic liberation and progress,[18] offers a potentially important platform for coordinated diplomacy on issues of democracy and human rights, but momentum seems to be stalled.[19] Coordinated action by IBSA countries began to occur, for example, during the July 2013 crisis in Egypt, but to little effect. The BRICS framework, well endowed by China's deep pockets, appears to be overshadowing the group, intentionally or not. An invigorated and/or expanded IBSA, to include states like Indonesia, Mexico, and South Korea, could forge an alternative and complementary path toward international support for democracy. If paired with a more coercive approach led by established democracies, such a group could serve a salutary "good cop, bad cop" function, like the role Indonesia and ASEAN played in Myanmar vis-à-vis the sanctions regime of the West.

The Arab Spring once presented a positive narrative that underscored the universal nature of democracy and human rights and the importance of popular will in the definition and legitimacy of national sovereignty. According to some polls, large majorities in the Arab world continue to express strong support for democracy, with or without political Islam,[20] reinforcing universal aspirations for more open and accountable governance and human rights. The Arab region may still offer a unique opportunity for swing states, individually and as a group, to take the lead in sharing their own recent experiences of democratic transition within a context of multilateral cooperation and respect for human rights, which the United States and Europe should encourage. The protracted instability of these transitions, however, may discourage states, both established and rising democracies, from making the long-term investments needed to stabilize them on a democratic track. Kidnappings and killings of foreign aid workers in the region are bloody reminders of the high risks of engaging some countries in the region. Another option would be to collaborate on support for positive trends of democratization in Africa.

Regional organizations, for better and worse, are becoming key players in the democracy and human rights sphere. The growth in declarations and mechanisms like human rights commissions and courts, anti-coup clauses,[21] and technical assistance activities, even in bodies composed of a high number of non-democracies like the Arab League, the Organization of Islamic Cooperation (OIC), and ASEAN, is positive but has not always been matched by a rise in quality or seriousness in implementation. In some cases, like ASEAN, international human rights norms are being eroded and come with little to no independent monitoring or enforcement mechanisms; even more established systems, like the Inter-American Commission and Court on Human Rights, have come under attack by states opposed to human rights scrutiny; however, this has largely been pushed back.[22]

Within this sphere, there is a growing tendency by swing states to insist on deference to regional organizations as gatekeepers to wider international interventions in political crises. This position has the dual benefit, in their view, of limiting Western involvement and reinforcing their own roles as leaders in their respective regions. In many ways, the emergence of regional organizations as key components of the democracy and human rights architecture has propelled positive outcomes, particularly in Europe, Africa, and Latin America. The rise of the Union of South American States (UNASUL) and the Community of Latin American and Caribbean States (CELAC), however, has brought a more passive, noncritical approach to democratic backsliding in states like Venezuela and Nicaragua, for example. The decision in 2012 to deep-freeze the Southern African Development Community Tribunal, which would allow individuals to bring human rights claims against member states to the court, was the result, in part, of South Africa's concern that it would impose onerous conditions on the region's development; negotiations for a revised mandate are likely to result in a much weaker court with no recourse for human rights complaints. But regional opinions can cut both ways. For example, to the surprise of many observers, the Arab League endorsed NATO intervention in Libya, and the African Union and the Economic Community of West African States supported the UN intervention force in Côte d'Ivoire (and more recently to deal with democratic rupture and violence in Mali and Burkina Faso). These moves have led swing states to go along with outright interventions in these countries in the name of protecting civilians and offer important precedents toward more robust international action.

As regional organizations proliferate and strengthen, it is imperative that both regional and international standards be strengthened and not dissipated into a patchwork of soft and ineffective rules that serve as roadblocks to action. A concerted effort should be made to construct an international expert body on regional organizations composed of diplomats, lawyers, academics, and civil society that would meet regularly to set standards and share lessons learned from their common experience in dealing with human rights and democracy issues.[23] Leading institutions like International IDEA, the Community of Democracies Permanent Secretariat, and OHCHR could team up to convene such an effort, thereby also helping to bridge the democracy and human rights communities, share best practices, and raise standards. A good starting point for such a body would be for India, as it steps up its leadership of the South Asian Association for Regional Cooperation (SAARC),[24] to convene a lessons learned exercise with other regional organizations and UN experts.

In sum, the challenge before Western democracies is to work with rising democracies wherever possible to reinforce the core international standards for human rights, expand them where possible in areas responsive to their priorities, and construct cross-regional coalitions at the UN and elsewhere on such issues. They should also encourage parallel but complementary efforts by newer democracies to share their own experiences with others, a step that may entail less control but greater acceptance by both givers and receivers of such assistance and, therefore, greater effectiveness on the ground.

Rising democracies for their part need to reconcile their status and values as democracies with their other national interests. They could continue as fence-sitters or followers of one regional or ideological camp or another to avoid jeopardizing other national interests or domestic constituencies. Or they could choose to become leaders in multilateral fora and take positions that more closely match their own values and experiences as democracies, including a more robust role in conflict prevention and resolution that leads to more peaceful democratic outcomes. They could proactively find ways to bridge the gap between economic and political rights by championing hybrid initiatives that advance both sets of norms. Most important, all democracies need to get their own internal houses in order if they are to lead the international community toward a vision of democratic peace. This means much greater attention to the full range of civil, political, economic, social, and cultural rights. In addition to greater coherence between domestic and international positions, rising democracies could do more to contribute both financial and technical resources to key pillars of the international human rights and democracy order, for example, the UN human rights system, the UN Democracy Fund, and regional human rights mechanisms.

Against this backdrop, the following section offers some specific areas of collaboration that would advance a progressive global human rights and democracy agenda in the coming years.

AREAS OF CONVERGENCE

In the broad and diverse array of issues on the international democracy and human rights agenda, it can be enormously difficult to identify the top priorities that would have the most impact across the board, let alone to figure out the processes that would give such goals the legitimacy and buy-in they would need to advance. Where big transnational campaigns have succeeded in the past, they have tended to be around very specific targets, like the campaigns against land mines and torture or, in the environmental sphere, prohibiting ozone-depleting chemicals.[25] Broader themes like women's and children's rights, corruption, responsibility to protect, and the International Criminal Court (ICC) have also generated big-tent coalitions to move an agenda forward in some concrete ways. Many of these issues are still divisive, and progress is incomplete; they therefore remain front-burner items for the wider international community as evidenced by the continuation of national and global efforts, coordinated or otherwise, toward specific goals.[26] The informal coalition that formed in 2005–06 to ensure a positive outcome to the proposals launched by Kofi Annan, including the creation of the new Human Rights Council, is a good example of a global architecture problem that elicited wide and diverse participation and generally positive results. There is growing concern, however, that the sheer volume of human rights and democracy-oriented initiatives is swamping the field and dissipating its effectiveness.[27]

Looking forward, the crowded democracy and human rights agenda would benefit from an effort to identify a manageable set of priorities that cut across the entire sector and would thereby attract support from a wide variety of stakeholders, including both established and rising democracies. These should include defending and strengthening civil society, expanding the right to information and Internet freedom, and confronting corruption. These issues have both intrinsic and instrumental values in building national and international liberal orders as they directly affect the health of open societies and the ability of multiple communities to do their work. On specific thematic topics, a grand coalition to promote respect for the core fundamental right to quality of life—the rights to food, water, shelter, and health—as well as equal access to quality education would yield political, economic, and social dividends that would directly advance an even broader agenda of peace, development, and security. Much of this agenda can be found in the post-2015 Sustainable Development Goals, a potential breakthrough opportunity to bring all countries together around a set of common benchmarks to lift the standards of living of millions of people around the world; many other avenues can be pursued, as well. Barring a major economic depression, current and projected economic growth rates and some fiscal stability—along with the requisite political will—should allow for enough liquidity in the system to allow states to accelerate their attention to these demands. For starters, governments should double their financial commitments to the pathetically underfunded UN human rights pillar, which currently garners only 3 percent of the UN's regular budget, and marry its efforts to the SDG implementation process.

Promoting and Defending Civil Society

> This growing crackdown on civil society is a campaign to undermine the very idea of democracy. And what's needed is an even stronger campaign to defend democracy.
>
> President Obama *to Clinton Global Initiative,*
> *September 23, 2014*

Around the world, civil society—the loose collection of nongovernmental organizations, think tanks, journalists, trade unions, business associations, religious communities, academics, indigenous groups, and volunteer citizen associations—has grown dramatically, thanks in large part to the creation of new avenues for citizen activism in more competitive and open societies and the growing awareness that they are essential components of a vibrant democratic society. Civil society expresses bedrock freedoms enshrined in the Universal Declaration of Human Rights— freedoms of association, of assembly, of expression, and the right to participate in political and civic affairs—as well as advances a host of wider freedoms.[28]

As it has grown in size and effectiveness, however, civil society faces a mounting counterattack. In authoritarian states, civil society at best is circumscribed to groups that rely on the state for funding and do not openly criticize the regime, giving rise to the phrase governmental NGOs, or GONGOs. Critics that openly complain about or organize against governmental policies are typically considered enemies of the state with severe punishments for anyone who crosses the line. If they receive foreign funding, they are labeled as mercenaries and spies. Even in transitioning and some consolidated democracies like India, civil society organizations face a litany of challenges: scarce funding, onerous registration and tax laws, restrictions on receiving funds from international sources, harassment and demonization by politicians and bureaucrats, and apathetic citizens. The determination by international funders, both governmental and nongovernmental, to focus attention on the NGO sector as agents of social and political change is stirring controversy, particularly in societies suspicious of ulterior motives. Conservative forces opposed to gender equality, LGBT rights, and children's rights are speaking out against international initiatives that they feel threaten their traditional way of life.[29]

Any initiative to advance democracy and human rights depends inherently on animating and mobilizing opinion for or against a particular goal. In this sense, civil society is the lifeblood of the democracy and human rights ecosystem. Hence, its protection and promotion must stand high on the list of priorities for anyone interested in addressing a range of societal problems, from inadequate social services to unfair elections.

Some efforts are already under way to tackle the constricting space for civil society and deserve greater support and attention from both established and emerging democracies. For example, in 2010, the UN Human Rights Council established a special rapporteur mandate on peaceful freedom of assembly and of association. Maina Kiai, the first mandate holder, has issued a string of important reports and recommendations to protect these rights in the context of elections, multilateral institutions, reprisals against activists, and access to financial resources.[30] The Community of Democracies has established a civil society working group composed of both government and nongovernmental representatives to support civil society through quiet diplomacy, advocacy, and technical assistance.[31] In a number of cases, their interventions to prevent restrictive NGO laws have led to better outcomes.[32] The UN Human Rights Council encourages NGOs to submit their views for each state's universal periodic review and now webcasts its sessions, opening a new window into its work and empowering civil society groups to monitor and hold governments accountable to their international commitments. Retaliation against activists for cooperating with the UN system is gaining focused attention in Geneva, as well.[33]

Every public agency or organization, at the local, national, and multilateral levels, should likewise open their doors to engagement with interested citizens and the media. IBSATI countries of late have a disappointing record on these issues (India's latest actions to harass NGOs is particularly troublesome but not unique) and should reconsider how they can better lead by example. Regular consultation with independent civil society groups on both domestic and foreign policies should become standard practice in all democracies. Advisory councils composed of experts, activists, and other stakeholders should be established as avenues for consultation on foreign policy and human rights, as done in Brazil and South Africa.

To that end, the Community of Democracies, which has one of the more welcoming environments for civil society, and other international organizations should initiate a process to set global standards and exchange best practices for ensuring civil society participation becomes institutionalized at the national and international levels. Such standards should protect the rights of civil society organizations to receive information and resources from whatever source as long as they are not abused for criminal activities. As Louise Arbour, former high commissioner for human rights, has eloquently argued, civil society networks from North and South need to focus on strengthening local knowledge of international human rights norms so that implementation on the ground has meaning and connects back to elite decisionmaking circles in Geneva and New York.[34] Democracies should also take on a long overdue reform of the UN Committee on Non-Governmental Organizations, which continues to harass and deny accreditation to NGOs on political rather than technical grounds.[35]

Right to Access Information

In a similar vein, a modern democracy and human rights system requires access to information held by governments on equal and enforceable terms.[36] Here, the international movement toward adoption of right to information laws and procedures is encouraging and should be expanded.[37] In the debate over the post-2015 Sustainable Development Goals, for example, a majority of stakeholders from both North and South agreed in principle that access to information, including better quality, coverage, and availability of disaggregated data, is critical to monitor and hold states accountable to implementation of the goals.[38] As digital technology expands, governments and citizens are finding it easier to make access to information a reliable and effective tool for improving governance, both domestic and foreign. Big gaps between developed and developing countries in accessing data and technology, however, raise a host of important moral, political, economic, and security issues, a concern raised by Secretary General Ban Ki-moon in his report on the post-2015 agenda.[39]

While implementation of right to information laws deserves more attention, practice is slowly catching up with theory in innovative ways. In Brazil, for example, public participation in local government budgeting (known as "participatory budgeting") has expanded thanks to a combination of civil society activism and technological innovations.[40] Similarly, NGOs like Conectas Direitos Humanos have used Brazil's new access to information law successfully to demand information regarding Brazil's human rights and foreign policy positions.[41] The National Security Archive, a nonprofit research organization in Washington, D.C., specializes in obtaining declassified documents through the U.S. Freedom of Information Act and uses digital technology to construct databases easily searchable by anyone in the world. These databases are being tapped by activists, journalists, and historians to advance claims for truth, reconciliation, and accountability for past human rights violations in places like El Salvador, Peru, and Brazil. These are just a tiny sample of the many ways in which advocates and researchers are able to exercise the right to access information to advance wider causes around more open governance, accountability, and human rights. Each of the IBSATI countries has constitutional and/or legal provisions that recognize the right to information and are at varying levels of implementation and enforcement; these common experiences offer a platform for stronger international leadership by them on these issues.

Freedom of the Internet

The spread of information technologies, principally the Internet, has revolutionized global communications. The Internet has become so integral to the basic functions of modern governance, business, and human rights that its protection as an open worldwide platform accessible to all is of paramount importance. It promotes other public goods like transparency and public accountability of state action and offers a lifeline to activists on the front line who are documenting violations. Unfortunately, it too is under rising pressure from governments that want greater control of the information that flows to and between citizens.

A wave of disputes is roiling this fast-moving field, from the closure of Internet space in places such as China and Iran to the attacks on Twitter and YouTube by President Erdoğan of Turkey. The revelations by Edward Snowden and others that U.S. intelligence agencies were spying on U.S. and foreign citizens, including the president of Brazil and the chancellor of Germany, prompted demands for demoting U.S. leadership in favor of multilateral bodies, a step that could result in less digital freedom. Other breaches of privacy, including the use of "big data" to collect and deploy information about users' information consumption patterns and criminal networks' brazen theft of purportedly secure financial data, along with the growing use of cyberwarfare to disrupt rivals' security plans and infrastructure, implicate a range of human rights in multiple ways. Censorship is prevalent in closed societies, where the simple act of communicating via Internet about "taboo" subjects like universal values, criticism of the government, or elections can land someone in prison in countries like China, Cuba, and Iran.[42]

President Obama's decision in November 2014 to call for domestic regulation of the Internet as a public utility like water and electricity rather than as a private enterprise reflects a paradigm shift toward understanding the Internet as a public good that delivers multiple benefits— political, economic, educational, social, and cultural—to vast numbers of individuals around the world. The notion of the Internet as a public good should be the starting point for a common set of principles for Internet governance around the world. As two democratic societies with well-advanced laws and practices regarding Internet governance and freedom, Brazil and the United States are particularly well positioned to lead a global campaign to defend and strengthen a free, diverse, neutral, and open Internet system.[43] As leaders in the software and ICT industries, Brazil and the United States, along with India and Germany, can play an important role in building consensus for a set of universal norms that would protect and promote an open and free Internet in the public interest. Building on the multistakeholder approach endorsed by Brazil, the outcomes of the NETMundial conference on Internet governance in São Paolo in 2014, and efforts at the UN Human Rights Council to elaborate the right to privacy in the digital age, democratic states from North and South should take the lead in ensuring human rights underpin Internet governance principles.[44] Work under way by the Council of Europe and the Internet Governance Forum to identify best practices is another step in the right direction.[45] Universal access to fast and affordable networks, a trend already under way in less developed countries benefiting from the spread of mobile phone systems, should become a signature goal of the international community.

Essential Elements of the Right to Life—Food,
Water, Health, Shelter

It is long past time to reaffirm in normative and practical terms the core ingredients that make up the fundamental right to quality of life—adequate and nutritious food, safe water and sanitation, emergency shelter, and access to quality health care for all—as indivisible and equal to other aspects of the larger human rights agenda. The long-standing distinctions in international law between civil and political rights, on the one hand, which afford immediate legal remedies, and the "progressive realization" of economic, social, and cultural rights, on the other, have generated grievances that developed countries unfairly prioritize the former over the latter.[46] Human rights champions like Aryeh Neier have long argued that economic and social rights do not merit the same attention from the international community given their inherently "nonjusticiable" and negotiable nature.[47] Government officials and rights activists alike in the global South, which faces grinding poverty, are quick to remind others, however, that human rights in their societies first and foremost mean the right to survival in basic human terms. The shadow of the Cold War, which pitted guaranteed delivery of certain economic and social rights under communist systems against the protection of political and civil rights of market democracies, poisoned this debate for decades. And the recurrent questions around the high costs of delivering a minimum standard of economic and social rights, particularly for low-income countries, have blocked a meaningful debate about what the state owes its citizens as part of a social contract that puts this broader concept of human rights at its center.

Despite the history of conflict over these concepts, there are positive signs of an emerging global consensus that the effective implementation of economic and social rights deserves attention on par with political and civil rights. A growing movement of advocates from the rights and development communities, in both developed and developing countries, is taking its demands for enforcement of rights to a minimum quality of life to the chambers of executive power, parliaments, and courts, with some success.[48] In the IBSATI countries, for example, courts are finding that access to adequate emergency medical services is a guaranteed right under both national and international law.[49] On the political advocacy front, Brazil under President Lula made ending hunger one of its signature national and international initiatives and has led an effort at the Food and Agricultural Organization (FAO), now headed by a Brazilian, for "making peoples' right to a healthy diet a global reality."[50] In 2014, India won U.S. support for bending rules at the World Trade Organization to exempt its new massive food subsidy program, part of the National Food Security Act adopted by the Indian Parliament in September 2013, to make the right to food a meaningful reality across the subcontinent. Indonesia has made significant progress in reducing the level of hunger in the country, exceeding its MDG target, as recognized by the FAO.[51] These examples demonstrate that IBSATI countries are starting to take leadership positions on human rights and development issues responsive to their own domestic priorities and are especially well positioned to do more on these issues internationally.[52]

Signs are emerging that the United States is also rethinking its approach to the issue. For several decades, U.S. diplomats voted against UN resolutions regarding economic and social rights on grounds that they are not recognized by U.S. law.[53] Under the Obama administration, this has begun to change, with multiple U.S. votes in favor of resolutions and mandates on rights to food, water, and health.[54] President Obama's signature achievement to provide affordable health care to all Americans, while generally not framed in rights language, in effect brings the United States closer to compliance with international norms in this regard. In a 2014 visit to Detroit facilitated by the State Department, UN special rapporteurs on the rights to water and to housing called on the city to comply with international norms by restoring access to water for citizens unable to pay their bills.[55] Advocates are effectively using the nondiscrimination and equality provisions of UN treaties and other UN processes to lobby for greater U.S. compliance with international economic and social rights norms.[56]

To build on this momentum, the United States should actively reach out to IBSATI countries to identify common priorities on the economic and social rights front. Explicit support for the UN mandates on rights to food, water, health, and housing through joint resolutions and allocation of resources to support their work and invitations for country visits would be a modest but symbolically important way to cooperate on this front.

One of the more promising vehicles for elevating and unifying the broader human rights agenda is the post-2015 Sustainable Development Goals. While the Millennium Development Goals are viewed positively as a galvanizing force for reallocating political and financial resources toward achieving common development targets, they said little about the importance of accountable institutions and rights-based approaches to these issues. Some argue that goal-setting exercises preferred by development practitioners water down a more rights-driven approach that goes to the causes of poverty and inequality rather than the symptoms.[57]

While official adoption of a rights-based approach to development is still contentious, the UN Development Program and other international aid organizations have embraced principles of accountability, transparency, participation, and inclusion as integral to their missions. As a 2014 Carnegie Endowment report explains, these concepts have intrinsic value as ways of respecting human dignity and individual autonomy. "The four principles together in effect form a new conventional wisdom about development, one with interlinked normative and instrumental rationales and one that promises to bridge long-standing divides both within aid organizations as well as between donors and recipients."[58] Despite fissures in this consensus, they do provide a broader platform for mainstreaming normative political values into the global development agenda.

The SDG process opens the door for validating and deepening the emerging consensus on the links between governance, rights, and development. It also affords an opportunity to explicitly reassert economic and social rights per se as essential for realizing progress toward universal norms articulated more than sixty years ago in the Universal Declaration of Human Rights. The High-Level Panel on the Post-2015 Development Agenda, cochaired by Susilo Bambang Yudhoyono, then president of Indonesia, Ellen Johnson Sirleaf, president of Liberia, and David Cameron, U.K. prime minister, tackled this challenge explicitly, calling for a "transformative shift" in the way the international community addresses poverty and development. One of its top five recommendations was to "build peace and effective, open and accountable institutions for all":

People the world over expect their governments to be honest, accountable, and responsive to their needs. We are calling for a fundamental shift—to recognise peace and good governance as core elements of wellbeing, not optional extras. This is a universal agenda, for all countries. Responsive and legitimate institutions should encourage the rule of law, property rights, freedom of speech and the media, open political choice, access to justice, and accountable government and public institutions. We need a transparency revolution, so citizens can see exactly where and how taxes, aid and revenues from extractive industries are spent. These are ends as well as means.[59]

The high-level panel's report is replete with references to the rights to food, water, education, and gender equality as universal norms. "Many people living in poverty have not had a fair chance in life because they are victims of illness or poor healthcare, unemployment, a natural disaster, climate change, local conflict, instability, poor local leadership, or low-quality education—or have been given no schooling at all. Others face discrimination. Remedying these fundamental inequalities and injustices is a matter of respect for people's universal human rights."[60] A rights-based approach to development was also strongly endorsed in Secretary General Ban Ki-moon's 2013 report on *A Life of Dignity for All*. His Rights UpFront initiative, launched in late 2013, is designed to mainstream human rights across the UN's core development and peace and security missions.[61] A broad coalition of rights and development organizations strongly endorsed and elaborated on this approach and urged governments to put human rights at the core of the SDG vision.[62] Unfortunately, however, this big-tent approach to articulating the global development agenda in human rights terms did not fully carry over to subsequent rounds of negotiations among governments at the UN. The final version of the Sustainable Development Goals, for example, sidelined rights and governance language to only one of its seventeen draft goals, which states, "Promote peaceful and inclusive societies for sustainable development, provide access to justice for all and build effective, accountable and inclusive institutions at all levels." Nonetheless, these are positive steps toward integrating the development, justice, and accountability agendas; the real challenge will be in translating them into measurable targets.

The SDG process is a litmus test for whether the international community can move beyond traditional debates about the right to development and obligations to transfer resources from North to South,[63] on the one hand, and nonrecognition of fundamental components of the right to life, on the other. A failure to incorporate goals and targets in the SDG process that explicitly refer to human rights and accountable and transparent institutions would be a lost opportunity. But it does not mean the end of the road for the elevation of economic and social rights on both national and international agendas. Concerted efforts by developed and rising democracies to carve out common ground on implementation of the rights to food, water, health, and housing would go a long way toward defusing old tensions between North and South and East and West and would breathe new life into the global human rights movement. On the other hand, failure to find a consensus backed up by sustainable development financing could encourage these states to head for the exits of the multilateral development system.[64] Sustainable financing is inevitably a core concern, but with an estimated $22 trillion in annual global savings (public and private), there should be little argument that the money is not available.[65]

Right to Education for Women and Girls

Among the many rights set forth in the economic and social rights sphere, the right to education is probably the most broadly accepted and understood around the world. Education, as articulated by the UN Committee on Economic, Social, and Cultural Rights, is both a human right in and of itself and an "empowerment right" that enables people to realize a host of other rights, including the ability of "all persons to participate effectively in a free society."[66] Evidence also suggests that states with high measures of gender equality are less likely to encounter civil war, interstate war, or widespread human rights abuses than states with low measures.[67] In the first years of the covenant's adoption, priority was placed on the provision of free compulsory primary education for all, regardless of a country's resources or level of development. States also agreed to make secondary education generally available and accessible to all, and higher education equally accessible to all on the basis of capacity. The first UN special rapporteur on the right to education, Katarina Tomasevski, promoted a widely held consensus defining the contours of the right to education around the four "As"—availability, accessibility (without discrimination), acceptability (in substance and form), and adaptability.[68] Recent case law in the five IBSATI countries reaffirms and broadens the right to education to include exemption from religious instruction (Turkey), mandates to increase budgetary resources for education to 20 percent of the national budget (Indonesia), free and compulsory education for children ages six to fourteen (India), the prohibition of corporal punishment (South Africa), and the use of racial quotas in universities for black, indigenous, and mixed-race students (Brazil).[69]

Despite the broad recognition of the universal right to education,[70] and the substantial advancement toward realizing the right in practical terms, millions of children and adults are still deprived of their right to a quality education and suffer the consequences for their entire lives. Less than one half of countries have achieved universal primary education under the Education for All 2000–2015 initiative, according to the 2015 UNESCO Global Monitoring Report.[71] The disappointing results are particularly evident when it comes to education for women and girls. By

2015, according to UNESCO, only 70 percent of countries are expected to reach gender parity in primary enrollment; at current rates, girls from the poorest households in sub-Saharan Africa will not achieve universal primary school completion until 2086.[72] Illiterate girls in South and West Asia stand a much higher chance than literate girls of getting married by age fifteen. Teacher training, absenteeism, and ability to teach core subjects like math and computer science are major challenges in countries like Indonesia and Brazil. India is still very far from achieving an adult literacy target of at least 95 percent by 2015.[73] And as we know from the tragic kidnapping of girls in northern Nigeria and the compelling story of Malala Yousafzai, the Pakistani teenage girl who won the Nobel Peace Prize for her efforts to demand equal access to education for girls and boys, those brave enough to campaign for such a basic right risk violent attacks by groups bent on keeping women and girls behind.

We know from years of social science research that an investment in quality education for women and girls directly contributes to improved family living standards, reduced poverty, higher incomes, better health, more civic participation, less corruption, and less violence.[74] More generally, one additional year of education in developing countries adds about 10 percent to a person's earnings.[75] In South Africa, every additional year of education was linked with a 7 percent lower probability of being infected with HIV.[76] Both the MDGs and the SDGs contain tangible goals for finally ensuring quality education for all, including that "all girls and boys complete free, equitable and quality primary and secondary education" by 2030.[77] This goal alone should merit creation of a grand coalition of stakeholders from both developed and developing democracies to cooperate on a series of measures designed to dramatically increase the resources and capabilities for achieving it in full and on time. More specific concerns around early marriage, child labor (including forced recruitment for armed conflict), privatization of education,[78] and access to appropriate sexual education could also be addressed as part of such a global campaign to make fulfillment of the right to a quality education for all a signature achievement of the next two decades.

Business and Human Rights

From a macro perspective of where economic and political power reside in the current global order, one must point to the rise of transnational corporations as one of the big stories of the last few decades. To illustrate the point, consider that Amazon's gross revenue of $74.45 billion in 2013 was larger than the gross national income of 150 countries.[79] Tata, the massive Indian conglomerate, grew in value from $96 billion in 2013 to $113 billion as of September 2015, which would give it the world's fifty-second largest gross national income if it were a country.[80] Countries clamor to attract foreign direct investment (and the accompanying tax revenue) to their domains, spurring a complex web of cross-border corporate structures and networks that demand proper monitoring and accountability for the adverse human rights impacts, intentional or otherwise, of their activities.

Given their outsized influence on human rights conditions on the ground and in the halls of power, advocates for human rights from the global South and North have long argued for greater regulation of their operations and financial flows in human rights terms. After several attempts resulted in rancorous debates and failure,[81] the "end of the beginning" arrived in 2011 with the adoption of the UN Guiding Principles on Business and Human Rights.[82] The Guiding Principles were the result of six years of consultations and debate led by the Special Representative of the Secretary General, John Ruggie, to devise a set of guidelines to help fill this gap in the international human rights architecture. While international law imposes direct legal duties mainly on states, private enterprise, like any recognized juridical entity, has both a legal duty to obey domestic laws and a moral duty to promote respect for the rights and freedoms enunciated in the Universal Declaration of Human Rights.[83] The Guiding Principles elaborate on states' roles in regulating and adjudicating corporate activities, particularly those corporations that have direct ties to government, clarify standards of corporate responsibility and accountability for respecting human rights, and offer best practices for accessing effective remedies through both judicial and nonjudicial mechanisms. The Human Rights Council endorsed the guidelines and established a follow-on Working Group to promote their dissemination and implementation, support capacity building at the national level, and conduct country visits.[84] In 2014, the Council agreed by consensus on a resolution cosponsored by twenty-three countries to renew the Working Group's mandate for another three years and called on states to adopt national action plans to ensure implementation of the guidelines.[85] The Working Group convenes an annual forum in addition to regional meetings and country visits with the aim of rapidly escalating awareness and adoption of the Guiding Principles.

After the many years of contentious debate on the matter, these steps were modest but decent progress. In 2014, however, the fragile consensus broke when Ecuador and South Africa, joined by Bolivia, Venezuela, and Cuba, tabled a resolution calling for negotiations to begin toward "an international legally binding instrument on transnational corporations and other business enterprises with respect to human rights." The resolution passed by a vote of twenty in favor, including South Africa, India, and Indonesia, fourteen against (mainly OECD countries), and thirteen abstentions, including Brazil.[86] Hundreds of NGOs from around the world applauded the decision to move toward treaty-based regulation of transnational corporations, but other constituencies, including the business community and John Ruggie, came out strongly against the exercise as problematic in scope and a divisive distraction from the more practical work of getting states and businesses to implement the guidelines.[87] Notably, the proposed treaty would only cover corporations of a transnational character, exempting national businesses from the exercise. Negotiations to begin the process of elaborating the treaty, meanwhile, got under way in the summer of 2015.

While positions on how best to mainstream human rights in the corporate sector are clearly divided between North and South, reasonable efforts should be made to bridge these differences given the importance of the business sector to human rights. This could be done by convening a small working group of stakeholders from the United States and the European Union and the IBSATI countries to craft elements of a compromise approach that would allow concrete steps toward implementation of the Guiding Principles while negotiations on a treaty slowly churn away in Geneva. The group could lead by example by becoming early adopters of national action plans as well as leaders of such initiatives as the Open Government Partnership, the Extractive Industries Transparency Initiative, and the Publish What You Pay campaign.

Controlling Corruption

Corruption of government officials, which results in theft of public resources or their diversion for private gain, is a fundamental challenge to the quality and credibility of democratic governance. It is also of serious concern to the independence of judicial systems that depend on objective and principled application of the law. Corruption, legal and illegal, in the conduct of elections and political campaigns goes to the heart of the integrity of free and fair elections, a bedrock principle of representative democracy. Its proliferation saps public confidence in government and politicians, impedes and distorts economic activity, fuels criminal enterprises, and falls disproportionately on the poor. Corruption has direct effects on the enjoyment of human rights, particularly on the delivery of social rights in exchange for bribes.[88] It also threatens public and national security in multiple ways.[89]

In response, both governmental and nongovernmental initiatives have begun to make headway toward controlling corruption, which continues to resonate widely as a rallying cry in political campaigns from India to Indonesia to Guatemala and Brazil. Transparency International, an international coalition campaigning against corruption, began its work in 1993 and now has more than 100 chapters tackling the issue in their respective countries. In near record time, the United Nations negotiated and adopted a Convention against Corruption, which entered into force in 2005 with 174 parties, including all five IBSATI countries.[90] The Convention requires countries to establish criminal and other offences to cover a wide range of acts of corruption and to cooperate to prevent, investigate, and prosecute offenders, including mutual legal assistance in gathering and transferring evidence for use in court.[91] The Organization of American States has adopted an Inter-American Convention against Corruption ratified by all its members except Cuba and Barbados.

Strong endorsement and support of global initiatives to combat the resource course—Publish What You Pay and the Extractive Industries Transparency Initiative, for example—are well-tested areas for common endeavors. In 2011, the United States and Brazil joined forces to launch the Open Government Partnership, a voluntary initiative designed to encourage states to adopt national action plans to make government more transparent, including by adopting robust anticorruption policies, ensuring transparency in the management of public finances and purchases, making public information on the income and assets of high-ranking public officials, and protecting whistle-blowers. In a related vein, former South African president Thabo Mbeki has convened a High-Level Panel on Illicit Financial Flows sponsored by UNECA and the African Union to raise awareness about public assets stolen from Africa and hiding in financial centers around the world.[92] Banking and law enforcement authorities in developed countries have a critical role to play in working with African countries to combat these crimes. The United Kingdom's

Department for International Development, for example, is funding law enforcement investigations of political figures from third countries using UK banks for money laundering.[93] Similarly, former UN secretary general Kofi Annan, who chairs the African Progress Panel, has called for a rules-based global system on tax transparency.[94] These initiatives, while not binding, do create the right environment for raising the bar for both national and collective action against gross corruption and should be expanded. Given the cross-border nature of illicit finances, it may be time to consider appointing a high-level official at the UN whose primary role would be to coordinate and promote various initiatives on anticorruption and the rule of law.[95] Political will at the local, national, and global levels is the driver of change in this arena, and judging from the growing public demands in both North and South for more honest government, this issue will only increase in importance in the decades ahead.

CONCLUSION

In the contentious domain of international cooperation for democracy and human rights, there are as many divergent as convergent paths to take. Like so many issues of international affairs, political will is paramount in order to achieve progress. It is particularly challenging, however, when the issues concern such fundamental questions as the structure of governance, the relationship between citizens and the state, and basic respect for human life and dignity. The triumph of the modern human rights era—to break away from the stifling control of the state to place the human being at the center of public life in accordance with a widely adopted set of international norms—is an extraordinary testament to the human spirit to overcome conflict and live in peace. But the promise of the post–World War II human rights revolution remains unfulfilled for millions of people around the world.

In the current context of the return of geopolitics and realism, it is important to underscore that democracies, given their inherent nature as governments accountable to their citizens, have a special role to play in fostering a more stable and secure democratic peace. The fate of that vision depends heavily on the role of both established and rising democratic powers that have demonstrated, through the delivery of both substantive and procedural rights, that government of, by, and for the people is the most legitimate way to prevent conflict and protect the progress made over the last seventy years. It is long past time for these democracies to leverage their special influence and experience to move beyond past prejudices and find common ground around a set of priorities like those outlined in this chapter and thereby fortify the international liberal order for future generations.

Notes

PREFACE AND ACKNOWLEDGMENTS

1. *The Foreign Policies of Emerging-Market Democracies: What Role for Human Rights and Democracy? Report of Proceedings, April 14–15, 2011* (Brookings, 2011), www.brookings.edu/~/media/research/files/reports/2011/6 /human-rights-piccone/06_human_rights_piccone.pdf.

2. Ted Piccone, *Democracy, Human Rights and the Emerging Global Order: Workshop Summary, November 29–30, 2012, Greentree* (Brookings, 2013), www.brookings.edu/~/media/research/files/reports/2013/04/10-democracy -human-rights-piccone/10-democracy-human-rights-piccone.pdf.

CHAPTER 1

1. UCDP Battle-Related Deaths Dataset v.5–2014, Uppsala Conflict Data Program, Uppsala University, www.pcr.uu.se/digitalAssets/124/124920_1code book_ucdp_prio-armed-conflict-dataset-v4_2014a.pdf.

2. United Nations, *The Millennium Development Goals Report 2015* (New York: United Nations, 2015), www.un.org/millenniumgoals/2015_MDG _Report/pdf/MDG%202015%20rev%20(July%201).pdf; see also Mark Leon Goldberg, "7 Humanity Affirming Charts from the UN's Final MDG Progress Report," UN Dispatch, July 7, 2015, www.undispatch.com/7-humanity-affirming -charts-from-the-uns-final-mdg-progress-report/.

3. Freedom House, *Electoral Democracies: Freedom in the World 1989– 2014*, www.freedomhouse.org/report-types/freedom-world#.VE-6xfldVSE.

4. A significant majority of more than 82 percent said their opinion of having a democracy govern their country was good or very good. The five rising democracies examined here had results consistent with these global trends.

World Values Survey, Wave 6 2010–2014, Official Aggregate v.20141107, World Values Survey Association (www.worldvaluessurvey.org). Aggregate File Producer: Asep/JDS, Madrid, Spain.

5. The consensus around these principles of liberal democracy can be found in international agreements covering nearly every region of the world. See, for example, UN General Assembly resolution 55/2, *United Nations Millennium Declaration*, A/RES/55/2 (September 18, 2000), paras. 6 and 24; UN General Assembly resolution 60/1, *2005 World Summit Outcome*, A/RES/60/1 (October 24, 2005); UN General Assembly resolution 62/7, *Support by the United Nations System of the Efforts of Governments to Promote and Consolidate New or Restored Democracies*, A/RES/62/7 (November 8, 2007); UN General Assembly resolution 55/96, *Promoting and Consolidating Democracy*, A/RES/55/96 (February 28, 2001); Community of Democracies, *Final Warsaw Declaration: Toward a Community of Democracies* (June 27, 2000); Organization of American States, Inter-American Democratic Charter (September 11, 2001); African Union, *Constitutive Act of the African Union* (July 11, 2000); Organization for Security and Cooperation in Europe, *Document of the Copenhagen Meeting of the Conference on the Human Dimension of the CSCE* (June 29, 1990); South Asian Association for Regional Cooperation, *SAARC Charter of Democracy* (February 9, 2011); The Commonwealth, *Harare Commonwealth Declaration* (October 20, 1991) and *Aso Rock Commonwealth Declaration on Development and Democracy* (December 8, 2003).

6. Francis Fukuyama, *The End of History and the Last Man* (New York: Free Press, 1992).

7. World Bank. GDP per capita is measured in current U.S. dollars.

8. United Nations, "Millennium Development Goals Indicators," http://mdgs .un.org/unsd/mdg/Data.aspx. Indonesia lagged slightly behind the world average in the percentage of its population with improved drinking water sources, and India lagged a bit on reducing child mortality. Both countries still made marked improvements from their starting benchmarks—for example, India more than halved its child mortality rate. As figures 1-7 and 1-8 show, China performed better than IBSATI on the rate of improvement on access to clean drinking water and has lower child mortality than any IBSATI country or the world average.

9. Sumit Ganguly, "The Story of Indian Democracy," Foreign Policy Research Institute, June 2011, www.fpri.org/articles/2011/06/story-indian-democracy.

10. Ibid. See also Mukul Kesavan, "India's Model Democracy," BBC News, August 15, 2007, http://news.bbc.co.uk/2/hi/south_asia/6943598.stm.

11. For example, the Supreme Court ruled in March 2014 that the constitution requires state intervention to end the practice of "manual scavenging"—the cleaning by hand of human waste by members of communities considered low caste. In April 2014, the Supreme Court recognized transgender individuals as a third gender eligible for quotas in jobs and education. The Supreme Court ruled in 2012 that the "rarest of rare" case standard for death penalty sentences had not been applied uniformly and required review; it later commuted the death sentence of fifteen prisoners (*World Report 2015: India*, Human Rights Watch).

12. Mihai Macovei, "Growth and Economic Crises in Turkey: Leaving behind a Turbulent Past?," *Economic Papers* 386 (October 2009), European Commission, http://ec.europa.eu/economy_finance/publications/publication16004_en.pdf.

13. For example, as Amnesty International reported in its 2015 annual report: "Following the 2013 Gezi protests and the rupture with former ally Fethullah Gülen, the authorities became more authoritarian in responding to critics. They undermined the independence of the judiciary, introduced new restrictions on internet freedoms and handed unprecedented powers to the country's intelligence agency. The rights of peaceful demonstrators were violated and police officers enjoyed near-total impunity for the use of excessive force. Unfair trials continued, especially under anti-terrorism laws, but the excessive use and length of pre-trial detention declined." See Amnesty International, *Amnesty International Report 2014/15: The State of the World's Human Rights* (London: Peter Benson House, 2015), www.amnesty.eu/content/assets/Annual_Report/Annual_Report_-_English_-_AIR1415.pdf.

14. Economist Intelligence Unit, *Democracy Index 2014: Democracy and Its Discontents*, www.sudestada.com.uy/Content/Articles/421a313a-d58f-462e-9b24-2504a37f6b56/Democracy-index-2014.pdf.

15. Indonesia fell back to partly free in Freedom House's report in 2014 as a result of a lower civil liberties score stemming from a restrictive NGO law that requires commitment to the national ideology of Pancasila and restricted funding. Freedom House, "Indonesia," *Freedom in the World 2014*, www.freedomhouse.org/report/freedom-world/2014/indonesia-0#.VFFkiPldVSE. Its relatively successful national elections held in 2014, however, and the decision to overturn attempts to restrict direct voting for governors and mayors suggest it remains on a solidly democratic track.

16. Polity IV data cover the period through 2012. For more recent trends, see Freedom House, "Turkey," *Freedom in the World 2014*, https://freedomhouse.org/report/freedom-world/2014/turkey#.VOYLrvnF-1Y.

17. Monty G. Marshall and Keith Jaggers, *Polity IV Project: Dataset Users' Manual*, 2002, 27, http://www3.nd.edu/~mcoppedg/crd/PolityIVUsersManualv2002.pdf. Postapartheid South Africa, however, has not yet experienced a transfer of power from the dominant African National Congress party.

18. Freedom House, *Freedom of the Press 2014*, http://freedomhouse.org/report/freedom-press-2014/press-freedom-rankings.

19. *World Economic Forum Global Gender Gap Report 2014*, 75, www3.weforum.org/docs/GGGR14/GGGR_CompleteReport_2014.pdf. See also the Inter Parliamentary Union's *Women in National Politics* statistical database as of May 1, 2014, http://www.ipu.org/wmn-e/arc/classif010514.htm.

20. United Nations, *Millennium Development Goals*, 5.

21. Indonesia is the exception. World Bank Country Dataset, *Military Expenditures as a % of GDP*, http://data.worldbank.org/indicator/MS.MIL.XPND.GD.ZS. Note Brazil data begin in 1988.

22. International Institute for Strategic Studies, *The Military Balance* (London: Taylor & Francis 1981–2015), vols. 81–115.

23. As of December 2014. See www.un.org/en/peacekeeping/resources /statistics/contributors.shtml.

24. South Africa was the exception.

25. Bertelsmann Stiftung, *Bertelsmann Transformation Index Dataset— 2014, BTI Project*, www.bti-project.org/index/status-index. Bertelsmann Stiftung, *Bertelsmann Transformation Index Dataset—2006, BTI Project*, http://bti2006 .bertelsmann-transformation-index.de/fileadmin/pdf/BTI_2006_Detailed _Ranking.pdf.

26. Transparency International changed its methodology in 2012 such that scores before that date are not comparable to scores afterward. However, since 2012, Brazil, India, Indonesia, and South Africa have improved slightly; Turkey's perceived levels of corruption have gotten somewhat worse. Transparency International, "Corruption Perceptions Index 2014: Results," www.transparency .org/cpi2014/results. (On a scale of 0 to 100, 0 is the highest level of perceived corruption and 100 is the lowest level.)

27. Bertelsmann Stiftung, *Bertelsmann Transformation Index Dataset— 2014*. BTI's 2006 report covers 2005, and its 2014 report covers 2013.

28. Heritage Foundation, *Index of Economic Freedom Dataset—2015*, www .heritage.org/index/explore?view=by-region-country-year.

29. James Gwartney, Robert Lawson, and Joshua Hall, "2014 Economic Freedom Dataset," *Economic Freedom of the World: 2014 Annual Report* (Vancouver: Fraser Institute, 2012), 44, 89, 90, 151, and 167, www.freetheworld .com/datasets_efw.html. A higher point score indicates more open and liberal economic structures.

30. The Fraser Institute's *Economic Freedom of the World* report of 2012 bases its comparative analysis on data from the World Bank, Freedom House, and Transparency International (ibid.).

31. Recent research conducted by the Legatum Institute on indicators of prosperity largely confirm these findings of a leveling off in recent years across such categories as entrepreneurship, personal freedom, governance, and social capital, although Indonesia continues to improve. Legatum Institute, *2014 Legatum Prosperity Index*, http://media.prosperity.com/2014/pdf/publications/PI2014Brochure _WEB.pdf; Legatum Institute, *Legatum Prosperity Index*, www.prosperity .com/#!/.

32. An average of 79.2 percent of respondents in IBSATI countries felt that democracy was a "very good" or "fairly good" system of governance for their country. An average of 73.1 percent of respondents rated the importance of living in a democratic system at least a 7 on a 1–10 scale, where 1 is "not at all" and 10 is "absolutely important."

33. An average of 61.2 percent of respondents rated the importance to democracy of "civil rights protect people from state oppression" at least a 7 on a 1–10 scale, where 1 is "not at all" and 10 is "absolutely important." An average of 38.4 percent of respondents rated the importance to democracy of "the army takes over when government is incompetent" at least a 7 on the same 1–10 scale.

34. On a 1–10 scale of how essential a characteristic of democracy a given factor was, where 1 is "not at all" and 10 is "absolutely important," 74.2 percent

of Brazilians ranked "people choose their leaders in free elections" as at least a 7; 76.7 percent of Indonesians ranked "women have the same rights as men" as at least a 7; and 70.8 percent of Turks ranked "the state makes people's incomes equal" as at least a 7.

35. World Values Survey, Waves 5–6 2005–2009, 2010–2014, Official Aggregate v.20141107, World Values Survey Association (www.worldvaluessurvey .org). Aggregate File Producer: Asep/JDS, Madrid, Spain.

36. In 2003, 27.4 million individual beneficiaries were part of Brazil's Bolsa Familia program. This equates to 16 percent of the population. The expenditure (measured in R$ of 2009) was R$2.5 billion, or 0.3 percent of GDP. By 2009, the number of beneficiaries had expanded to 41.2 million (22.2 percent of the population) and the budget expenditure had grown to R$3.14 billion, or 0.4 percent of GDP. See Sergei Soares, "Bolsa Familia, Its Design, Its Impacts and Possibilities for the Future," Working Paper 89 (International Policy Centre for Inclusive Growth, February 2012), 6, www.ipc-undp.org/pub/IPCWorking Paper89.pdf. According to the World Bank, Bolsa Familia "now reaches nearly 14 million households—50 million people or around ¼ of the population, and is widely seen as a global success story, a reference point for social policy around the world" (Deborah Wetzel, "Bolsa Familia: Brazil's Quiet Revolution," *Valor Econômico*, November 4, 2013, www.worldbank.org/en/news/opinion/2013 /11/04/bolsa-familia-Brazil-quiet-revolution).

37. World Health Organization, "Country Cooperation Strategy at a Glance: Turkey," May 2013, www.who.int/countryfocus/cooperation_strategy/ccsbrief _tur_en.pdf.

38. Beneficiaries can buy up to 5 kilograms of subsidized rice, wheat, and coarse grains every month. Preetika Rana, "Fact Sheet: India's Food Security Bill," *Wall Street Journal*, August 7, 2013.

39. When South Africa is removed from the set, life expectancy actually grew to an average of 71.3 years in the remaining four countries when comparing T1-4 with 2012.

40. UNESCO Institute for Statistics, "Gross Enrolment Rate, Tertiary, Female (%)," "Percentage of Students in Secondary Education Who Are Female (%)," and "Percentage of Students in Tertiary Education Who Are Female (%)," www.uis.unesco.org/Pages/default.aspx.

41. United Nations, *Millennium Development Goals*.

42. Over the time period of 2000 to 2010 and on an index scale of 0 to 100 with 100 being the strongest performance, SERF utilizes a number of indicators to measure access to education, health care, housing, food, and decent work. By this measure, Brazil performs especially well in education, earning 97.4 in 2010, the highest of the IBSATI countries that year; the IBSATI countries each scored at least 85 or higher in 2010. (For comparison, the United States earned an 83.) Brazil was also the strongest performer in health, scoring a 90.8 compared with India, which scored 74.8, and South Africa, which scored the lowest at 59.4. Turkey was the strongest performer in housing and work, earning 90.8 and 91.1, respectively. (For comparison, in 2010 China scored a 68.5 on right to work and the United States scored a 37.5 in the same area.) Sakiko Fukuda-Parr, Terra

Lawson-Remer, and Susan Randolph, *The International SERF Index Dataset Version 2011.1*, www.serfindex.org/data/.

43. Indonesia hosted the founding Bandung conference of the NAM, and three of the five IBSATI countries were active members. (South Africa did not become a member until 1994, and Brazil has observer status.)

44. Morton H. Halperin, Joseph T. Siegle, and Michael J. Weinstein, *The Democracy Advantage* (New York: Routledge, 2005), 33–34.

45. United Nations Development Programme, *Human Development Report 2013—The Rise of the South: Human Progress in a Diverse World* (New York: United Nations Development Programme, 2013), 2, http://hdr.undp.org/sites /default/files/reports/14/hdr2013_en_complete.pdf.

46. World Bank, "World Development Indicators," http://data.worldbank.org/.

47. Calculations based on quarterly trade data (nominal U.S. dollars) from IMF's Direction of Trade Statistics.

48. Ibid. India in particular experienced a sharp increase in imports from the MENA region in the past decade, coinciding with its growing appetite for energy.

49. "Top 5 Trading Partners—Imports," *CIA World Fact Book*, 1982–2013, www.theodora.com/wfb/abc_world_fact_book.html.

50. "Top 5 Trading Partners—Exports," *CIA World Fact Book*, 2013, www .cia.gov/library/publications/the-world-factbook/fields/2050.html.

51. United Nations Conference on Trade and Development, *Bilateral FDI Statistics 2014*, April 2014, http://unctad.org/en/Pages/DIAE/FDI%20Statistics /FDI-Statistics-Bilateral.aspx.

52. Development Initiatives, Global Humanitarian Assistance Program, *Global Humanitarian Assistance Report 2014*, 128, 130 (based on OECD data), www.globalhumanitarianassistance.org/wp-content/uploads/2014/09/GHA -Report-2014–interactive.pdf.

53. Ibid.

54. Brazil and India were among the top twenty recipients of ODA in 2012—Brazil received $1.3 billion, and India received $1.7 billion (ibid., 131, based on OECD data). No 2013 data were available for ODA recipients.

55. As measured by Freedom House's scores of "not free" and "partly free," 50 percent of IBSATI trade is with countries in these two categories as of 2014, and an increasing proportion of IBSATI trade has been with emerging economies since 2000.

56. More than 2.8 million Brazilians live outside Brazil, 1 million of which live in the United States. More than 21 million nonresident Indians (NRIs) were living overseas as of May 2012. According to government estimates, 4.3 million Indonesian migrant workers live overseas. Turkey's Ministry of Foreign Affairs estimates that approximately 5 million Turks live abroad, mostly in Western Europe, and some South Africans live abroad, primarily in other Commonwealth countries such as the United Kingdom and Australia. Brasileiros no Mundo, Ministério das Relações Exteriores, "Estimativas populacionais das comuni- dades," www.brasileirosnomundo.itamaraty.gov.br/a-comunidade/estimativas -populacionais-das-comunidades/; Ministry of Overseas Indian Affairs, "Popu-

lation of Non-Resident Indians (NRIs): Country Wise," http://moia.gov.in
/writereaddata/pdf/NRISPIOS-Data(15–06–12)new.pdf; International Organization for Migration, "Indonesia," www.iom.int/countries/indonesia/general
-information; Republic of Turkey Ministry of Foreign Affairs, "Turkish Citizens
Living Abroad," www.mfa.gov.tr/the-expatriate-turkish-citizens.en.mfa; International Organization for Migration, "World Migration—Outward, South Africa," www.iom.int/world-migration.

57. Turkey stands out as the exception in the group, with a significant decline
in remittances from T1-4 to 2013. This may be explained by Turkey's high economic growth rates at home, dampening demands for seeking jobs elsewhere or
for remittances.

58. The author wishes to thank Kemal Kirişci at Brookings for illuminating
this point.

59. See, for example, Kofi Annan, "The Global Order Can Only Be Saved If
New Powers Are Let In," *Project Syndicate*, January 29, 2015.

60. See, for example, Jorge Castañeda, "Not Ready for Prime Time," *Foreign Affairs*, September–October 2010, www.foreignaffairs.com/articles/south
-africa/2010-09-01/not-ready-prime-time.

61. "The will of the people shall be the basis of the authority of government;
this will shall be expressed in periodic and genuine elections which shall be by
universal and equal suffrage and shall be held by secret vote or by equivalent
free voting procedures" (article 21[3] of the Universal Declaration of Human
Rights). See also Final Warsaw Declaration: Toward a Community of Democracies (June 27, 2000) ("The will of the people shall be the basis of the authority
of government, as expressed by exercise of the right and civic duties of citizens
to choose their representatives through regular, free and fair elections with universal and equal suffrage, open to multiple parties, conducted by secret ballot, mon-
itored by independent electoral authorities, and free of fraud and intimidation");
and article 3 of the Inter-American Democratic Charter of the Organization of
American States.

62. Areas of potential convergence are set forth in chapter 8.

CHAPTER 2

1. For a compilation of views on the resurgence of authoritarianism, see
Journal of Democracy 26, no. 2 (2015).

2. See www.youtube.com/watch?v=9F5yeW6XFZk. In 2014, she became
the youngest person to receive the Nobel Peace Prize and is featured in "He
Named Me Malala," a new documentary released worldwide through National
Geographic.

3. "Kony 2012," Invisible Children, invisiblechildren.com/kony-2012/.

4. Invisible Children, *Invisible Children 2012 Annual Report*, 29, files
.invisiblechildren.com/annualreport2012/index.html#p=74.

5. "#BBCtrending: Five Facts about #BringBackOurGirls," *BBC Trending*,
May 13, 2014, www.bbc.com/news/blogs-trending-27392955. From November
3 to December 3, 2014, the hashtag was used more than 43,000 times, a testament

to the durability of the campaign. "Tweets per Day: #bringbackourgirls," Topsy Analytics, topsy.com/analytics?q1=%23bringbackourgirls&via=Topsy.

6. "The People's Republic of China is a socialist state under the people's democratic dictatorship led by the working class and based on the alliance of workers and peasants"; chapter 1, article 1 of the Constitution of the People's Republic of China, the Constitute Project, www.constituteproject.org/consti tution/China_2004.pdf. China's leaders see political rights and participation "as privileges to be negotiated based on the needs and conditions of the nation" (Eric X. Li, "Why China's Political Model Is Superior," *New York Times*, February 16, 2012).

7. Michael W. Doyle, "Three Pillars of the Liberal Peace," *American Political Science Review* 99, no. 3 (2005): 463.

8. Michael W. Doyle, *Liberal Peace: Selected Essays* (New York: Routledge, 2011); and Henry S. Farber and Joanne Gowa, "Polities and Peace," *International Security* 20, no. 2 (1995): 123–46.

9. Ibid., 465.

10. Daniel M. Kliman, *Fateful Transitions: How Democracies Manage Rising Powers, from the Eve of World War I to China's Ascendance* (University of Pennsylvania Press, 2015), 1–2.

11. White House, "Remarks by the President to the UN General Assembly," White House press release, September 25, 2012, www.whitehouse.gov/the-press -office/2012/09/25/remarks-president-un-general-assembly. Previous administrations have likewise espoused the importance of democracy expansion. See William J. Clinton, *A National Security Strategy of Engagement and Enlargement* (Washington, D.C.: White House, 1994), 18–20, nssarchive.us/NSSR/1994.pdf; Inaugural Address of George W. Bush, Washington, D.C., January 20, 2005, www.inaugural.senate.gov/swearing-in/address/address-by-george-w-bush-2005.

12. SIPRI Yearbook 2015, Summary, Stockholm International Peace Research Institute, 7, www.sipri.org/yearbook/2015/downloadable-files/sipri-yearbook -2015-summary-pdf.

13. The Universal Declaration of Human Rights holds the Guinness World Record for the most translated document in the world. "The Universal Declaration of Human Rights Is the Most Universal Document in the World," Office of the High Commissioner for Human Rights, www.ohchr.org/EN/UDHR/Pages /WorldRecord.aspx.

14. Freedom House, *Freedom in the World 2015*, https://freedomhouse.org /report-types/freedom-world.

15. This concept is enshrined in Article 21(3) of the Universal Declaration of Human Rights, which reads: "The will of the people shall be the basis of the authority of government; this will shall be expressed in periodic and genuine elections which shall be by universal and equal suffrage and shall be held by secret vote or by equivalent free voting procedures."

16. For an assessment of collective responses to disruptions to democratic rule, see Morton H. Halperin and Mirna Galic, *Protecting Democracy: International Responses* (Oxford: Lexington Books, 2005), especially the chapter by Ken Gude (63–99).

17. "We recommit ourselves to actively protecting and promoting all human rights, the rule of law and democracy . . . The universal nature of these rights and freedoms is beyond question" (2005 World Summit Outcome, paras. 119–120, UN General Assembly Resolution A/RES/60/1 [October 24, 2005]).

18. International Convention on the Elimination of All Forms of Racial Discrimination (adopted December 1965, 177 parties/82 ratifications); International Covenant on Civil and Political Rights (adopted December 1966, 168 parties/68 ratifications); International Covenant on Economic, Social, and Cultural Rights (adopted December 1966, 164 parties/64 ratifications); Convention on the Elimination of All Forms of Discrimination against Women (adopted December 1979, 189 parties/96 ratifications); Convention against Torture and Other Cruel, Inhuman, or Degrading Treatment or Punishment (adopted December 1984, 158 parties/72 ratifications); Convention on the Rights of the Child (adopted November 1989, 196 parties/138 ratifications); International Convention on the Protection of the Rights of All Migrant Workers and Members of Their Families (adopted December 1990, 48 parties/20 ratifications); Convention on the Rights of Persons with Disabilities (adopted December 2006, 159 parties/132 ratifications); International Convention for the Protection of All Persons from Enforced Disappearance (adopted December 2006, 51 parties/44 ratifications). All states parties dated as of October 12, 2015. See the United Nations Treaty Collection, treaties.un.org/Home.aspx?lang=en.

19. For a concise history of the role these states played in supporting international involvement in internal affairs, see Marc Limon and Hilary Power, "History of the United Nations Special Procedures Mechanism: Origins, Evolution and Reform," *Universal Rights Group*, September 2014, www.universal-rights .org/urg-policy-reports/history-of-the-united-nations-special-procedures -mechanism-origins-evolution-and-reform/.

20. See "Towards a Community of Democracies," a statement issued at the first ministerial meeting of the Community of Democracies held in Warsaw, Poland, on June 25–27, 2000 (otherwise referred to as "the Warsaw Declaration"), www.community-democracies.org/Visioning-Democracy/To-be-a-Democracy -The-Warsaw-Declaration.

21. Provisions in the Warsaw Declaration went beyond norms previously expressed in international agreements, including respect for freedom of the press, independent electoral observation, civilian democratic control of militaries, and so on. For more, see the Warsaw Declaration at www.community-democracies .org/Visioning-Democracy/To-be-a-Democracy-The-Warsaw-Declaration.

22. For a critique of the Community of Democracies' early years and of proposals for a U.S.-led "League of Democracies," see Ted Piccone, "Democracies: In a League of their Own? Lessons Learned from the Community of Democracies," Foreign Policy Paper Series 8, Brookings, October 2008, www.brookings .edu/research/papers/2008/10/democracy-piccone.

23. International Advisory Committee, *Community of Democracies Invitation Process: Statement and Recommendations on Government Invitations*, March 2009, www.bti2010.bertelsmann-transformation-index.de/fileadmin /pdf/IAC_Brochure_2009.pdf.

24. "Democracies at UN Gather for First Caucus," *New York Times*, October 7, 2000, www.nytimes.com/2000/10/07/world/07CAUC.html.

25. See press release, "The Governing Council of the Community of Democracies Suspends Mali's Membership," July 10, 2012, www.community-democracies .org/index.php?option=com_content&view=article&id=351:the-governing -council-of-the-community-of-democracies-suspends-malis-membership.

26. Mali was reinstated to the Governing Council in September 2014, after restoring civilian rule and presidential elections. A special Community of Democracies Group of Friends led by Canada and Nigeria assisted in this process; see "Press Release—Mali Returns to the Governing Council of the Community of Democracies," Community of Democracies, September 25, 2014, www .community-democracies.org/Talking-Democracy/Press-Announcements-and -Statements/Press-Release-Mali-Returns-to-the-Governing-Counci.

27. See "Remarks Given by Secretary Clinton at the Community of Democracies Governing Council," Ulaanbaatar, Mongolia, July 9, 2012, www.state .gov/secretary/20092013clinton/rm/2012/07/194784.htm.

28. The White House, Fact Sheet: U.S. Support for Civil Society, September 23, 2014, www.whitehouse.gov/the-press-office/2014/09/23/fact-sheet-us-support -civil-society.

29. UNDEF, "Contribution Table," www.un.org/democracyfund/contribution-table.

30. For more on UNDEF's current and past projects, see "Projects," UN Democracy Fund, www.un.org/democracyfund/projects.

31. For more on UNDEF's governance and partners, see "UNDEF Governance and Partners," UN Democracy Fund, www.un.org/democracyfund/undef -governance-and-partners.

32. In the founding Warsaw Declaration, participating governments promised to "collaborate on democracy-related issues in existing international and regional institutions, forming coalitions and caucuses to support resolutions and other international activities aimed at the promotion of democratic governance."

33. For more information on the Community of Democracies, see www .community-democracies.org/.

34. Working Group mandate is available at www.community-democracies .org/index.php?option=com_content&view=article&id=261&Itemid=158.

35. A high-level panel on a post-MDG agenda appointed by UN Secretary General Ban Ki-moon and cochaired by the heads of state and government of Indonesia, Liberia, and the United Kingdom released their report in May 2013. One of the five transformative shifts they called for was "effective, open and accountable institutions": "People the world over expect their governments to be honest, accountable, and responsive to their needs. We are calling for a fundamental shift—to recognize peace and good governance as a core element of wellbeing, not an optional extra" (www.post2015hlp.org/featured/high-level-panel -releases-recommendations-for-worlds-next-development-agenda/).

36. Eighty-eight countries hosted national consultations; a survey available online in seventeen languages asked respondents around the world about their highest development priorities, and the UNDP hosted a variety of events, includ-

ing a global dialogue on rule of law in September 2013. UNDP, "Post-2015 Development Agenda," www.undp.org/content/undp/en/home/mdgoverview/mdg _goals/post-2015-development-agenda.html; The World We Want, "Global Consultation on Governance and the Post-2015 Framework," www.worldwewant2015 .org/governance; and UNDP Democratic Governance and the Post-2015 Development Framework Issue briefs, www.undp.org/content/undp/en/home /librarypage/democratic-governance/dg-publications/governance-and-the-post -2015-development-framework.html.

37. Twenty-six percent of the 2011 budget contributed to "fostering democratic governance." UNDP, *Annual Report 2011/2012: The Sustainable Future We Want* (New York: UNDP, 2012), 5, www.undp.org/content/dam/undp/library/corporate /UNDP-in-action/2012/English/UNDP-AnnualReport_ENGLISH.pdf.

38. Since 2012, 15 to 17 percent of the budget has gone to democratic governance projects, while 26 to 35 percent of the budget has gone to "responsive institutions" projects. Responsive institutions projects include battling corruption and increasing the capacity of local governments to provide services and preserve peace. UNDP, "Our Projects," February 28, 2015, open.undp.org/#2015; UNDP, "Responsible and Accountable Institutions," www.undp.org/content /undp/en/home/ourwork/democratic-governance-and-peacebuilding/responsive -and-accountable-institutions.html.

39. "'Human Rights Up Front' Initiative," United Nations, www.un.org/sg /rightsupfront/.

40. "About Us," UN High Commissioner for Refugees, www.unhcr.org /pages/49c3646c2.html.

41. "Introducing UNESCO," United Nations Educational, Scientific, and Cultural Organization, en.unesco.org/about-us/introducing-unesco.

42. "Special and Personal Representatives, Envoys and Advisers of the Secretary-General," United Nations, www.un.org/sg/srsg/other.shtml.

43. "Human Rights—New York Statements," Office of the High Commissioner for Human Rights, www.ohchr.org/EN/NewYork/Pages/Statements .aspx; "Human Rights," Security Council Report, www.securitycouncilreport .org/human-rights/index.php?page=1.

44. See the Santiago Resolution (1991), www.au.af.mil/au/awc/awcgate /sa95/sach06f2.html; the Protocol of Amendment to the Charter of the Organization of American States, "The Protocol of Washington" (1992), www.oas .org/dil/treaties_A-56_Protocol_of_Washington.htm; and the Inter-American Democratic Charter (2001), www.oas.org/charter/docs/resolution1_en_p4 .htm.

45. See PM 382/10—Indigenous Communities of the Xingu River Basin, Pará, Brazil, April 1, 2011, www.oas.org/en/iachr/indigenous/protection/precautionary .asp, and Report 64/04, Petition 167/03 on admissibility, the Kichwa Peoples of the Sarayaku Community and Its Members, Ecuador, October 13, 2004, www .cidh.oas.org/annualrep/2004eng/Ecuador.167.03eng.htm. For more on inter-American standards on forced disappearance, see paras. 23–27 of Inter-American Commission on Human Rights, "Statement on the Duty of the Haitian State to Investigate the Gross Violations of Human Rights Committed during the Regime

of Jean-Claude Duvalier," www.oas.org/en/iachr/docs/other/Haiti2011.asp, and Inter-American Court of Human Rights Case of La Cantuta v. Peru. Merits, Reparations and Costs. Judgment of November 29, 2006. Series C no. 162, para. 225, www.corteidh.or.cr/docs/casos/articulos/seriec_162_ing.pdf.

46. Permanent Council of the Organization of American States, Special Working Group to Reflect on the Workings of the Inter-American Commission on Human Rights, final report (December 13, 2011), scm.oas.org/IDMS/Redirectpage.aspx ?class=GT/SIDH-&classNum=13&lang=e; *Aportes DPLF, Magazine of the Due Process of Law Foundation (DPLF)* 19, no. 7 (2014), www.dplf.org/sites/default /files/aportes_19_english.pdf.

47. See the Harare Commonwealth Declaration (1991), thecommonwealth .org/sites/default/files/history-items/documents/Harare%20Common- wealth%20Declaration%201991.pdf; the Commonwealth Ministerial Action Group that deals with violations of the Harare Declaration (established 1995), www.thecommonwealth.org/Internal/190945/190842/the_commonwealth _ministerial_action_group_s__cmag/; "Pakistan Suspended from the Common- wealth," 1999, thecommonwealth.org/history-of-the-commonwealth/pakistan -suspended-commonwealth-0; "Nigeria Suspended from the Commonwealth," 1995, thecommonwealth.org/history-of-the-commonwealth/nigeria-suspended -commonwealth; "Zimbabwe Is Suspended from the Councils of the Common- wealth," 2002, thecommonwealth.org/history-of-the-commonwealth/zimbabwe -suspended-councils-commonwealth.

48. Peter Griffiths, "Commonwealth Suspends Maldives from Rights Group, Seeks Elections," *Reuters*, February 23, 2013, in.reuters.com/article/2012/02 /22/maldives-commonwealth-idINDEE81L0JO20120222; for more, see recent CMAG statements at www.thecommonwealth.org/Internal/190945/190842 /141670/list_of_meetings/.

49. "SAARC Charter of Democracy," South Asian Association for Regional Cooperation, www.saarc-sec.org/SAARC-Charter-of-Democracy/88/.

50. "ASEAN Human Rights Declaration," ASEAN, November 19, 2012, www.asean.org/news/asean-statement-communiques/item/asean-human-rights -declaration. For a summary of reactions to the declaration, see "ASEAN Human Rights Declaration," *Wikipedia*, last modified August 3, 2015, en.wikipedia .org/wiki/ASEAN_Human_Rights_Declaration.

51. Article 17 of the Rome Statute. For the full statute, see www.icc-cpi.int /nr/rdonlyres/add16852-aee9-4757-abe7-9cdc7cf02886/283503/romestatuteng1 .pdf.

52. As of October 2015, twenty-three cases in eight countries have been brought before the ICC: the Central African Republic, Côte d'Ivoire, the Democratic Republic of the Congo, Kenya, Libya, Mali, Sudan (Darfur), and Uganda. For more on these cases, see "Situations and Cases," ICC, www.icc-cpi.int/en _menus/icc/situations%20and%20cases/Pages/situations%20and%20cases .aspx. It should be noted that six of these eight countries requested the ICC's intervention. See Kenneth Roth, "The End of Human Rights?," *New York Review of Books*, October 23, 2014, www.nybooks.com/articles/archives/2014/oct /23/end-human-rights/.

53. United National Treaty Collection, "Rome Statute of the International Criminal Court," treaties.un.org/Pages/ViewDetails.aspx?src=TREATY&mtdsg_no=XVIII-10&chapter=18&lang=en.

54. Statement by Dilip Lahiri, additional secretary (UN), "Explanation of Vote on the Adoption of the Statute of the International Criminal Court," July 17, 1998, www.un.int/india/ind272.htm.

55. Margareth S. Aritonang, "Govt Officially Rejects Rome Statute," *Jakarta Post*, May 21, 2013, www.thejakartapost.com/news/2013/05/21/govt-officially-rejects-rome-statute.html.

56. Ercan Yavuz, "Turkey's Planned Ratification of Rome Statute Stirs Debate," *Today's Zaman*, August 22, 2008, www.todayszaman.com/news-150927-turkeys-planned-ratification-of-rome-statute-stirs-debate.html.

57. Thomas Carothers and Richard Youngs, *Looking for Help: Will Rising Democracies Become International Democracy Supporters?* (Washington, D.C.: Carnegie Endowment for International Peace, 2011), 11.

58. Decision Ext/Assembly/AU/Dec.1 (Oct. 2013), "Decision on Africa's Relationship with the International Criminal Court (ICC)," Extraordinary Session of the Assembly of the African Union, October 12, 2013, Addis Ababa, Ethiopia.

59. Norimitsu Onishi, "Omar al-Bashir, Leaving South Africa, Eludes Arrest Again," *New York Times*, June 15, 2015, www.nytimes.com/2015/06/16/world/africa/omar-hassan-al-bashir-sudan-south-africa.html?_r=0.

60. "Intensely Debating Targeted Country Reviews, Third Committee Approves Draft Texts on Iran, Syria, Democratic People's Republic of Korea," General Assembly meetings coverage, November 18, 2014, www.un.org/press/en/2014/gashc4122.doc.htm. Typically, in Third Committee resolutions that come to a vote, Brazil and Turkey vote in favor of resolutions that condemn the human rights situation in North Korea while India, Indonesia, and South Africa typically abstain. Third Committee resolutions on DPRK in 2012 and 2013 were passed by consensus and did not come to a vote.

61. For the full breakdown of votes, see the voting record for A/C.3/L.63, available at www.un.org/en/ga/third/69/docs/voting_sheets/L.63.pdf.

62. See "The Responsibility to Protect," Office of the Special Adviser on the Prevention of Genocide, www.un.org/en/preventgenocide/adviser/responsibility.shtml and paras. 138–140 of Resolution 60/1, adopted October 24, 2005, www.un.org/en/preventgenocide/adviser/pdf/World%20Summit%20Outcome%20Document.pdf#page=30.

63. Madeleine K. Albright and Richard S. Williamson, *The United States and R2P: From Words to Action* (Washington, D.C.: United States Institute of Peace, 2013).

64. Ted Piccone, report of Brookings Workshop held November 29–30, 2012, "Democracy, Human Rights and the Emerging Global Order," Brookings, April 2013, www.brookings.edu/research/reports/2013/04/10-democracy-human-rights-piccone.

65. See, for example, European Commission "European Instrument for Democracy & Human Rights (EIDHR)," ec.europa.eu/europeaid/how/finance/eidhr_en.htm; Thomas Carothers, "Revitalizing Democracy Assistance: The

Challenge of USAID," Carnegie Endowment, 2009, carnegieendowment
.org/files/revitalizing_democracy_assistance.pdf; Thomas Carothers, "Democracy Aid at 25: Time to Choose," *Journal of Democracy* 26, no. 1 (2015):
59–73.

66. "About MCC," Millennium Challenge Corporation, www.mcc.gov/pages
/about.

67. Carothers and de Gramont, *Development Aid Confronts Politics*.

68. "Democracy and the United Nations," United Nations, www.un.org/en
/globalissues/democracy/democracy_and_un.shtml.

69. Funding for advancing democracy is found in the State and Foreign Operations budget under Governing Justly and Democratically, and is further broken
out into subareas of rule of law and human rights, good governance, political
competition and consensus building, and civil society. U.S. Department of State,
*Congressional Budget Justification: Foreign Assistance Summary Tables, Fiscal
Year 2016*, February 27, 2015, 22, www.state.gov/f/releases/iab/fy2016cbj/pdf
/index.htm.

70. European External Action Service, "Instrument for Democracy and
Human Rights Worldwide Multiannual Indicative Programme (2014–2017),"
33, www.eeas.europa.eu/human_rights/docs/eidhr-mip-2014-2017_en.pdf.

71. Richard Youngs, "Accessing the EU's New Democracy and Human Rights
Action Plan," Carnegie Europe, July 23, 2015, carnegieeurope.eu/strategiceu-
rope/?fa=60822; European Endowment for Democracy, "More Synergies in EU-
US Democracy Support?," February 21, 2014, www.democracyendowment.eu
/news/more-synergies-in-eu-us-democracy-support/.

72. Tsveta Petrova, *From Solidarity to Geopolitics: Support for Democracy
among Postcommunist States* (Cambridge University Press, 2014).

73. Robert G. Herman and Theodore J. Piccone, eds., *Defending Democracy: A Global Survey of Foreign Policy Trends, 1992–2002* (Washington, D.C.:
Democracy Coalition Project, 2002), 4.

74. Daniel Calingaert, Arch Puddington, and Sarah Repucci, "The Democracy Support Deficit: Despite Progress, Major Countries Fall Short," in *Supporting
Democracy Abroad: An Assessment of Leading Powers*, Freedom House, November 2014, freedomhouse.org/sites/default/files/GSD_Overview_and_Country
_Reports.pdf. The author served as an adviser to the report's authors.

75. Tsveta Petrova, "From Recipients to Donors: The New Role of East Eu-
ropeans in Democracy Promotion," presentation at the National Endowment for
Democracy, July 18, 2012, www.ned.org/sites/default/files/Tsveta-Petrova
-PowerPoint-Slideshow.pdf.

76. Ted Piccone, "Do New Democracies Support Democracy: The Multilateral Dimension," *Journal of Democracy* 22, no. 4 (2011): 139–54.

77. Richard Gowan, "Who Is Winning on Human Rights at the UN?," European Council on Foreign Relations, September 24, 2012, ecfr.eu/content/entry
/commentary_who_is_winning_on_human_rights_at_the_un.

78. UN Security Council Resolution 1970, February 26, 2011.

79. UN Security Council Resolution 1975, March 30, 2011, para. 6.

80. Ibid.; for more information on Brazil's stance on protection of civilians, see *Responsibility while Protecting: Elements for the Development and Promotion of a Concept*, annex to the letter dated November 9, 2011, from the Permanent Representative of Brazil to the UN addressed to the secretary general, official UN Doc: A/66/551-S/2011/701.

81. At the launch of the UN Democracy Fund, Prime Minister Singh stated: "India has been sharing its rich experience, institutional capabilities and training infrastructure with nations that share our values and beliefs and request our assistance. We are prepared to do much more" (quoted in Jan Cartwright, "India's Regional and International Support for Democracy: Rhetoric or Reality?," *Asian Survey* 49, no. 3 [2009]: 420).

82. William Dalrymple, "A Deadly Triangle: Afghanistan, Pakistan, & India," Brookings, June 25, 2013, www.brookings.edu/research/essays/2013 /deadly-triangle-afghanistan-pakistan-india-c.

83. C. Raja Mohan, "Balancing Interests and Values: India's Struggle with Democracy Promotion," *Washington Quarterly* 30, no. 2 (2007): 110.

84. Simon Denyer, "As Middle East Erupts in Protest, India Finds Comfort on the Fence," *Washington Post*, February 19, 2011, www.washingtonpost.com /wp-dyn/content/article/2011/02/18/AR2011021802699.html.

85. "Krishna Describes Egypt as Internal Affair," *Sify News*, February 1, 2011, www.sify.com/news/krishna-describes-egypt-crisis-its-internal-affair-news -international-lcbt4dahajj.html.

86. Ambassador Manjeev Sigh Puri, Explanation of Vote on the Resolution Adopted Concerning Libya, the UN Security Council, March 17, 2011.

87. P. R. Ramesh, "India Supports African Union Stand on Libya Crisis," *Economic Times*, May 25, 2011, articles.economictimes.indiatimes.com/2011 -05-25/news/29581862_1_libya-crisis-african-union-africa-india-summit.

88. Nidhi Verma, "Exclusive: India to Slash Iran Oil Imports to Meet Nuclear Deal Parameters—Sources," *Reuters*, March 11, 2014, www.reuters.com /article/2014/03/11/us-india-iran-imports-idUSBREA2A0TU20140311.

89. Devon Maylie and Patrick McGroarty, "Mugabe Tightens Grip on Power after Disputed Zimbabwe Vote," *Wall Street Journal*, August 4, 2013, online.wsj .com/article/SB10001424127887323514404578647732249178720.html?mod =googlenews_wsj.

90. "South Africa Calls on Egyptians to Refrain from Violence," *DIRCO*, July 30, 2013, www.info.gov.za/speech/DynamicAction?pageid=461&sid=38401 &tid=114871.

91. Susilo Bambang Yudhoyono, Keynote Address, World Movement for Democracy, 6th Meeting, April 12, 2010, Jakarta, Indonesia, www.wmd.org /assemblies/sixth-assembly/remarks/keynote-speech-dr-susilo-bambang -yudhoyono.

92. For example, Indonesia in 2008 launched the Bali Democracy Forum as a way to talk about democratic principles and practices in an inclusive dialogue among equals; it has drawn a significant number of heads of state and ministers, including from China.

93. "Indonesia Urges UN to Bring Peace to Egypt," *Antara News*, August 15, 2013, www.antara.co.id/en/news/90258/indonesia-urges-un-to-bring-peace-to-egypt.

94. CNN World, "Indonesia's President: 'We Can Be Model for Islam and Democracy,'" June 15, 2011, articles.cnn.com/2011-06-15/world/indonesia.president.yudhoyono_1_indonesia-president-suharto-islam-and-democracy?_s=PM:WORLD.

95. Address by H. E. Recep Tayyip Erdoğan at Harvard University Kennedy School of Government, January 30, 2003, in *Journal of Turkish Weekly*, www.turkishweekly.net/2004/10/12/article/erdogan-democracy-in-the-middle-east-pluraliism-in-europe-turkish-view/.

96. "Turkey Calls Morsi's Removal 'Unacceptable Coup,'" *Voice of America*, July 4, 2013, www.voanews.com/content/turkey-morsi-reaction/1695408.html; Daniel Dombey, "Erdoğan Attacks West's Reaction to Morsi's Overthrow," *Financial Times*, July 5, 2013, www.ft.com/intl/cms/s/0/b8396b56-e582-11e2-ad1a-00144feabdc0.html#axzz2bDwuyQ3k.

97. Turkey was not sitting on the UN Security Council at the time and thus did not have a vote on the resolution.

98. "Erdoğan Warns Assad against Division of Syria," *Today's Zaman*, May 2, 2011, www.todayszaman.com/news-242543-erdogan-warns-assad-against-division-of-syria.html.

99. Global Humanitarian Assistance Report 2014, www.globalhumanitarianassistance.org/wp-content/uploads/2014/09/GHA-Report-2014-interactive.pdf, 28 and 128; see table 10.2 "Top 20 Government Donors, Plus EU Institutions, International Humanitarian Assistance, 2004–2013."

CHAPTER 3

1. "Abstract of Speakers' Strengths of Languages and Mother Tongues—2001," Census of India. The Indian Census does not recognize ethnic groups, but does consider Scheduled Castes (654 groups) and Scheduled Tribes (744 groups).

2. Sunil Khilnani and others, *Nonalignment 2.0: A Foreign and Strategic Policy for India in the Twenty First Century*, January 2012, 7, ris.org.in/images/RIS_images/pdf/NonAlignment.pdf.

3. Author interview, October 2012.

4. For a fascinating account of India's diplomatic role at the founding of the United Nations and Gandhi and Nehru's vision of global order, see Manu Bhagavan, *Peacemakers: India and the Quest for One World* (Delhi: HarperCollins Publishers India, 2012); see also Mark Mazower, *No Enchanted Palace: The End of Empire and the Ideological Origins of the United Nations* (Princeton University Press, 2009), 167–89.

5. Encyclopaedia Britannica Online, s.v. "Mohandas Karamchand Gandhi," www.britannica.com/EBchecked/topic/225216/Mohandas-Karamchand-Gandhi.

6. Article 2 (7) of the UN Charter states: "Nothing contained in the present Charter shall authorize the United Nations to intervene in matters which are essentially within the domestic jurisdiction of any state or shall require the Mem-

bers to submit such matters to settlement under the present Charter; but this principle shall not prejudice the application of enforcement measures under Chapter VII."

7. Jawaharlal Nehru and Sarvepalli Gopal, *Selected Words of Jawaharlal Nehru, Ser. 2, Vol. 1* (New Delhi: Jawaharlal Nehru Memorial Fund, 1984), 437. See also Mazower, *No Enchanted Palace*, 177n33.

8. "Proceedings of the Joint Meetings of the States Committee of the Constituent Assembly and the States Negotiating Committee of the Chamber of Princes" (hereafter "Joint Proceedings"), February–March 1947, in B. Shiva Rao, ed., *The Framing of India's Constitution: Select Documents* (New Delhi: Universal Law Publishing, 2006), 1:677, quoted in Bhagavan, *Peacemakers*, 102.

9. Bhagavan, *Peacemakers*, 97.

10. Nitin Pai, "India and International Norms: R2P, Genocide Prevention, Human Rights and Democracy," in *Shaping the Emerging World*, ed. Waheguru Pal Singh Sidhu, Pratap Bhanu Mehta, and Bruce Jones (Brookings, 2013), 307.

11. Upon the Bangladeshi Supreme Court's issuance of the death penalty for fundamentalist Jamaat e Isalmi leader Abdul Quadar Mollah for war crimes committed in 1971, a spokesperson for India's External Affairs Ministry stated, "This is an internal matter for Bangladesh and for the people of Bangladesh." See "Bangladesh War Crimes Trial an Internal Matter: India," *Economic Times*, September 18, 2013, articles.economictimes.indiatimes.com/2013-09-18/news /42182977_1_internal-matter-abdul-quader-mollah-death-sentence.

12. Oliver Stuenkel, "Rising Powers and the Future of Democracy Promotion: The Case of Brazil and India," *Third World Quarterly* 32, no. 2 (2013): 347.

13. Indrani Bagchi, "Maldivian President Yameen to Visit India on December 22," *Times of India*, December 3, 2013, timesofindia.indiatimes.com/india /Maldivian-President-Yameen-to-visit-India-on-December-22/articleshow /26805321.cms.

14. "Second Thoughts: The Maldives and India," *The Economist*, February 23, 2013.

15. "India, Maldives Ink 3 MoUs, to Resolve GMR Issue," *Economic Times*, January 2, 2014, articles.economictimes.indiatimes.com/2014-01-02/news/457 99601_1_maldives-government-indian-ocean-indian-high-commission.

16. "Was 'Hurt' That Narendra Modi Could Not Visit: Maldives," *Deccan Herald*, March 17, 2015, www.deccanherald.com/content/466155/was-hurt -narendra-modi-could.html.

17. Shashi Tharoor, *Pax Indica* (New Delhi: Allen Lane, 2012), 397.

18. Thin Thin Aung and Soe Myint, "India-Burma Relations," in *Challenges to Democratization in Burma* (Stockholm: International Institute for Democracy and Electoral Assistance, 2001), 87.

19. UN General Assembly resolution 47/144, *Situation in Myanmar*, A/ RES/47/144 (December 18, 1992).

20. Author interview with former Indian diplomat, October 2012.

21. Pratap Bhanu Mehta, "Reluctant India," *Journal of Democracy* 22, no. 4 (2011): 103.

22. Author interview with Indian government official, October 2012.

23. Ibid.

24. UN General Assembly resolution 66/230, *Situation of Human Rights in Myanmar*, A/RES/266/230 (December 24, 2011), unbisnet.un.org:8080/ipac20 /ipac.jsp?profile=voting&index=.VM&term=ares66230.

25. "Timeline: Myanmar's Reforms under Civilian Control," Reuters, October 14, 2011, www.reuters.com/article/2011/10/14/us-myanmar-timeline -idUSTRE79D19720111014.

26. Author interview with Harsh Shringla, MEA, October 15, 2012 (then joint secretary, Bangladesh-Sri Lanka-Myanmar-Maldives division); "PM's Address to Think-Tank's and Business Community at an Event Organized by Myanmar Federation of Chambers of Commerce and Industry and the Myanmar Development Resource Institute in Yangon," Ministry of External Affairs, Government of India, May 29, 2012, www.mea.gov.in/outgoing-visit-detail .htm?19749/PMs+address+to+thinktanks+and+business+community+at+an +event+organized+by+Myanmar+Federation+of+Chambers+of+Commerce +and+Industry+and+the+Myanmar+Development+Resource+Institute+in +Yangon.

27. "Modi Meets Aung San Suu Kyi, Describes Her as 'Symbol of Democracy,'" *F.India*, November 12, 2014, www.firstpost.com/world/modi-meets -aung-san-suu-kyi-describes-symbol-democracy-1799947.html.

28. With hydropower potential measured at an estimated 83,000 MW, India sees high growth potential in the hydropower sector in Nepal. "Nepal Hydropower Overview," Hydroelectricity Investment and Development Company, www.hidcl.org.np/nepal-hydropower.php. More significantly, India's interest in establishing contracts and filling a technical vacuum ahead of China is a large contributor to the clamor surrounding hydroelectric development. For more, see Russell Sticklor, "The Race to Harness Himalayan Hydropower," *Stimson Center*, October 4, 2012, www.stimson.org/spotlight/the-race-to-harness-himalayan -hydropower/.

29. Author interview with Lalit Mansingh, former foreign secretary, October 2012.

30. Prime Minister Manmohan Singh speech at India Today Conclave, February 25, 2005, pmindia.gov.in/speech-details.php?nodeid=73.

31. Saeed Naqvi, Observer Research Foundation, comments at Brookings-FICCI dialogue on U.S.-India Strategic Partnership, October 10, 2012.

32. As Bharat Karnad of the Centre for Policy Research has stated, India can promote democracy rhetorically (unless doing so endangers India's national interest or realization of strategic priorities) but otherwise should leave countries to "discover the joys of democracy themselves," with the possible exception of China. Bharat Karnad at CNAS/GWU Conference on "Rising Powers" in Washington, D.C., January 23–24, 2012, bharatkarnad.com/2012/01/27/bharat -karnad-at-cnasgwu-conference-on-rising-powers-in-washington-dc-january -23-24-2012/.

33. President Karzai signed three MoUs during his first official state visit to India in 2006, intended to promote rural development, education, and standardization. In the same year, India pledged $50 million to promote bilateral busi-

ness between the two countries and raised its aid package to $750 million from $150 million. During the 2008 SAARC conference, India pledged an additional $450 million for reconstruction and training projects. By August 2013, $321 million in food assistance and school construction had been disbursed, $250 million had been spent on construction of the Salma Dam Power Project and a power line from Puli Khumri to Kabul, and $150 million was spent on rehabilitating the Delaram-Zaranj road. See "Summary of MoUs Signed by India and Afghanistan during the State Visit of President Hamid Karzai to India," Ministry of External Affairs, Government of India, April 10, 2006; "India Announces $100 mln More Aid for Afghanistan," Reuters, January 23, 2007; Amin Tarzi, "Afghanistan: Kabul's India Ties Worry Pakistan," Radio Free Europe/Radio Liberty, April 16, 2006; "India Announces More Afghan Aid," BBC, August 4, 2008; and Gareth Price, "India's Policy towards Afghanistan," Chatham House, ASP 2013/04, August 2013.

34. Text of Agreement on Strategic Partnership between the Republic of India and the Islamic Republic of Afghanistan, October 4, 2011, mfa.gov.af/en/news /3867.

35. It is commonly cited that Indian firms are deeply involved in the development of mineral deposits estimated to be worth $1 trillion. See the Economist Intelligence Unit, *Afghanistan 4th Quarter 2013 Country Report.*

36. Dipanjan Roy Chaudhury, "S M Krishna Condemns Ex-Afghan President Burhanuddin Rabbani's Assassination," *India Today*, September 21, 2011, http://indiatoday.intoday.in/story/s-m-krishna-condemns-burhanudin-rabbani -killing/1/152079.html.

37. Cynthia English, "U.S. Leadership More Popular in Asia than China's, India's," *Gallup World*, November 5, 2010, www.gallup.com/poll/144269 /Leadership-Popular-Asia-China-India.aspx.

38. For example, in a sample of voting behavior at the Human Rights Council from 2004 to 2010, on country-specific issues India voted no 48 percent of the time, abstained 30 percent of the time, and voted yes only 22 percent of the time, one of which was a vote to block consideration of a resolution on Zimbabwe and another of which was a no-action motion on Belarus. For more, see the Democracy Coalition Project, www.scribd.com/DemocracyCoalition. A Human Rights Watch survey showed that from 2012 to 2014, India abstained from or voted no on a majority of country-specific resolutions at the Human Rights Council. It was also one of only two member states that did not cosponsor any country-specific resolutions in 2012 or 2013. It voted in favor of two out of three resolutions regarding Sri Lanka and the human rights situation in Palestine and other occupied Arab territories. For more, see "Vote Count," Human Rights Watch, votescount.hrw.org/page/India; "Country Voting History Portal," Universal Rights Group, www.universal-rights.org/country-voting-history -portal/.

39. In the Charter, member states agreed to "encourage all democratic forces in South Asia, including elected representatives of the people, to unite against any unconstitutional change in government in any South Asian country, and work towards the restoration of democracy in keeping with the SAARC Charter."

South Asian Association for Regional Cooperation, *SAARC Charter of Democracy* (February 9, 2011), www.saarc-sec.org/SAARC-Charter-of-Democracy/88/.

40. Khilnani and others, *Nonalignment 2.0,* 15–16.

41. "India's Foreign Policy Priorities and India-U.S. Relations," Brookings, September 2014, www.brookings.edu/research/opinions/2014/09/23-india-fore ign-policy-priorities-sidhu; W. P. S. Sidhu, "India's Multiple Multilateral Opportunities," *Mint*, November 6, 2014, www.livemint.com/Opinion/lXLwNRGD0 PJnaEJEZPuAIM/Indias-multiple-multilateral-opportunities.html.

42. Sumit Ganguly and Eswaran Sridharan, "The End of India's Sovereignty Hawks?," *Foreign Policy*, November 7, 2013, www.foreignpolicy.com/articles /2013/11/07/the_end_of_indias_sovereignty_hawks_human_rights.

43. Khilnani and others, *Nonalignment 2.0,* 17.

44. Robert G. Herman and Theodore J. Piccone, *Defending Democracy: A Global Survey of Foreign Policy Trends, 1992–2002* (Washington, D.C.: Democracy Coalition Project, 2002), 97–98.

45. "PM Modi Seeks Stronger Ties with Fiji; Announces a 75 Million Dollar Credit Line," *Indian Express*, November 19, 2014, indianexpress.com/article /india/india-others/india-extends-75-million-dollar-credit-line-to-fiji/.

46. Author interview with Indian government official, October 2012.

47. Khilnani and others, *Nonalignment 2.0,* 37.

48. Sundeep Waslekar, "Credible India?," *Forbes India* 4, no. 18 (2012): 44–55.

49. Excerpts of prime minister's address at the Annual Conclave of Indian Ambassadors/High Commissioners Abroad in New Delhi, November 4, 2013, pmindia.nic.in/speech-details.php?nodeid=1387.

50. "Migrants from Developing Countries to Send Home $414 Billion in Earnings in 2013," World Bank, October 2, 2013, www.worldbank.org/en/news /feature/2013/10/02/Migrants-from-developing-countries-to-send-home-414 -billion-in-earnings-in-2013.

51. Author interview with former Indian diplomat, October 2012.

52. Author interview with Indian government official, October 2012.

53. Ibid.

54. *Report of the Working Group on the Universal Periodic Review: India*, A/HRC/21/10, July 9, 2012, daccess-dds-ny.un.org/doc/UNDOC/GEN/G12 /151/08/PDF/G1215108.pdf?OpenElement.

55. As of October 2015, another twelve requests for country visits have been requested but not accepted. See "Country and Other Visits by Special Procedures Mandate Holders since 1998," Office of the High Commissioner for Human Rights, www.ohchr.org/EN/HRBodies/SP/Pages/CountryvisitsF-M.aspx.

56. See wghr.org/?page_id=615; author interview with Miloon Kothari, convener of the Working Group on Human Rights, October 2012.

57. Author interview with Indian government official, October 2012.

58. "India: Govt. Blocks Greenpeace's Foreign Funding, Activists Raise Concerns over Freedom of Expression," Business and Human Rights Resource Center, April 12, 2015, business-humanrights.org/en/india-govt-blocks-greenpeaces -foreign-funding-activists-raise-concerns-over-freedom-of-expression.

59. Open Letter to the Honorable Prime Minister of India, May 8, 2015, author's files.

60. "Amnesty International Criticises Modi Govt's Rights Record" *Hindu*, February 25, 2015, www.thehindu.com/news/international/world/amnesty -international-criticises-modi-govts-rights-record/article6931794.ece.

61. Sonia Faleiro, "India's Attack on Free Speech," *New York Times*, October 2, 2015, http://www.nytimes.com/2015/10/04/opinion/sunday/sonia-faleiro -india-free-speech-kalburgi-pansare-dabholkar.html?_r=0.

62. "Amnesty International Reports Nun Murder as the Fourth Activist Killing in India This Year," Amnesty International, November 17, 2011, www .amnestyusa.org/news/press-releases/amnesty-international-reports-nun -murder-as-the-fourth-activist-killing-in-india-this-year. See also Amnesty International's 2011 annual report on India, *Annual Report: India 2011*, May 28, 2011, www.amnestyusa.org/research/reports/annual-report-india-2011.

63. Author interview with Indian government official, October 2012.

64. Government of India, Ministry of Home Affairs, "Abstract of Speaker's Strength of Languages and Mother Tongues—2001," www.censusindia.gov.in /Census_Data_2001/Census_Data_Online/Language/Statement1.aspx.

65. "Population by Ethnic Group According to Districts, 2012," Government of Sri Lanka, Department of Census and Statistics, www.statistics.gov.lk /PopHouSat/CPH2011/index.php?fileName=pop42&gp=Activities&tpl=3.

66. Ian Hall, "Tilting at Windmills? The Indian Debate over the Responsibility to Protect after UNSC Resolution 1973," *Global Responsibility to Protect 5* (2013): 90.

67. UN Human Rights Council resolution A/HRC/S-11/2, *Report of the Human Rights Council on Its Eleventh Special Session* (June 26, 2009), http:// daccess-dds-ny.un.org/doc/UNDOC/GEN/G09/144/09/PDF/G0914409.pdf ?OpenElement; Human Rights Watch, "Sri Lanka: UN Rights Council Fails Victims," May 27, 2009, https://www.hrw.org/news/2009/05/27/sri-lanka-un -rights-council-fails-victims.

68. "India Votes against Sri Lanka at UNHRC, DMK Slams Govt for Diluting Resolution," *Times of India*, March 21, 2013, articles.timesofindia.india times.com/2013-03-21/india/37902646_1_llrc-unhrc-sri-lanka.

69. Author interview with Meenakshi Ganguly, Human Rights Watch, October 2012.

70. India also voted in favor of Resolution 22/1 in 2013, which had a similar vote tally of 25-13-8. However, at the last minute, the United States significantly weakened the language in this resolution in six distinct places, most tellingly by deleting a paragraph calling for "unfettered access" in Sri Lanka by international observers and specialists, resulting in the dilution of the previously condemnatory tone of the text. Affirmative statements acknowledging progress made on such issues as holding elections and resettling internally displaced persons were also added. For more, see Narayan Lakshman, "Has U.S. Watered Down Sri Lanka UNHRC Resolution?," *Hindu*, March 20, 2013, www.thehindu .com/news/international/has-us-watered-down-sri-lanka-unhrc-resolution /article4528023.ece.

71. Canadian prime minister Stephen Harper and Mauritian prime minister Navin Ramgoolam also boycotted the summit. All three executives sent their foreign ministers instead. "Mauritian PM to Join Sri Lanka Commonwealth Summit Boycott," BBC, November 12, 2013, www.bbc.com/news/world-asia -24918261.

72. Author interview with Indian business executive, October 2012.

73. Waslekar, "Credible India," 44.

74. "The German Missions Abroad," Federal Foreign Office, www .auswaertiges-amt.de/EN/AAmt/Auslandsvertretungen/Uebersicht_node.html.

75. For example, the United States recorded 285 mission facilities worldwide in 2015. It also recorded employing 13,385 foreign service officers a few years prior. "About Diplomatic Security—Frequently Asked Questions," U.S. Department of State, www.state.gov/m/ds/about/faq/index.htm#13; Paul Webster Hare, *Making Diplomacy Work: Intelligent Innovation for the Modern World* (Los Angeles, Calif.: CQ Press, 2015), 18.

76. Author interview with Indian diplomat, October 2012.

77. "I also recognize that your efforts must be supported by adequate and timely availability of resources. I would urge you, however, to prioritize the use of our limited financial and human resources in the most efficient and effective manner." PM Manmohan Singh, "India in the Changing World: Priorities and Principles," speech to the Annual Conclave of Indian Ambassadors/High Commissioners abroad in New Delhi, November 4, 2013.

78. W. P. S. Sidhu and Shruti Godbole, "Bold Initiatives Stymied by Systemic Weakness," in *Modi's Foreign Policy @365: Robust Engagement* (Brookings India, 2015), 4.

79. U.S. Department of State, *Trafficking in Human Persons Report June 2013*, 195, www.state.gov/j/tip/rls/tiprpt/2013/.

80. NHRIs promote and monitor the effective implementation of international human rights standards at the national level. To be accredited by the UNHRC through a peer review process, NHRIs must comply with the Paris Principles, an internationally agreed-on list of characteristics that guide the role, composition, status, and functions of NHRIs and ensure their independence and credibility. For more, see "OHCHR and NHRIs," United Nations Office of the High Commissioner for Human Rights, www.ohchr.org/en/countries/nhri /pages/nhrimain.aspx.

81. National Human Rights Commission of India, "Text of Speech by Justice K. G. Balakrishnan, Chairperson, NHRC on Human Rights Day Function of NHRC," nhrc.nic.in/Documents/Speech_By_Chairperson_NHRC_On _HumanRightsDay2013.pdf.

82. For more on the MEA organization and portfolios, see "Organization Structure," Ministry of External Affairs, Government of India, www.mea.gov .in/organization-structure.htm.

83. S. Jaishankar, foreign secretary, Ministry of External Affairs, "India, the United States and China," IISS-Fullerton Lecture, Singapore, July 20, 2015, www.iiss.org/en/events/events/archive/2015-f463/july-636f/fullerton-lecture -jaishankar-f64e.

84. Rajiv Kumar, "India 2015: Towards Economic Transformation," *Legatum Institute Transitions Forum*, April 2015, 6.

85. Ibid., 3.

86. Prime Minister's address to Parliament of Sri Lanka, March 13, 2015, Ministry of External Affairs, http://www.mea.gov.in/outgoing-visit-detail.htm ?24938/Prime+Ministers+address+to+Parliament+of+Sri+Lanka+March+13 +2015.

87. Ministry of External Affairs Media Center, "Prime Minister's Interview to the TIME Magazine," May 8, 2015, www.mea.gov.in/interviews.htm?dtl /25211/Prime+Ministers+interview+to+the+TIME+Magazine.

88. Remarks by prime minister in the Mongolian Parliament, May 17, 2015, Ministry of External Affairs, www.mea.gov.in/outgoing-visit-detail.htm?25254 /Remarks+by+Prime+Minister+in+the+Mongolian+ParliamentMay+17+2015.

89. Kadira Pethiyagoda, "Modi Deploys His Culture Skills in Asia," in *Modi's Foreign Policy @365: Robust Engagement* (Brookings India, 2015), 15.

90. Modi speech to UNGA, September 27, 2014. See "Full Text of PM Modi's Speech at UNGA," *Business Standard*, September 27, 2014, www.business -standard.com/article/current-affairs/full-text-of-pm-modi-s-speech-at-unga -114092800002_1.html; see also UN General Assembly resolution, *International Day of Yoga*, A/RES/69/131 (December 11, 2014), www.un.org/en/ga/search /view_doc.asp?symbol=A/RES/69/131.

91. David Barstow and Suhasini Raj, "Mob Attack, Fueled by Rumors of Cow Slaughter, Has Political Overtones in India," *New York Times*, October 4, 2015, http://www.nytimes.com/2015/10/05/world/asia/mob-attack-over-rumors -of-cow-slaughter-has-political-overtones-in-india.html.

92. For a discussion on the growing influence of local forces on Indian politics, see William Antholis, *Inside Out India and China: Local Politics Go Global* (Brookings, 2013). The author is also indebted to Samir Saran of the Observatory Research Foundation for his insights on India's evolving foreign policy ecosystem.

CHAPTER 4

1. As Antonio de Aguiar Patriota, Brazil's ambassador to the UN and former foreign minister put it, under Presidents Lula and Rousseff, 40 million Brazilians have been brought out of poverty. "Perhaps even more significantly, the recent improvements in Brazil's Human Development Index have taken place in a fully democratic environment." Antonio de Aguiar Patriota, "Brazil and the Shaping of a Cooperative Multilateral Order: Reflections on the Emerging World Order and Kissinger's World Order," *Horizons* 2 (2015): 229.

2. For a general assessment of Brazil's global ambitions, see Harold Trinkunas, "Do Brazil's Capabilities Match Its Global Ambitions?," *Americas Quarterly* 9, no. 1 (2015): 52–58.

3. Mac Margolis, "Why Venezuela's Neighbors Keep Quiet," *Bloomberg View*, March 8, 2015, www.bloombergview.com/articles/2015-03-08/why -venezuela-s-neighbors-might-stay-quiet-after-unasur.

4. Oliver Stuenkel, "Brazil," in *Supporting Democracy Abroad: An Assessment of Leading Powers*, ed. Daniel Calingaert, Arch Puddington, and Sarah Repucci (Washington, D.C.: Freedom House, 2014), 9–14.

5. According to the Constitution of the Federative Republic of Brazil, article 4, "The international relations of the Federative Republic of Brazil are governed by the following principles:

I. national independence;

II. prevalence of human rights;

III. self-determination of the peoples;

IV. non-intervention;

V. equality among the states;

VI. defense of peace;

VII. peaceful settlement of conflicts;

VIII. repudiation of terrorism and racism;

IX. cooperation among peoples for the progress of mankind;

X. granting of political asylum.

The Federative Republic of Brazil shall seek the economic, political, social and cultural integration of the peoples of Latin America, viewing the formation of a Latin-American community of nations."

6. Celso Lafer, "Brazil and the World," in *Brazil: A Century of Change*, ed. Ignacy Sachs, Jorge Wilheim, and Paul Sérgio Pinheiro (University of North Carolina Press, 2009), 110.

7. Lincoln Gordon, *Brazil's Second Chance: En Route toward the First World* (Brookings, 2001), 195.

8. Tullo Vigevani and Gabriel Cepaluni, *Brazilian Foreign Policy in Changing Times: The Quest for Autonomy from Sarney to Lula*, trans. Leandro Moura (Lanham, Md.: Lexington Books, 2009), xiv. Lafer viewed Brazilian foreign policy as Grotian, falling between the realist Hobbesian tradition and the universalist Kantian tradition, and felt Brazilian autonomy could only be maintained "through active participation in the elaboration of norms and agendas managing the world order" ("Brazil and the World," 116). Fernando Henrique Cardoso would deepen Lafer's framework during his brief tenure as foreign minister from October 1992 to May 1993 (Vigevani and Cepaluni, *Brazilian Foreign Policy*, 47).

9. Jânio Quadros, "Brazil's New Foreign Policy," *Foreign Affairs* 20, no. 1 (1961): 19–27.

10. White House, Memorandum for the President's File, "The President's Private Meeting with British Prime Minister Edward Heath on Monday, December 20, 1971, 1:30–5:00 p.m., in the Sitting Room of Government House, Bermuda," December 20, 1971, www2.gwu.edu/~nsarchiv/NSAEBB/NSAEBB71/doc15.pdf; and White House, Memorandum for the President's File, "Meeting with President Emílio Garrastazú Médici of Brazil on Thursday, December 9, 1971, at 10:00 a.m., in the President's Office, the White House," December 9, 1971, www2.gwu .edu/~nsarchiv/NSAEBB/NSAEBB282/Document%20143%2012.9.71.pdf.

11. Olga Nazario, "Brazil's Rapprochement with Cuba: The Process and the Prospects," *Journal of Interamerican Studies and World Affairs* 28, no. 3 (1986): 67.

12. Antonio Azeredo da Silveira, Ministério das Relações Exteriores, broadcast speech, March 28, 1974, *Resenha de Política Exterior do Brasil* 1 (1974): 23.

13. Lafer, "Brazil and the World," 112.

14. Bertha K. Becker and Claudio A. G. Egler, *Brazil, a New Regional Power in the World-Economy* (Cambridge University Press, 1992), 107.

15. Lafer, "Brazil and the World," 112.

16. Nazario, "Brazil's Rapprochement with Cuba," 67.

17. "Brazil Country Profile," Nuclear Threat Initiative, www.nti.org/country -profiles/brazil/; "Treaty for the Prohibition of Nuclear Weapons in Latin America and the Caribbean (Treaty of Tlatelolco)," State Department, February 14, 1967, www.state.gov/p/wha/rls/70658.htm.

18. Vigevani and Cepaluni, *Brazilian Foreign Policy*, 14.

19. Sean Burges and Jean Daudelin, "Brazil: How Realists Defend Democracy," in *Promoting Democracy in the Americas*, ed. Thomas Legler, Sharon F. Lean, and Dexter S. Boniface (Johns Hopkins University Press, 2007), 3.

20. Vigevani and Cepaluni, *Brazilian Foreign Policy*, 16.

21. In 1991, the OAS General Assembly passed resolution 1080, which instructs the secretary general to convene a meeting of the Permanent Council in cases of "sudden or irregular interruption of the democratic political institutional process." The Inter-American Democratic Charter, adopted in 2001, allows for the suspension of an OAS member state by special session of the General Assembly in the event of "an unconstitutional interruption of the democratic order or an unconstitutional alteration of the constitutional regime that impairs the democratic order in a member state." The Ushuaia Protocol on Democratic Commitment of Mercosul likewise permits state parties to take measures, including suspension, against other state parties "in the event of a breakdown of democracy." OAS General Assembly, AG/RES. 1080 (XXI-O/91), "Representative Democracy," www.oas.org/juridico/english/agres1080.htm; Organization of American States, "Inter-American Democratic Charter," September 11, 2001, www.oas.org/charter/docs/resolution1_en_p4.htm; Mercosul, Protocolo de Ushuaia sobre compromise democrático en el Mercosur, la República de Bolivia y la República de Chile, July 24, 1998.

22. For an excellent summary of the main trends in Brazil's human rights policies abroad, see Par Engstrom, "Brazilian Foreign Policy and International Human Rights Promotion: Existing Tensions and Future Prospects," in *Shifting Power and Human Rights Diplomacy: Brazil*, ed. Thijs van Lindert and Lars van Troost (Amsterdam: Amnesty International Netherlands, 2014), 15–23, www.amnesty.nl/RisingPowerBrazil.

23. Vigevani and Cepaluni, *Brazilian Foreign Policy*, 57.

24. Ibid., 58.

25. Fernando Henrique Cardoso, "Democracy as a Starting Point," *Journal of Democracy* 12, no. 1 (2001): 5–14; Fernando Henrique Cardoso, "Brazil and a New South America," *Valor*, August 30, 2000.

26. OAS Resolution 1080, "Representative Democracy."

27. At the inaugural summit meeting in Brazil in 2000, the group decided that participation in future summits would depend on respect for democratic

institutions and the rule of law. UNASUR's implementation of this principle, however, has been shaky, at best.

28. Fernando Henrique Cardoso and Mauricio A. Font, *Charting a New Course: The Politics of Globalization and Social Transformation* (Lanham, Md.: Rowman and Littlefield, 2001), 255–56. Excerpted from a lecture at the University of Witwatersrand, Johannesburg, South Africa, on November 27, 1996.

29. For a cogent overview of the OAS response to such crises, see Ruben M. Perina, "The Role of the Organization of American States," in *Protecting Democracy: International Responses*, ed. Morton H. Halperin and Mirna Galic, 127–71 (Lanham, Md.: Lexington Books, 2005).

30. Robert G. Herman and Theodore J. Piccone, *Defending Democracy: A Global Survey of Foreign Policy Trends, 1992–2002* (Washington D.C.: Democracy Coalition Project, 2002), 56–60.

31. The Initiative for the Integration of Regional Infrastructure in South America (IIRSA) was launched in 2000 to more closely connect the economies of South America by constructing roads and waterways. Lula's development agenda complemented these aims. Vigevani and Cepaluni, *Brazilian Foreign Policy*, 66; Pitou van Dijck, *The Impact of the IIRSA Road Infrastructure Programme on Amazonia* (New York: Routledge, 2013), 20–21.

32. Sean W. Burges, "Brazil as Regional Leader: Meeting the Chavez Challenge," *Current History* 109 (2010): 53–59. The Brazilian Senate was initially opposed to Venezuela's entry in Mercosul on democracy and human rights grounds but eventually relented in part owing to Brazilian business interests in Venezuela.

33. "Chavez is without a doubt Venezuela's best president in the last 100 years"—from interview with Jens Glüsing and Helene Zuber, *Der Spiegel*, May 10, 2008, www.spiegel.de/international/world/spiegel-interview -with-brazilian-president-lula-we-want-to-join-opec-and-make-oil-cheaper-a -552900.html. In response, former president Cardoso told the press that Lula was "very indulgent" with Chávez. "The region has recovered the machinery of democracy, yes, but not the soul of it. Much remains to be done to ensure equality before the law and equal opportunities" (from interview with Fernando Gualdoni, *El País Internacional*, June 15, 2010, internacional.elpais.com/internacional /2010/06/15/actualidad/1276552817_850215.html).

34. Maria Teresa Romero, "Brazil and Venezuela: The Discrete Fallout of Two Strategic Partners," *PanAm Post*, November 7, 2013, panampost.com /maria-teresa-romero/2013/11/07/brazil-and-venezuela-the-discrete-fallout-of -two-strategic-partners/.

35. Brian Winter, "Brazil Grows Weary of Venezuela under Maduro, Reduces Support," Reuters, March 28, 2014.

36. Author interview with foreign diplomat, Brazil, May 2011.

37. Oliver Stuenkel, "Rising Powers and the Future of Democracy Promotion: The Case of Brazil and India," *Third World Quarterly* 24, no. 2 (2013): 344; Marcelo Ballve, "Lula Steps In: Brazil Fills Vacuum Left by American Disengagement," *World Politics Review*, September 18, 2008.

38. Oliver Stuenkel, "Is Brazil the New Regional Champion of Democracy?," *Americas Quarterly* 7, no. 4 (2013): 32–36, www.americasquarterly.org/content /brazil-new-regional-champion-democracy.

39. At the June 2005 General Assembly meeting in Florida, the United States proposed creating a mechanism within the IADC to allow OAS member states to intervene in nations to foster or strengthen democracy. "OAS Members Balk at U.S. Intervention Plan," CNN International, June 7, 2005.

40. OAS, the EU, and Carter Center all canceled their electoral observation missions. Peter J. Meyer, "Honduran Political Crisis, June 2009–January 2010," Congressional Research Service, February 1, 2010, www.fas.org/sgp/crs/row /R41064.pdf.

41. Oliver Stuenkel, "Brazil at the Eye of the Storm: Lula, Zelaya and Democracy in Central America," *Post-Western World*, June 28, 2014, www.post westernworld.com/2014/06/28/democracy-central-america/.

42. The OAS sent a delegation to Paraguay in July 2012 to investigate the events resulting in President Lugo's dismissal and released a public report to that effect on July 10, 2012. The next day, the assistant secretary for the Bureau of Western Hemisphere Affairs at the U.S. State Department, Roberta Jacobson, spoke at a press briefing where she asserted that there was no reason to suspend Paraguay from the OAS and that the most important action to take was "to look for constructive ways moving forward to engage with the Paraguayans, including with the Franco government, to get to the elections next year." U.S. Department of State, "Overview of Recent Travel to Central America and the Western Hemisphere Affairs Agenda, Roberta S. Jacobson," July 11, 2012, fpc.state.gov/194826.htm.

43. Stuenkel, "Brazil."

44. "Tightening the Grip: Concentration and Abuse of Power in Chávez's Venezuela," Human Rights Watch, July 17, 2012, https://www.hrw.org/report /2012/07/17/tightening-grip/concentration-and-abuse-power-chavezs -venezuela.

45. Author interview with U.S. diplomat, May 2011.

46. Cardoso, *The Accidental President of Brazil*, 223.

47. Ibid., 224.

48. Ibid., 224–25.

49. "Lula Ends Delicate Cuban Trip," BBC News, September 27, 2003, news .bbc.co.uk/2/hi/americas/3143108.stm; Mauricio Vicent, "Los intercambios económicos marcan la visita de Lula a Cuba," *El País*, September 28, 2003.

50. According to Brazil's ambassador to Cuba, "Tax and tariff exemptions in the zone will allow Brazilian agribusiness, food and tobacco companies to exploit Cuba's educated and low-cost labour force to gain a competitive edge in the US and Caribbean markets" (Anatoly Kurmanaev, "Boat-Lift Memories Fade at Cuban Port Poised for Trade Boom," *Bloomberg Business*, December 26, 2014, www.bloomberg.com/news/articles/2014-12-26/boat-lift-memory-fades -in-cuba-with-biggest-port-poised-for-boom).

51. Brascuba, a joint cigarette and cigar venture between Souza Cruz (Brazil) and Tabacuba (Cuba), is poised to expand production significantly in coming

years, according to Brazilian diplomatic sources, with an eye to the Brazilian and global markets.

52. "We have to respect the decisions of the Cuban legal system and the government to arrest people on the laws of Cuba, like I want them to respect Brazil," said Lula ("Brazil's Lula Criticized for Cuba Dissidents Comment," BBC News, March 11, 2010, news.bbc.co.uk/2/hi/8561718.stm).

53. Haroon Siddique, "Fidel Castro Holds 'Emotional' Meeting with Brazilian President," *The Guardian*, February 25, 2010, www.theguardian.com/world /2010/feb/25/fidel-castro-cuba-lula-brazil.

54. Raul Castro, meanwhile, blamed the activist's death on the U.S. embargo ("Brazil's Lula Criticized").

55. Author interviews with Brazilian officials.

56. The three-year contract for medical services provides $8.5 billion in revenue to Cuba, according to Brazilian diplomatic sources (author interview).

57. "Brazil Increases Pressure on Venezuela to Set Election Date," Reuters (U.K.), May 8, 2015, uk.reuters.com/article/2015/05/08/uk-venezuela-brazil -idUKKBN0NT01Y20150508.

58. Winter, "Brazil Grows Weary."

59. Celso Amorim, "Brazilian Foreign Policy under President Lula (2003–2010): An Overview," *Revista Brasileira de Política Internacional* 53 (2010): 231. As one Brazilian scholar observed, South-South cooperation was Lula's strategy to counterbalance the agenda of developed nations (Vigevani and Cepaluni, *Brazilian Foreign Policy*, xii).

60. Amorim, "Brazilian Foreign Policy," 225; italics in original.

61. Ibid., 234.

62. "Home," IBSA Fund, tcdc2.undp.org/IBSA/Default.aspx.

63. Stuenkel, "Brazil," 2.

64. As of March 2015, IBSA had not held a summit since 2011 while BRICS ministerials are still occurring annually; the Seventh BRICS Summit was held in July 2015 in Ufa, Russia.

65. Robert F. Worth and Nazila Fathi, "Protests Flare in Tehran as Opposition Disputes Vote," *New York Times*, June 13, 2009, www.nytimes.com/2009 /06/14/world/middleeast/14iran.html?pagewanted=all&_r=0.

66. For the murder of her husband, Sakineh Mohammadi Ashtiani was sentenced to prison for ten years. For adultery, she was sentenced to death by stoning. Her execution was stayed indefinitely, and she was pardoned and released on good behavior in March 2014.

67. Alexei Barrionuevo, "Brazil's President Offers Asylum to Woman Facing Stoning in Iran," *New York Times*, August 1, 2010.

68. Lally Weymouth, "An Interview with Dilma Rousseff, Brazil's President-Elect," *Washington Post*, December 3, 2010.

69. "President Rousseff's Foreign Policy 'Will Emphasize Human Rights (South and North),'" *MercoPress*, April 4, 2011.

70. In its Explanation of Vote for resolution A/HRC/28/L.17, "Situation of Human Rights in the Islamic Republic of Iran," Brazil indicated it had abstained because Iran had demonstrated a renewed engagement with the human rights system

by participating in the UPR and extending invitations to the High Commissioner for Human Rights, Special Rapporteur on the right to food, and the Special Rapporteur on the right to health to visit Iran. As of May 2015, none of these visits had been made; see www.ohchr.org/EN/HRBodies/SP/Pages/CountryvisitsF-M.aspx.

71. Conectas Direitos Humanos, "Foreign Policy and Human Rights: Strategies for Civil Society Action," June 2013, 19–20, http://www.conectas.org/arquivos/editor/files/CONECTAS%20ing_add_LAURA.pdf.

72. UN General Assembly, "Report of the Commission of Inquiry on Human Rights in the Democratic People's Republic of Korea," A/HRC/25/63, February 7, 2014; UN General Assembly "Report of the Detailed Findings of the Commission of Inquiry on Human Rights in the Democratic People's Republic of Korea," A/HRC/25/CRP.1, February 7, 2014, www.ohchr.org/EN/HRBodies/HRC/CoIDPRK/Pages/ReportoftheCommissionofInquiryDPRK.aspx; "UN General Assembly Seeks North Korea ICC Charges," BBC News, December 18, 2014, www.bbc.com/news/world-asia-30540379.

73. The UN General Assembly Third Committee deals with matters of social and humanitarian affairs and human rights.

74. "Haiti Earthquake Memorial (January 2010)," United Nations, www.un.org/en/memorial/haiti/.

75. Statement by H. E. Dilma Rousseff, President of the Federative Republic of Brazil at the Sixty-Sixth Session of the UN General Assembly, New York, September 21, 2011.

76. For an earlier take on the importance of Africa to Brazil's foreign and development policy, see the article by then president Jânio Quadros, "Brazil's New Foreign Policy," *Foreign Affairs* 40, no. 1 (1961): 24–26.

77. "Brazil Census Shows Africa-Brazilians in the Majority for the First Time," *The Guardian*, November 17, 2011, www.theguardian.com/world/2011/nov/17/brazil-census-african-brazilians-majority.

78. Christina Stolte, "Brazil in Africa: Just Another BRICS Country Seeking Resources?," Chatham House Briefing Paper, November 2012.

79. Ibid.

80. "Latin America and Mercosur, Priorities of Brazil Foreign Policy Ratifies Rousseff," *MercoPress*, June 17, 2013.

81. Brazil mining giant Vale opened a $1.7 billion coal mine in Mozambique in May 2011; Odebrecht is the largest private employer in Angola with activities in food and ethanol production, factories, and supermarkets. Stuart Grudgings, "As Rich World Sputters, Brazil Looks to Africa," reuters.com, November 17, 2011. See also Nikolas Kozloff, "Is Brazil the Inheritor of the Portuguese Empire in Africa?," *Al Jazeera*, September 30, 2012.

82. Brazil has served as the chair of the Guinea-Bissau country-specific configuration at the UN Peacebuilding Commission from its addition to the PBC agenda in 2007. At the time of the crisis, Ambassador Maria Luiza Ribeiro Viotti served as chairperson; since 2013, Ambassador Antonio de Aguiar Patriota has held the position.

83. "Guinea-Bissau," *Security Council Report Update Report* 1, May 4, 2012; and "Resolução sobre a situação na Guiné-Bissau," adopted at the VIII

Extraordinary Meeting of the Council of Ministers of the CPLP, April 14, 2012, www.itamaraty.gov.br/index.php?option=com_content&view=article&id =3023&catid=42&Itemid=280&lang=pt-br.

84. Ted Piccone, "The Multilateral Dimension," *Journal of Democracy* 22, no. 4 (2011): 139–52, www.journalofdemocracy.org/article/do-new-democracies -support-democracy-multilateral-dimension.

85. "Brazil—Votes Count," Votes Count: Monitoring the UN HRC, vote-scount.hrw.org/page/Brazil.

86. It abstained, however, in 2015.

87. "25th Session of the Human Rights Council Comes to an End," Conectas, April 3, 2014, www.conectas.org/en/actions/foreign-policy/news/17002 -25th-session-of-the-human-rights-council-comes-to-an-end.

88. Ibid.

89. "24th Session of the UN Human Rights Council Comes to an End," Conectas, October 8, 2013, www.conectas.org/en/actions/foreign-policy/news/3392 -24th-session-of-the-un-human-rights-council-comes-to-an-end.

90. UN Human Rights Council resolution 17/19, *Human Rights, Sexual Orientation and Gender Identity*, A/HRC/17/L.9/Rev.1 (July 14, 2011); and "Combatting Discrimination Based on Sexual Orientation and Gender Identity," OHCHR, www.ohchr.org/EN/Issues/Discrimination/Pages/LGBT.aspx.

91. "27th Session of the UN Human Rights Council Comes to an End," Conectas, October 3, 2014, www.conectas.org/en/actions/foreign-policy/news/26391 -27th-session-of-the-un-human-rights-council-comes-to-an-end.

92. Statement by H. E. Dilma Rousseff, President of the Federative Republic of Brazil, at the Sixty-Eighth Session of the UN General Assembly, September 24, 2013.

93. UN Human Rights Council resolution, *The Right to Privacy in the Digital Age*, A/HRC/28/L.27, ap.ohchr.org/documents/alldocs.aspx?doc_id=24720, March 23, 2015.

94. Harold Trinkunas and Ian Wallace, "Converging on the Future of Global Internet Governance: The United States and Brazil," Brookings, July 2015; Maria Laura Canineu and Eileen Donahoe, "Brazil as the Global Guardian of Internet Freedom?," in *Shifting Power and Human Rights Diplomacy: Brazil*, ed. Thijs van Lindert and Lars van Troost (Amsterdam: Amnesty International Netherlands, 2014), www.amnesty.nl/RisingPowerBrazil.

95. Ministry of External Relations, Government of Brazil, "Situation in Egypt, Tunisia, and Yemen," note 31, January 28, 2011, www.itamaraty.gov.br /sala-de-imprensa/notas-a-imprensa/situacao-no-egito-na-tunisia-e-no-iemen.

96. Ibid.

97. A week before Mubarak stepped down, Itamaraty (shorthand for Brazil's Foreign Ministry) reaffirmed Brazil's "solidarity and friendship toward the Egyptian people and expect[ed] that this moment of instability be overcome shortly under a framework of institutional and democratic improvement in Egypt." Ministry of External Relations, Government of Brazil, "Situation in Egypt," note 41, February 2, 2011, www.itamaraty.gov.br/sala-de-imprensa/notas-a-imprensa/sit uacao-no-egito-1.

98. Sebastiao Martins, "Brazil," *Pulsamerica*, February 2, 2011, www
.pulsamerica.co.uk/?p=3514.

99. Ministry of External Relations, Government of Brazil, "Political Situation
in Egypt," note 54, February 11, 2011, www.itamaraty.gov.br/sala-de-imprensa
/notas-a-imprensa/situacao-politica-no-egito.

100. "Brazil Foreign Minister Visits Egypt; Urges Arab Support for UN FAO
Candidate," *BBC Monitoring Latin American*, May 10, 2011.

101. Ministry of External Relations, Government of Brazil, "Minister Antonio de Aguiar to Visit Egypt," note 179, May 6, 2011, www.itamaraty.gov.br
/sala-de-imprensa/notas-a-imprensa/visita-do-ministro-antonio-de-aguiar
-patriota-ao-egito-2013-cairo-7-e-8-de-maio-de-2011.

102. "Brasil demonstra preocupação com golpe de Estado no Egito," *O
Globo*, July 3, 2013, oglobo.globo.com/mundo/brasil-demonstra-preocupacao
-com-golpe-de-estado-no-egito-8901866.

103. UN Security Council resolution 1975, March 30, 2011, para. 6, S/RES/
1975.

104. Statement by H. E. Ambassador Maria Luiza Ribeiro Viotti, Permanent
Representative of Brazil to the United Nations, *The Situation in Côte d'Ivoire*,
March 30, 2011, www.un.int/brazil/speech/11d_mlrv_Cote_Ivoire-explanation
-vote.html.

105. Statement by H. E. Ambassador Maria Luiza Ribeiro Viotti, Permanent
Representative of Brazil to the United Nations, *The Situation in Libya*, March 17,
2011, www.un.int/brazil/speech/11d-mlrv-on-situation-in-libya.html.

106. Author interview with senior US diplomat.

107. Ibid.; for more information on Brazil's stance on protection of civilians,
see *Responsibility while Protecting: Elements for the Development and Promotion of a Concept*, annex to the letter dated November 9, 2011, from the
permanent representative of Brazil to the UN addressed to the secretary general, A/66/551-S/2011/701.

108. "Brazil Makes Intervention in Libya Conditional on UN Approval,"
BBC Monitoring Latin America, March 7, 2011.

109. Ministry of External Relations, Government of Brazil, "Situation in
Syria," note 161, April 25, 2011, www.itamaraty.gov.br/sala-de-imprensa/notas
-a-imprensa/situacao-na-siria.

110. Ibid.

111. Ministry of External Relations, Government of Brazil, "Actions against
Protesters in Hama, Syria," note 286, August 1, 2011, www.itamaraty.gov.br
/sala-de-imprensa/notas-a-imprensa/acao-contra-manifestantes-em-hama
-siria.

112. Statement by H. E. Dilma Rousseff, President of the Federative Republic of Brazil, at the Sixty-Sixth Session of the UN General Assembly, September 21, 2011.

113. Colum Lynch, "New UN Bloc Finds Constraining the West Preferable
to Restraining Syria," *Foreign Policy*, August 10, 2011, turtlebay.foreignpolicy
.com/posts/2011/08/10/new_un_bloc_finds_constraining_the_west_preferable
_to_restraining_syria.

114. International Service for Human Rights, "Human Rights Council Holds Special Session on Syria," May 2, 2011, www.ishr.ch/council/376-council/1055 -human-rights-council-holds-special-session-on-syria. The Human Rights Council convened subsequent special sessions on Syria in August and December 2011 but Brazil was no longer a member of the Council.

115. Column Lunch, "UN Security Council Condemns Syria's Campaign against Protesters," *Foreign Policy*, August 3, 2011, turtlebay.foreignpolicy.com /posts/2011/08/03/un_security_council_condemns_syrias_campaign_against _protesters.

116. Amal Hasson, "Syria, Brazil Launch Business Council to Encourage Economic, Trade Cooperation," *Global Arab Network*, November 20, 2011, www.english.globalarabnetwork.com/201011308249/Economics/syria-brazil -launch-business-council-to-encourage-economic-trade-cooperation.html.

117. Ministry of External Relations, Government of Brazil, "Situation in Bahrain," note 64, February 17, 2011, www.itamaraty.gov.br/sala-de-imprensa /notas-a-imprensa/situacao-no-bareine.

118. Ministry of External Relations, Government of Brazil, "Situation in Bahrain," note 102, March 17, 2011, www.itamaraty.gov.br/sala-de-imprensa /notas-a-imprensa/situacao-no-bareine-1.

119. Brazil imports less than 2 percent of its total oil and other liquids consumption. U.S. Energy Information Administration, *Background Analysis on Brazil*, January 2011, www.eia.gov/countries/cab.cfm?fips=BR.

120. Eduarda Passarelli Hamann, "The Protection of Civilians in Armed Conflict and Brazil's 'Responsibility while Protecting,'" NOREF Policy Brief, October 2012.

121. Bruce Jones, *Still Ours to Lead* (Brookings, 2014), 136.

122. Ibid.

123. Brazil abstained on a UN Security Council vote to condemn Russia's violation of Ukraine's territorial integrity. See UN General Assembly resolution 68/262, *Territorial Integrity of Ukraine*, A/RES/68/262 (March 27, 2014); and Somini Sengupta, "Vote by UN General Assembly Isolates Russia," *New York Times*, March 27, 2014, www.nytimes.com/2014/03/28/world/europe/General -Assembly-Vote-on-Crimea.html?_r=0.

124. The name *Itamaraty* refers to the building in Rio de Janeiro that housed the first Foreign Ministry (Conectas strategy report, 7n1).

125. Author interview with Sergio Amaral, former deputy foreign minister, May 2011.

126. Jose Sarney, "Brazil: A President's Story," *Foreign Affairs* 56, no. 1 (1986): 101–17.

127. E. Bradford Burns, "Tradition and Variation in Brazilian Foreign Policy," *Journal of Inter-American Studies* 9, no. 2 (1967): 196–98.

128. Jeffrey W. Cason and Timothy J. Power, "Presidentialization, Pluralization, and the Rollback of Itamaraty: Explaining Change in Brazilian Foreign Policy Making in the Cordoso-Lula Era," *International Political Science Review* 30, no. 2 (2009): 117–40.

129. Author interview with Sergio Fausto, Instituto Fernando Henrique Cardoso, May 2011.

130. Guadalupe González González, Jorge A. Schiavon, David Crow, and Gerardo Maldonado, *The Americas and the World 2010–2011, CIDE* (Mexico City: Centro de Investigación y Docencia Económicos, 2011), www.wilsoncenter.org/sites/default/files/The%20Americas%20and%20the%20World%202010-2011%20%283%29.pdf.

131. Simon Kemp, "Digital, Social, & Mobile in 2015," *We Are Social*, January 2015, Slides 71–81, de.slideshare.net/wearesocialsg/digital-social-mobile-in-2015?ref=http://wearesocial.net/blog/2015/01/digital-social-mobile-worldwide-2015/.

132. Ted Piccone, "The Middle Classes and Foreign Policy: Engaging in It but Not Changing It . . . Yet," *Americas Quarterly*, November 5, 2012, www.americasquarterly.org/middle-classes-and-foreign-policy-engaging-it-not-changing-ityet.

133. Lucia Nader and Laura Trajber Waisbich, "The Long March towards the Democratization of Brazilian Foreign Policy," in *Shifting Power and Human Rights Diplomacy: Brazil*, ed. Thijs van Lindert and Lars van Troost (Amsterdam: Amnesty International Netherlands, 2014), 92, www.amnesty.nl/RisingPowerBrazil.

134. Fiona Macaulay, "The Impact of Domestic Politics on Brazil's Foreign Policy on Human Rights," in *Shifting Power and Human Rights Diplomacy: Brazil*, ed. Thijs van Lindert and Lars van Troost (Amsterdam: Amnesty International Netherlands, 2014), 82–83.

135. Author interview with former Brazilian official, May 2011.

136. For a summary of the foreign policy work of Conectas Direitos Humanos, see "Foreign Policy and Human Rights: Strategies for Civil Society Action," June 2013, www.conectas.org/arquivos/editor/files/CONECTAS%20ing_add_LAURA.pdf.

137. Ibid., 20.

138. "Foreign Policy, Human Rights and Elections: Ten Proposals for the Presidential Candidates," Conectas, September 26, 2014, www.conectas.org/en/actions/foreign-policy/news/25418-foreign-policy-human-rights-and-elections.

139. *Report of Strategy Meeting on Emerging Democratic Powers: Civil Society Engagement in Multilateral, Regional and Bilateral Foreign Policy on Human Rights*, hosted by Conectas Direitos Humanos, May 25–26, 2011, São Paolo, 12 (author's files).

140. "Foreign Policy and Human Rights," 19, 24.

141. See Nader and Trajber Waisbich, "The Long March," 87–95.

142. "International Mobility of Students in Brazil," *UN Chronicle* L, no. 4 (2013): 42–44, unchronicle.un.org/article/international-mobility-students-brazil/.

143. Two Brazilian institutions were ranked in the top thirty-five of non-U.S. think tanks in the world, and three were listed in the top eleven think tanks in Central and South America. See James G. McGann, "2014 Global Go-To Think Tank Index Report," Think Tanks and Civil Societies Program, University of Pennsylvania, January 22, 2015, repository.upenn.edu/think_tanks/8/.

144. "Drug Policy," Igarapé Institute, www.igarape.org.br/en/drug-policy/.

145. Author interview with Sergio Amaral, former deputy foreign minister, May 2011.

146. Author interview with Collor de Mello, chair of Senate Committee on Foreign Affairs, May 2011.

147. de Aguiar Patriota, "Brazil and the Shaping of a Cooperative Multilateral Order," 230.

148. Author interview with Itamaraty diplomats, May 2011. In the 2014–15 training course for new diplomats, the Rio Branco Institute offered a course specifically in human rights and social issues, as well as continuing education opportunities in the same vein. "Perguentas Frequentes," Instituto Rio Branco, Ministry of External Relations, Government of Brazil, www.Institutoriobranco.mre.gov.br/pt-br/o_curso_de_formacao.xml.

149. Author interview with Marco Aurelio Garcia, foreign policy adviser to the president of Brazil, May 2011.

150. Ibid.

151. Gabriela Terenzi and José Marques, "Não vamos aceitar regras do governo cubano, diz Aécio sobre Mais Médicos," *Folha*, July 16, 2014, www1.folha.uol.com.br/poder/2014/07/1486716-nao-vamos-aceitar-regras-do-governo-cubano-diz-aecio-sobre-mais-medicos.shtml; Anderson Atunes, "5 Reasons Why Aécio Neves Should Be Elected the Next President of Brazil," *Forbes*, October 22, 2014, www.forbes.com/sites/andersonantunes/2014/10/22/5-reasons-why-aecio-neves-should-be-elected-the-next-president-of-brazil/; Brianna Lee, "Aécio Neves, Brazil's Market-Minded Presidential Challenger, in Virtual Tie with Incumbent ahead of Oct. 26 Vote," *International Business Times*, October 16, 2014, www.ibtimes.com/aecio-neves-brazils-market-minded-presidential-challenger-virtual-tie-incumbent-ahead-oct-1705681.

CHAPTER 5

1. As the Indian delegation in New York warned, "If the belief that there is to be one standard of treatment for the White races and another for the non-White continues to gain strength among the latter, the future for solidarity among the Members of the United Nations and, consequently, for world peace, will indeed be dark"; see www.sahistory.org.za/topic/united-nations-and-apartheid-timeline-1946-1994.

2. In 1952, the UN General Assembly agreed to establish a three-member commission to study the racial situation in South Africa by a vote of 35 to 1, with 23 abstentions. UN General Assembly resolution A/RES/616(VII), *The Question of Race Conflict in South Africa Resulting from the Policies of Apartheid of the Government of the Union of South Africa*, A/RES/616(VII) (December 5, 1952), aww.un.org/en/ga/search/view_doc.asp?symbol=A/RES/616(VII).

3. In 1963, the UN Special Committee against Apartheid first met; it was followed by the creation of the UN Centre against Apartheid in 1976. "The United Nations: Partner in the Struggle against Apartheid," United Nations, www.un.org/en/events/mandeladay/apartheid.shtml; and UN General Assembly

resolution 1761 (XVII), *The Policies of Apartheid of the Government of the Republic of South Africa* (November 6, 1962), daccess-dds-ny.un.org/doc/RES OLUTION/GEN/NR0/192/69/IMG/NR019269.pdf?OpenElement. For an extensive account of the ANC's campaign against apartheid at the United Nations, see Mfanafuthi Johnstone Makhatini, Special Representative of the African National Congress to the United Nations (1977–87), *Diplomacy for Democracy*, November 2012, www.dfa.gov.za/docs/2013/johnny_makhathini_artwork.pdf.

4. By many accounts, the Cuban military involvement in Angola in 1988 was a key factor in drawing South Africa to the negotiating table and ultimately led to its withdrawal from Angola, the independence of Namibia, and the withdrawal of Cuban troops from Angola by 1991.

5. United Nations Security Council resolution S/RES/554, *South Africa* (August 17, 1984), www.un.org/en/ga/search/view_doc.asp?symbol=S/RES/554(1984).

6. Congress overrode Reagan's veto days later, but the damage with the antiapartheid movement was already done.

7. Address by President Nelson Mandela of South Africa to the Forty-Ninth Session of the General Assembly of the United Nations, October 3, 1994, db .nelsonmandela.org/speeches/pub_view.asp?pg=item&ItemID=NMS204 &txtstr=united%20nations.

8. Chris Landsberg, "Promoting Democracy: The Mandela-Mbeki Doctrine," *Journal of Democracy* 11, no. 3 (2000): 108.

9. Ibid.

10. Author interview with Sydney Mufamadi, ANC activist and cabinet minister under both Presidents Mandela and Mbeki, December 2011.

11. Department of Foreign Affairs, Discussion Paper on South Africa's Foreign Relations, Fourth Draft, January 16, 1996, 7, quoted in Chris Landsberg and Jo-Ansie van Wyk, *South African Foreign Policy Review—Volume I* (Pretoria: Africa Institute of South Africa, 2012), 3.

12. Landsberg, "Promoting Democracy," 109.

13. Address by Deputy President Thabo Mbeki, "South Africa: A Year of Democracy," Bruno Kreisky Forum, Vienna, August 28, 1995, www.polity.org .za/polity/govdocs/speeches/1995/sp0828.html.

14. Author interview, November 2011.

15. Robert G. Herman and Theodore J. Piccone, eds., *Defending Democracy: A Global Survey of Foreign Policy Trends, 1992–2002* (Washington, D.C.: Democracy Coalition Project, 2002), 179.

16. Ibid., 180.

17. Aziz Pahad, then deputy minister of foreign affairs, Foreign Policy Workshop Concluding Remarks, Pretoria, September 9–10, 1996, quoted in Landsberg and van Wyk, *South African Foreign Policy Review*, 7.

18. See, for example, remarks of Tjiurimo Hengari in response to Salil Shetty, secretary general of Amnesty International, South African Institute of International Affairs, Pretoria, October 10, 2014, http://www.saiia.org.za/events /foreign-policy-and-human-rights-the-role-of-south-africa.

19. Author's calculations based on data from the Chinese National Bureau of Statistics. See figure 1-9 on page 26.

20. Foreign Policy Workshop, Opening Address by Minister Alfred B. Nzo, Pretoria, September 9–10, 1996, quoted in Landsberg and van Wyk, *South African Foreign Policy Review*, 6.

21. Nelson Mandela, speech to UN General Assembly, October 3, 1994, www.unric.org/en/images/stories/in-focus/Mandela_landmark_speech_to_the _UN.pdf.

22. "Building a Better World: The Diplomacy of Ubuntu," White Paper on South Africa's Foreign Policy, Final Draft, May 13, 2011.

23. President Jacob Zuma, State of the Nation Address to the Joint Sitting of Parliament, Cape Town, February 12, 2015, www.gov.za/president-jacob-zuma -state-nation-address-2015.

24. African National Congress (ANC), *International Relations Policy Discussion Document*, March 2012, 3, 6, www.anc.org.za/docs/discus/2012 /internationalb.pdf.

25. Ibid., 6.

26. Remarks by Ambassador Ebrahim Rasool at launch of Report on Supporting Democracy Abroad, Freedom House, November 13, 2014.

27. Statement by Oliver Tambo at the plenary meeting of the United Nations General Assembly, October 26, 1976, www.anc.org.za/show.php?id=4331.

28. Remarks by Foreign Minister Maite Nkoana Mashabane, University of Pretoria, September 11, 2012, reprinted in SAFPI. Nkoana goes on to note that South Africa's conduct is also based on fundamental values and principles in South Africa's constitution, notably human dignity, equity, human rights, non-racialism, nonsexism, democracy, and rule of law.

29. South African Foreign Policy Initiative, "South Africa's Role in the World: A Public Opinion Survey," SAFPI Policy Brief 55 (December 2013), 4.

30. Ibid., 7.

31. Ibid., 10.

32. Herman and Piccone, *Defending Democracy*, 178.

33. Article 4, subsection (g) of the SADC Protocol on Politics, Defence, and Security Co-operation (2001) stipulates that one of SADC's objectives is to "promote the development of democratic institutions and practices within the territories of State Parties and encourage the observance of universal human rights." Furthermore, the SADC Principles and Guidelines Governing Democratic Elections (2004) outlines the rights and responsibilities of host countries and observation missions in ensuring free and fair elections. Both are being reevaluated in 2015 through consultative workshops to enhance the principles and guidelines. SADC, "Protocol on Politics, Defence, and Security Co-operation," August 14, 2001, www.sadc.int/files/3613/5292/8367/Protocol_on_Politics _Defence_and_Security20001.pdf; "SADC Principles and Guidelines Governing Democratic Elections," Office of the United Nations High Commissioner for Human Rights, www2.ohchr.org/english/law/compilation_democracy/sadcprinc .htm; "SEAC Consultative Workshop on the Revision of the SADC Principles and Guidelines Governing Democratic Elections," SADC News, July 15, 2015, www.sadc.int/news-events/news/seac-consultative-workshop-revision-sadc -principles-and-guid/.

34. "Lesotho Elections Transparent and Fair, Says SADC," *Mail and Guardian Online*, March 2, 2015, mg.co.za/article/2015-03-02-lesotho-elections -transparent-and-fair-says-sadc.

35. Landsberg, "Promoting Democracy," 112.

36. Ibid., 113.

37. Ibid.

38. The Commonwealth observation mission concluded that "the conditions in Zimbabwe did not adequately allow for a free expression of will by the electors." "Zimbabwe Presidential Election, 9 to 11 March 2002: Report of the Commonwealth Observer Group," Commonwealth Secretariat, 44, archive .kubatana.net/docs/elec/commwrep0203.pdf. The Zimbabwe Election Support Network (a coalition of thirty NGOs) asserted that the elections were tainted by violence and threats. "The Zimbabwe Electoral Environment Post March 2002— Any Changes for Better or Worse," Zimbabwe Election Support Network, ace-project.org/regions-en/countries-and-territories/ZW/reports/Zimbabwe%20 -%20Environment%20Post%20Presidential%202002%20election%20Assement .doc. The South African observation mission, on the other hand, concluded that the regulatory system threatened the integrity of the electoral process, but that the outcome of the election was legitimate. Sam Motsuenyane, "Interim Statement by the South African Observer Mission to the Zimbabwean Presidential Elections," DIRCO, March 13, 2002, www.dfa.gov.za/docs/2002/zimb1303.htm.

39. Herman and Piccone, *Defending Democracy*, 179.

40. Landsberg, "Promoting Democracy," 116–19.

41. Paul Graham, "South Africa," in *Supporting Democracy Abroad: An Assessment of Leading Powers*, ed. Daniel Calingaert, Arch Puddington, and Sarah Repucci (Washington, D.C.: Freedom House, 2014), 3–4; Arrigo Pallotti, "Human Rights and Regional Cooperation in Africa: SADC and the Crisis in Zimbabwe," *Strategic Review for Southern Africa* 35, no. 1 (2013): 32–33.

42. ANC, *International Relations Policy Discussion Document*, 30.

43. Heather Saul, "South African President Jack Zuma Congratulates Robert Mugabe on His Landslide Victory in Zimbabwe Elections," *Independent*, August 4, 2013, www.independent.co.uk/news/world/africa/south-african -president-jacob-zuma-congratulates-robert-mugabe-on-his-landslide-victory -in-zimbabwe-elections-8745168.html.

44. Pallotti, "Human Rights and Regional Cooperation," 26–27.

45. Lesley Wentworth, "South Africa and the Regional Economic Integration Agenda: Priorities and Perspectives," presentation at SAIIA Eightieth Anniversary Conference on Agenda 2063, www.saiia.org.za/doc_download/604 -saiia-80conf-pres-day-3-wentworth-regional-economic-integration.

46. Reports include deaths and kidnappings of opposition leaders, media harassment, and abuse of state resources. Amy Poteete, "Does Botswana Deserve Its Reputation as a Stable Democracy?," *Washington Post*, October 20, 2014, www.washingtonpost.com/blogs/monkey-cage/wp/2014/10/20/does-botswana -deserve-its-reputation-as-a-stable-democracy/.

47. Paul-Henri Bischoff, "What's Been Built in Twenty Years? SADC and Southern Africa's Political and Regional Security Culture," *Strategic Review for*

Southern Africa 34, no. 2 (2012): 63–91; Bertha Z. Osei-Hwedie, "The Question for Peace and Security: The Southern African Development Community (SADC) Organ on Politics, Defence and Security," in *Democracy, Human Rights and Regional Cooperation in Southern Africa*, ed. Dominic Milazi, Munyae Mulinge, and Elizabeth Mukamaambo (Pretoria: Africa Institute of South Africa, 2002), 154–72.

48. Article 30 of the Constitutive Act of the African Union states: "Governments which shall come to power through unconstitutional means shall not be allowed to participate in the activities of the Union." Adopted at AU Summit on July 11, 2000, in Lome, Togo, www.au.int/en/sites/default/files/Constitutive_Act_en_0.htm#top.

49. African Charter on Democracy, Elections, and Governance, articles 17–25, www.ipu.org/idd-E/afr_charter.pdf.

50. As of May 2015, South Africa had signed and ratified the Charter on Democracy, along with twenty-two others. Another twenty-three states have signed but not ratified, and eight have done neither. African Union, *List of Countries Which Have Signed, Ratified/Acceded to the African Charter on Democracy, Elections and Governance*, February 3, 2014, www.au.int/en/sites/default/files/Charter%20on%20Democracy%20and%20Governance.pdf. The charter, which was adopted in January 2007, entered into force in February 2012. By comparison, all fifty-four African states except newly independent South Sudan have signed and ratified the African Charter on Human and Peoples' Rights, which came into effect in 1986. "Ratification Table: African Charter on Human and Peoples' Rights," African Commission on Human and Peoples' Rights, www.achpr.org/instruments/achpr/ratification/.

51. Bashir Adigun, "Ecowas Criticises SA Warship off West Africa," *Mail and Guardian Online*, February 9, 2011, http://mg.co.za/article/2011-02-09-ecowas-criticises-sa-warship-off-west-africa/.

52. Siphokazi Mthathi, "President Zuma Should Be on the Side of Justice in Ivory Coast," *New Age (South Africa)*, February 22, 2011. A similar view was espoused by the International Crisis Group. "Côte d'Ivoire: Is War the Only Option?," *Africa Report* 171, March 3, 2011, www.crisisgroup.org/en/regions/africa/west-africa/cote-divoire/171-cote-divoire-is-war-the-only-option.aspx.

53. ANC, *International Relations Policy Discussion Document*, 11.

54. The ICC trial against Gbagbo and a close aide is scheduled to commence in November 2015.

55. Graham, "South Africa," 5.

56. Jo-Ansie van Wyk, "South African Soft Power and Its Regional Leadership: The Use of Special Envoys," presentation at SAIIA's Eightieth Anniversary Foreign Policy Conference, Pretoria, October 28–30, 2014.

57. "South Africa in BRICS," Fifth BRICS Summit, Durban, South Africa, March 26–27, 2013, DIRCO, www.brics5.co.za/about-brics/south-africa-in-brics/.

58. Ibid.

59. The treaty entered into force on December 24, 2014, with sixty ratifications (seventy-two as of August 2015), including South Africa's. "The Arms

Trade Treaty," United Nations Office for Disarmament Affairs, www.un.org /disarmament/ATT/.

60. Salil Shetty, secretary general of Amnesty International, "Foreign Policy and Human Rights: The Role of South Africa," remarks to South African Institute of International Affairs, Pretoria, October 10, 2014.

61. Nahla Valji and Dire Tladi, "South Africa's Foreign Policy: Between Idealism and the Realpolitik of Being an Emerging Power," *openGlobalRights*, June 19, 2013.

62. "Human Rights? What's That?," *The Economist*, October 14, 2010, www.economist.com/node/17259138.

63. Shetty, "Foreign Policy and Human Rights," 8.

64. Ted Piccone, "Do New Democracies Support Democracy?: The Multilateral Dimension," *Journal of Democracy* 22, no. 4 (2011): 144.

65. Eduard Jordaan, "South Africa and the United Nations Human Rights Council," *Human Rights Quarterly* 36, no. 1 (2014): 92.

66. Shetty, "Foreign Policy and Human Rights," 9.

67. Jordaan, "South Africa," 113.

68. Author interview with Pitso Montwedi, DIRCO chief director of human rights and humanitarian affairs, December 2011.

69. Jordaan, "South Africa," 115.

70. See "South Africa: Twenty Years after Apartheid," Panel IV on "South Africa as a Beacon for Human Rights?," Roosevelt House, New York, September 19, 2014, www.roosevelthouse.hunter.cuny.edu/events/south-africa-twenty -years-apartheid/.

71. Shetty, "Foreign Policy and Human Rights," 13.

72. South African Department of International Relations and Cooperation (DIRCO), Media Statement on the situation in Egypt, January 31, 2011, www .dfa.gov.za/docs/2011/media0131.html.

73. "Zuma: Mubarak Made Correct Decision," February 11, 2011, *Mail and Guardian Online*, mg.co.za/article/2011-02-11-zuma-mubarak-made-correct -decision.

74. Statement by President Jacob Zuma at Joint Sitting of Parliament, February 10, 2011.

75. Graham, "South Africa," 4–5.

76. DIRCO, Media Statement on the situation in Libya, February 21, 2011, www.dfa.gov.za/docs/2011/libya0221.html.

77. Statement in Explanation of Vote by Ambassador Baso Sangqu on Resolution on Libya in the UN Security Council, New York, February 26, 2011, www.dfa.gov.za/docs/2011/unsc0226.html.

78. DIRCO, "South Africa Welcomes and Supports the UN Security Council's Resolution on No Fly Zone in Libya," March 18, 2011, www.dfa.gov.za /docs/2011/liby0318.html.

79. Ibid.

80. Wyndham Hartley, "Government Slated for Being Soft on Libya," *Business Day*, June 1, 2011, www.businessday.co.za/articles/Content.aspx?id=144404.

81. "South Africans Protest NATO Bombing of Libya," Associated Press, July 6, 2011.

82. Communique of the 265th Meeting of the African Union Peace and Security Council, March 10, 2011.

83. Ibid.

84. "Libya: Zuma Weighs In on NATO Bombings," *All Africa*, June 15, 2011, allafrica.com/stories/201106150501.html.

85. "Libyan Rebels Reject African Union Road Map," *Al Jazeera*, April 12, 2011, english.aljazeera.net/news/africa/2011/04/201141116356323979.html; see also Peter Fabricus, "What Ended Zuma's Mediation in Libya?," Institute for Security Studies, May 28, 2015, www.issafrica.org/iss-today/what-ended-zumas-mediation-in-libya.

86. DIRCO, Minister's Media Conference on Climate Change and Libyan Issues, June 16, 2011, www.dfa.gov.za/docs/2011/liby0616.html.

87. Some leading observers of South Africa's foreign policy do not consider its policy on the Libya intervention as inconsistent or random. Instead, as Adam Habib suggests, South Africa's endorsement of the intervention in Libya at the UNSC, and its subsequent criticism of NATO's actions, can be interpreted as South Africa's attempt to reconcile its desire to ensure that the international community does not neglect its humanitarian responsibilities—as it did in Rwanda—and its fear that intervention can be manipulated for political gain—as it was in Iraq. Adam Habib, "Is South African Foreign Policy at a Crossroads in Libya?," *New Age*, 2011, www.thenewage.co.za/blogdetail.aspx?mid=186&blog_id=548.

88. Speech by Ebrahim Ebrahim, "Libya, the United Nations and the African Union and South Africa: Wrong Moves?," September 15, 2011, http://www.dfa.gov.za/docs/speeches/2011/ebra0915a.html.

89. Ibid.

90. Ibid.

91. In July 2013, Ebrahim asserted, "The consistent failure of the UNSC to address the situation in Syria has reinforced our belief on the urgent need for the reform of the Council" ("Celebrating 19 Years of South Africa's Foreign Policy," public lecture by Deputy Minister of International Relations and Cooperation, H. E. Ebrahim Ebrahim to SAIIA, July 4, 2013, 5, www.dfa.gov.za/docs/speeches/2013/ebra0704.html).

92. ANC, *International Relations Policy Discussion Document*, 12.

93. DIRCO, "South Africa Is Concerned about the Situation in Syria," August 1, 2011, www.dfa.gov.za/docs/2011/syri0802.html.

94. Ibid.

95. Statement by Deputy Minister Ebrahim after bilateral meeting with Syrian counterpart, Mr. Mikad, August 8, 2011, www.dfa.gov.za/docs/speeches/2011/ebra0808.html.

96. South Africa abstained on the vote in the UN Security Council on the situation in Syria, October 5, 2011.

97. In July 2012 South Africa again joined Russia, China, and Pakistan against a UNSC resolution condemning human rights abuses in Syria.

98. "Statement by South Africa on Other Weapons of Mass Destruction during the Thematic Debate of the 2013 UN First Committee," United Nations, October 24, 2013, www.un.org/disarmament/special/meetings/firstcommittee/68/pdfs/TD_24-Oct_OWMD_South-Africa.pdf.

99. Author interview with Ebrahim Rasool, South African ambassador to the United States, November 2011.

100. Press TV, "South Africans Stage Anti-KSA rally," June 3, 2011, http://edition.presstv.ir/detail/183082.html.

101. U.S. Energy Information Administration, *Background Analysis on South Africa*, October 2011, www.eia.gov/countries/cab.cfm?fips=SF.

102. South Africa Department of Trade and Industry, *Statistics by Country*, apps.thedti.gov.za/econdb/raportt/rapcoun.html.

103. U.S. Energy Information Administration, *Background Analysis on South Africa*, October 2011.

104. South Africa Department of Trade and Industry, *Statistics by Country.*

105. U.S. Energy Information Administration, *South Africa*, April 29, 2015, 8–9, www.eia.gov/beta/international/analysis_includes/countries_long/South_Africa/south_africa.pdf.

106. "Africa Creates TFTA—Cape to Cairo Free-Trade Zone," BBC News, June 10, 2015, www.bbc.com/news/world-africa-33076917.

107. Address by Deputy Minister Marius Llewellyn Fransman during a Panel Discussion on South Africa's Second Term on the UN Security Council, Center for Human Rights, University of Pretoria, March 30, 2011, www.dfa.gov.za/docs/speeches/2011/cmchr0331.html.

108. Deputy Minister Marius Llewellyn Fransman, speech entitled "South Africa's Role in the International Arena," May 12, 2011, www.dfa.gov.za/docs/speeches/2011/frans0512.html.

109. Author interview with senior South African diplomat, November 2011.

110. Mandela's official statement at the time also expressed gratitude for Taiwan's "generous contribution" to South Africa's transition to democracy. Office of the President, "Statement by President Nelson Mandela on South Africa's Relations with the Greater China Region," November 27, 1996, www.mandela.gov.za/mandela_speeches/1996/961127_china.htm.

111. Tseliso Thipanyane, "South Africa's Foreign Policy under the Zuma Government," Africa Institute of South Africa, Briefing 64, December 2011, 5.

112. Peter Kenny, "Nobel Laureates' Conference Cancelled in South Africa over Dalai Lama Visa," *Presbyterian Church USA*, October 15, 2014, www.pcusa.org/news/2014/10/15/nobel-laureates-conference-cancelled-south-africa-/; and "Nobel Laureates Cancel South Africa Meeting," Associated Press, October 2, 2014, www.ndtv.com/world-news/nobel-laureates-cancel-south-africa-meeting-674210.

113. Author interview with former senior South African diplomat, December 2011.

114. Shetty, "Foreign Policy and Human Rights," 9–10.

115. Nelson Mandela, "Speech at the Rally in Cuba," July 26, 1991, db.nelsonmandela.org/speeches/pub_view.asp?pg=item&ItemID=NMS1526.

116. Dirk Kotze, "South Africa's Foreign Policy and International Relations during 2012," *South African Yearbook of International Law* 37 (2012): 368; Elizabeth Sidiropoulos, "Emerging 'Donor,' Geopolitical Actor: South Africa in the Global Terrain," in *International Development Policy: Aid, Emerging Economies and Global Policies*, ed. Gilles Carbonnier (London: Palgrave McMillan, 2012), 97.

117. "S. Africa Gives Cuba \$31 Million Economic Aid," *Voice of America*, September 27, 2014, www.voanews.com/content/south-africa-gives-cuba-31 -million-economic-aid/2464428.html.

118. Landsberg, "Promoting Democracy," 120.

119. Figures reflect conversion rates using a yearly average that coincides with South Africa's fiscal year (March 31–April 1). Republic of South Africa National Treasury, *Budget 2014, Estimates of National Expenditure: Vote 5, International Relations and Cooperation*, February 26, 2014, www.treasury.gov.za/documents /national%20budget/2014/enebooklets/Vote%205%20International%20Relations%20and%20Cooperation.pdf; and Republic of South Africa National Treasury, *Budget 2015, Estimates of National Expenditure: Vote 6, International Relations and Cooperation*, February 25, 2015, www.treasury.gov.za /documents/national%20budget/2015/enebooklets/Vote%206%20International%20Relations%20and%20Cooperation.pdf.

120. Graham, "South Africa," 4.

121. Graham, "South Africa"; Republic of South Africa National Treasury, *Budget 2015*, 18–19.

122. Projects have been funded in Haiti, Sierra Leone, and Vietnam, among other countries, and the fund was awarded the UN's MDG award in 2010 for its creative approach to eradicating poverty and hunger worldwide. "The IBSA Fund," IBSA, www.ibsa-trilateral.org/about-ibsa/ibsa-fund.

123. ANC, *International Relations Policy Discussion Document*, 5.

124. The Freedom Charter of 1955 is known for its commitment to a nonracial South Africa founded on democracy and human rights, and it served as the basis for most of modern South Africa's constitution. African National Congress, "The Freedom Charter," June 26, 1955, www.anc.org.za/show.php?id=72.

125. See, for example, Kotze, "South Africa's Foreign Policy," 358–59.

126. "In terms of policy hierarchy, the decisions of the ANC's National Conference are very important and influential in macro-policymaking" (ibid., 362).

127. Lesley McMasters, "Opening the 'Black Box': South African Foreign Policy-Making," in *South African Foreign Policy Review—Volume I, Africa Institute of South Africa*, ed. Chris Landsberg and Jo-Ansie van Wyk (Pretoria: Africa Institute of South Africa, 2012), 26.

128. Ibid., 23.

129. Kotze, "South Africa's Foreign Policy," 366.

130. SAICOR is expected to be formally launched in 2015. Parliamentary Monitoring Group, "Diplomacy Strategy and Functioning of South Africa Council on International Relations: DIRCO Input," NCOP Trade and International Relations Committee meeting summary, February 18, 2015, pmg.org.za/committee -meeting/20001/.

131. McMasters, "Opening the 'Black Box,'" 32.

132. The Geneva Conventions Act 8 of 2012 states that "any South African court may try any person for any offence or omission under the Act even if it was committed outside the Republic. Kotze, "South Africa's Foreign Policy," 360.

133. ANC, *International Relations Discussion Document*, 25–26.

134. Parliamentary Monitoring Group, DIRCO briefing on White Paper on South Africa's Foreign Policy, March 12, 2014, www.pmg.org.za.

135. See Parliamentary Monitoring Group, "What Is the PMG?," pmg.org.za/page/what-is-pmg.

136. The South Africa Institute for International Affairs, International Global Dialogue, and the Institute for Security Studies are cited most frequently as the leading international relations think tanks in the country. The Southern Africa Liaison Office conducts research, dialogue, and advocacy on African issues and is close to the ANC. Eight of the top twenty ranked think tanks in sub-Saharan Africa are found in South Africa, according to the *2014 Global Go-To Think Tank Index Report*, Think Tanks and Civil Societies Program, University of Pennsylvania, January 22, 2015, 69.

137. "COSATU Backs Satawu on China Ship with Zim Arms," COSATU press statement, April 18, 2008, www.cosatu.org.za/show.php?ID=1490.

138. Conectas Human Rights, "BRICS Summit Ends with Progress on Syria and Uncertainty on New Bank," March 27, 2013, www.conectas.org/en/actions/foreign-policy/news/brics-summit-ends-with-progress-on-syria-and-uncertainty-on-new-bank.

139. The South African government was reluctant to get involved at first, but after quiet lobbying from the United States, and a more vigorous campaign by NGOs, the ANC and then the diplomats came around. Author interview with anonymous sources.

140. McMasters, "Opening the 'Black Box,'" 34.

141. "South Africa/Zimbabwe: Challenging the NPA's Refusal to Act in Terms of the ICC Act," Southern Africa Litigation Centre, www.southernafricalitigationcentre.org/cases/completed-cases/challenging-the-npas-refusal-to-act-in-terms-of-the-rome-statute-act/.

142. Fernando Henrique Cardoso, *The Accidental President of Brazil: A Memoir* (New York: Public Affairs, 2006), 213–14.

143. See, for example, Sarah Boseley, "Mbeki AIDS Denial 'Caused 300,000 Deaths,'" *The Guardian*, November 26, 2008.

144. Cardoso, *The Accidental President of Brazil*, 217.

145. "About Us," Treatment Action Campaign, www.tac.org.za/about_us.

146. "South Africa," *Freedom of the Press 2014 Report on South Africa*, Freedom House, freedomhouse.org/report/freedom-press/2014/south-africa#.VQnmVPPD_cs.

147. ANC, *International Relations Discussion Document*, 26.

148. "South Africa and the Pursuit of Inclusive Growth," *Democracy Works Country Report*, Legatum Institute and Centre for Development and Enterprise, 2014, 36.

149. Brent Swails, "Xenophobic Killing in South African Township Caught by Photographer," CNN, April 21, 2015, www.cnn.com/2015/04/20/africa /south-africa-xenophobia-killing-photos/.

150. "New $25 Million Fund for South African Civil Society Groups Working to Advance Constitutionalism," Ford Foundation Newsroom, February 5, 2015.

CHAPTER 6

1. Gavin D. Brockett, *How Happy to Call Oneself a Turk: Provincial Newspapers and the Negotiation of a Muslim National Identity* (University of Texas, 2011), 32–63; Erik J. Zürcher, *Turkey: A Modern History* (New York: Tauris, 2004), 180.

2. Bernard Lewis, *The Emergence of Modern Turkey* (Oxford University Press, 1968), 315.

3. Zürcher, *Turkey*, 208.

4. Lewis, *The Emergence of Modern Turkey*, 305.

5. Ibid., 309; Brockett, *How Happy*, 67.

6. Lewis, *The Emergence of Modern Turkey*, 312.

7. Kerem Öktem, *Turkey since 1989: Angry Nation* (London: Zed Books, 2011), 44.

8. Ibid., 41.

9. "GDP per Capita (Current US$)," World Bank Development Indicators, data.worldbank.org/country/turkey.

10. Erdoğan was sentenced to ten months in prison in 1999 for "inciting religious hatred" by reading a poem at a rally written in 1912 by Turkish nationalist Ziya Gökalp at a rally: "The mosques are our barracks / The domes our helmets / The minarets our bayonets / And the believers our soldiers." The conviction also banned Erdoğan from participation in parliamentary elections.

11. Ted Piccone and Ashley Miller, "The Path to Progress? How Democratic Development Drives Five Rising Leaders," *Görüş*, December 2013, www .brookings.edu/research/articles/2013/12/democratic-development-five -countries-piccone-miller; Sebnem Y. Geyikci, "The Impact of Parties and Party Systems on Democratic Consolidation: The Case of Turkey," University of Essex, Doctoral Discussion Paper, 2, www.lse.ac.uk/europeaninstitute/research/contem poraryturkishstudies/papersyg20111.pdf.

12. The Sèvres Syndrome, which originates from the Treaty of Sèvres of the 1920s partitioning the Ottoman Empire among Armenia, Greece, Britain, France, and Italy, refers to the notion that foreign actors, notably the West, are continuing to conspire against the integrity of Turkey.

13. Alexander Murinson, "The Strategic Depth Doctrine of Turkish Foreign Policy," *Middle Eastern Studies* 42, no. 6 (2006): 945–64.

14. Selim Deringil, *Turkish Foreign Policy during the Second World War: An "Active" Neutrality* (Cambridge University Press, 1989), 7.

15. Richard Weitz, *Turkey's New Regional Security Role: Implications for the United States* (Strategic Studies Institute and U.S. Army War College Press, 2014), 3.

16. Ibid. See also William Hale, *Turkish Foreign Policy Since 1774*, 3rd ed. (Abingdon: Routledge, 2013), 135.

17. Soli Özel and Gencer Özcan, "Turkey's Dilemmas," *Journal of Democracy* 22, no. 4 (2011): 126.

18. Aybars Görgülü, "The Litmus Test for Turkey's New Foreign Policy: The Historical Rapprochement with Armenia," in *Another Empire?: A Decade of Turkey's Foreign Policy Under the Justice and Development Party,* ed. Karem Öktem, Ayşe Kadıoğlu, and Mehmet Karlı (Istanbul Bilgi Üniversitesi, 2012), 282. As Özel and Özcan point out, Turkey's main priority was economic growth, prompting some analysts to conclude Turkey had shifted from being a "national security state" to a "trading state." Kemal Kirişci, "Turkey's Foreign Policy in Turbulent Times," Chaillot Paper 92, September 2006; and Kemal Kirişci, "The Transformation of Turkish Foreign Policy: The Rise of the Trading State," *New Perspectives on Turkey* 40 (2009): 29–57.

19. Ahmet Davutoğlu, *Stratejik Derinlik: Turkiye'nin Uluslararasi Konumu* (Istanbul: Küre Yayinlari, 2001).

20. Ahmet Davutoğlu, interview by *Cairo Review of Global Affairs*, March 12, 2013, www.mfa.gov.tr/interview-by-mr_-ahmet-davutoğlu-published-in-auc-cairo-review-_egypt_-on-12-march-2012.en.mfa.

21. Ahmet Davutoğlu, "Turkey's Zero-Problems Foreign Policy," *Foreign Policy*, May 20, 2010, www.foreignpolicy.com/articles/2010/05/20/turkeys_zero_problems_foreign_policy.

22. Özel and Özcan, "Turkey's Dilemmas," 131.

23. Senem Aydın-Düzgit and E. Fuat Keyman, "Democracy Support in Turkey's Foreign Policy," Carnegie Endowment for International Peace, March 25, 2014, carnegieendowment.org/2014/03/25/democracy-support-in-turkey-s-foreign-policy/h5ne.

24. "Davutoğlu Rejects Neo-Ottoman Label Using 'Neo-Roman' Analogy," *Today's Zaman*, March 3, 2013, www.todayszaman.com/news-308703-davutoglu-rejects-neo-ottoman-label-using-neo-roman-analogy.html.

25. Ahmet Davutoğlu, "Turkish Foreign Policy at a Time of Global and Regional Transformation: Vision and Challenges," address, Brookings Institution, Washington, D.C., November 18, 2013, www.brookings.edu/events/2013/11/18-turkey-transformation-challenges-davutoglu.

26. "Commission Opinion on Turkey's Request for Accession to the Community," Commission of the European Communities, Brussels, December 20, 1989, aei.pitt.edu/4475/1/4475.pdf; see also Metin Heper and Sabri Sayari, *The Routledge Handbook of Modern Turkey* (New York: Routledge, 2012), 237.

27. Davutoğlu, "Turkish Foreign Policy," 9.

28. Author interview with Volkan Bozkir, chairman, Foreign Relations Committee, Grand National Assembly, Ankara, October 2011. Meltem Müftüler-Baç has written extensively on Turkish-European relations. See, for example, Meltem Müftüler-Baç and Yannis A. Stivachtis, eds., *Turkey-European Union Relations: Dilemmas, Opportunities and Constraints* (Lanham, Md.: Lexington Books, 2008); Meltem Müftüler-Baç, *Enlarging the European Union: Where Does Turkey*

Stand? (Istanbul: Turkish Social Economic Studies Foundation [TESEV], 2002).

29. E. P. Licursi, "The Ergenekon Case and Turkey's Democratic Aspirations," Freedom House, February 7, 2012, freedomhouse.org/blog/ergenekon -case-and-turkey%E2%80%99s-democratic-aspirations#.VY1sFiFVhHw; and "Timeline: Turkey's 'Ergenekon' Trial," *Al Jazeera*, August 5, 2013, www .aljazeera.com/news/europe/2013/08/20138512358195978.html. In 2007, an alleged plot to foment a military coup was uncovered, and by the end of the investigation and trial in 2013 there were 275 defendants, including opposition parliamentarians, academics, politicians, and journalists. A number of defendants were sentenced to prison for conspiring to overthrow the government, whereas others were acquitted. The case drew its name from an alleged clandestine network of ultranationalists, Ergenekon, that supposedly aims to overthrow the AKP and has been characterized as a modern iteration of former clandestine networks that previously made up the "deep state."

30. "The Silent Revolution," AK Parti, April 4, 2014. Erdoğan and the AKP have published three editions of *The Silent Revolution: Turkey's Democratic Change and Transformation Inventory: 2002–2012* to highlight Turkey's democratic progress under the AKP.

31. "No Way Forward, No Way Back?," *Economist Intelligence Unit*, October, 15, 2014.

32. "Legislating Autocracy? Recent Legal Developments in Turkey," Bipartisan Policy Center, April 3, 2014, bipartisanpolicy.org/library/legislating-autocracy -recent-legal-developments-turkey/.

33. Human Rights Watch, "Turkey: Spy Agency Law Opens Door to Abuse," April 29, 2014, https://www.hrw.org/news/2014/04/29/turkey-spy-agency-law -opens-door-abuse.

34. "Legislating Autocracy?"

35. "Turkey's Internet Crackdown," *New York Times*, February 21, 2014.

36. Ryan Mauro, "Erdoğan Bans Twitter, Vows to Show 'Power of Turkish Republic,'" *Clarion Project*, March 23, 2014, www.clarionproject.org/analysis /erdogan-bans-twitter-vows-show-power-turkish-republic#.

37. For the second year running, Turkey's Freedom House Press Freedom score in 2014 was not free and it has been steadily declining for the past five years. Reporters without Borders ranked Turkey 154th out of 180 countries, based on pluralism, media independence, environment and self-censorship, legislative framework, transparency and infrastructure, and violence against journalists.

38. Turan Kayaoğlu, "Turkey: Not a Leader for Democracy in the Middle East," *Al Arabiya*, May 18, 2012, www.brookings.edu/research/opinions/2012 /05/19-turkey-democracy-kayaoglu; Human Rights Watch, "Turkey: UPR Submission 2014," December 19, 2014, www.hrw.org/news/2014/06/16/turkey-upr -submission-june-2014.

39. Mustafay Aykol, "Turkey's Maturing Foreign Policy: How the Arab Spring Changed the AKP," *Foreign Affairs*, July 7, 2011, www.foreignaffairs .com/articles/turkey/2011-07-07/turkeys-maturing-foreign-policy.

40. Ahmet Davutoğlu, *Principles of Turkish Foreign Policy and Regional Political Structuring*, Turkish Policy Brief Series, International Policy and Leadership Institute, 3rd ed. (Ankara: Economic Policy Research Foundation of Turkey [TEPAV], 2012), 2.

41. H. E. Ahmet Davutoğlu, minister of foreign affairs of the Republic of Turkey, "Turkish Foreign Policy at a Time of Global and Regional Transformation: Vision and Challenges," Brookings Institution transcript, November 18, 2013, 14–16.

42. Robert G. Herman and Theodore J. Piccone, *Defending Democracy: A Global Survey of Foreign Policy Trends, 1992–2002* (Washington, D.C.: Democracy Coalition Project, 2002), 198.

43. Özel and Özcan, "Turkey's Dilemma," 134.

44. Ahmet Davutoğlu, "Turkey's Zero-Problems Foreign Policy," *Foreign Policy*, May 20, 2010, www.foreignpolicy.com/articles/2010/05/20/turkeys_zero_problems_foreign_policy.

45. "Turkey's $20 Billion Tourism Industry under Threat," *Sydney Morning Herald*, June 12, 2013; Kemal Kirişci, "Turkey's ISIL Dilemma: To Fight or Not to Fight," *Brookings UpFront*, October 3, 2014, www.brookings.edu/blogs/up-front/posts/2014/10/03-turkey-isil-dilemma-kirisci.

46. Thomas de Waal, *Great Catastrophe: Armenians and Turks in the Shadow of Genocide* (Oxford University Press, 2015); Tim Arango, "Turkey's Century of Denial about an Armenian Genocide," *New York Times*, April 16, 2015.

47. One of the most prominent groups, the Turkish Foundation for Human Rights and Freedoms and Humanitarian Relief, has been caught up in a variety of controversies, notably its flotilla in 2010 to evade Israel's blockade of the Gaza Strip, which Israel attacked, killing nine activists.

48. As of December 2014, 2015 UNHCR country operations profile—Turkey, www.unhcr.org/pages/49e48e0fa7f.html.

49. Ministry of Foreign Affairs, Republic of Turkey, "Responsibility and Vision: Turkish Foreign Policy in 2014," 3 (author's files).

50. In 2014, the court overturned Erdoğan's attempts to ban Twitter and YouTube and annulled parts of a law that gave the justice minister sweeping powers over the body that appoints judges and public prosecutors. In 2015, the court ruled against the AKP's attempt to ban private supplemental education services, a veiled attack against Erdoğan's erstwhile enemy, the Gülen movement, which sponsors a substantial minority of such schools.

51. Ömer Taşpinar, for example, argues that Turkey is not an appropriate model for democratizing Middle Eastern countries in "The End of the Turkish Model," *Survival: Global Politics and Strategy* 56, no. 2 (2014): 49–64, www.iiss.org/en/publications/survival/sections/2014-4667/survival—global-politics-and-strategy-april-may-2014-3f8b/56-2-06-taspinar-220c.

52. "ANA Trust Fund," NATO, updated February 27, 2015, www.nato.int/nato_static_fl2014/assets/pdf/pdf_2015_02/20150227_2015-02-ANA-TF.pdf. For more information on Turkey's troop contributions to NATO's mission in Afghanistan, see "Troop Numbers and Contributions," NATO Afghanistan

Resolute Support, www.rs.nato.int/troop-numbers-and-contributions/index
.php.

53. While Turkey's development aid budget has grown significantly since
then, the share devoted to Afghanistan has markedly declined. "Annual Report
2013," Turkish Cooperation and Coordination Agency (TÍKA), 192, www.tika
.gov.tr/upload/publication/TIKA%20ANNUAL%20REPORT%202013.pdf.

54. Turkey has been a contributor to and participant in NATO's Training
Mission in Iraq since 2005, hosting specialized courses to train security officers.
General Michael D. Barbero, "Turkey, NATO, and Iraq: 2011 and Beyond,"
speech, Center for Middle East Strategic Studies, October 12, 2011, www.arrc
.nato.int/training_mission_iraq/page88203640.aspx. In cooperation with the
UN Assistance Mission in Iraq, Turkey hosted a conference on Iraq's constitution in 2006 that brought together members of all Iraq's political parties. In
addition, Turkey initiated the Neighboring Countries Process, a forum that
brings together Iraq, its neighbors, and others for ministerial consultations to
support Iraq's democratic transition. For more information, see "Relations between Turkey and Iraq," Ministry of Foreign Affairs, Republic of Turkey, www
.mfa.gov.tr/turkey_s-contributions-to-iraq.en.mfa; and "3 November 2007, Final
Communiqué of the Ministerial Conference of the Neighboring Countries of
Iraq, Egypt, and Bahrain and the Permanent Members of the UN Security
Council and the G-8," Ministry of Foreign Affairs, Republic of Turkey, www
.mfa.gov.tr/3-november-2007_-final-communique-of-the-ministerial
-conference-of-the-neighboring-countries-of-iraq_-egypt-and-bahrain-and
-the.en.mfa.

55. Şaban Kardaş, "Is Turkey's Long Game in Iraq a Success?," *Al Jazeera*,
September 3, 2014, www.aljazeera.com/indepth/opinion/2014/09/turkey-long
-game-iraq-success-2014939291192517.html.

56. Özel and Özcan, "Turkey's Dilemma," 128.

57. The share of Turkey's foreign aid budget allocated to Palestine jumped
from 2.2 percent in 2008 to 18 percent in 2013. "Annual Report 2013," Turkish Cooperation and Coordination Agency (TÍKA), 18, 135, www.tika.gov.tr
/upload/publication/TIKA%20ANNUAL%20REPORT%202013.pdf. TÍKA's
reporting on aid to Palestine, however, is not consistent. One report states that
Palestine was the largest recipient in 2013 with 20.2 percent of Turkey's $3.3
billion foreign assistance budget. A companion report states that it was sixth on
the list (*Turkish Development Assistance 2013*, 10–11, 90, www.tika.gov.tr
/upload/publication/KYR_FRAE_2013_uyg9.pdf).

58. Özel and Özcan, "Turkey's Dilemma," 128–29.

59. Paul Salem, "Turkey's Image in the Arab World," TESEV Foreign Policy
Program (May 2011), www.tesev.org.tr/Upload/Publication/de444c67-2c2d
-4312-bb59-e902eb944e50/Paul_Salem_FINAL.pdf.

60. Mensur Akgün and Sabiha Senyücel Gündoğar, "The Perception of Turkey in the Middle East 2012," TESEV Foreign Policy Program (December 2012),
www.tesev.org.tr/assets/publications/file/Perception%20of%20Turkey%20
2011_IIBASIM.pdf.

61. Ibid.

62. Mensur Akgün, Sabiha Senyücel Gündoğar, Aybars Görgülü, and Erdem Aydin, "Foreign Policy Perceptions in Turkey," TESEV Foreign Policy Program (May 2011), 23.

63. Joshua Keating, "Erdoğan's Cairo Speech," *Foreign Policy*, February 2, 2011, blog.foreignpolicy.com/posts/2011/02/02/erdogans_cairo_speech.

64. Benjamin Harvey, "Erdoğan Says Turkey Sides with the Egyptian People," Bloomberg News, February 1, 2011, www.bloomberg.com/news/2011-02-01 /erdogan-says-turkey-sides-with-the-egyptian-people-update1-.html.

65. "Turkey Calls for Constitutional Democracy in Egypt," Reuters, February 12, 2011, www.reuters.com/article/2011/02/12/us-egypt-turkey-idUSTRE 71B0OZ20110212.

66. The former prime minister of Belgium and Liberal Group chairman of the European Parliament, Guy Verhofstadt, dubbed Erdoğan's call for Mubarak to step down "the only European reaction so far" ("Erdoğan's Egypt Remarks Teach EU Lesson on Democracy," *Today's Zaman*, February 12, 2011, www .todayszaman.com/news-235374-erdogans-egypt-remarks-teach-eu-lesson-on -democracy.html).

67. Author interview with Bulent Aras, Strategic Planning Office, Ministry of Foreign Affairs, Republic of Turkey, Ankara, October 2011.

68. Steven Cook, "Erdoğan's Middle Eastern Victory Lap," *Foreign Affairs*, September 15, 2011.

69. Egypt was also in discussions to secure a $4.8 billion loan from the IMF, negotiations that later failed. Matt Bradley, "Turkey to Provide Egypt $2 Billion in Aid," *Wall Street Journal*, September 15, 2012, www.wsj.com/articles/SB100 00872396390444517304577653852418813354; "Turkey to Give Egypt Rest of $2bln Loan within 2 Months—Sources," Reuters, April 17, 2013, www.reuters .com/article/2013/04/17/egypt-turkey-loan-idUSL5N0D41QX20130417; Daniela Huber, *Democracy Promotion and Foreign Policy: Identity and Interests in US, EU and Non-Western Democracies* (New York: Palgrave Macmillan, 2015), 158.

70. "Turkey Says Egypt's Coup Unacceptable, Calls for Return to Democracy," *Today's Zaman*, July 4, 2013, www.todayszaman.com/latest-news _turkey-says-egypts-coup-unacceptable-calls-for-return-to-democracy _319980.html.

71. "Turkish PM Defends Egypt and Syria Stance, Criticizes EU at Ambassadors' Iftar Dinner," *Hurriyet Daily News*, July 19, 2013, www.hurriyetdailynews .com/turkish-pm-defends-egypt-and-syria-stance-criticizes-eu-at-ambassadors -iftar-dinner.aspx?pageID=238&nID=51007&NewsCatID=338.

72. "Turkey's Erdoğan Slams World's 'Double Standards,'" Reuters, July 29, 2013.

73. Jared Malson, "Egyptian Court Sentences Morsi to Death," *New York Times*, May 17, 2015, 4.

74. "Davutoğlu Dismisses Claims Turkey Silent over Tunisia, Egypt," *Today's Zaman*, February 2, 2011, www.todayszaman.com/news-234221-davutoglu -dismisses-claims-turkey-silent-over-tunisia-egypt.html.

75. Ibid.

76. Ministry of Foreign Affairs, Republic of Turkey, "No. 364, Press Release Regarding the First Round of Presidential Elections of Tunisia Held on 23 November 2014," November 26, 2014, www.mfa.gov.tr/no_-364_-26-november -2014_-press-release-regarding-the-first-round-of-presidential-elections-of -tunisia-held-on-23-november-2014.en.mfa.

77. According to the Turkish Foreign Ministry, the volume of trade between Turkey and Tunisia increased from $357 million in 2004 to $995 million in 2010. Although this increase is large, it amounts to less than 1 percent of Turkey's export volume annually.

78. "Turkey-Egypt Economic and Trade Relations," Ministry of Foreign Affairs, Republic of Turkey, www.mfa.gov.tr/turkey_s-commercial-and-economic -relations-with-egypt.en.mfa.

79. For more information on Turkey's economic relations with Libya, see the Turkish Foreign Ministry's website: www.mfa.gov.tr/turkey_s-commercial-and -economic-relations-with-libya.en.mfa.

80. Turkey was not sitting on the UN Security Council at the time and thus did not have a vote on the Libya resolution. It should also be noted that Erdoğan had recently received a human rights award from Qaddafi himself.

81. Özel and Özcan, "Turkey's Dilemma," 135.

82. "Turkey's PM Erdoğan Urges Colonel Muammar Gaddafi to Quit," BBC News, May 3, 2011, www.bbc.co.uk/news/world-europe-13265825.

83. Zaid Sabah and Kim Chipman, "Turkey Recognizes Libyan Rebels, Gives $300 Million," Bloomberg News, July 3, 2011, www.bloomberg.com/news/2011 -07-03/turkey-recognizes-libyan-rebels-gives-300-million-ap-reports.html.

84. Fahim Taştekin has written on this topic; see, for example, Fahim Taştekin, "Turkey's War in Libya," *Al-Monitor*, December 4, 2014, www.al-monitor.com /pulse/originals/2014/12/turkey-libya-muslim-brotherhood.html.

85. For more information on Turkish-Syria economic relations, see the Turkish Ministry of Foreign Affairs website: www.mfa.gov.tr/turkey_s-commercial -and-economic-relations-with-syria.en.mfa.

86. Fahim Taştekin, "Iraq, Syria Crises Cost Billions for Turkey," *Al-Monitor*, April 30, 2015, www.al-monitor.com/pulse/originals/2015/04/turkey-iraq-syria -cost-of-crisis-16-billion.html.

87. "Erdoğan Warns Assad against Division of Syria," *Today's Zaman*, May 2, 2011, www.todayszaman.com/news-242543-erdogan-warns-assad-against -division-of-syria.html.

88. Ibid.

89. Ministry of Foreign Affairs, Republic of Turkey, "Press Release Regarding Recent Developments in Syria, No. 178," July 31, 2011, www.mfa.gov.tr/no_178_ -31-july-2011_-press-release-regarding-the-recent-developments-in-syria.en.mfa.

90. Nada Bakri, "Casting Aside Criticism, Syria Invades Town," *New York Times*, August 3, 2011, www.nytimes.com/2011/08/04/world/middleeast/04syria .html.

91. Simon Cameron-Moore, "Turkey's Friendship with Syria Nears Breaking Point," Reuters, August 8, 2011, www.reuters.com/article/2011/08/08/us-turkey -syria-idUSTRE7773J320110808.

92. Fareed Zakaria, Interview with Turkish Prime Minister Erdoğan, September 25, 2011, CNN, www.youtube.com/watch?v=cb_44XNqFeU.

93. "Erdoğan Tells Assad to Draw Lessons from Fate of Gaddafi, Hitler," *Today's Zaman*, November 22, 2011, www.todayszaman.com/news-263554 -erdogan-tells-assad-to-draw-lessons-from-fate-of-gaddafi-hitler.html.

94. Ministry of Foreign Affairs, Republic of Turkey, "Press Statement by Mr. Ahmet Davutoğlu Regarding Measures Adopted vis-à-vis the Syrian Administration," November 30, 2011, www.mfa.gov.tr/press-statement-by-h_e_ -mr_-ahmet-davutoglu_-minister-of-foreign-affairs-of-the-republic-of-turkey_ -regarding-measures-adopted.en.mfa.

95. Ibid.

96. Halil M. Karaveli, "Turkey, the Unhelpful Ally," *New York Times*, March 1, 2013, www.nytimes.com/2013/02/27/opinion/turkey-the-unhelpful-ally.html.

97. Lally Weymouth, "Turkish President Abdullah Gül: Assad Must Go," *Washington Post*, September 23, 2013.

98. "Davutoğlu Visits Crisis Spots on Day of Whirlwind Diplomacy," *Today's Zaman*, April 7, 2011, www.todayszaman.com/newsDetail_getNewsById .action?newsId=240409.

99. Bulent Aras, "Turkey and Iran: Facing the Challenge of the Arab Spring," *On Turkey Analysis*, German Marshall Fund of the United States, February 19, 2013, 2.

100. "Back to Zero Problems? Recent Developments in Turkish Foreign Policy," Bipartisan Policy Center, April 2014, 16.

101. Weitz, *Turkey's New Regional Security Role*, 85.

102. Ibid., 82.

103. See, for example, Amberin Zaman, "Human Rights Situation Worsens in Azerbaijan," *Al Monitor*, February 13, 2013, www.al-monitor.com/pulse /culture/2013/02/azerbaijan-human-rights-turkey.html#; "Open Letter Regarding the Human Rights Situation in Azerbaijan," Freedom House, April 13, 2015, freedomhouse.org/article/open-letter-regarding-human-rights-situation -azerbaijan#.VT645_PD_cs.

104. Bayram Balci, "Strengths and Constraints of Turkish Policy in the South Caucasus," *Insight Turkey* 16, no. 12 (2014): 45.

105. Weitz, *Turkey's New Regional Security Role*, 87–89.

106. According to Weitz (ibid., 91), Turkey already has some $11 billion in combined trade and investments in Central Asia, approximately $1 billion in Eximbank loans, and some $30 billion in contracts to almost 2,000 Turkish firms.

107. Ibid., 89. See also author interview with Minister of Development Cevdet Yılmaz, Ankara, October 2011.

108. Anadolu Agency, "Turkey, Kazakhstan Aim to Increase Trade Volume to $10 Billion," *Hurriyet Daily News*, April 16, 2015.

109. Özel and Özcan, "Turkey's Dilemma."

110. Hugh Pope, International Crisis Group, "The New Turkey and the Old Middle East: The Limits of Ambitions," April 15, 2015, www.youtube.com /watch?v=2EyKKBU9EDI&utm_campaign=website&utm_source=sendgrid .com&utm_medium=email.

111. "In the lands where it was once present, the Ottoman Empire has built the infrastructure, water systems, bridges, madrasahs, mosques, hamams for the benefit of local people" ("Turkey-Africa Relations," Ministry of Foreign Affairs, Republic of Turkey, www.mfa.gov.tr/turkey-africa-relations.en.mfa).

112. Ibid.

113. Ibid.

114. "Back to Zero Problems?," 14.

115. Bayram Balci, "The Gülen Movement and Turkish Soft Power," Carnegie Endowment for International Peace, February 4, 2014, carnegieendowment.org/2014/02/04/g%C3%BClen-movement-and-turkish-soft-power.

116. Richard Lough, "Turkey Tries Out Soft Power, Hard Cash in Somalia," Reuters, June 3, 2012.

117. "Back to Zero Problems?," 14–15.

118. "Turkish President Pledges More Investment for War-Torn Somalia," *Agence France Presse*, January 25, 2015.

119. Turkish officials were quick to deny any ulterior motive to realign Turkey away from its traditional security relationship with NATO.

120. "Responsibility and Vision: Turkish Foreign Policy in 2014," Ministry of Foreign Affairs, Republic of Turkey, 15.

121. "Turkey Collects $3 Million in Aid for Myanmar's Rohingya Muslims," *RTT News*, August 14, 2012, www.rttnews.com/1947307/turkey-collects-3-million-in-aid-for-rohingya-muslims.aspx?type=in&utm_source=google&utm_campaign=sitemap.

122. He also struck a critical note against the abuses of colonial rule and "deliberate attempts to keep 'the natives' uneducated and insecure," as well as the bipolar competition of the Cold War. Ahmet Davutoğlu, "A New Vision for Least Developed Countries," Center for Strategic Research Vision Paper 4 (July 2012), 7–8.

123. Ibid., 10.

124. "Responsibility and Vision: Turkish Foreign Policy in 2014," Ministry of Foreign Affairs, Republic of Turkey, 23.

125. Harut Sassounian, "Why the UN Rejected Turkey's Bid for a Security Council Seat," *Huffington Post*, October 28, 2014.

126. Ted Piccone, "Do New Democracies Support Democracy? The Multilateral Dimension," *Journal of Democracy* 22, no. 4 (2011): 145–46.

127. Mensur Akgün and others, "Foreign Policy Perceptions in Turkey," 23.

128. Author interview with analysts at TESEV, October 2012.

129. Among those that saw Turkey as a political model, 16 percent cited Turkey's democratic regime and another 16 percent cited its political attitude. Those believing that Turkey could be a model in economic and cultural terms emphasized the country's economic power (30 percent) and cultural history (35 percent), respectively. Mensur Akgün and others, "Foreign Policy Perceptions in Turkey," 24.

130. Author interview with Abdülhamit Bilici, *Zaman* newspaper group, October 2011.

131. Author interview, October 2011.

132. Author interview with Mehmet Celalettin Lekesiz, governor of Hatay, October 2011.

133. Crisis Action memo, January 2013, author's files.

134. Author interviews at Mustafa Kemal University, Hatay, Turkey; and Turget Özal University, Ankara, October 2011.

135. For summaries of the Ergenekon case, see, for example, Licursi; "Timeline: Turkey's 'Ergenekon' Trial"; and "Justice or Revenge?," *The Economist*, August 10, 2013, www.economist.com/news/europe/21583312-harsh-verdicts -are-handed-down-ergenekon-trial-justice-or-revenge.

136. The lead defendant, former general İlker Başbuğ, appealed his life sentence to the Constitutional Court, which in March 2014 ruled in his favor.

137. Onur Ant, "Turkey's Corruption Probe Turns into Plot and Power for Erdoğan," *BloombergBusiness*, January 8, 2015, www.bloomberg.com/news /articles/2015-01-08/turkey-s-corruption-probe-turns-into-plot-and-power-for -erdogan.

CHAPTER 7

1. Islam, Hinduism, Catholicism, Protestantism, Buddhism, and Confucianism.

2. From 2008 to 2014, Indonesia has consistently scored 2 on a 1–5 scale, indicating "latent conflict," according to qualitative assessments issued by the Economist Intelligence Unit's Country Analysis team. Of the five democracies examined in this book, only Brazil performs better, consistently scoring a 1 on internal conflict, indicating no conflict. Institute for Economics and Peace, *Global Peace Index 2014*, June 2014, economicsandpeace.org/wp-content /uploads/2015/06/2014-Global-Peace-Index-REPORT_0-1.pdf.

3. Kanupriya Kapoor and Gayatri Suroyo, "In Victory for Widodo, Indonesia Parliament Backs Direct Regional Vote," Reuters, January 20, 2015, www .reuters.com/article/2015/01/20/us-indonesia-elections -idUSKBN0KT0ON20150120. Polling conducted in October 2014 found high support (86.5 percent) for direct elections of district heads and mayors and for Yudhoyono's decision (79.6 percent) to cancel the opposition-controlled Parliament's attempt to install indirect elections. SaifulMujani Research and Consulting, "Citizens' Preferences at the Outset of the Jokowi Presidency: A National Opinion Survey," October 2–4, 2014, origin.library.constantcontact .com/download/get/file/1103854201467-1618/USINDO+DC+Conference _Prof.+Liddle.pdf.

4. Poverty headcount at less than $2 a day (PPP) was 81.55 percent of the population in 1999 and 43.33 percent in 2011, the most recent year for which World Bank data are available. Poverty as measured by the percentage of the population living at the national poverty line has also been cut in half in that time period—in 1999 it was 23.4 percent, while in 2013 it was 11.4 percent, as recorded by the World Bank.

5. Newley Purnell, "Facebook Users in Indonesia Rise to 69 Million," *Wall Street Journal*, June 27, 2014, blogs.wsj.com/digits/2014/06/27/facebook-users -in-indonesia-rise-to-69-million/.

6. "Leading Countries Based on Number of Facebook Users as of May 2014 (in Millions)," Statista, www.statista.com/statistics/268136/top-15-countries -based-on-number-of-facebook-users/; "A World of Tweets," www.aworldoft weets.frogdesign.com.

7. By GDP in 2014. World Development Indicators database, World Bank, July 2015, databank.worldbank.org/data/download/GDP.pdf.

8. Foreign Minister Marty Natalegawa, "The Garuda and the Eagle: Forging a Balanced U.S.-Indonesian Partnership for the Future," *Jakarta Globe*, March 18, 2010, quoted in Anne Marie Murphy, "Democratization and Indonesian Foreign Policy," *Asia Policy* 13 (2012): 89.

9. Saiful-Mujani Research and Consulting, "Citizens' Preferences at the Out-set of the Jokowi Presidency: A National Opinion Survey," October 2–4, 2014, http://origin.library.constantcontact.com/download/get/file/1103854201467 -1618/USINDO+DC+Conference_Prof.+Liddle.pdf

10. In addition, "Indonesia has the two largest member-based Islamic civil society organizations in the world, both of which have taken strong positions against Indonesia as an Islamic state and the establishment of sharia as the *only* source of law" (Mirjam Kunkler and Alfred Stepan, eds., *Democracy and Islam in Indonesia* [Columbia University Press, 2013], 7–10).

11. In 1985, for example, all organizations were required to adopt Pancasila as their sole ideological foundation (*asas tunggal*). A similar law was passed in 2013 that included elements of the 1985 Law on Social Organizations. Despite calls for its repeal, it still stands. Bob Hadiwinata, *The Politics of NGOs in Indonesia: Developing Democracy and Managing a Movement* (New York: Routledge, 2003), 53; "Indonesia: Amend Law on Mass Organizations," Human Rights Watch, July 17, 2013, www.hrw.org/news/2013/07/17/indonesia-amend -law-mass-organizations.

12. Quoted in Leo Suryadinata, *Indonesia's Foreign Policy under Suharto: Aspiring to International Leadership* (Singapore: Times Academic Press, 1996), 25.

13. Joshua Oppenheimer, the director of two high-profile documentaries on the perpetrators of the 1965 killings, reflected on the unreconciled horrors of the Indonesian genocide in several 2015 interviews; see Adam Shatz, "Joshua Oppenheimer Won't Go Back to Indonesia," *New York Times Magazine*, July 9, 2015, www.nytimes.com/2015/07/12/magazine/joshua-oppenheimer-wont -go-back-to-indonesia.html.

14. For the text of the 1945 Constitution of the Republic of Indonesia, including the four amendments, see www.wipo.int/wipolex/en/text.jsp?file_id=200129.

15. Dewi Fortuna Anwar, "Megawati's Search for an Effective Foreign Policy," in *Governance in Indonesia: Challenges Facing the Megawati Presidency*, ed. Hadi Soesastro, Anthony L. Smith, and Han Mui Ling (Singapore: Institute of Southeast Asian Studies, 2003), 74.

16. Ibid., 85.

17. Ibid., 85–86.

18. "Asian-African Summit 2005 and the Anniversary of the Golden Jubilee of the Asian-African Conference," Museum Konperensi Asia-Afrika, April 22–24, 2005, asianafricanmuseum.org/en/konferensi-tingkat-tinggi-asia-afrika-2005-dan-peringatan-50-tahun-konferensi-asia-afrika/.

19. Quoted in Rizal Sukma, "Indonesia Finds a New Voice," *Journal of Democracy* 22, no. 4 (2011): 112.

20. Ibid.; see also Anwar, "Megawati's Search," 75.

21. Brunei Darussalam joined in 1984, Vietnam in 1995, Laos PDR and Myanmar in 1997, and Cambodia in 1999.

22. Leo Suryadinata, *Indonesia's Foreign Policy under Suharto: Aspiring to International Leadership* (Singapore: Times Academic Press, 1996), 68.

23. Author interview, April 2010.

24. Yongwook Ryu and Maria Ortuoste, "Democratization, Regional Integration, and Human Rights: The Case of the ASEAN Intergovernmental Commission on Human Rights," *Pacific Review* 27, no. 3 (2014): 376.

25. The ASEAN Political-Security Community Blueprint, 2009, www.asean.org/archive/5187-18.pdf, and the ASEAN Economic Community and Socio-Cultural Community Blueprint, 2009, www.asean.org/archive/5187-19.pdf, were adopted at the same time, all designed to lead to the ASEAN Community in 2015.

26. The inclusion of universal norms is notable given ASEAN's previous prioritization of "Asian values." ASEAN Political-Security Community Blueprint, 2009, www.asean.org/communities/asean-political-security-community.

27. ASEAN Political-Security Community Blueprint, A.1.5. These initiatives have made little progress. The ASEAN Commission on the Promotion and Protection of the Rights of Women and Children (ACWC) was established in 2010 and has two representatives from each of the ten member states. In 2007, the ASEAN Committee on Migrant Workers was established by the ASEAN Foreign Ministers; its mandate is to implement the Declaration on the Protection and Promotion of the Rights of Migrant Workers. It has since established a task force to draft an ASEAN framework instrument for migrant worker rights, but the task force has yet to establish consensus among all ten member states. For more, see "ASEAN Commission on the Rights of Women and Children," humanrightsinasean.info/asean-commission-rights-women-and-children/about.html, and "ASEAN Committee on Migrant Workers," humanrightsinasean.info/asean-committee-migrant-workers/about.html.

28. "Each ASEAN Member State shall appoint a Representative to the AICHR who shall be accountable to the appointing Government" (Terms of Reference of the ASEAN Intergovernmental Commission on Human Rights [2009], art. 5.2); also see AICHR booklet (23).

29. ASEAN Human Rights Declaration para. 7, adopted November 19, 2012, www.asean.org/news/asean-statement-communiques/item/asean-human-rights-declaration.

30. ASEAN Human Rights Declaration, para. 8.

31. A coalition of Asian and international human rights groups strongly criticized the ASEAN Declaration on Human Rights. See "Civil Society Denounces

Adoption of Flawed ASEAN Human Rights Declaration," November 19, 2012, www.hrw.org/news/2012/11/19/civil-society-denounces-adoption-flawed-asean-human-rights-declaration.

32. For a more optimistic view, see Yongwook Ryu and Maria Ortuoste, "Democratization, Regional Integration, and Human Rights: The Case of the ASEAN Intergovernmental Commission on Human Rights," *Pacific Review* 27, no. 3 (2014): 362.

33. Surin Pitsuwan, "A Caring ASEAN Community," *Jakarta Post*, September 9, 2014.

34. *Mainstreaming the Responsibility to Protect in Southeast Asia: Pathway towards a Caring ASEAN Community*, Report of the High-Level Advisory Panel on the Responsibility to Protect in Southeast Asia, September 9, 2014.

35. Interview with author, April 2010.

36. "ASEAN Turns Deaf Ear to Concerns on Rights in Thailand," *Bangkok Post*, August 17, 2014.

37. Donald E. Weatherbee, "Southeast Asia and ASEAN—Running in Place," *Southeast Asian Affairs*, 3, referenced in Alice D. Ba, *[Re]Negotiating East and Southeast Asia: Region, Regionalism, and the Association of Southeast Asian Nations* (Stanford University Press, 2009), 222. Rizal Sukma, a leading adviser to President Jokowi, has been critical of Indonesia's failed efforts to forge consensus within ASEAN and argued for a post-ASEAN foreign policy as far back as 2009. See, for example, Rizal Sukma, "Insight: Without Unity, No Centrality," *Jakarta Post*, July 17, 2012.

38. Some assert that China's rise, ASEAN's desire to appease Western powers, and the West's own backsliding on human rights have undermined a regional and global human rights agenda. See, for example, Shuan Narine, "Human Rights Norms and the Evolution of ASEAN: Moving in a Changing Regional Environment," *Contemporary Southeast Asia* 34, no. 3 (2012): 365–88.

39. In December 1993, for example, a delegation from the State Law and Order Restoration Council, the military regime in Myanmar, went to Jakarta to study the dual function of the Indonesian military—its simultaneous role in defense and in politics—to adopt a similar position for itself back home. Andreas Harsono, "Love at First Sight Slorc Meets Abri," *Inside Indonesia* 52 (October–December 1997), www.insideindonesia.org/weekly-articles/love-at-first-sight-slorc-meets-abri. See also Catherine Shanahan Renshaw, "Democratic Transformation and Regional Institutions: The Case of Myanmar and ASEAN," *Journal of Current Southeast Asian Affairs* 32, no. 1 (2013): 44–45.

40. Ulf Sundhaussen, "Indonesia's New Order: A Model for Myanmar?," *Asian Survey* 35, no. 8 (1995): 771–72, www.jstor.org/stable/pdfplus/2645735.pdf?&acceptTC=true&jpdConfirm=true.

41. Note, however, that the Burmese military failed miserably to emulate the high economic growth rates of Suharto's New Order system. The author wishes to thank Lex Reiffel for drawing this distinction.

42. Harsono, "Love at First Sight."

43. Ibid.

44. Greg Sheridan, "ASEAN: An Image Problem," *Southeast Asian Affairs* 25, no. 1 (1998): 37–45.

45. Ibid.

46. Robin Ramcharan, "ASEAN and Non-Interference: A Principle Maintained," *Contemporary Southeast Asia* 22, no. 1 (2000): 60–88.

47. Tom Wingfield, "Myanmar: Political Statis and a Precarious Economy," *Southeast Asian Affairs* (2000): 212–13.

48. "Megawati's Diplomatic 'Coup' in Freeing Suu Kyi," *Jakarta Post*, July 31, 2013, www.thejakartapost.com/news/2003/07/30/megawati039s-diplomatic -039coup039-freeing-suu-kyi.html.

49. Ibid.

50. "Megawati Urges Security Steps at ASEAN Meeting," *Taipei Times*, July 1, 2004, www.taipeitimes.com/News/world/archives/2004/07/01/2003177252.

51. "Indonesian Caucus on Myanmar Launched," *Asian Tribune*, February 4, 2005, www.asiantribune.com/news/2005/02/04/indonesian-caucus-myanmar -launched; "Caucus Launch, Indonesia," *ASEAN Parliamentarians for Human Rights*, February 3, 2005, www.aseanmp.org/?p=611; and "Indonesian Caucus on Myanmar Launched," *ASEAN Parliamentarians for Human Rights*, September 10, 2008, www.aseanmp.org/?p=1194.

52. Ron Corben, "ASEAN Foreign Ministers Postpone Decision on Burma's Chairmanship," U.S. Fed News Service, April 11, 2005.

53. "Myanmar Gives Up 2006 ASEAN Chairmanship," *New York Times*, July 26, 2005, www.nytimes.com/2005/07/26/world/asia/26iht-web.0726asean .html; Corben, "ASEAN Foreign Ministers Postpone Decision."

54. Rob Corben, "Burma to Remain Focus of Attention at ASEAN Summit, but Tangible Moves for Reform Unlikely," *Voice of America News*, December 7, 2005.

55. Ruukun Katanyuu, "Beyond Non-Interference in ASEAN: The Association's Role in Myanmar's National Reconciliation and Democratization," *Asian Survey* 46, no. 6 (2006): 825–45.

56. Ibid.

57. Ibid.

58. Ibid.

59. "Antara (Indonesia): RI-Myanmar Joint Commission to Hold First Meeting in Bali," *BurmaNet News*, March 20, 2006, www.burmanet.org/news /2006/03/20/antara-indonesia-ri-myanmar-joint-commission-to-hold-first -meeting-in-bali/.

60. Ron Corben, "VOA News: Burma Postpones ASEAN Visit Meant to Assess Its Progress toward Democracy," U.S. Fed News Service, January 7, 2007.

61. Ridwan Max Sijabat, "ASEAN Caucus Slams Indonesia's Lack of Resolve on Myanmar Issue," *Jakarta Post*, January 16, 2007, www.thejakartapost.com /news/2007/01/16/asean-caucus-slams-indonesia039s-lack-resolve-myanmar -issue.html; "Security Council Fails to Adopt Draft Resolution on Myanmar, Owing to Negative Votes by China, Russian Federation," Security Council Press Release, January 12, 2007, www.un.org/press/en/2007/sc8939.doc.htm.

62. Sijabat, "ASEAN Caucus."

63. Ibid.

64. Ibid.

65. Ibid.

66. Governing Council on IPU, "Myanmar," resolution adopted by the IPU Governing Council, May 4, 2007, www.ipu.org/hr-e/180/Myn04.htm.

67. Agung Laksono, "Seminar: Burma at the Inter-Parliamentary Union (IPU) Assembly—Item Three," speech delivered at 116th Assembly of the Inter-Parliamentary Union, Nusa Dua Bali, April 29, 2007, www.aseanmp.org/?p=29.

68. Ridwan Max Sijabat, "Indonesia President asked to bring Myanmar issue to the front at UN assembly," *Jakarta* Post, September 24, 2007, buddhistchannel.tv/index.php?id=83,4941,0,0,1,0.

69. Statement by H. E. Dr. Susilo Bambang Yudhoyono at the General Debate Session of the Sixty-Second UN General Assembly, New York, September 25, 2007, www.un.org/webcast/ga/62/2007/pdfs/indonesia-en.pdf.

70. Hamish McDonald, "What Indonesia can teach Burma," *Sydney Morning Herald*, March 13, 2010, www.smh.com.au/federal-politics/political-opinion/what-indonesia-can-teach-burma-20100312-q40v.html.

71. Dr. Dino Patti Djalal, "An Independent, Active and Creative Foreign Policy for Indonesia," *Strategic Review: The Indonesian Journal of Leadership, Policy and World Affairs* 2, no. 1 (2012): 40–46.

72. Daniel Schearf, "Southeast Asian Politicians Urge ASEAN to Suspend Burma, Consider Sanctions," *Voice of American News*, May 26, 2009.

73. Feng Yinqui, "Roundup: Indonesian President's Myanmar Visit to Further Bilateral Ties, Cooperation," *World News*, April 23, 2013.

74. "ASEAN Leaders Approve Burma Chairmanship Bid," BBC News Asia, November 17, 2011.

75. Zaw Win Than, "Indonesia Pledges US$1m for Rakhine Aid," *Myanmar Times*, January 14, 2013, www.mmtimes.com/index.php/national-news/3770-indonesia-pledges-us-1m-rakhine-aid.html.

76. "Indonesian President's State Visit to Myanmar Highlights Cooperation," *Global Times*, April 24, 2013, www.globaltimes.cn/content/777160.shtml. Another group of political prisoners was released in January 2012 and opposition parties led by Aung San Suu Kyi won forty-three out of forty-five seats in parliamentary by-elections in April 2013, among other signs of progress.

77. "Day 2 SEA Visit: SBY Returns to Myanmar," Cabinet Secretariat of the Republic of Indonesia, April 26, 2013, setkab.go.id/en/international-8409-.html.

78. In September 2011, President Thein Sein suspended construction of controversial Chinese-funded Myitsone hydroelectric dam, a move seen as showing greater openness to public opinion. "Timeline: Reforms in Myanmar," BBC News, November 11, 2014, www.bbc.com/news/world-asia-16546688.

79. "Myanmar's Foreign Minister Visits the Institute for Peace and Democracy," Institute for Peace and Democracy, www.ipd.or.id/myanmars-foreign-minister-visits-the-institute-for-peace-and-democracy.htm.

80. This event was organized by the Indonesian Foreign Ministry, the Myanmar Foreign Ministry, the Institute for Peace and Democracy, and the Myan-

mar Institute for Strategic and International Studies. See "Indonesia Supports Democratic Reform and Reconciliation in Myanmar," Embassy of the Republic of Indonesia, Sana'a, Yemen, June 26, 2013, www.kemlu.go.id/sanaa/Pages /News.aspx?IDP=6321&l=en.

81. Hassan Wirajuda, "Indonesia's Role in the Promotion of Democracy," speech delivered at the Brookings Institution, Washington, D.C., April 18, 2014.

82. "Rohingya Refugees in Indonesia Await Resettlement That Never Comes," *Irin News*, April 25, 2014, www.irinnews.org/report/99991/rohingya -refugees-in-indonesia-await-resettlement-that-never-comes.

83. In August 2012, Vice President Jusuf Kalla led an Indonesian Red Cross delegation to deliver aid, and in January 2013, Foreign Minister Natalegawa visited Rohingya communities and pledged $1 million to help rebuild shelters and schools. Ismira Lutfia Tisnadibrata, "Burma Welcomes Indonesia's Engagement: Natalegawa," *Khabar Southeast Asia*, January 16, 2013, khabarsoutheas-tasia.com/en_GB/articles/apwi/articles/features/2013/01/16/feature-03.

84. Joe Cochrane, "Indonesia and Malaysia Agree to Care for Stranded Migrants," *New York Times*, May 20, 2015, www.nytimes.com/2015/05/21/world /asia/indonesia-malaysia-rohingya-bangladeshi-migrants-agreement.html?_r=0.

85. Vietnam joined ASEAN in 1995, Laos in 1997, and Cambodia in 1999.

86. "Indonesia 'Deeply Concerned' over Thai Martial Law," *GlobalPost*, May 20, 2014, www.globalpost.com/dispatch/news/afp/140520/indonesia-deeply -concerned-over-thai-martial-law.

87. Kerstin Radtke, "Thailand's Coup—Will ASEAN Answer?," *Diplomat*, May 30, 2014, thediplomat.com/2014/05/thailands-coup-will-asean-answer/; Nyan Lynn Aung, "Why ASEAN Stays Quiet as the Thai Military Seizes Control," *Myanmar Times*, June 23, 2014, www.mmtimes.com/index.php/national-news /10777-why-asean-stays-quiet-as-the-thai-military-seizes-control.html. Natalegawa also stated that the coup was a setback to ASEAN efforts to promote democracy in the region and "certainly would be inconsistent with ASEAN's collective support for democratic principles and constitutional government" ("U.S., Other Nations Express Concerns over Thai Coup," Associated Press, May 23, 2014, bigstory.ap.org/article/us-other-nations-express-concerns-over-thai-coup).

88. Radtke, "Thailand's Coup."

89. Ibid.

90. Aung, "Why ASEAN Stays Quiet."

91. Opening Statement by H. E. Dr. Susilo Bambang Yudhoyono at Inaugural Session of Bali Democracy Forum, December 10, 2008.

92. Minggu, "Bali Democracy Forum Ends with Calls for Continuation," *Antara News*, October 12, 2014, www.antaranews.com/en/news/96016/bali -democracy-forum-ends-with-calls-for-continuation.

93. I Ketut Putra Erawan, "Indonesia," in *Supporting Democracy Abroad: An Assessment of Leading Powers*, ed. Daniel Calingaert, Arch Puddington, and Sarah Repucci (Washington, D.C.: Freedom House, 2014), 9–16.

94. Ted Piccone, "The Multilateral Dimension," *Journal of Democracy* 22, no. 4 (2011): 139–52, www.journalofdemocracy.org/article/do-new-democracies -support-democracy-multilateral-dimension.

95. Ibid., 147–50.

96. "Votes Count: Monitoring the UN HRC," Indonesia analysis, Human Rights Watch, votescount.hrw.org/#/; and "Country Voting History Portal," Indonesia analysis, Universal Rights Group, www.universal-rights.org/country -voting-history-portal/country/?country=indonesia.

97. "Bali Democracy Forum III (10–11 December, 2010)," Bali Democracy Forum, bdf.kemlu.go.id/index.php?option=com_content&view=article&id=451 &Itemid=381&lang=en; Fiji was not invited to the previous two, but it has been invited to subsequent ones.

98. The Melanesian Spearhead Group includes Fiji, Papua New Guinea, Solomon Islands, Vanuatu, and the Front de Libération Nationale Kanak et Socialiste (FLNKS). According to a Lowy Institute publication, "The presence of a political group such as FLNKS is unusual and reflects the historical and political roots of the MSG. Newly independent Melanesian countries came together in a spirit of ethnic and cultural solidarity with an express commitment to working to ensure the liberation of their kanaky brethren." Indonesia's bid for observer status was motivated by its desire to gain influence in the group (Tess Newton Cain, "The Melanesian Spearhead Group: What Is It? And What Does It Do?," *Interpreter*, March 14, 2014, www.lowyinterpreter.org/post/2014/03 /14/The-Melanesian-Spearhead-Group-What-is-it-and-what-does-it-do.aspx).

99. Johnny Blades, "Fiji's Military Ruler Uses Melanesian Spearhead Group to End Pariah Status," *The Guardian*, April 26, 2011, www.theguardian.com /world/2011/apr/26/melanesia-fiji-frank-bainimarama-blades.

100. "Fiji Opens Embassy in Indonesia to Boost Bilateral Ties," *Xinhua Net*, April 6, 2011, news.xinhuanet.com/english2010/world/2011-04/06/c_13815725 .htm.

101. "Democratic Transition in Fiji," *Institute for Peace and Democracy*, November 1, 2012, www.ipd.or.id/democratic-transition-in-fiji.htm.

102. Bruce Hill, "Can Fiji Learn from Indonesia about Returning to Democracy?," Radio Australia, March 26, 2013, www.radioaustralia.net.au /international/radio/program/pacific-beat/can-fiji-learn-from-indonesia-about -returning-to-democracy/1107474. Erawan also spoke of the importance of students and the media in the democratization process.

103. "Fiji: Indonesia to Intensify Contact," *Cook Islands News*, June 21, 2014, www.cookislandsnews.com/item/47260-fiji-indonesia-to-intensify-contact /47260-fiji-indonesia-to-intensify-contact. In his keynote speech at the second Pacific Islands Development Forum (PIDF) hosted in Nadi, Fiji, Yudhoyono outlined four central goals:

> 1. Increase Indonesian involvement with Pacific nations, including $20 million pledge to the Pacific Island countries over the course of the next five years to help them face common goals, such as the protection of marine resources and the challenges presented by natural disasters
> 2. Boost connectivity and the interaction of peoples between Indonesia and the South Pacific region
> 3. Strengthen economic ties with the PIDF countries, tripling their trade over the coming years

4. Serve as a bridge between Pacific and Indian Ocean states (Susilo Bambang Yudhoyono, "Keynote Address," Second Summit of the Pacific Islands Development Forum, Nadi, June 19, 2014, pacificidf.org/his-excellency-prof-dr-susilo-bambang-yudhoyono-president-of-the-republic-of-indonesia-keynote-address-at-the-second-summit-of-the-pacific-islands-development-forum/).

104. "Indonesia to Co-Lead Election Observer Group for Fiji Elections," *Pacific Islands News Association*, June 19, 2014, www.pina.com.fj/?p=pacnews&m=read&o=27580040953a26fd26aa3f7d382ce2. The other co-leaders are Australia, Papua New Guinea, and India; the other observer countries are Israel, South Africa, Brazil, Russia, Turkey, Japan, New Zealand, Korea, Iran, and the United Kingdom. "A-G, Miles Sign Observer Group Terms for Elections," *Fiji Sun Online*, August 13, 2014, www.fijisun.com.fj/2014/08/13/a-g-miles-sign-observer-group-terms/.

105. Nick Perry and Pita Ligaiula, "International Monitors Endorse Fiji Election as Credible," Associated Press, September 18, 2014, bigstory.ap.org/article/6e44f8f77b6e4c0e867b9d8750689e5b/international-monitors-endorse-fiji-election; "Preliminary Statement 18 September 2014," Multinational Observer Group, September 18, 2014, www.mog.org.fj/index.php/media-center/item/41-preliminary-statement-18-september-2014.

106. Joe Cochrane, "Indonesian Militants Join Foreigners Fighting in Syria," *New York Times*, January 31, 2014, www.nytimes.com/2014/02/01/world/asia/indonesian-militants-join-fight-in-syria.html?_r=0.

107. Jennifer Campbell, "Indonesia-Canada Relations Thrive; Foreign Minister Also Discusses Arab Spring, Human Trafficking and Faith-Related Violence," *Ottawa Citizen*, September 5, 2012.

108. "Indonesia-Tunisia Capacity Building Partnership for Democracy," Institute for Peace and Democracy, Bali, May 10–16, 2013, www.ipd.or.id/indonesia-tunisia-capacity-building-partnership-for-democracy.htm.

109. Karen Brooks, "Indonesia's Lessons for Egypt," Council on Foreign Relations, February 17, 2011, www.cfr.org/indonesia/indonesias-lessons-egypt/p24156.

110. Ted Piccone and Emily Alinikoff, *Rising Democracies and the Arab Awakening: Implications for Global Democracy and Human Rights* (Brookings, 2012).

111. "Egypt-Indonesia Dialogue on Democratic Transition," Institute for Peace and Democracy, www.ipd.or.id/egypt-indonesia-dialogue-on-democratic-transition.htm.

112. "Indonesians Show Solidarity with Egyptian People," *Antara News*, August 18, 2013, www.antaranews.com/en/news/90305/indonesians-show-solidarity-with-egyptian-people; Bagus B. T. Saragih and Margareth S. Aritonang, "RI Calls for Peaceful Transition," *Jakarta Post*, July 5, 2014, www.thejakartapost.com/news/2013/07/05/ri-calls-peaceful-transition.html.

113. Piccone and Alinikoff, *Rising Democracies.*

114. "Editorial: RI's Activism on Syria," *Jakarta Post*, January 9, 2013, www.thejakartapost.com/news/2013/01/09/editorial-ri-s-activism-syria.html. See

also Ismira Lutfia, "Egypt Asks for Indonesia's Help in Implementing Democracy," *Jakarta Globe*, May 29, 2011, www.thejakartaglobe.com/archive/egypt -asks-for-indonesias-help-in-implementing-democracy/432215/.

115. According to the Kuwait News Agency, Yudhoyono said that "President Assad should step down as Syria is in need of a new leader that loves his people, and would pave efforts to create peace in the country" ("Indonesian President Calls on Al-Assad to Step Down," *Kuwait News Agency*, January 7, 2013, www .kuna.net.kw/ArticleDetails.aspx?id=2285246&language=en).

116. Bagus B. T. Saragih, "SBY Now Says Assad Should Step Down," *Jakarta Post*, January 8, 2013, www.thejakartapost.com/news/2013/01/08/sby-now -says-assad-should-step-down.html.

117. "Indonesia Critical of United Nations Syrian Resolution Elements," *Jakarta Globe*, May 17, 2013, www.thejakartaglobe.com/news/indonesia-critical -of-united-nations-syrian-resolution-elements/.

118. "Human Rights Council Debates Situation of Human Rights in Libya," Office of the High Commissioner for Human Rights, February 25, 2011, www .ohchr.org/EN/NewsEvents/Pages/DisplayNews.aspx?NewsID=10766 &LangID=E.

119. UN General Assembly resolution 65/265, *Suspension of the Rights of Membership for the Libyan Arab Jamahiriya in the Human Rights Council*, A/ RES/65/265, March 3, 2011. For more see the General Assembly 76th plenary meeting notes for March 1, 2011, A/65/PV.76, www.un.org/en/ga/search/view _doc.asp?symbol=A/65/PV.76, and "General Assembly Suspends Libya from Human Rights Council," General Assembly Meetings Coverage, March 1, 2011, www.un.org/press/en/2011/ga11050.doc.htm.

120. In 2014, Indonesia spent $7.02 billion on military expenditures, number 29 in the world in terms of dollars spent, or $27.80 per capita, number 108 in the world. All data from the Stockholm International Peace Research Institute (SIPRI) *Military Expenditure Database, 1988–2014*, www.sipri.org/research /armaments/milex.

121. As a percentage of GDP. See Shubham Chaudhuri, "Indonesia: 2015 and Beyond," World Bank Presentation to USINDO Conference, December 11, 2014, origin.library.constantcontact.com/download/get/file/1103854201467 -1619/Dr.+Chaudhuri.pdf.

122. Speech by President Susilo Bambang Yudhoyono at the general debate of the Sixty-Ninth Session of the UN General Assembly, "Making the Right Choice at History's Cross Road," September 24, 2014.

123. SaifulMujani Research and Consulting, "Citizens' Preferences at the Outset of the Jokowi Presidency: A National Opinion Survey," October 2–4, 2014, origin.library.constantcontact.com/download/get/file/1103854201467 -1618/USINDO+DC+Conference_Prof.+Liddle.pdf.

124. Eighty-one percent of Indonesians prefer direct elections to elections by regional council, a poll released in September 2014 showed. Kennial Caroline Laia and Carlos Paath, "Home Ministry Flip-Flips on Election Bill," *Jakarta Globe*, September 10, 2014, thejakartaglobe.beritasatu.com/news/home-ministry -flip-flops-election-bill/.

125. "Opening Statement by Dr. Susilo Bambang Yudhoyono, President RI," in Bali Democracy Forum VII, Bali, Indonesia, October 10–11, 2014, Cabinet Secretariat, Republic of Indonesia, October 10, 2014, setkab.go.id/ opening-statement-by-dr-susilo-bambang-yudhoyono-president-ri-in-bali-democracy-forum-vii-bali-indonesia-10-11-october-2014-10-10/.

126. Ben Otto and I Made Sentana, "Indonesia President Plans Decree Aimed at Restoring Regional Elections," *Wall Street Journal*, September 30, 2014, online .wsj.com/articles/indonesia-president-plans-decree-aimed-at-restoring-regional-elections-1412101313; Ina Parlina, "SBY Bids to Save Direct Elections," *Jakarta Post*, October 1, 2014, www.thejakartapost.com/news/2014/10/01/sby-bids-save-direct-elections.html; "SBY Issues Perppu to Defend Direct Election of Regional Leaders," *Jakarta Post*, October 2, 2014, www.thejakartapost.com/news/2014/10/02/sby-issues-perppu-defend-direct-election-regional-leaders.html.

127. This development was highlighted by Freedom House to explain the decline in Indonesia's ranking from free to partly free in 2013. "Indonesia," *Freedom in the World 2014*, Freedom House, freedomhouse.org/report/freedom-world/2014/indonesia-0.

128. Author's notes from meeting with IPD and government officials, April 3, 2013.

129. Paige Johnson Tan, "Navigating a Turbulent Ocean: Indonesia's Worldview and Foreign Policy," *Asian Perspective* 31, no. 3 (2007): 150.

130. Ibid., 150–51.

131. Kai He, "Indonesia's Foreign Policy after Suharto: International Pressure, Democratization and Policy Change," *International Relations of the Asia Pacific* 8 (2008): 264.

132. Only one of the eighteen individuals tried for the 1999 abuses in East Timor was convicted, though his conviction was later overturned, and a warrant for the arrest of General Wiranto, chief of the armed forces during 1998–99, was never executed. As former East Timor president Jose Ramos-Horta said in 2006, "In today's Indonesia or in the foreseeable future, there will be no leader strong enough who can bring to court and prison senior military officers who were involved in violence in the past . . . they are still too powerful" (Colum Lynch and Ellen Nakashima, "E. Timor Atrocities Detailed," *Washington Post*, January 21, 2006, www.washingtonpost.com/wp-dyn/content/article/2006/01/20/AR2006012001811.html, quoted in Ted Piccone and Bimo Yusman, "Indonesian Foreign Policy: 'A Million Friends and Zero Enemies,'" *Diplomat*, February 14, 2014, http://thediplomat.com/2014/02/indonesian-foreign-policy-a-million-friends-and-zero-enemies/). For more, see "Justice Denied for East Timor," Human Rights Watch, December 20, 2002, www.hrw.org/reports/2002/12/20/justice-denied-east-timor; "Indonesia Frees Militia Leader," *Al Jazeera*, April 7, 2008, www.aljazeera.com/news/asia-pacific/2008/04/200861423337328531.html; "Indonesia and East Timor: Against Impunity, for Justice," *APSNet Policy Forum*, April 24, 2008, nautilus.org/apsnet/indonesia-and-east-timor-against-impunity-for-justice/.

133. Markus Junianto Sihaloho, "Defense Minister Dodges Question on Blocking ICC Treaty's Ratification," *Jakarta Globe*, May 21, 2013, www

.thejakartaglobe.com/news/defense-minister-dodges-question-on-blocking-icc
-treatys-ratification/.

134. Daniel Calingaert, Arch Puddington, and Sarah Repucci, *Supporting Democracy Abroad: An Assessment of Leading Powers* (Washington, D.C.: Freedom House, 2014).

135. Rizal Sukma, *Islam in Indonesian Foreign Policy* (London: Routledege-Curzon, 2003), 123–39.

136. Yuliasri Perdani and Ina Parlina, "Govt Bans Support, Endorsement of ISIL," *Jakarta Post*, August 5, 2014, www.thejakartapost.com/news/2014/08 /05/govt-bans-support-endorsement-isil.html; Rizal Sukma, *Islam in Indonesian Foreign Policy*; and Dominic Berger, "Why Indonesia Banned ISIS," *New Mandala*, October 1, 2014, asiapacific.anu.edu.au/newmandala/2014/10/01/why -indonesia-banned-isis/.

137. For a comprehensive review of domestic factors of Indonesia's foreign policy decisionmaking under Yudhoyono, see Dewi Fortuna Anwar, "The Impact of Domestic and Asian Regional Changes on Indonesian Foreign Policy," *Southeast Asian Affairs* (2010): 126–41.

138. Iis Gindarsah, "Democracy and Foreign Policy-Making in Indonesia: A Case Study of the Iranian Nuclear Issue, 2007–08," *Contemporary Southeast Asia* 34, no. 3 (2012): 423.

139. Ibid., 416–37.

140. Anwar, "The Impact of Domestic and Asian Regional Changes," 130–31.

141. "Country Voting History Portal"; Rabu, "Indonesia Welcomes Iran's Nuclear Agreement," *Antara News*, July 15, 2015, www.antaranews.com/en /news/99513/indonesia-welcomes-irans-nuclear-agreement; Kamis, "Iran, Indonesia Discuss Cooperation Plans," *Antara News*, July 30, 2015, www .antaranews.com/en/news/99717/iran-indonesia-discuss-cooperation-plans.

142. Margareth S. Aritonang, "RI Postpones Plans for Representative Office," *Jakarta Post*, August 3, 2012, www.thejakartapost.com/news/2012/08 /03/ri-postpones-plans-representative-office.html.

143. Anwar, "The Impact of Domestic and Asian Regional Changes," 131.

144. Greta Nabbs-Keller, "Reforming Indonesia's Foreign Ministry: Ideas, Organization and Leadership," *Contemporary Southeast Asia* 35, no. 1 (2013): 67–70.

145. The missions consist of ninety-five embassies, three permanent missions to the United Nations (New York and Geneva) and ASEAN (Jakarta), thirty-one Consulates General, and three Consulates. Indonesia also has sixty-four honorary Consuls. For more, see the "Mission," Ministry of Foreign Affairs, Republic of Indonesia, www.kemlu.go.id/Pages/Mission.aspx?l=en.

146. Dino Patti Djalal, "An Independent, Active and *Creative* Foreign Policy for Indonesia," *Strategic Review: The Indonesian Journal of Leadership, Policy and World Affairs* 2, no. 1 (2012): 40–46.

147. Rushida Majeed, "The Gecko's Bite," Democracy Lab, *Foreign Policy*, July 24, 2015, foreignpolicy.com/2015/07/24/the-geckos-bite/.

148. Ibid.

149. Since 1999, Indonesia has signed and ratified the International Convention on the Protection of the Rights of All Migrant Workers and Members of Their Families (2004; 2012); the Optional Protocol to the Convention on the Rights of the Child on the involvement of children in armed conflict (2001; 2012); the Optional Protocol to the Convention on the Rights of the Child on the sale of children, child prostitution, and child pornography; and the Convention on the Rights of Persons with Disabilities (2007, 2011). It has also acceded to several treaties, including the International Covenant on Civil and Political Rights (2006); the International Convention on the Elimination of All Forms of Racial Discrimination (1999); and the International Covenant on Economic and Social Rights (2006). Indonesia country page, "Status of Ratifications," OHCHR, tbinternet.ohchr.org/_layouts/TreatyBodyExternal/Treaty.aspx?CountryID=80&Lang=EN.

150. Author interview with Hassan Wirayuda, April 2010.

CHAPTER 8

1. For an assessment of what ails the democracy promotion community, see Larry Diamond, "Chasing Away the Democracy Blues," *Foreign Policy Democracy Lab*, October 24, 2014, www.foreignpolicy.com/articles/2014/10/24/chasing_away_the_democracy_blues. The *Journal of Democracy*'s twenty-fifth anniversary edition contains a number of articles that argue both sides of the proposition. See also Christian Caryl, "The Beacon Dims," *Foreign Policy Democracy Lab*, October 31, 2014, www.foreignpolicy.com/articles/2014/10/31/the_beacon_dims_america_democracy. For a critique of the current state of international human rights law, see Eric Posner, "The Case against Human Rights," *The Guardian*, December 4 2014, www.theguardian.com/news/2014/dec/04/-sp-case-against-human-rights?utm_source=Sailthru&utm_medium=email&utm_term=%2ADemocracy%20Lab&utm_campaign=DemLab%20Weekly%20Brief%2012%2F8. For an incisive analysis of the fraying liberal democratic bargain, see William A. Galston, "The New Challenge to Market Democracies," Brookings Institution, October 2014, www.brookings.edu/research/reports2/2014/10/new-challenge-market-democracies.

2. Stephen Hopgood, *The Endtimes of Human Rights* (Cornell University Press, 2013); Eric Posner, *The Twilight of Human Rights Law* (Oxford University Press, 2014).

3. See, for example, Mark Lagon and Anthony Clark Arend, eds., *Human Dignity and the Future of Global Institutions* (Georgetown University Press, 2014).

4. Statement by UN High Commissioner for Human Rights Zeid Ra'ad Al Hussein, Presentation of report on OHCHR activities, Human Rights Council session in Geneva, March 3, 2015, www.ohchr.org/EN/NewsEvents/Pages/DisplayNews.aspx?NewsID=15642&LangID=E.

5. The UN Convention against Torture and Other Cruel, Inhuman, or Degrading Treatment or Punishment, which includes the United States among its 158 states parties, is considered a principle of customary international law. The treaty permits no invocation of exceptional circumstances to justify torture nor

may orders from superior authorities be invoked as justification for such acts. Parties must criminalize such acts under their national laws and take steps to investigate and, if the facts warrant, to prosecute such acts or extradite the defendant to another jurisdiction that will. Convention against Torture and Other Cruel, Inhuman, or Degrading Treatment or Punishment, adopted by UN General Assembly resolution 39/46 on December 10, 1984, www.ohchr.org/EN /ProfessionalInterest/Pages/CAT.aspx. U.S. law prohibits torture and cruel and unusual punishments under the Eighth Amendment to the U.S. Constitution and subsequent laws. See, for example, 18 U.S.C. sec. 2340.

6. See Ted Piccone, "Senate GOP Failed on Disability Rights," CNN Opinion, December 8, 2012, www.cnn.com/2012/12/08/opinion/piccone-senate -rights/index.html.

7. Chandran Nair, "Foreign Lives Matter," *Foreign Policy*, April 30, 2015, foreignpolicy.com/2015/04/30/foreign-lives-matter-american-racism-foreign -policy-baltimore-ferguson/.

8. The United States has the highest incarceration rate in the world. It also has the highest number of guns per capita and ranks fifth in the world in the number of prisoners put to death.

9. For a recent classical liberalist critique of the dysfunction of American and European democracy, see John Micklethwait and Adrian Wooldridge, *The Fourth Revolution: The Global Race to Reinvent the State* (New York: Penguin Press, 2014).

10. Freedom House data for 2014 can be found at freedomhouse.org/report -types/freedom-world#.VNt2ffnF-1Y; its analysis of the general decline for the last nine years can be found in its 2015 report: Arch Puddington, "Discarding Democracy: A Return to the Iron Fist," Freedom House, freedomhouse.org/report /freedom-world-2015/discarding-democracy-return-iron-fist#.VNt2DfnF-1Y.

11. "Globally, More Say China Does Not Respect Personal Freedoms," Pew Research Center, Spring 2015, www.pewresearch.org/fact-tank/2015/06/23/key -takeaways-on-how-the-world-views-the-u-s-and-china/ft_15-06-23 _chinafreedoms/. The latest Pew Center polling shows positive opinions in Africa toward the state of "personal freedoms" in China.

12. Rosemary Foot and Rana Siu Inboden, "China's Influence on Asian States during the Creation of the UN Human Rights Council: 2005–2007," *Asian Survey* 54, no. 5 (2014): 849–68. See also Andrew J. Nathan, "The Authoritarian Resurgence: China's Challenge," *Journal of Democracy* 26, no. 1 (2015): 156–70.

13. Christopher Walker and Robert W. Orttung, "Breaking the News: The Role of State Run Media," *Journal of Democracy* 25, no. 1 (2014): 71–85.

14. "Like Minded Group Joint Statement," Ministry of Defense Sri Lanka, last modified September 27, 2014, www.defence.lk/new.asp?fname=Like_Minded _Group_Joint_Statement_20140927_06.

15. For an analysis of the growing convergence within the international human rights community, see Louis Bickford, "Convergence towards the Global Middle: An Emerging Architecture for the International Human Rights Movement," openGlobalRights, January 19, 2015, www.opendemocracy.net

/openglobalrights/louis-bickford/convergence-towards-global-middle-emerging
-architecture-for-internat; see also Richard Youngs, "Can Non-Western Democracy Help to Foster Political Transformation?," openDemocracy, October 5,
2015, https://www.opendemocracy.net/transformation/richard-youngs/can-non
-western-democracy-help-to-foster-political-transformation; Thomas Carothers, Richard Youngs, Oliver Stuenkel, Claudio Fuentes, Niranjan Sahoo, I Ketut
Putra Erawan, Maiko Ichihara, Tjiurimo Alfredo Hengari, Sook Jong Lee, Senem
Aydin-Düzgit, and Tsveta Petrova, "Non-Western Roots of International Democracy Support," Carnegie Endowment for International Peace, June 3, 2014, carn-
egieendowment.org/2014/06/03/non-western-roots-of-international-democracy
-support; Thomas Carothers, "The Elusive Synthesis," *Journal of Democracy* 21,
no. 4 (2010): 12–26, www.ndi.org/files/JoD_Carothers_Oct2010.pdf.

16. This could include leading one of its various working groups, staffing
technical assistance missions, contributing funds to the UN Democracy Fund,
working proactively to coordinate positions at the UN, and providing personnel
and resources to its secretariat in Warsaw.

17. The resolution was initiated by Peru, Norway, Morocco, Republic of
Korea, Romania, and Tunisia and adopted by a vote of thirty-five yes and twelve
abstentions. UN Human Rights Council resolution 28/L.24, *Human Rights,
Democracy and the Rule of Law*, A/HRC/28/L.24 (March 23, 2015), www.ishr
.ch/sites/default/files/documents/resolution_on_human_rights_democracy_and
_the_rule_of_law.pdf.

18. Mandeep Tiwana, "Can Emerging Powers Break Out of Narrow Strategic Imperatives and Reboot the Global Human Rights Narrative?," openGlobal-
Rights, June 10, 2014, www.opendemocracy.net/openglobalrights/mandeep
-tiwana/can-emerging-powers-break-out-of-narrow-strategic-imperatives
-and-re.

19. "The group's founding in itself made a strong statement about the ambitions of emerging powers to seize a greater role in shaping the Western-dominated
international order, as well as their willingness to work within that system . . .
Yet concrete successes in promoting trade or spurring joint diplomatic efforts
have remained largely elusive" (Oliver Stuenkel, "The Uncertain Future of
IBSA," Carnegie Endowment for International Peace, February 18, 2015, carn-
egieendowment.org/2015/02/18/uncertain-future-of-ibsa).

20. According to the Arab Barometer, in all but one country surveyed, three-
quarters or more of respondents in the third wave of surveys (late 2012–14)
agree or strongly agree with the statement "a democratic system may have problems, yet it is better than other political systems." This belief is most widespread
in Lebanon (85 percent) and Egypt (84 percent), followed by Tunisia (83 percent),
Algeria (82 percent), Jordan (81 percent), and Palestine (81 percent). Although
lowest among the countries surveyed, overwhelming majorities also favor democracy in Iraq (76 percent) and Yemen (73 percent). See Michael Robbins,
"After the Arab Spring: Support for Democracy High, Political Islam in Decline," *Democracy Digest*, October 29, 2014, demdigest.net/blog/arab-spring
-support-democracy-high-political-islam-decline/. Such surveys do not always
define democracy in specific terms.

21. For a comprehensive overview of international responses to interruptions to democratic rule, see Morton H. Halperin and Mirna Galic, eds., *Protecting Democracy: International Responses* (Lanham, Md.: Lexington Books, 2005).

22. For a comprehensive treatment of the topic, see "La reforma de la Comisión Interamericana de Derechos Humanos," *Aportes DPLf* (Magazine of the Due Process of Law Foundation) 19 (2014), www.dplf.org/sites/default /files/aportes_19_web_0.pdf.

23. See, for example, the ongoing series of talks between the Organization of American States and the African Union on democracy and human rights and the Inter-Regional Dialogue on Democracy convened by International IDEA.

24. See, for example, W. P. S. Sidhu, "India's Multiple Multilateral Opportunities," *Live Mint*, November 6, 2014, www.livemint.com/Opinion/lXLwNR GD0PJnaEJEZPuAIM/Indias-multiple-multilateral-opportunities.html.

25. According to the International Campaign to Ban Landmines, 80 percent of states have joined the treaty. "Home," International Campaign to Ban Landmines, www.icbl.org/en-gb/home.aspx. For a summary of the success of the antitorture campaign, see Walter Kälin, "The Struggle against Torture," *International Review of the Red Cross*, March 9, 1988, www.icrc.org/eng/resources /documents/misc/57jpg5.htm. On the success of international efforts to combat depletion of the ozone, see Peter M. Morrisette, "The Evolution of Policy Responses to Stratospheric Ozone Depletion," *Natural Resources Journal* 29 (1989): 793–820, www.ciesin.org/docs/003-006/003-006.html.

26. See, for example, the ongoing efforts to stop use of land mines, which the United States adopted in October 2014 (with the exception of the Korea Peninsula), "United States Landmine Policy: Questions and Answers, " Human Rights Watch, October 3, 2014, www.hrw.org/news/2014/10/03/united-states-landmine -policy-questions-and-answers, and the campaign to build support for R2P, Stanley Foundation, "The Responsibility to Protect in the Next Decade," April 2, 2015, www.stanleyfoundation.org/publications/policy_memo/R2PintheNext Decade_PolicyMemo415.pdf.

27. On the growing demand for Special Procedures, for example, see Ted Piccone and Marc Limon, "Human Rights Special Procedures: Determinants of Influence," Universal Rights Group and the Brookings Institution, March 2014, www.brookings.edu/~/media/research/files/reports/2014/03/19-un-human -rights-experts-evaluation-piccone/un-human-rights-experts-evaluation -piccone.pdf; and Subhas Gujadhur and Toby Lamarque, "Ensuring Relevance, Driving Impact: The Evolution and Future Direction of UN Human Rights Council's Resolution System," Universal Rights Group, January 2015, www .universal-rights.org/wp-content/uploads/2015/02/URG_Report_ERDI -Jan2015-print_layout.pdf.

28. See, for example, Vladimir Tismaneanu's *Reinventing Politics* (New York: Free Press, 1992), about the direct role played by underground civil society, and by the 1975 Helsinki agreements that catalyzed and legitimized their activities, in the fall of the communist regimes of Eastern Europe.

29. For a summary of recent trends restricting civil society space, see Sarah E. Mendelson, "Why Governments Target Civil Society and What Can Be Done in Response," Center for Strategic and International Studies April 2015, 1–3.

30. "Annual Reports," UN Human Rights Council, www.ohchr.org/EN /Issues/AssemblyAssociation/Pages/AnnualReports.aspx.

31. "Working Group on Enabling and Protecting Civil Society," Community of Democracies, www.community-democracies.org/Working-for-Democracy /Initiatives/Governmental-Bodies/Working-Group-on-Enabling-and -Protecting-Civil-Soc.

32. "Stand with Civil Society: Best Practices," USAID, January 2014, www .usaid.gov/sites/default/files/documents/1866/SWCS%20Best%20Practices%20 Publications%20Final%20%281%29.pd; and "ICNL NGO Law Monitor," International Center for Not-for-Profit Law, www.icnl.org/research/monitor/.

33. "Human Rights Council: 28th Session Adopts 5 Resolutions of Significance to Human Rights Defenders," International Service for Human Rights, April 2, 2015, www.ishr.ch/news/human-rights-council-28th-session-adopts-5 -resolutions-significance-human-rights-defenders.

34. Louise Arbour, "North-South Solidarity Is Key," *Sur International Journal on Human Rights* 11, no. 20 (2014): 539–44, www.conectas.org/en/actions /sur-journal/issue/20/1007395-%E2%80%9Cnorth-south-solidarity-is -key%E2%80%9D.

35. The committee, which includes states such as China, Cuba, Pakistan, Russia, Sudan, and Venezuela, has repeatedly delayed or blocked action on applications for consultative status by NGOs whose work these governments oppose, including on defending persons arbitrarily detained and protecting rights of LGBT persons. Denials are often appealed to the full Economic and Social Committee, which usually overrides the committee's vote, but only after years of time and labor are wasted in the process. See, for example, "Media Release: UN Grants Freedom Now Consultative Status," Freedom Now, July 20, 2015, www.freedom-now.org/news/media-release-un-grants-freedom-now -consultative-status/.

36. Article 19 of the UDHR and ICCPR states: "Everyone shall have the right to freedom of expression; this right shall include freedom to seek, receive and impart information of all kinds, regardless of frontiers, either orally, in writing or in print, in the form of art or through any media of his choice." According to the UN Special Rapporteur on Freedom of Opinion and Expression, "The right to seek, receive and impart information imposes a positive obligation on States to ensure access to information, particularly with regard to information held by Government in all types of storage and retrieval systems" (UN Doc. E/CN.4/1998/40, Report of the Special Rapporteur on the promotion and protection of the right to freedom of opinion and expression, January 28, 1998, para. 14).

37. As of September 2014, at least 100 countries have adopted some form of national right to information laws or decrees. See Toby McIntosh, "Paraguay Is 100th Nation to Pass FOI Law, but Struggle for Openness Goes On," *The Guardian*, September 19, 2014, www.theguardian.com/public-leaders-network

/2014/sep/19/paraguay-freedom-information-law-transparency; and "Access to Information Laws: Overview and Statutory Goals," Right2INFO.org, modified January 20, 2012, www.right2info.org/access-to-information-laws.

38. See Open Working Group proposal for Sustainable Development Goals, para. 17 (November 9, 2014); zero draft of the outcome document for the UN Summit to adopt the Post-2015 Development Agenda, para. 39, Goal 6.10 ("Ensure public access to information . . ."); see also paras. 17, 18 (June 2015).

39. See UNSG report on post-2015 agenda, "The Road to Dignity by 2030: Ending Poverty, Transforming All Lives and Protecting the Planet," A/69/700 (December 4, 2014), para. 125.

40. At least one study of Brazil's experience with participatory budgeting found that it often results in more equitable public spending, greater governmental transparency and accountability, and increased levels of public participation and citizenship education. See Brian Wampler, *Participatory Budgeting in Brazil: Contestation, Cooperation and Accountability* (Pennsylvania State University Press, 2007).

41. "Foreign Policy and Human Rights: Strategies for Civil Society Action," Conectas Direitos Humanos, June 2013, 11–12, http://www.conectas.org/arquivos/editor/files/CONECTAS%20ing_add_LAURA.pdf.

42. *World Report 2014*, Human Rights Watch, www.hrw.org/world-report/2014.

43. For a comprehensive assessment of the converging paths of both countries' policies on Internet governance, see Harold Trinkunas and Ian Wallace, "Converging on the Future of Global Internet Governance: The United States and Brazil," Brookings, July 2015, http://www.brookings.edu/~/media/research/files/reports/2015/07/internet-governance-brazil-us/usbrazil-global-internet-governance-web-final.pdf.

44. In the wake of the Snowden revelations, and under the leadership of Brazil and Germany, the UN General Assembly adopted a resolution in November 2013 declaring the rights held by people off-line must also be protected online. It called upon all states to respect and protect the right to privacy in digital communication and to review their procedures, practices, and legislation related to communications surveillance, interception, and collection of personal data. "The Right to Privacy in the Digital Age," Office of the High Commissioner for Human Rights, www.ohchr.org/EN/Issues/DigitalAge/Pages/DigitalAgeIndex.aspx.

45. See "Best Practice Forums," Internet Governance Forum, www.intgovforum.org/cms/best-practice-forums; "Internet Governance," Council of Europe, www.coe.int/t/informationsociety.

46. "All human rights are universal, indivisible and interdependent and interrelated" (Vienna Declaration and Programme of Action, para. 5 [1993], www.ohchr.org/EN/ProfessionalInterest/Pages/Vienna.aspx).

47. Aryeh Neier, "Social and Economic Rights: A Critique," *Human Rights Brief* 13, no. 2 (2006): 1–3.

48. For a comprehensive discussion of the growing collaboration between international human rights and development communities, see Paul J. Nelson and

Ellen Dorsey, *The New Rights Advocacy: Changing Strategies of Development and Human Rights NGOs* (Georgetown University Press, 2009).

49. See, for example, the constitution of South Africa, which states that "no one may be refused emergency medical treatment" (chap. 2 [27][3] of constitution of the Republic of South Africa, www.constitutionalcourt.org.za /site/theconstitution/thetext.htm). The South African court defined this term in the case of *Soobramoney v. Minister of Health (Kwazulu-Natal)* as "a sudden catastrophe which calls for immediate medical attention." Indian courts have ruled that hospitals cannot refuse to provide emergency services unless it requires technical expertise; see *Parmanand Katra v. Union of India (1989 4SCC 286).* In *Alyne da Silva Pimentel v. Brazil,* the UN Committee on the Elimination of Discrimination against Women held that governments have an obligation to provide emergency care to all women. Committee on the Elimination of Discrimination against Women, Communication 17/2008 (September 27, 2011), www.ohchr.org/Documents/HRBodies/CEDAW/Jurisprudence/CEDAW-C-49 -D-17-2008_en.pdf.

50. Jose Graziano da Silva and Margaret Chan, "Now Is the Time to Tackle Malnutrition and Its Massive Human Costs," Inter Press Service, November 13, 2014, www.ipsnews.net/2014/11/opinion-now-is-the-time-to-tackle-malnutrition -and-its-massive-human-costs/.

51. FAO data showed that the hunger level in the country decreased from 19.9 percent between 1990 and 1992 to about 8.6 percent in 2010–12, surpassing the MDG target of 9.9 percent (Food and Agriculture Organization of the United Nations, "The State of Food Insecurity in the World 2012," 48, www.fao .org/docrep/016/i3027e/i3027e.pdf, and "38 Countries Meet Anti-Hunger Targets for 2015," June 12, 2013, www.fao.org/news/story/en/item/177728/icode/).

52. According to the Index of Social and Economic Rights Fulfillment (SERF Index), which measures the fulfillment of economic and social rights, considering both the perspective of the rights-holding individuals and the duty-bearing governments, IBSATI countries perform well. See Susan Randolph and Patrick Guyer, The International SERF Index Historical Trends Dataset Version 2012.1, www.serfindex.org/serf-index-historical-trends-downloads.

53. The United States is one of only six countries that have not ratified the UN Convention on Economic, Social, and Cultural Rights. "International Covenant on Economic, Social, and Cultural Rights," United Nations Treaty Collection, treaties.un.org/pages/viewdetails.aspx?chapter=4&lang=en&mtdsg _no=iv-3&src=treaty.

54. In 2009, the United States joined consensus on a nonbinding resolution on right to food for the first time. "Explanation of Position By Craig Kuehl, United States Advisor, on Resolution L.30, Rev. 1—The Right to Food, in the Third Committee of the Sixty-Fourth Session of the United Nations General Assembly," United States Mission to the United Nations, November 19, 2009, usun.state.gov/briefing/statements/2009/132187.htm. In 2012, it again joined consensus on HRC's resolution on the right to food, despite concerns about the jurisdiction of the HRC vis-à-vis trade negotiations. "Explanation of Position by the United States of America, Resolution: The Right to Food, UN Human

Rights Council—19th Session," Mission of the United States, Geneva, Switzerland, geneva.usmission.gov/2012/03/22/us-joins-consensus-on-hrc-resolution-on-the-right-to-food/. In March 2013, the U.S. delegation supported a draft resolution of Human Rights Council "Action on a Resolution on a Right to Food" "because it recognized the importance of maintaining the world community's focus on the right to food" but believed the scope was beyond that of the Human Rights Council. "Call on Sri Lanka to Conduct Investigation into Alleged Violations of Human Rights and Humanitarian Law, Extends Mandates on Human Rights and Counter-Terrorism and Right to Food," Office of the High Commissioner for Human Rights, March 21, 2013, www.ohchr.org/en/NewsEvents/Pages/DisplayNews.aspx?NewsID=13167.

55. "In Detroit, City-Backed Water Shut-Offs 'Contrary to Human Rights,' Say UN Experts," UN News Centre, October 20, 2014, www.un.org/apps/news/story.asp?NewsID=49127.

56. The United States, for example, accepted several ESC-related recommendations resulting from the UPR. Risa Kaufman, "Framing Economic, Social, and Cultural Rights at the UN," *Northeastern University Law Journal* 4, no. 2 (2012): 418–19, nulj.org/sites/default/files/files/NULJ-ESC-Risa-E-Kaufman.pdf.

57. Nelson and Dorsey, *The New Rights Advocacy*, 116–17.

58. Thomas Carothers and Saskia Brechenmacher, "Accountability, Transparency, Participation and Inclusion: A New Development Consensus?" Carnegie Endowment for International Peace, October 2014, 3–6, http://carnegieendowment.org/files/new_development_consensus.pdf.

59. "A New Global Partnership: Eradicate Poverty and Transform Economies through Sustainable Development—Report of the High-Level Panel of Eminent Persons on the Post-2015 Development Agenda," United Nations, 2013, para. 5, www.un.org/sg/management/pdf/HLP_P2015_Report.pdf.

60. Ibid., 7.

61. "New UN 'Rights Up Front' Strategy Seeks to Prevent Genocide, Human Rights Abuses," UN News Centre, December 18, 2013, www.un.org/apps/news/story.asp?NewsID=46778#.VbpFE5NViko; United Nations, General Assembly, *A Life of Dignity for All: Accelerating Progress towards the Millennium Development Goals and Advancing the United Nations Development Agenda beyond 2015; Report of the Secretary-General*, July 26, 2013, A/68/202, www.un.org/millenniumgoals/pdf/A%20Life%20of%20Dignity%20for%20All.pdf.

62. "The Post-2015 Agenda Won't Deliver without Human Rights at the Core," Open Letter to UN Secretary General Ban Ki-moon and others, September 29, 2014, signed by the Post-2015 Human Rights Caucus, www.cesr.org/article.php?id=1648; see also reflections from co-conveners, "The Post-2015 Agenda Won't Deliver without Human Rights at the Core," Center for Economic and Social Rights, September 29, 2014, www.cesr.org/downloads/HRsCaucus Reflections-Post2015-Sept2014.pdf.

63. For a chronology of the development of the right to development norm within the UN system from 1944 to 2015, see "Development Is a Human Right for All," Office of the High Commissioner for Human Rights, www.ohchr.org

/EN/Issues/Development/Pages/Landmarksintherecognitiondevelopmentasahu manright.aspx.

64. Alex Evans and David Steven, "What Happens Now? Time to Deliver the Post-2015 Development Agenda," New York University Center on International Cooperation, April 2015, cic.nyu.edu/sites/default/files/evans_steven_what _happens_now_time_deliver_april2015.pdf.

65. A report of the Intergovernmental Committee of Experts on Sustainable Development Financing, published in August 2014, argues that the world is awash with finance, with $22 trillion in annual global savings and domestic and international financial flows all growing considerably since the MDGs were agreed. "The problem was not a lack of money, then, but rather the challenge of directing investment towards sustainable development opportunities that delivered less attractive short-term returns than less sustainable alternatives" (Evans and Steven, "What Happens Now?," 8).

66. UN Committee on Economic, Social, and Cultural Rights, General Comment on Article 13, para. 1; Article 13, International Covenant on Economic, Social and Cultural Rights, www.ohchr.org/en/professionalinterest/pages/cescr .aspx.

67. *SIPRI Yearbook 2015, Summary*, Stockholm International Peace Research Institute, 6, www.sipri.org/yearbook/2015/downloadable-files/sipri -yearbook-2015-summary-pdf.

68. Katarina Tomasevski, *Human Rights Obligations: Making Education Available, Accessible, Acceptable and Adaptable* (Gothenburg: Novum Grafiska AB, 2001), www.right-to-education.org/sites/right-to-education.org/files /resource-attachments/Tomasevski_Primer%203.pdf. Tomasevski served as special rapporteur from 1998 to 2004.

69. *Teaching and Learning: Achieving Quality for All, Education for All Global Monitoring Report 2013/4*, United Nations Educational, Scientific, and Cultural Organization, 2014, unesco.nl/sites/default/files/dossier/gmr_2013-4. pdf?download=1.

70. In addition to the UN treaty on the subject, the European Convention on Human Rights, the African Charter on Human and People's Rights, and the Inter-American Protocol of San Salvador all recognize the right to education.

71. "Education for All 2000–2015; Achievements and Challenges," UNESCO, 2015, unesdoc.unesco.org/images/0023/002322/232205e.pdf.

72. *Teaching and Learning*.

73. Ibid., 75.

74. See 2014 Legatum Prosperity Index, Legatum, 21–22, media.prosperity .com/2014/pdf/publications/PI2014Brochure_WEB.pdf ("many experts, academics and institutions—including the World Bank in its 2014 report—agree that improving the agency of women as well as access to opportunities is crucial for development and prosperity around the world"). Transparency International, "Gender, Equality and Corruption: What Are the Linkages?," Policy Brief, April 7, 2014, www.transparency.org/whatwedo/publication/policy_position_01 _2014_gender_equality_and_corruption_what_are_the_linkage; The Millennium

Development Goals Report 2015, United Nations, mdgs.un.org/unsd/mdg/Resources/Static/Products/Progress2015/English2015.pdf.

75. Jenny Perlman Robinson, *A Global Compact on Learning: Taking Action on Education in Developing Countries*, Brookings Institution, June 8, 2011, www.brookings.edu/research/reports/2011/06/09-global-compact.

76. *Teaching and Learning*, 165.

77. Proposal for Sustainable Development Goals, Goals and Targets 4.1.

78. See statement by the special rapporteur on the right to education at the Sixty-Ninth Session of the UN General Assembly, October 27, 2014, www.ohchr.org/EN/NewsEvents/Pages/DisplayNews.aspx?NewsID=15213&LangID=E.

79. "Annual Financials for Amazon.com Inc.," Market Watch, www.marketwatch.com/investing/stock/amzn/financials; World Bank Development Indicators, databank.worldbank.org/data/download/GNI.pdf.

80. "Tata Group Market Value Nears Rs. 6 Trillion," *Hindu*, September 1, 2013, www.thehindu.com/business/Industry/tata-group-market-value-nears-rs-6-trillion/article5082104.ece; "Market Capitalization of Tata Companies as on July 23, 2015," Tata, www.tata.com/article/inside/Market-capitalisation-of-Tata-companies.

81. For example, see failed efforts by UN Commission on Transnational Corporations to negotiate a code of conduct to govern multinational corporations, which were abandoned in the early 1990s (see Theodore H. Moran, "The United Nations and Transnational Corporations: A Review and a Perspective," United Nations Conference on Trade and Development, 2009, 1–22) and by a subsidiary body of the UN Commission on Human Rights to promote the "Norms on Transnational Corporations and Other Business Enterprises with Regard to Human Rights," E/CN.4/Sub.2/2003/12/Rev.2, which was rejected by the Commission in 2004. UN Document E/CN.4/DEC/2004/116 (April 20, 2004). See, for example, Tagi Sagafi-nejad and John H. Dunning, *The UN and Transnational Corporations: From Code of Conduct to Global Compact* (Indiana University Press, 2008), 41–123; and Theodore H. Moran, "The United Nations and Transnational Corporations: A Review and a Perspective," *Transnational Corporations* 2 (2009): 91–97, unctad.org/en/docs/diaeiia200910a4_en.pdf.

82. United Nations Human Rights Office of the High Commissioner, *Guiding Principles on Business and Human Rights* (Geneva: Publishing Service United Nations, 2012), www.ohchr.org/documents/publications/GuidingprinciplesBusinesshr_en.pdf.

83. Navanethem Pillay, UN High Commission for Human Rights, "The Corporate Responsibility to Respect: A Human Rights Milestone," *Annual Labour and Social Policy Review*, 2, www.ohchr.org/Documents/Press/HC_contribution_on_Business_and_HR.pdf.

84. Human Rights Council, A/HRC/RES/17/4, "Human Rights and Transnational Corporations and Other Business Enterprises," July 6, 2011.

85. Human Rights Council, A/HRC/26/L.1, "Human Rights and Transnational Corporations and Other Business Enterprises," June 23, 2014.

86. A/HRC/26/L.22/Rev.1, "Elaboration of an International Legally Binding Instrument on Transnational Corporations and Other Business Enterprises with Respect to Human Rights," June 25, 2014.

87. John G. Ruggie, "Quo Vadis? Unsolicited Advice to Business and Human Rights Treaty Sponsors," Institute for Human Rights and Business, September 9, 2014, www.ihrb.org/commentary/quo-vadis-unsolicited-advice-business.html.

88. Anne Peters, "Corruption and Human Rights," Working Paper No. 20 (Basel Institute on Governance, 2015), 11.

89. See, for example, Sarah Chayes, *Thieves of State: Why Corruption Threatens Global Security* (New York: W. W. Norton, 2015).

90. "United Nations Convention against Corruption, Signature and Ratification Status as of 1 April 2015," United Nations Office on Drugs and Crime, www.unodc.org/unodc/en/treaties/CAC/signatories.html.

91. "United Nations Convention against Corruption," United Nations Office on Drugs and Crime, www.unodc.org/unodc/en/treaties/CAC/.

92. According to UNECA, it is estimated that Africa loses $50 billion a year in illicit financial flows that find their way to developed countries, draining the continent of much-needed resources for governance and economic development. This estimated amount exceeds the official development assistance to the continent, which stood at $46.1 billion in 2012. "The High Level Panel on Illicit Financial Flows Meets in Lusaka," UN Economic Commission for Africa, June 19, 2013, www.uneca.org/stories/high-level-panel-illicit-financial-flows-meets-lusaka.

93. Alessandra Fontana, "Making Development Assistance Work at Home: DfID's Approach to Clamping Down on International Bribery and Money Laundering in the UK," *U4 Practice Insight*, May 2011, www.u4.no/publications/making-development-assistance-work-at-home-dfid-s-approach-to-clamping-down-on-international-bribery-and-money-laundering-in-the-uk/.

94. "Kofi Annan," *Africa Progress Panel*, www.africaprogresspanel.org/panelmember/kofi-annan/.

95. My Brookings colleague Bruce Jones suggests a more expansive idea to establish a UN high commissioner for the rule of law, with a focus on institution building for political, security, and justice institutions. Bruce Jones, "The Last Mile: Laying the Political and Security Foundations First for Peace, Then Development," *Future Development*, July 28, 2015, www.brookings.edu/blogs/future-development/posts/2015/07/28-peace-development-last-mile-jones.

Index

Figures and tables are indicated by "f" and "t" following page numbers. Surnames starting with al- are alphabetized by the subsequent part of the name.

Asia, financial crisis (1997), 9
Asia-Africa (Bandung) Conference, 193–194
Asia Democracy Network, 45
Asia Pacific Economic Cooperation forum (APEC), 191
Aslan, Süleyman, 181
al-Assad, Bashar, 68, 121, 122, 175–176, 209–210. *See also* Syria
Association of Southeast Asian Nations. *See* ASEAN
Atatürk, Mustafa Kemal, 11, 162, 164
AU. *See* African Union
Aung San Suu Kyi, 77, 78, 93, 200, 203
Authoritarian/autocratic states, 35–36, 57–58, 223
Auto-golpes, 105
Aydın-Düzgit, Senem, 165
Azerbaijan: Turkey and, 178; UNDEF support for, 44; on UN Human Rights Council, 40
Azeredo da Silveira, Antonio Francisco, 101

Baha'i community, in Brazil, 125–126
Bahrain: Brazil's actions on, 117, 122; India's actions on, 62; Indonesia's actions on, 65; South Africa and, 150; Turkey and, 177–178
Balance of power, 106, 112, 136, 224, 228
Bali Democracy Forum (BDF), 194, 205–06, 207
Bali terrorist attacks, 213
Baltic states, promotion of democracy in, 56
Bambang, Susilo, 195
Ban, Ki-moon, 47, 241
Bandung Conference, 193–194
Bangladesh: Pakistani recognition of, 76; SAARC and, 49, 83
al-Bashir, Omar, 41, 51, 52, 144–145, 157
BDF (Bali Democracy Forum), 194, 205–06, 207

Belarus, at HRC, 40, 145
Belo Monte hydroelectric dam (Brazil), 110–111
Ben Ali, Zine El Abidine, 173–174
Bengali state, campaign for, 75–76
Bertelsmann Transformation Index, 13, 16, 17, 222
Bharatiya Janata Party (BJP, India), 72, 92
Bhinneka Tunggal Ika (Unity in Diversity), 190
Big data, 236–237
"The Birth of *Pancasila*" (Sukarno), 189, 192–193, 211, 218
Boko Haram, 32–33
Bolivarian Alliance for the Peoples of our America (ALBA), 106
Bolivia, 106, 245
Bollywood films, 28
Bolsa Familia program (Brazil), 20
Border Roads Organization (Indian army), 81
Botswana, 140
Branco, Rio, 98–99
Brazil, 97–128; Arab Spring and, 118–123; Bertelsmann Transformation Index on, 16; on business and human rights, UN actions on, 245; child mortality rates, 23f; China as trade partner of, 26, 27; civil society advisory councils, 234; Community of Democracies and, 42–43; conclusions on, 127–128; energy imports, 26; FDI from China, 26, 26f; Foreign Ministry (Itamaraty), 119, 122, 123, 124, 126, 127; foreign policy, domestic politics and, 123–127; foreign policy, global focus of, 111–118; foreign policy, under Lula administration, 105–111; girls' education in, 243; HIV/AIDS crisis, response to, 157–158; human rights and democracy order, impact on, 59–60; hunger, initiatives on ending, 238; ICC and, 51; indicators on, 15,

UN Convention against Corruption,
246
UN Convention against Torture, 101
UN Convention to Eliminate Racial
Discrimination, 144
UN Covenant on Economic, Social, and
Cultural Rights, 23
UN Democracy Fund (UNDEF), 44,
45f, 60, 82
UN Development Program (UNDP), 21,
25, 46–47, 55, 240
UNECA (United Nations Economic
Commission for Africa), 246
Unemployment rates, 19
UNESCO, 47, 242–243
UN Food and Agricultural
Organization (FAO), 113, 119, 238
UN General Assembly (UNGA): Brazil
at, 114; India at, 78, 82; Indonesia at,
206, 210; Libya, action on, 210;
Malala's speech at, 32; Mandela at,
131; Obama at, 36; Rousseff at, 115,
118; South Africa, actions on, 130;
Third Committee, 52, 58t, 64, 114,
149–150; Turkey at, 183; Yousafzai
at, 32; Yudhoyono at, 211
UN Guiding Principles on Business and
Human Rights, 244
UN High Commissioner for Human
Rights, 38, 221
UN High Commissioner for Refugees
(UNHCR), 47
UN Human Rights Council (HRC):
Brazil's actions on, 114, 117, 118,
126; China at, 223; Commission of
Inquiry on Syria, 65; creation of, 39,
219, 232; funding for, 233; India
and, 82; Indonesia at, 206–07, 209,
210, 215; Libya's suspension from,
210; on right to privacy, 237; South
Africa and, 145, 149, 152; Special
Procedures, 86; special rapporteur
mandate on peaceful freedom of
assembly, 234; Sri Lanka, resolution
on, 89; Syria, Brazil on special

session on, 121–122; Turkey and,
183; Universal Periodic Review
mechanism, 39, 40, 86–87, 217, 227,
234; Working Group on Guiding
Principles, 244
UN International Covenant on Civil
and Political Rights, 166
UN International Covenant on
Economic, Social, and Cultural
Rights, 166
Union of South American Nations
(UNASUL), 104, 107, 108
Union of South American States
(UNASUR), 60, 230
United Democratic Movement (South
Africa), 147
United Kingdom: Department for
International Development, 247;
South Africa, actions on, at UN, 130
United Nations: Côte d'Ivoire, actions
on, 141; Democracy Caucus,
attempts at formation of, 44–45;
human rights at, 39–41, 52, 57, 58t,
64; India's role at, 60–62, 82;
Indonesia at, 206–07; Indonesia's
role at, 65; mainstreaming of
democracy and rights, 46–50;
peacekeeping missions, civilian
protection as feature of, 47; South
Africa, actions on, 10–11, 73–74,
129–130; South Africa at, 63–64;
Turkey and, 162–163, 182. See also
entries beginning "UN"
United States: Brazil and, 99, 101, 118;
Central and South America,
interventions in, 105; democratic
processes, support for, 36, 54–55;
globalization and, 25; Honduras
coup, actions on, 107; India's role
with, 61; Indonesia's relationship
with, 194; international human
rights order, construction of role in,
37; Internet, as defender of, 237;
Latin America and, 48; moral
standing, loss of, 220–222; Paraguay,

actions on, 108; political system, dysfunctionality of, 221–222; regime change, support for, 80; on right to quality of life, 239; Rome Statute, failure to ratify, 51; RWP, response to, 123; Senate report on torture, 221; South Africa, actions on, 11, 130; Sri Lanka, actions on, 89; Sukarno, actions against, 212; UNDEF, support for, 44. See also *specific presidents*

Unity in Diversity (*Bhinneka Tunggal Ika*), 190

Universal Declaration of Human Rights: APSC and, 197; civil society and, 233; description of, 37; India and, 74; private enterprises and, 244; SDG and, 240; SERF as measurement of adherence to, 23; South Africa and, 131; UN and, 38

Universal norms, 73–75

Universal Periodic Review (UPR) mechanism (UN Human Rights Council), 39, 40, 86–87, 217, 227, 234

Universal suffrage, 72

UN Office of the High Commissioner for Human Rights, 39, 47, 117, 230

UN Peacebuilding Commission, 113

UN Security Council (UNSC): Brazil's campaign for permanent seat on, 106, 113, 115; on Brazil's response to Syria, 121–122; China at, 223; Guinea-Bissau, actions on, 116; Haiti, actions on, 115; human rights, attention to, 47–48; ICC and, 50, 52; Indonesia at, 201, 207, 214, 215; Iran, actions on, 113; Libya, resolutions on, 53, 61, 146–147; Office of the High Commissioner for Human Rights and, 47; Qaddafi regime, sanctions against, 57; Resolution 1970, 61, 146–147; Resolution 1973, 53; rising democracies and, 29, 228; Russia at,

223; South Africa and, 64, 130, 134, 141–142, 143, 152; Syria, actions on, 149; Turkey on, 165, 183; Zimbabwe, actions on, 139

UN Special Rapporteurs, 86, 239, 242

UPR (Universal Periodic Review) mechanism (UN Human Rights Council), 39, 40, 86–87, 217, 227, 234

Uruguay, 101

Vannuchi, Paulo de Tarso, 49

Védrine, Hubert, 42

Vegevani, Tulio, 99

Venezuela: Brazil, relationship with, 106, 111; on business and human rights, actions on, at UN, 245; Community of Democracies and, 42; Mercosul membership, 108–09; on UN Human Rights Council, 40

Video, power of, 33

Vietnam, 204

Violence against women, 87

Voice and accountability, World Bank Institute indicators of, 14–16

Wahid, Abdurrahman, 10, 194, 200, 213, 215

Wall Street Journal/Heritage Foundation, 17

Warmongering, 35

Wars, interstate, 33

Warsaw Declaration, 42

Washington Post, Rousseff remarks in, 114

Waslekar, Sundeep, 85, 90

Water, as essential element of right to life, 237–242

Weitz, Richard, 179

Welfare Party (Turkey), 12

West Asia, education of girls in, 243

West Papua, autonomy movement, 190

White Paper on Foreign Policy (DIRCO, South Africa), 155, 156

Wibisono, Makarim, 198